BottomLine
BANKING

Meeting the Challenges for Survival & Success

John B. McCoy

Larry A. Frieder

Robert B. Hedges, Jr.

IRWIN
Professional Publishing®
Chicago • London • Singapore

ISBN 0-7863-1112-6

Printed in the United States of America

BB

1 2 3 4 5 6 7 8 9 0

To my father John G. McCoy, my grandfather John H. McCoy, and my uncle Charles W. McCoy, all of whom dedicated their lives to enhancing the financial services industry.

John B. McCoy

To my mother Marian M. Frieder, my late father Alvin I. Frieder, and my brother, "Coach" William S. Frieder, all of whom have constantly inspired me.

Larry A. Frieder

To my ever-patient wife Christie and our three young children Connor, Ryan, and Kara, all of whom have come to believe that weekends are for book writing. We need to change that.

Robert B. Hedges, Jr.

Contents

List of Exhibits

Sidebar Contributors

The following authors have contributed sidebar articles throughout this book.

Foreword

In *Bottomline Banking*, John B. McCoy, Larry A. Frieder, and Robert B. Hedges, Jr., lay out the blueprint for transitioning to a new financial services paradigm. The three authors are uniquely qualified for the task. Their writing not only brings important insights, but an all too often missing sense of urgency.

Dramatic change has marked the beginning of the 1990s. Worldwide political and economic events filled newspaper headlines with stories of Eastern Europe, the Soviet Union, and the United States. We wrestle with the need to maintain the competitiveness of the U.S. economy. In the most recent presidential election, all three major candidates spoke of "the need for change" and debated who was best equipped to "manage change." Nowhere are there to be found proponents of maintaining the status quo.

On the scale of change, the banking industry, perhaps more than any other industry, is evolving at a revolutionary pace. Market forces first released by significant deregulatory moves in the early 1980s are transforming the industry and its institutions. Managing change has become the hallmark of the effective financial services executive. It is a challenge, however, that few were prepared for by tradition or training.

Across the banking industry, BANC ONE stands out in consistently delivering above-average performance in this era of change. For over 10 years in studying the industry's top performers, we at First Manhattan Consulting Group (FMCG) have been asking BANC ONE's CEO, John B. McCoy, how they had so consistently beaten the odds stacked against them. Early on, John responded with one word—"MIS." He went on to describe how BANC ONE installed their management information system in new affiliates. Then by examining an affiliate's performance on key measures relative to their best affiliates, they could determine what marketing, pricing, and productivity steps should be taken to increase shareholder value. Moreover, executives running BANC ONE's units were empowered and encouraged to act on this MIS-derived information. This "systematic management" approach to running a regional bank was and continues to be very powerful for BANC ONE. It produces greater returns than the typical bank. It is this management approach that has been so successfully explored by the authors.

We are very fortunate to have the author team of John B. McCoy, Larry Frieder, and Bob Hedges to explore and explain the phenomenon of the superregional banking entity. John, as CEO of one of this new breed of financial institution, is at the forefront of this dramatic industry change. Both BANC ONE's performance and John's thinking reflect the bank's and John's personal role as industry leader. Larry, a distinguished professor at Florida A&M, is deeply rooted in regional and interstate banking. He has been an industry observer for decades. In the structure of the consolidation landscape, you can see the mark of Larry's thinking. Bob, formerly my colleague at FMCG, is an experienced consultant who knows first-hand the strategy and tactics required for success in today's demanding environment. Now at Shawmut National Corporation, he is one of the industry pioneers on the forefront of change. The three are uniquely qualified to share important perspectives with their readers.

Much has been recently written on turmoil in the banking industry. This book does more than recount the performance problems of the 1980s; it points out what it will take to compete and succeed in the future. The emphasis is on what management must do, not how history has treated the industry. In an era when management is going to make the difference, I believe this work has something to teach to all executives involved in the financial services arena.

In our consulting and research at FMCG, we find tremendous differences in management effectiveness across banks today. Some have a knowledge of their businesses' economics that is used with credibility throughout the bank. Some have already empowered their people to use MIS information to turn the various dials that can maximize the shareholder value potential of each business. Many of these have instigated focused programs and have improved the profitability of their units.

To dissect their profitability by business and maximize each unit's value, banks need to create an income statement and a balance sheet for each business unit. They need to adopt a process of corporate governance that uses insights related to business unit profitability, combined with marketing perspectives derived from understanding target customer segments and how to meet market needs more effectively. *Bottomline Banking* presents the essence of this shareholder value approach.

Leading banks are now better poised to face the key challenge that must be dealt with to win in the 1990s—that is, finding new sources of revenue growth. This is because many traditional lines of business are mature and actually shrinking on an inflation-adjusted basis. Moreover, these same progressively managed institutions tend to already earn a higher return on equity, enjoy superior stock prices, and are those that have the currency to acquire others in the next inevitable wave of bank consolidations.

Those not facing today's environmental and performance challenges armed with information and progressive management are inevitably still hoping that "somehow it will all work out." Unarmed with business, product, and market segment MIS, they compete broadly, price at the market level, and periodically cut costs, hoping that their results will be satisfactory. This approach becomes more problematic with every passing day.

On the other hand, the best managed banks use information and analysis persuasively. They:

- Calculate risk-adjusted rates of return for business units, products, and customer relationships;

- Use forecasting models to project the impact of macroeconomic forces on each business, and thereby set growth targets in line with market realities;

- Make decisions on how much capital and other resources to commit to businesses as a function of profitability potential;

- Evaluate merger economics by calculating the return on the acquisition investment as a function of expense savings, revenue potential, balance sheet restructuring opportunities, and growth potential;

- Use pricing models, key performance measures, and various early-warning indicators to manage day-to-day;

- Determine capital and loss-revenue needs based on an actuarial perspective on expected loss levels and the degree of volatility anticipated by business and credit grade of customer.

Ultimately, the fate of bankers who don't adapt their management methods to the changing requirements of their markets will be death by acquisition. Indeed, FMCG analysis indicates that half of the top 200 banks will disappear through mergers over the next five years, taken over by better-managed banks. That will be best for all concerned.

The 1990s should end with the U.S. banking industry stronger and more profitable than it is today, and with customers paying less for a variety of financial services than they are paying today. This book shows the way in great detail. What we at FMCG call "systematic management," and John B. McCoy, Larry

Frieder, and Bob Hedges describe as the perspectives and techniques used to effect higher performance, are right on point.

If one looks out across the U.S. banking industry today, one can begin to see the outline for a restructured industry. Market forces have indeed produced the evolutionary "Darwinian" environment that had been earlier predicted. Out of this environment, a new set of competitors is emerging; institutions disciplined by the marketplace and fueled by ambition to successfully compete. Already some of these institutions—BANC ONE, BankAmerica, NationsBank—are becoming recognized as new household names for the 1990s. More importantly, these successful competitors are defining the new paradigm for a restructured banking industry. John, Larry, and Bob have done us all a great favor by sharing that future with us today.

James M. McCormick
President
First Manhattan Consulting Group
New York, NY

Some Opening Remarks

Since the onset of deregulation in the early 1980s, much has been written about the trials and tribulations of the banking industry. Despite all the pages of prose, the literature generally falls into two categories. One set of writings focuses on scandal, mismanagement, and the misdeeds of the industry (and more specifically the S&L industry) as it sought to deal with the challenge of deregulation. The second set can be broadly categorized as self-help books, usually dedicated to specific tactical issues. For example, how to improve the quality of customer service, or how to build a sales culture. If you are writing to sell books, either approach makes sense. In the first case, tabloid sizzle sells. In the second case, a clear market niche can be targeted. In neither case, however, are real insights into the industry's struggle necessarily shared. Nor is the industry's real story, that of an industry in transition, told. Neither set of writings focuses on the profound paradigm shift that is currently underway in the banking industry.

Great drama marks the banking industry over the past decade. Within the context of this drama, individual institutions have both thrived and failed. More broadly, however, the drama is not about the success and failure of individual institutions, but an industry in naturally chaotic transition. Regulatory change, increased competition and the resulting operating revolution have kicked the transition into motion. It is a transition of objectives and tactics. The industry's underlying economics, approach to competition, stock market scrutiny, and, ultimately, management mindset have all had to move in response to underlying environmental pressures. At any given moment, the change may appear to be temporary or incremental, but measured across time, it is compelling and, to some, overwhelming.

Today, in response to these pressures, a new management philosophy is emerging. The new management approach is performance-driven and more activist. The bank executive of the '90s invites stock market scrutiny rather than yearning for the era when banks were generally sheltered from it. In this new era, banks must be market-driven, rather than regulation-oriented. To survive, one must be lean, adaptable and aggressive. To develop and nurture the required management instincts, one seeks exposure to the rigors of the market, rather than the protection of regulatory shelter.

Most fundamentally, in this period of change, there is growing recognition that the bank executive must be a leader, rather than just a steward or caretaker. Vision and leadership are imperatives. Courage is probably also a good word to describe an important attribute of today's banking leaders. History can provide guidance and context, but today's industry faces performance challenges never seen before. No longer can a bank management team rely on being a collection of "good customer people." When the decade closes, it will be those institutions that embraced the future that have fared the best. Change will not have been something resisted, but harnessed. For an institution to survive, it must be led with this perspective. In a period of consolidation, there will be no survivors among the banks that attempt to muddle through, or worse, to hide.

Leadership in the face of change is not an easy order. For those lacking a sense of direction, there are no blueprints; it may simply be an impossible challenge. Leadership is not about charisma, but instinct. The industry does not need more larger-than-life personalities, but rather a stronger sense and firmer grip on what is required to succeed. And when the environmental changes destroy the logic of the old business paradigm, the leadership challenge may become daunting. Everyone is in a race for answers.

Bottomline Banking seeks to meet this need for both context and strategic vision. This book is the story of an industry in transition, where old rules are no longer reliable and a new conventional wisdom has not yet emerged. At the same time, it is written with great urgency based on an awareness that the current decade may not be kind to all our readers. Rather than offer scandal-based analysis or a laundry list of "self-help" tips to ensure survival, we have tried to serve a greater need—to provide an objective appraisal of the forces of change and offer a prognosis for the industry which we hope will be received as a call to action.

For every force of change in the industry today, there is an appropriate institutional response. Of course, developing an integrated strategic program to address the forces of change is a significant management challenge. While *Bottomline Banking* is not meant to be a definitive blueprint, it offers a clear vision for what will be required to build and sustain strategic leadership. A new industry paradigm is beginning to emerge; one can see its early outline. We encourage readers to press on with the difficult pioneering work of making this vision a successful reality.

Acknowledgments

As with any undertaking this large, we are indebted to many, many people who supported our work over the project's more than two years' life. As we now complete the effort, it is most appropriate that we offer our thanks to all.

In particular, two people made invaluable contributions to the project—John Russell, Chief Communication Officer of BANC ONE and Ralph C. Kimball, Professor of Finance at Babson College. John was always accessible to make sure that the broad resources of BANC ONE were available for the project, and he personally contributed several key insights and suggestions, not the least of which was his sidebar essay which appears in Chapter 8. Ralph served as the project's senior technical consultant. In this role, he frequently critiqued the broad conceptual frameworks we hoped to use. His contributions are probably best identified in Chapter 9's discussion on the topic of product versus relationship management strategies.

Special thanks is expressed to the senior management team of BANC ONE. These individuals, who by definition are incredibly busy, never were too busy to address our inquiries and reflect on the large number of hypotheses developed over the course of our research. Specifically, we wish to thank: John G. McCoy, Donald McWhorter, William Boardman, John Westman, Paul Walsh, George Meiling, Tom Hoaglin, Roman Gerber, David Van Lear (now Chairman of EPS, Inc.), Tom Young and Phil Weaver. Two other members of the BANC ONE staff also helped greatly in keeping the ball rolling; John McCoy's Administrative Executive Secretary, Laura Gray, and John Russell's Executive Secretary, Louise Sladoje.

This project required significant data collection and research assistance. In this regard, we owe special gratitude to three people who hung in there with us—Steve W. Bensko, Irwin C. Loud, and Gordon Goetzmann. We tested the patience of each of these outstanding individuals.

We are appreciative to John Baker of the Midwest Bank Fund, Chicago Corporation, Lyle Logan of Continental Bank, and George Gregorash of the Federal Reserve Bank of Chicago; all generously contributed as critical reviewers of the numerous drafts that circulated over the last two years.

The presentation of *Bottomline Banking* relied heavily on data and graphics support. We had a number of organizations help us develop over 80 exhibits. First Manhattan Consulting Group (FMCG) was most generous in this regard. FMCG contributed the insights of its partners, data analysis support, and long hours of research and production assistance. Special thanks to Jim McCormick for his personal support of the project. Other firms or individuals who supplied important data or allowed reproduction of their research include: SNL Securities, Gemini Consulting Group, First Boston, Salomon Brothers, Kidder Peabody, Goldman Sachs, Keefe, Bruyette & Woods, Montgomery Securities, Merrill Lynch, FDIC, Board of Governors of the Federal Reserve, Office of Thrift Supervision, Federal Reserve Bank of Chicago, Federal Reserve Bank of St. Louis, Federal Reserve Bank of Kansas City, IBC Donoghue, David Cates, Loan Pricing Corporation, BANC ONE, DRI, Investment Company Institute, Wells Fargo, and *Bank Management.*

From the beginning, we decided that we would invite some of the banking industry's top thinkers to write essays or "sidebars" on topics that we felt were crucial to the delivery of the book's message. We were most fortunate that the following executives contributed outstanding works: John Medlin of Wachovia; Harvey Rosenblum of the Federal Reserve Bank of Dallas; Waite Rawls of the Chicago Corporation; John Singleton of ISSC; Jim McDermott and Dick Stillinger of Keefe, Bruyette & Woods; John Russell of BANC ONE; Anat Bird of BDO Seidman; Paul Ross of DRI (McGraw Hill); and Dick Fredericks of Montgomery Securities.

The production work on the project was endless. To meet this challenge we received great support from the School of Business and Industry (SBI), Florida A and M University, and the First Manhattan Consulting Group. We thank SBI's Dean, Dr. Sybil C. Mobley who has been a terrific supporter of this project. Numerous individuals at each of these institutions always "turned the work" for which we are grateful. Special thanks to FMCG's Diana Hakim and Florida A and M's Tracie Wynn.

We wish to express our appreciation to the following individuals at Probus who taught us something about deadlines: Jim McNeil, Kevin Thornton, and Judy Brown.

As we express appreciation to all those who helped make *Bottomline Banking* happen, we regret that we cannot mention individually the great number of people who have influenced our thinking over the years. Each of us has spent virtually all of our adult life "in banking" and in doing so, we have had a chance to work with many outstanding people who have a similar passion for the industry. Undoubtedly, many of the ideas we put forth emanate from various discussions, projects, and panels that we have enjoyed with our professional colleagues. To each of them a sincere "thanks" and we look forward to continued associations in the future.

If we have inadvertently omitted anyone, we apologize in advance.

John B. McCoy
Columbus, OH

Larry A. Frieder
Tallahassee, FL

Robert B. Hedges, Jr.
New Canaan, CT

1

Paradigm Lost

Industry change is never sudden. Rather like continental drift, change occurs gradually. Plate tectonics is not a spectator event. Stresses in an evolving system only occasionally flash dramatic; but it is slow, gradual change that is most profound. Evolutionary change can be seductively dangerous: seductive because everyone talks about the pressures for change, and yet only moderate incremental change may be necessary to appear abreast of the new requirements for success; dangerous because, while incremental moves may temporarily suffice, they will not adequately address the ultimate need for more pervasive, fundamental change.

Change, however, is never required for change's sake. In the case of the banking industry, change has been inspired by the need for increased marketplace and financial competitiveness. With regulatory protection gone, the industry has been working hard to meet both stringent competition from nonbanks and the performance standards of the stock market.

The performance challenges facing the banking industry are significant. They can be fundamentally defined as the need to meet both the product and capital market standards of competitiveness. From a capital market perspective, banks' ability to create value for their shareholders must receive the highest attention. Business portfolio composition, acquisition strategies, and investor relations all represent opportunities that need to be more aggressively managed. Four specific areas of product-market concern demand increased performance: cost management, distribution management, relationship management, and credit risk management. The struggle to step up to these performance challenges has marked the first part of the 1990s. The management mettle of the industry is being tested.

In the popular language of management, the word *paradigm* has caught on as a useful term for describing a business system or way of managing. Webster's defines paradigm as "a pattern, example, or model; an overall concept accepted by most people . . . because of its effectiveness in explaining a complex process." Historically, banks operated under a relatively stable business paradigm.

Regulatory guidelines and constraints that ensured competitive and operating stability were the foundation of the banking industry paradigm. Regulations drove product, pricing, place, and promotion decisions. From the perspective of the classic marketer, banks were greatly restricted in their ability to compete freely against the usual relevant criteria. Market share was fragmented and controlled. Pricing regulations set revenues, and regulated revenues provided the context for cost management. Adequate managers were widely available. This business paradigm produced industry stability and consumer confidence. And management did not play a particularly activist role. Because most institutions then were relatively small, as compared to today's, they required little access to capital markets. The paradigm was simple, stable, and, for most participants, secure.

This paradigm held, in general, for nearly 50 years—into the 1980s. Throughout this period, however, important environmental forces were at work eroding the banking industry's traditional business system. Outside the structure of banking regulation, nonbank competitors offered product and service alternatives to banks and were able to attract consumers. Underlying the success of nonbanks was their willingness to compete along dimensions that were obvious and impossible to ignore: product, price, and place, with significant cost and risk implications. Nonbanks were simultaneously changing the basis of competition, as well as getting a head start in developing the capabilities required to compete in the new world they were helping to create.

The regulatory response to the outbreak of nonbank competition was, first, to delay it, then ignore it, and then reluctantly seek to emulate it. Regulators initially failed to recognize nonbanks as a natural marketplace reaction to their historic failure to promote competition. Given the banking industry's dominance through regulatory history, nonbanks were not seen as a significant force.

In addition to the competitive threat that nonbanks represented, their operational tactics promoted significant advancement for the role of technology. Application of financial service technology resulted both in greater economies of scale and greater consumer access to their funds. As banks began to introduce new forms of technology, they also sought to exert influence over changing consumer behavior. The combination of competition and technology was changing market performance and expectations. From a regulatory perspective, the genie was essentially out of the bottle.

It was no longer possible to control external marketplace forces, and, given options, consumers were demanding that financial service providers compete. At best, regulators could redefine their own roles as referees. The new focus of regulatory activity

The regulatory response to the outbreak of nonbank competition was, first, to delay it, then ignore it, and then reluctantly seek to emulate it. Regulators initially failed to recognize nonbanks as a natural marketplace reaction to their historic failure to promote competition.

was establishing a more even playing field. In the parlance of paradigms, a shift was clearly under way.

The most important, but not unexpected, impact of expanded competition was increasing pressure on bank profitability. Exhibit 1.1 illustrates the extent to which the industry long-term average return on equity failed to exceed its cost of equity in the 1980s. With product margins under considerable pressure, the resulting revenue-cost squeeze should have been anticipated. The banking industry's infrastructure and cost dynamics had evolved in a noncompetitive environment. The industry's cost structure was largely fixed and somewhat inflexible. This led to an ever increasing importance of productivity and cost performance. Wrestling with costs has become a litmus test issue of management's will to survive in a deregulated environment.

In a few cases, budget discipline and belt-tightening have been sufficient to maintain competitiveness. For most banks, however, the past decade has been marked by growing acceptance of the need to implement uncharacteristically tough measures. Cost and resource allocation have required new discipline. In no other

It was no longer possible to control external market-place forces, and, given options, consumers were demanding that financial service providers compete. At best, regulators could redefine their own roles as referees.

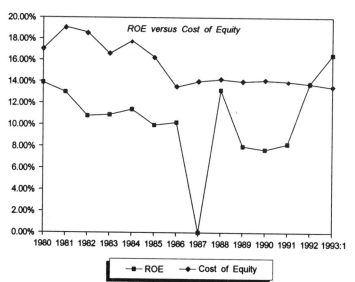

Exhibit 1.1

**COMMERCIAL BANKING INDUSTRY ROE
FAILED TO EXCEED ITS COST OF EQUITY IN THE 1980s**

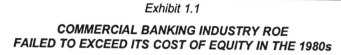

Note: The cost of equity, as calculated by Merrill Lynch, equals the 30-year Treasury bond yield plus 5.6% equity risk premium.
Sources: FDIC, Merrill Lynch

area has the gentlemanly culture of the banking industry faced greater challenge.

Most important, belt-tightening alone has not been enough. It has been necessary to slash staff and service levels to bring costs in line with available revenues. An industry that was accustomed to closing its doors at three o'clock in the afternoon has had to develop a new work ethic in order to contend with competitors unbound by banking's culture and traditions. This fundamental realignment with marketplace reality has resulted in significant pain and loss of face for some management teams.

But even the most draconian cost reductions are inadequate to meet the continuing challenges facing the industry. Tremendous economies of scale, coupled with existing excess capacity, suggest dramatic restructuring as the only acceptable solution to the industry's revenue-cost dilemma.

But even the most draconian cost reductions are inadequate to meet the continuing challenges facing the industry. Tremendous economies of scale, coupled with existing excess capacity, suggest dramatic restructuring as the only acceptable solution to the industry's revenue-cost dilemma. To address the industry's cost challenge with draconian, rather than revolutionary, approaches will be by definition to fall short of the challenge.

By the mid-1980s, some initial attempts at restructuring were beginning to provide both relief for individual institutions and broader leadership for the industry as a whole. The best early examples of restructuring include:

- the exit of Banker's Trust from retail banking, including the sale of its New York branch network;

- Continental Bank's divestiture of its credit card business (the first of many banks to do so);

- the general retreat of U.S. banks from international Eurodollar lending in the mid-1980s.

One bank, one product line at a time—restructuring is a slow process. And while the glacial pace of restructuring implicitly suggested that the competitive environment would allow banks the necessary time, a more correct interpretation was that pressure for restructuring was building rapidly. Much heralded budget discipline at many institutions was equivalent to rearranging the deck chairs on the *Titanic* as the band played its final tune. Performance pressures and expectations were building, and not all institutions were ready to address them. The pace of paradigm change accelerated in the 1980s, but even the most astute industry observers were not yet prepared to declare that the traditional paradigm was lost.

The pace of paradigm change accelerated in the 1980s, but even the most astute industry observers were not yet prepared to declare that the traditional paradigm was lost.

Today's consolidation wave is in response to both the need for dramatic industry restructuring and the scarcity of management required to do the job. Consolidation is the inevitable response to the necessity to reduce costs, the real absence of market sources for revenue growth, and the overhang of excess capacity. At the same time, the most limited resource today may be the management talent necessary to lead and restructure the large financial institutions that consolidation pressures have created. Management that both understands the complexity of the industry's performance challenges and embraces the need for change in response to those challenges may ultimately be the constrained resource around which the consolidating industry must be configured. The bottom line is that while there may be sufficient capital to go around, there may not be enough industry leadership.

Musical chairs is an apt analogy for the consolidation of the banking industry. Industry performance pressures and environmental shocks bring successive waves of merger and acquisition activity. Each wave sees shifts in market share and bank ownership. Bank names change and are mutated to reflect new alliances and ownership. The landscape evolves, and familiar institutions are eliminated with each successive wave. Emerging are stronger, more competitive, more responsive institutions designed to compete in this new era. For any management team to survive a wave of consolidation is a triumph. To think about surviving long term almost requires prescient knowledge of marketplace forces that no one professes to have. When the music stops, one should expect that there will be as many bank competitors as there are management teams up to the challenge. With equilibrium established, though probably not market stability, a new paradigm will eventually settle in.

Noted bank stock analyst, J. Richard Fredericks of Montgomery Securities has characterized the industry as being in an era of "Darwinian banking." The analogy is appropriate. Only the strongest, most fit competitors will survive. Moreover, fitness must be measured along multiple dimensions: profitability, capital, franchise strength, and management. From the capital market's perspective, deregulation and the resulting consolidation have created an environment in which attractive profitability and adequate capital are achievable. Consolidation activity and regulatory encouragement have allowed banks to gain strong market share positions and franchise strength in natural markets. With historical regulatory and structural constraints removed, and other things being equal, management becomes the crucial, deciding factor. In an industry long driven by regulation and tradition, management leadership becomes the critical differentiating factor between competitors.

In the 1960s and 1970s, industry regulators were the dominant personalities and driving forces in the banking industry. In the 1980s, competitive markets succeeded the regulators as the central, driving force. By the end of the 1990s, it will be forward-looking and creative bank executives who will be most responsible for writing the history of the industry's transition. Exhibit 1.2 presents the different eras of strategic emphasis through which the industry has recently passed.

> *Musical chairs is an apt analogy for the consolidation of the banking industry. Industry performance pressures and environmental shocks bring successive waves of merger and acquisition activity.*

Exhibit 1.2

RECENT ERAS OF STRATEGIC EMPHASIS

	1970s	1980s	First Half 1990s	Second Half 1990s
Industry Profitability	• Strong returns	• Declining returns	• Rebounding returns	• Strong returns
Management Orientation	• Growth	• Product/ market diversification	• Survival	• High performance
Strategic Focus	• Branch expansion • International banking	• New products • Expanded geographic coverage	• Cost reduction • Credit quality	• Earnings sustainability • Franchise strength
Acquisition Rationale	• Geographic expansion/ market coverage	• Grow to achieve scale	• Eliminate redundant capacity	• Diversification
Acquisition Targets	• Small bank branch networks	• Contiguous regional banks	• In-market competitors	• Nonbanks • New products
Regulatory Emphasis	• Expanded branch banking	• Deregulation • Market pricing	• Nationwide banking	• Stability • Fair lending/CRA

Today the banking industry is in a state most aptly described as *Paradigm Lost*. Lacking a protective regulatory structure, no new economic or competitive model has yet definitively emerged. While the playing field is not, and will never be, level, it has become more open. For institutions that are prepared, there is nothing to fear. A clean sheet of paper could provide an able management group the opportunity to redefine competition, more fluidly allocate resources, and restructure their internal economics. There is great opportunity to be found in a world where the once dominant business paradigm has been declared null and void.

An outline of the new paradigm is emerging. One can find some creative approaches by studying successful regional banks. The new paradigm is defined by market forces, customer needs, and a competitive environment not unlike musical chairs. It is a paradigm in which not all will succeed; it is not designed to be otherwise.

From careful analysis of the new, emerging paradigm, it is possible to discern the requirements for future success. Given that their source is today's competitive environment, these requirements will be neither easy to achieve, nor popular. For those who fail, it will become clear what they should have done to compete—but it will be too late.

Today one must manage through the period of transition with the highest standard of performance always as a guide. At some future date, after the fact, successful banks will have formally validated the new paradigm. Today's challenge is to make the cut. The focus of *Bottomline Banking* is not only the story of an industry in transition, but an account of how today's management can make or break the bank.

Moving to Address the Performance Challenges

The banking industry is witnessing a fundamental shift in strategic focus. The restructuring that is now well under way will continue into the next century—with the added complexity of more frequent consolidation maneuvering. The industry's strategic focus will shift from consolidation for the purpose of survival to restructuring for high performance. In this context, Wall Street is replacing regulators as the prime audience to satisfy.

In addition to traditional pressures, such as the prudent management of credit risk, banks today are under pressure from capital markets to exercise far more discipline and effectiveness in responding to fundamental industry forces. The capital markets' increasing emphasis on performing for shareholders will drive five major performance challenges throughout the current decade:

1. Acquisition and consolidation strategy: Mergers and acquisitions are a pivotal part of the restructuring occurring in the industry. Standards for assessing the value-creation potential of bank combinations have evolved. Reevaluation of the relative merits of interregional and interstate versus intrastate acquisitions is likely, and management's integration skills will continue to be critically important. A tolerance for higher dilution levels may emerge only if the potential for earn-back is apparent and attainable. While traditional rules regarding dilution and payback still cloud conventional wisdom, a more sophisticated strategic and financial framework for evaluating consolidation strategy is falling into place.

2. Resource allocation and cost management: Cost issues are still paramount, but banks gain few advantages by simply containing costs and reducing expenses. Success during the remaining 1990s depends on restructuring business processes to change the cost structures of business, achieving scale and scope economies in

Today one must manage through the period of transition with the highest standard of performance always as a guide.

the right businesses, and managing investment spending more strategically. Strategic cost management means knowing when to spend money.

3. Value-creating franchise management: Banks will shift the emphasis from expanding franchise size and concentrate more on effectively developing the franchise and exploiting market potential. The focus will be on levering the franchise to maximize profitability. With market revenue growth limited, new products, new channels, and overarching branding will be critical elements of the program. Strategies will focus on the two key franchise performance levers: distribution and relationship management.

4. Credit policy management: Stronger competition for customers both from within and without the industry has compressed pricing. Highly effective risk analysis systems and the use of portfolio (noncorrelated) risk selection are essential to address this pricing competition. Modern finance theory has dramatically changed the securities and investment management businesses. In the 1990s, this same revolution will occur in the banking industry.

5. Effective organization management and leadership: If the banking industry learned no other lesson during the 1980s, it saw a clear demonstration of the critical need for strong management. The volume, pace, and urgency of management decision making continues to accelerate. A profession that was once viewed commonly with managing a small family business has evolved into a complex, analytical undertaking with significant public policy implications. To establish the type of organization and management structure needed to succeed requires a higher level of CEO leadership than ever before. At the same time, this cultural revolution cannot be limited to the executive suite; it must be driven down into all levels of the organization to ensure a successful transformation.

Facing scrutiny from the capital markets in the 1980s, market forces that were neither kind nor gentle forced industrial corporations to restructure in order to enhance their market values or risk losing their independence. In the banking industry, well-capitalized institutions have only recently won high marks from the capital markets for solvency and the strength of their capital underpinnings. However, as the need for capital productivity continues to increase, capital markets of the 1990s will penalize institutions that are overcapitalized or have underleveraged assets. Simply building a conservative balance sheet will not be enough to ensure success.

During the past decade, executives of industrial corporations used a variety of restructuring techniques to alter their company's capital structure and/or its business profile significantly. Restructuring techniques used to alter the capital structure of industrial firms generally have not proven applicable to banks, which are naturally more highly leveraged relative to their industrial counterparts.

More important, banks generally have been slower to restructure because of the historic lack of capital market pressure. In banking, unfriendly tender offers and proxy fights have been the exception rather than the rule. Several reasons are generally cited to explain the historically privileged and protected position of the banking industry in the capital markets. While some are more legitimate than others, four reasons are most broadly accepted:

1. Regulatory hurdles and complications: The Federal Reserve merger approval process, combined with strict regulatory capital requirements, represents a formidable barrier to both banks and investor groups. Few CEOs or individual investors have the time, energy, or financial resources to overcome the regulatory hurdles that could exist in a hostile bank transaction.

2. Perception of limited break-up opportunities: Most banks are perceived to be fully integrated, full-service institutions. Moreover, as a result of the industry's cost structure, it is open to question whether or not the sum of the parts exceeds the value of the whole, which is often the case in the industrialized world. In addition, the analytics of break-up valuation aside, break-up moves would be extremely countercultural for the industry.

3. Inability to penetrate blind risk pools: Despite massive SEC disclosure requirements, bank balance sheets are not as transparent as industrialized balance sheets, and few outsiders are prepared to assume the risk inherent in loan and securities portfolios without an inside look. This has been a major issue in the bank merger-of-equals movement.

4. Inability to increase leverage: Although it is a frequently used technique in the industrial world, the banking industry is, as noted above, innately highly leveraged. Most banks have limited unused debt capacity. The type of leverage that was employed by indus-

trial corporations in the 1980s to support restructuring is simply not available to banks.

As a result of both regulation and industry tradition, the major force driving restructuring in the industrial world, capital market pressure, has historically been absent from the banking world. The record verifies this. During the 1980s, we saw 122 hostile bids (transactions exceeding value of $250 million) in the industrial world but only 19 unilateral attempts in the banking industry (only 11 were aimed at bank targets of greater than $250 million in market value). Of these, only seven have been successful. In Chapter 5, we will explore in more detail the banking industry's experience with hostile transactions.

The industry's slow response to performance challenges, however, cannot be fully explained by capital market conditions. Traditional industry management biases have also contributed. There are five common explanations:

1. Management's reluctance to downsize: A historical focus on size rather than profitability, and the accompanying concern of many bankers that revenues will drop faster than costs, have biased the industry against downsizing as a means to improve profitability. For banks with problem assets, shrinking the balance sheet magnifies the size of their potential revenue problem. Regulatory status, management ego, and bragging rights at the country club have also ruled out downsizing moves that might have been applauded by the capital markets.

2. Inadequate measures of line-of-business profitability: Lacking appropriate business line management information systems (MIS), management has been reluctant to make definitive resource allocation decisions. Historical resource alignments become relatively inert. If powerful management biases are driving most decision making, the absence of adequate MIS basically immobilizes the change process. Obtaining accurate line-of-business profitability is understandably difficult for banks for a variety of reasons.

   • The existence of a large base of indirect shared costs: Many banks have multiple lines of business yet limited ability to allocate costs adequately to individual lines or their components. Undoubtedly, certain lines of business absorb too great a share of the cost base, but little evidence of this allocation is included in the information that reaches management.

- Shared customers: Paralleling the shared cost problem, separate lines of business sharing common customers, further clouding revenue and cost allocations. Lacking a straightforward analytical resolution, many banks are forced to accept this constraint.

- Unintegrated and inadequate information systems: Bank management must receive adequate data and be able to analyze and synthesize basic revenue and cost dynamics. With both revenue and cost allocation complexities, systems must become fully integrated and supply information that is concise, timely, reconcilable, and comprehensible.

3. Perceived capital adequacy constraints: Although some banks have identified marginal or unprofitable activities that should be closed down or sold, they are unable or unwilling to take the capital write-down required, fearing loss of face and adverse stock market reactions. Accounting maneuvering, however, can make it possible to cover up economic losses.

4. Liquidity and funding considerations: Real or imagined, concerns regarding funding source diversification and asset origination sources (or diversification) have kept banks involved in some types of business long after management reporting information suggested that doing so was not in the best interests of shareholders. For example, some money centers were reluctant to divest their branch banking operations for fear they would be unable to fund the wholesale bank. Similarly, many regional banks maintain large, low-yielding securities portfolios for liquidity and balance sheet structure reasons. In today's capital market environment, this problem is probably much more imagined than real.

5. Slow pace of management decision making: Allocating indirect costs will never be popular with line managers. Moreover, rationalizing or divesting businesses has a high human cost and is not an easy decision to make. Banking's organizational structure has traditionally been highly pyramidal and hierarchical. In spite of new technologies that now make it possible to compress the decision-making process, this kind of structure, with its inherent rewards and breadth of control, can slow and stall decision making.

American industry, since the 1980s, has been marked by the popular, charismatic leader who took on difficult restructuring

When Cristopher Steffen, the crusading CFO of Kodak, departed the company for reasons of cultural incompatibility, it was no surprise that he was immediately recruited to Citicorp, certainly an institution facing a major restructuring challenge.

challenges. Lee Iaccoca at Chrysler, Jack Welch at General Electric, and most recently Lou Gerstner at IBM have all popularized the crusading, restructuring executive. Texas State Comptroller, John S. Sharp, has brought such leadership to state government. We have only just begun to see the emergence of similar leadership in the banking industry. When Cristopher Steffen, the crusading CFO of Kodak, departed the company for reasons of cultural incompatibility, it was no surprise that he was immediately recruited to Citicorp, certainly an institution facing a major restructuring challenge. Perhaps we are seeing the early signs of the new paradigm's priority on management talent and willingness to face capital market scrutiny head-on.

As deregulation unfolded during the 1980s, both real and imagined market and internal constraints on bank restructuring withered. Today few senior bank executives would argue that their institutions are any longer insulated from the pressures of capital markets. Additionally, congressional mandates emanating from the 1991 Federal Deposit Insurance Corporation Improvement Act (FDICIA) prevent capital forbearance and allow for more frequent and earlier regulatory intervention. Today's performance challenges are real and demand both appropriate strategies and effective management. In the current environment, these strategies must focus on building and leveraging shareholder value.

Institutional investors will increasingly exert pressure on the banking industry. In addition, reflecting today's low-revenue growth environment, many banks will need to make acquisitions in order to continue to grow. As the number of attractive candidates interested in selling dwindles, larger banks may utilize more hostile tactics to satisfy their strategic objectives. Without any doubt, the bank equity market environment of the 1990s will be markedly different from that of the 1980s.

Market Value: The Key to Survival and Success

In today's banking world, market value has become the ultimate performance measure. It is the enabler for participation in the industry's consolidation process. The most successful banks—those with strong market capitalizations—will have the currency to take advantage of opportunities generated by the evolving merger market.

Banks that, because of performance difficulties and consequent low valuations, do not enjoy a strong currency face dim prospects. Typically, weak banks find it advantageous to sell out. The Texas banking industry succumbed to out-of-state acquirers. The C&S/Sovran real estate credit problems led to its merger with NationsBank. Security Pacific's credit difficulties put it in the arms of BankAmerica. The Chemical-Manufacturers Hanover combination was a situation in which both partners were faced with low valuation and few strategic alternatives. Failure to generate adequate earnings and shareholder value has profound consequences.

At the same time, in the midst of the evolving banking environment, high-performing institutions continue to gain advantage. With the benefit of strong currency, they have the buying capacity to undertake value-creating mergers. The ability to absorb short-term dilution and maintain the confidence of the stock market is a critical strength. Strong banks realize a further advantage from their managements' ability to evaluate prospective partners or targets in terms of strategic fit and cost take-out. Too often an inadequate plan, or the missing will to restructure a new, combined entity, has soured the results of consolidation efforts. The inability to create value through consolidation results in a merger being a failure.

As the decade of the 1990s unfolds, weaker institutions will be increasingly subject to takeover and consolidation. Eventually, the landscape may be populated by only a handful of large banking survivors, each of whom commands major market share positions.

Manage Business Portfolio Mix as a Key Strategic Variable

Historically, banks have not completely understood the importance of business mix and performance within the mix as market value drivers. Reflecting the performance measurement problems discussed earlier, key performance levers too often remain disguised. Yet, from the capital market's perspective, business portfolio mix is a key strategic variable.

In today's management framework, each line of business must be rigorously evaluated, including a determination of which lines may disproportionately add to or detract from shareholder value. In this process it is necessary to assess the equity requirement for each business unit and establish full business unit P&Ls, including the assignment of indirect costs and risk adjustments. Those business units that do not enhance market value need to be scrutinized carefully and, in many cases, downsized or eliminated. Some banks may begin divesting even profitable and seemingly attractive businesses as long-term ROE projections drive home the link between a business line's prospective performance and its future stock price. Looking forward, bank management must decide the number of business lines that it can manage and grow profitably. Banks must be careful not to overextend management resources at the expense of performance. Even in the context of shareholder value analysis, management should be allocated as a limited resource.

Similarly, Signet divested a very profitable consumer finance subsidiary in 1988 after evaluating the productivity of the capital that this subsidiary required in comparison to alternative uses of the same capital.

The stock market's focus on capital allocation and performance will increasingly provide incentive for bank management teams to shift resources among their businesses based on each unit's earnings, growth prospects, and contribution to market value. For example, when U.S. Trust of New York elected to sell its marginally profitable commercial banking business in 1988, an almost 10 percent increase in share price occurred on the day of the announcement. As a second example, Michigan National's 1989 decision to sell its credit card business reflected a belief that the scale economics of that business would change materially in the future, and that alternative investments would represent a better use of capital. Similarly, Signet divested a very profitable consumer finance subsidiary in 1988 after evaluating the productivity of the capital that this subsidiary required in comparison to alternative uses of the same capital. At the same time, reflecting a different strategy and position on the business scale cost curve, Signet invested capital aggressively in the credit card business throughout the 1980s. This has proven to be a very valuable strategy.

Business portfolio analysis can identify the relative contribution that each line of business makes to a bank's overall market value by revealing which lines add to or detract from that value. In Chapter 4, Fifth Third, Wells Fargo, Banker's Trust, and State Street are broken up for illustrative purposes. These case study banks were found to have strong market capitalizations because they emphasize high-value-creating business lines.

If market value is the ultimate performance measure, then business portfolio mix is the critical management lever. Most banks have significant restructuring opportunities available. The 1990s should be the decade in which these opportunities are exploited.

Pursue Mergers and Acquisitions as a Source of Value

With growing recognition of the importance of having strong currency to support doing deals, it is increasingly asked whether acquisitions can be viewed as a source of value. In the earlier stages of the interstate merger process (1985–86), bank deals often involved double-digit dilution. In 1987–88 the equity markets adopted a lower standard of dilution tolerance to one approximating 5 to 6 percent. By 1988, this dilution standard was lowered to nearly zero as Wall Street became increasingly skeptical of interstate consolidation effects on shareholders.

In large part, the evidence covering mergers and acquisitions during this time period suggests most banks were not able to integrate the merged institutions well enough to justify taking earnings dilution. Several high-profile research studies, sponsored or conducted by organizations as diverse as the Bank Administration Institute, the Federal Reserve and the Harvard Business School, contributed evidence that supported the skeptics. Recent history, however, is beginning to tell a different story. High-profile transactions such as Society-Ameritrust and Barnett-First Florida Banks are demonstrating how value can be created. In fact, by the mid-1990s, well-managed superregionals that continue to make acquisitions as a result of their enhanced financing capacity should achieve higher market capitalization values than the largest remaining money-center banks.

In the future, a higher level of dilution may again become acceptable in the eyes of the market. Current standards fail to discriminate completely between mergers with varying underlying economic rationales. The stock market is sometimes too cynical about management's integration skills. Some banks have clearly developed stronger integration skills than others. As we move farther into the 1990s, the market's assessment of a merger's potential, along with the involved bank's management skills and resolve to exploit the value potential of a merged franchise, will become the key variables in establishing individualized dilution standards and future value. When that happens, the guidelines employed by bank analysts to evaluate acquisition economics will be replaced by the more discriminating assessments of the acquirer's management.

Against this backdrop, the value of intrastate transactions has risen in the 1990s, reflecting the inherent cost savings and other benefits that in-market deals offer. Out-of-state acquirers historically have paid an entry premium, offering about 12 percent more for the same institution than have competing in-state bidders. In the 1990s, in-state bidders' premiums have increasingly rivaled the premiums paid for interstate entry. The capital markets have reacted favorably to several deals patterned after the Wells Fargo absorption of Crocker, even though they often implied substantial up-front dilution. The compelling economics of in-market consolidations suggest such capital market support should continue.

In some geographical locations, thrifts are often the only available vehicle for either market entry or in-market consolidation. Notwithstanding some reservations, many banks have developed thrift-based expansion strategies. It is often simply less expensive to acquire a thrift than a commercial bank in order to gain market entry or market share. Moreover, the cost savings to be realized from the purchase of in-market thrifts can also be substantial. The Mellon-Meritor, PNC-First Federal of Pittsburgh, and First Union-DF Southeastern deals are examples of thrift-based market share strategies. The inclusion of thrifts and S&Ls into the

Current standards fail to discriminate completely between mergers with varying underlying economic rationales. The stock market is sometimes too cynical about management's integration skills. Some banks have clearly developed stronger integration skills than others.

banking industry paradigm reflects the collapse of the historical, regulatory separation and the strong logic of industry consolidation.

Commercial banks' experience with consolidation has often been disappointing. Mergers have not automatically produced increased share value. Market expectations for more efficient bank integration, however, are rising.

Effective integration is not easy, but it does hold the key to success. In the end, management's ability to work a merged franchise and achieve maximum value is even more important than whatever strategic logic might have led to a merger. The time the market allows for adjustments and phase-ins will be shorter, requiring banks to shift from simply acquiring attractive franchises to exploiting them effectively once they are on board. Managing the consolidation process to create value will be critical to success. Chapters 5 and 6 discuss industry consolidation and merger mechanics in detail. Included in Chapter 5 is a discussion of the survivor candidates and the probable consolidation scenarios to expect during the next 10 years.

Awareness and Acceptance of the Changing Banking Environment

Nonbank competitors, specifically mutual funds providers, offered much more favorably priced products. Deposit and investment product pricing narrowed considerably.

From the end of World War II through the 1970s, pricing regulations resulted in net interest margins remaining basically stable. Competition was oriented toward attracting customers by establishing convenient branch locations and improving personal service. Industry revenues were generated primarily from margin income, and other bank income elements were not thoroughly evaluated in terms of their potential or profitability.

In the 1980s, the banking industry found there was a wide range of challenges surrounding business mix and that certain important lines of business were not competitive. Product deregulation appeared to be only a limited panacea for the banking industry. Nonbank competitors, specifically mutual funds providers, offered much more favorably priced products. Deposit and investment product pricing narrowed considerably. Unfortunately, price deregulation served only to highlight the industry's profitability challenge further. As a result, significant revenue shortfall emerged relative to the existing cost structure of the industry. The need to address the basic disconnect between the industry's cost structure and the market's revenue potential became more acute.

Wrestle Successfully with Market Forces

From almost any perspective, the consolidation of the bank structure and the broadening of competition have dramatically changed the bank operating environment. Marketplace pressures are forcing managers of banks of all sizes to address a wide range of organizational and managerial issues. The emerging paradigm is requiring management attention and focus in areas previously left incompletely addressed:

- the need to manage costs instead of simply cutting costs;

- the need to rethink traditional branch distribution systems;

- the need to synthesize existing bank product and relationship strategies;

- the need to install more sophisticated credit management systems.

During this period of industry transition, operating decisions will be at least as important as corporate strategy decisions.

Replace Cost Reduction with Cost Management

Cost management is a complicated challenge because it is not well understood either by management or investment analysts. Banks need to rise above their preoccupation with cutting costs. Empirical evidence suggests that cost ratios and rates of expense growth do not always correlate closely with market value. Some banks that do not have low cost ratios or low expense growth rates have high stock market valuations.

As they progress through the 1990s, enlightened management teams will replace across-the-board cost-cutting and overcome their aversion to outlays that produce more strategic and opportunistic benefits. Chapter 7 identifies some different approaches that banks are using to manage costs effectively.

Rethink and Restructure Distribution Systems

It is increasingly accepted that the elaborate branch distribution systems of the past are not economically viable for the long term. Consumer usage patterns and buying behavior are shifting dramatically. Additionally, deregulation, technology, and nonbank competition have fundamentally changed the profitability equation of retail banking.

Banking's disadvantageous cost structure is increasingly problematic relative to the delivery systems of nonbanks. Accordingly, we present a number of suggestions related to addressing this competitive challenge. In Chapter 8, we argue that banks' delivery networks will be rationalized for customer usage patterns and combined with alternative delivery vehicles. Major restructuring of existing branch systems will occur. Managing this transition represents an enormous management challenge.

Transform to Relationship Banking

Despite the fact that many banks and bankers express their commitment to relationship banking, in truth they could still be classified as product-driven. As a general matter, the industry's cross-sell ratios are low, and most banks capture a relatively small percentage of their customers' wallets. At the same time, banks expend significant resources to acquire new customers while allowing large percentages of existing clientele to leave.

Despite the fact that many banks and bankers express their commitment to relationship banking, in truth they could still be classified as product-driven.

In Chapter 9, we analyze both product-driven and relationship banking. Some successful banks will be product-driven and will achieve volume from transaction-oriented customers. They will tend to have less dense distribution systems and lower levels of service and thus will have lower cost structures. Other banks, however, will pursue a more relationship-oriented approach. Capturing a greater share of existing customers' wallets through relationships has the potential of raising profitability significantly and locking in a bank's customer base. That is, if customers maintain several products and significant balances with a given bank, they will be less likely to switch to a competitor.

A relationship strategy is not a low-cost or scale-efficient approach. Rather, its potential profitability emanates from economies of scope. Ultimately, however, we see the current widespread distinction in banking between product-driven and relationship-driven banks as less relevant. Instead, in the pursuit of success, banks will synthesize both product and relationship management into new branding, segmentation, and channel management approaches. Chapter 9 presents our view of how this evolution will unfold.

Adopt New Credit Risk Management Approaches

Commercial banks have experienced a steady increase in their loan charge-off expense over the past several decades. The search for earning assets has led down several risky roads, including less developed countries (LDCs), highly leveraged transactions (HLTs), and commercial real estate lending. Banks are finding it increasingly difficult to transform their franchise deposit bases into high earning assets—at acceptable risk levels.

We argue that, in the face of pressure to generate higher earning assets, banks must be more effective in pricing and controlling credit risk. The answer is not to be more conservative, but rather more comprehensive and analytical in the approach to credit decision making. Banks must employ techniques involving more rigorous applications of quantitative portfolio theory.

Finally, some fundamental improvement in the diversification profile of bank loan portfolios will result from the formation of more intraregional, interregional, and nationwide banks. Both process and structured solutions are required for the diversification challenge. In Chapter 10, we put forward a comprehensive process for managing the loan portfolio.

Achieving the Desired Bottomline Impact

Following the industry's decade-long battle against myriad challenges, a set of institutions is beginning to emerge as high performers. Exhibit 1.3 lists some banks that have consistently performed well against key success factors of the 1990s.

Business portfolio mix is a critical trait of many successful institutions. The Northern Trust is very focused on private banking as well as trust and corporate services. J.P. Morgan has committed to providing investment banking and related commercial banking services to only the largest multinational corporations. The retail and small business focus of BANC ONE and Norwest certainly contributes significantly to their success.

NationsBank has excelled in creating value by seizing merger opportunities. Its First Republic and C&S/Sovran deals each added more than $1 billion to its market capitalization. NationsBank's more recent purchase of MNC may also prove to be quite valuable. An effective acquisition template is critical to bottomline success. BANC ONE and Norwest have two of the industry's better developed programs.

Given the industry's profitability pressures, cost discipline receives much attention as a key success factor. Fifth Third is by far the industry's leader in the practice of cost discipline. Other banks that have consistently performed well in this regard include PNC, Wells Fargo, and Republic New York.

CoreStates is one of the industry leaders in distribution effectiveness. Its channel management programs are focused and

Exhibit 1.3	
KEY SUCCESS FACTORS OF THE 1990s	
Key Success Factor	**Examples of Successful Banks**
Strategic business portfolio mix	J.P. Morgan, Northern Trust, Norwest, BANC ONE
Acquisition templates	BANC ONE, Norwest, NationsBank
Cost discipline	Fifth Third, Wells Fargo, PNC
Innovative retail distribution and marketing	CoreStates, BayBanks, Wells Fargo
Relationship banking	Norwest, J.P. Morgan, First American
Credit quality	Wachovia, NBD, Society

make aggressive use of technology. Some additional banks making a mark in this area include BayBanks and Wells Fargo.

We view relationship banking aimed at gaining a high share of wallet penetration as one key to high profitability. The approaches of Richard Kovacevich of Norwest and Dennis Bottorff of First American are notable in the level of intensity with which they have attempted to manage share of wallet.

Wachovia, NBD, and Society are examples of banks with outstanding credit management. A significant part of their superior performance over the years relates to their effectiveness in pricing and controlling credit risk.

Across all the different functional areas, one can find examples of success and excellence that reflect the emerging industry paradigm.

Management as the Critical Resource

An industry whose culture has always rewarded stability must now promote innovation. As a result, a strong, guiding corporate culture, which once may have been deemed only a soft consideration by some, could be a most decisive factor.

Spurred by regulatory changes, technological advances, and unexpected economic shocks, the banking industry is undergoing a period of rapidly intensifying competition and fundamental change. New products and services are both agents and consequences of change. An industry whose culture has always rewarded stability must now promote innovation. As a result, a strong, guiding corporate culture, which once may have been deemed only a soft consideration by some, could now be a most decisive factor. To a great extent it is important for the bank CEO to view his or her job as the manager of the bank's culture. For instance, at BANC ONE, as well as at many other banks, corporate culture is not just talked about, it is actively managed:

Even the most conservative observers predict that deregulation will eventually produce a banking industry structured dramatically differently from today's. Management's challenge lies in ensuring not only that a sound strategy exists at the broadest institutional level, but also that each individual component of the institution is making its largest possible contribution to shareholder value during this period of transition. Success depends ultimately on performance. And in the 1990s, an institution's performance will depend on its management. In Chapter 11, we discuss the critical strategic role of the CEO in communicating a bank's strategy and successes to the investment community; and then in Chapter 12, we focus on the management and leadership role of the CEO at the broadest level.

The Bottomline as We See It

As the structure of the industry has changed, so has the basis of competition. The historically stable banking environment allowed a conservative management orientation to generate adequate returns. The traditional banking success formula of conservative risk-taking and steady asset growth, along with government regulation of pricing, and thereby margins, is no longer of any relevance. As the 1990s continue to unfold, however, no new system of bank management has yet evolved. Years of success with the same management formula have atrophied the industry's ability to engage in meaningful self-assessment.

The fundamental challenge facing the banking industry is not the survival threat posed by deregulation. Neither are technological advances, in and of themselves, a problem. Emphasis on banks' difficulty in adapting to market changes begins to focus in on the banking industry dilemma more clearly. The real concern of the industry should be the quality of management and the quality of key management processes. A bank risks being overwhelmed by environmental change only if it lacks the necessary internal capabilities and systems to manage the required evolution. Much of the industry's turmoil in the 1980s can best be understood in this context.

Bank performance was once considered an almost exogenous variable by bank shareholders. Intensified competition, the introduction of new products and services, and increased resource demands have required that banks more explicitly manage performance. In the future, a bank's performance will no longer be simply the consequence of its balance sheet and market position, but rather the result of management leadership and effectiveness. This is the essence of the new paradigm.

The real concern of the industry should be the quality of management and the quality of key management processes. A bank risks being overwhelmed by environmental change only if it lacks the necessary internal capabilities and systems to manage the required evolution.

> ### Bottomline Banking:
> ### Meeting the Challenges for Survival and Success

Our purpose in this work is to provide a framework for examining critical issues arising within the changing banking landscape. We begin in Chapters 2 and 3 with an examination of the bank operating environment that includes analyses of deregulation, competition, and evolving reregulation. We then move on, in Chapter 4, to discuss a shareholder value framework and its application to four case study banks: Fifth Third, Wells Fargo, Banker's Trust, and State Street.

Chapter 5 explores merger issues that are integral to bank consolidation strategies. Using illustrative scenarios, we analyze possible options for different size regional banks. Then in Chapter 6, we analyze merger mechanics, placing emphasis on the need to determine what is required to ensure that deals create value. Some hypothetical potential mergers are examined.

Internal growth and profitability are the subjects of the second half of the book. We discuss some of the key levers that senior management can pull in order to enhance performance: cost management, distribution management, relationship management, and credit portfolio management. A chapter is dedicated to each topic.

We close with a sharp focus on management. Chapter 11 examines the requirements for successfully managing Wall Street. Then we explore the role of the CEO and senior management in Chapter 12. Our final discussion, in Chapter 13, synthesizes the major ideas developed throughout the text and identifies 10 fresh, guiding rules to help shape the new banking paradigm.

2

The Regulatory Forces of Change

In the public policy arena, an important and explicit tension exists between public and private interests. In free market economies, market forces are often deemed the natural regulators of this tension. Public policy, or regulatory, intervention occurs whenever the market fails to produce an outcome deemed to be in the public interest. The financial services marketplace is not exempt from this, at times, dialectic process. Indeed, regulation of the banking and financial industries has been the subject of spirited public debate since biblical times. We can see examples in the writings of William Shakespeare, Charles Dickens, and, most recently, film writer and director Oliver Stone's popular movie success, *Wall Street.*

Today's discussion is conducted simultaneously along several dimensions: equity versus efficiency; local versus national interests; and, in current populist terms, Main Street versus Wall Street. No single dimension best captures and depicts the age-old debate. While we do not plan to suggest any resolution to this perplexing problem, it is an important backdrop to any discussion of the financial services marketplace. Nowadays the equity versus efficiency debate is particularly high-profile. Product deregulation, interstate banking, and industry consolidation are all issues best viewed through this prism that has marked industry debate in the United States since Alexander Hamilton and Aaron Burr.

In this era of the superregional bank, our public policy debates have been fueled by the reality of the industry's evolving structure. Not always coherent, regulatory policy and action have been racing to keep up with an industry intent on resolving its fundamental structural economic problems. As the interstate environment evolves, the efficiency versus equity debate looms more important than ever before. During the current decade, a permanent structural solution to the banking industry's woes will be found. The policies and philosophies that will dominate remain to be worked out. These regulatory forces of change, however, are central to the paradigm shift now under way.

A Historical Perspective of Banking Regulation

Before legislation created the Federal Reserve System in 1913, banks functioned with fairly limited government intervention. For more than a hundred years following Hamilton's National Bank proposal, regulation of U.S. financial markets was minimal and primarily delegated to the states. A depression in 1883 and a financial panic in 1907 caused numerous bank failures and set the stage for financial reform.

Government's response, the Federal Reserve Act of 1913, has been characterized as the greatest piece of legislation, aside from wartime measures, of Woodrow Wilson's presidency. In establishing an independent Fed, the Act provided for flexible reserves and speedy collection of checks. Techniques and policy tools of modern monetary policy also came into being. In addition, for the first time, member banks were subject to federal government-mandated examinations.

Government policy toward banks changed dramatically in the 20-year period from 1913 to 1933. After World War I, America enjoyed an era of great optimism and rapid economic growth. Very few could have predicted the tragic events of the Depression era. The interrelationship between the economy and banks corresponded first with the economic growth and optimism and then with the economic collapse that followed the stock market crash in October 1929. Between 1929 and 1933 there were more than 9,000 bank failures. Bank loans shrank from $36 billion in 1929 to $11 billion in 1933. President Franklin D. Roosevelt shut down the entire banking system for several days as one of his first official acts after his March 1933 inauguration. This bank holiday was intended to allow widespread panic to subside. Additionally, Congress immediately held a series of hearings that culminated in reforms that have shaped the banking system ever since.

The 1933 Banking Act, popularly known as the Glass-Steagall Act, created the Federal Deposit Insurance Corporation (FDIC) as an official agency of the federal government, organized with the objectives of protecting bank depositors and promoting safe and sound banking practices. Payment of interest on demand deposits was also prohibited. Under the Glass-Steagall Act, banks were limited in their underwriting and prohibited from investing in any common stocks. The Banking Act of 1935 expanded on recently introduced rate restrictions by giving the Federal Reserve power to establish maximum interest rates that banks could pay on various savings and time deposits. Under this act the Federal Reserve established Regulation Q.

Since the creation of the Fed and the 1933 reform statutes, banks have operated under an umbrella of extensive regulations. Fashioned to protect the public interest, these regulations and prohibitions have been arguably more pervasive than those confronting the insurance and securities industries. Banks were prohibited from operating across state lines, selling or underwriting securities, or engaging in essentially any nonfinancial activities. To this day, at least from the bank executive's perspective, the proliferation of demands made on banks by regulations and regulators seems to be endless. Bank regulatory agencies increasingly require more reports, tighter controls on lending, and greater accountability by directors.

The early-1980s deregulation decisions that kicked into motion the forces of industry change were of immense significance. With changing financial markets, new competition from nonbanks, and rapid development of technology, it has become imperative to allow and even encourage banks to compete more actively in the marketplace. Deregulation has developed along three lines—price deregulation, product deregulation, and geographic deregulation. Price and product deregulation are addressed in this chapter. Geographic deregulation, as a regulatory response to the structural economic woes exposed by price and product deregulation, is discussed in Chapter 3.

Price Deregulation: Unleashing Market Forces

Price deregulation was an historical tradition in the financial services industry. In current history, the major form of price deregulation was the elimination of interest rate ceilings through the repeal of Regulation Q. Banks demanded this pricing deregulation to allow direct price competition with nonbank money market mutual funds (MMMFs). Before the 1980 Depository Institution Deregulation and Monetary Control Act (DIDMCA) and the subsequent Depository Institutions Act of 1982 (Garn-St Germain) abolishing Regulation Q interest rate ceilings, MMMFs were draining savings deposits traditionally kept in banks. Exhibit 2.1 presents the growth of MMMF deposits at the expense of bank deposits.

MMMFs were offering market rates of return, and banks were prohibited from offering similar, competitively priced products. Garn-St Germain gave banks money-fund equivalent powers, which enabled them to compete directly against money funds on the basis of price—in this case, yield. After enactment of Garn-St Germain in December 1982, nonbank money funds declined from approximately $240 billion to $160 billion, where they then stabilized. Bankers achieved the level playing field they had been seeking. At the same time, however, a permanent increase in the intensity of price competition and the resulting skyrocketing of banks' interest rate expense were the major impacts of abolishing Regulation Q.

This dramatic increase in interest expense produced a major profitability squeeze. The industry's traditional profit equation

Exhibit 2.1

RELATIVE GROWTH RATES: MUTUAL FUNDS VERSUS BANK DEPOSITS
1980–1993, QII

	IPC Deposits ($ Millions)	Growth Rate	Domestic Demand Deposits ($ Millions)	Growth Rate	Total Deposits ($ Millions)	Growth Rate	Money Market Funds ($ Millions)	Growth Rate	Total Mutual Funds ($ Millions)	Growth Rate
1980	1,118,042		431,540		1,481,163		76,400		134,800	
1981	1,104,245	-1.23%	384,201	-10.97%	1,588,895	7.27%	186,100	143.59%	241,400	79.08%
1982	1,214,542	9.99%	370,874	-3.47%	1,706,138	7.38%	219,800	18.11%	296,700	22.91%
1983	1,353,547	11.45%	389,471	5.01%	1,842,415	7.99%	179,400	-18.38%	293,000	-1.25%
1984	1,466,837	8.37%	414,171	6.34%	1,962,935	6.54%	233,500	30.16%	370,600	26.48%
1985	1,593,502	8.64%	451,005	8.89%	2,118,088	7.90%	243,800	4.41%	495,500	33.70%
1986	1,753,821	10.06%	510,810	13.26%	2,283,527	7.81%	292,100	19.81%	716,200	44.54%
1987	1,797,503	2.49%	455,826	-10.76%	2,335,441	2.27%	316,100	8.22%	769,900	7.50%
1988	1,922,494	6.95%	458,832	0.66%	2,431,724	4.12%	338,000	6.93%	810,300	5.25%
1989	2,045,830	6.42%	460,586	0.38%	2,548,485	4.80%	428,100	26.66%	982,000	21.19%
1990	2,170,761	6.11%	463,906	0.72%	2,650,095	3.99%	498,300	16.40%	1,066,800	8.64%
1991	2,205,255	1.59%	454,070	-2.12%	2,687,553	1.41%	539,600	8.29%	1,346,700	26.24%
1992	2,412,079	9.38%	511,090	12.56%	2,698,954	0.42%	543,500	0.72%	1,595,400	18.47%
6/93	N.A.		526,210	2.96%	2,680,386	-0.69%	558,500	2.76%	1,902,800	19.24%

Sources: Federal Reserve, FDIC, Investment Company Institute

was knocked out of equilibrium. Facing market share losses to nonbank competitors, the industry had pressed regulators to release these competitive constraints, perhaps without fully realizing the longer-term (and, in many cases, short-term) profitability consequences.

Competing without a Competitive Cost Structure

With banks paying higher interest rates as a result of the abolition of Regulation Q, awareness began to grow that long-term profitability effects could be devastating. From a revenue perspective, banks began charging for many services they had previously offered free and developed new products and services that could be provided for fee income. Banks intensified their demand for product deregulation. In the hope of generating greater fee income, they pursued additional powers in the areas of insurance, securities, and real estate.

Both revenue and cost solutions had to be pursued to reestablish adequate earnings. For the most part, however, cost reduction was not addressed strongly enough by banks, who were operating in a period of record economic growth immediately following 1980 and 1982 deregulation legislation. During the early 1980s, fueled by asset growth, this positive operating environment allowed banks to achieve modest profitability. Independent of the banks' disadvantaged structural economics, the industry attempted to live true to the old adage, "We'll make it up on volume." Exhibit 2.2 presents the industry's 15-year track record of operating performance. The 1979-1991 period reflects the long-term competitive effects of the nonbank challenge and the glaring need for fundamental industry restructuring. The industry's ROA declined from .80 percent to .53 percent until the 1992–1993 rebound.

A closer look at the comparative economics of the money market mutual fund illustrates banks' disadvantaged cost position. Operating as geographically defined utilities with profitability regulated by interest rate restrictions, banks found their products significantly disadvantaged relative to non-rate-regulated investment alternatives. A savings product can be delivered by the MMMFs at a direct cost of approximately 50 basis points as compared to typically more than 300 basis points in direct operating expense for savings products delivered by banks. This large mutual fund cost advantage translates into MMMFs being able to pay higher rates than commercial banks (Exhibit 2.3). In high rate environments, this spread widens on an absolute basis. Given an advantage of such magnitude, it is clear that over time money funds would inevitably gain market share. The rate-oriented consumer would move quickly. For the more conservative or traditional bank customer, other things being equal, it was only a matter of time.

Exhibit 2.2

COMMERCIAL BANK OPERATING PERFORMANCE
1979–1993

Year	ROA (Percent)	ROE (Percent)	Net Income ($ Millions)
1979	.80	13.91	12,839
1980	.79	13.68	14,010
1981	.76	13.04	14,722
1982	.70	12.02	14,844
1983	.66	11.09	14,931
1984	.64	10.53	15,502
1985	.69	11.12	17,977
1986	.61	9.92	17,419
1987	.09	1.55	2,804
1988	.81	13.16	24,814
1989	.48	7.76	15,574
1990	.48	7.56	16,001
1991	.53	8.01	18,047
1992	.96	13.35	32,245
1993	1.21	15.64	42,370*

* Net income annualized ($21.189 billion through June 30, 1993)
Source: FDIC

What is the source of MMMFs' advantages; or, more correctly, what is the source of banks' disadvantage? Reflecting competition in a different regulatory era, banks operate with relatively large numbers of employees and brick-and-mortar branches. The result is very expensive branch distribution networks. Mutual funds, on the other hand, operate with few clerical personnel and toll-free telephone numbers, which leads to a very low-cost structure. Even as banks are successful in closing uneconomic branches and eliminating people, their cost disadvantage may remain so great that it will continue to be a competitive problem.

Not only do banks face the need to adjust rapidly, but there is significant uncertainty about the direction in which they should seek to evolve. Some analysts of the money market fund challenge argue that to fairly compare banks and MMMFs, it is necessary to consider the potential advantage of FDIC insurance offered by banks. In our judgment, FDIC insurance does not seem to be a great equalizer because money funds can also offer an insurance option. In fact, some money funds—the Vanguard Group, for example—have offered their customers insurance for accounts up to the $250,000 level. This insurance can be purchased easily by

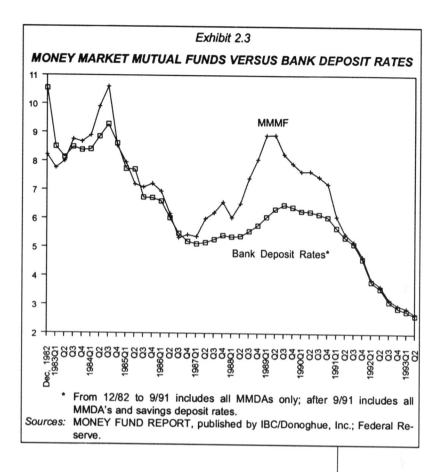

Exhibit 2.3

MONEY MARKET MUTUAL FUNDS VERSUS BANK DEPOSIT RATES

MMMF

Bank Deposit Rates*

* From 12/82 to 9/91 includes all MMDAs only; after 9/91 includes all MMDA's and savings deposit rates.

Sources: MONEY FUND REPORT, published by IBC/Donoghue, Inc.; Federal Reserve.

mutual funds at an additional cost of 40 to 55 basis points. However, when money fund customers are offered this supplemental insurance along with naturally higher yields than those provided by commercial banks, they generally reject the insurance feature in favor of capturing the highest possible yield. Although most consumers would rather pick up the additional 40 to 55 basis points in yield, it is important to note that MMMFs could provide insurance.

From the competitive perspective of most bank managements, FDIC insurance is viewed less as a potentially advantageous product feature and more as another government-mandated cost burden. More important, with the rise in both capital market depth and consumer sophistication, the relative benefits of the FDIC deposit insurance scheme have declined substantially. Because of the industry's credit problems, insurance rates have greatly increased.

Learning to Live in a Competitive Rate Environment

Inflation during the late 1970s and early 1980s actually caused and exacerbated the disintermediation problems faced by banks. High inflation drove market interest rates to record, double-digit levels. By the time regulators responded to quell the disintermediation of traditional banking customers by raising Regulation Q ceilings, a significant number of those customers had discovered an abundance of alternative nonbank savings vehicles.

The low-inflation economy of the early 1990s has provided incentive for yet another segment of traditional banking customers to turn away from banks. When rates are low, customers search to discover higher yield alternatives. In this environment, short- and intermediate-term bond funds and stock mutual funds are particularly attractive to savers. Additionally, individuals in search of 1980s-style returns are investing directly into the stock and bond markets. The mutual fund companies offering families of funds are particularly advantaged. Just as inflation and high interest rates were catalysts that drove segments of banking customers away from banks early in the 1980s, disinflation and low interest rates are having a similar effect in driving large numbers of traditional users of consumer banking services to seek other alternatives.

From a historical perspective, DIDMCA and the Depository Institutions Act of 1982 were the two critical pieces of legislation that launched this new era in banking. A very fundamental change occurred: banks were allowed to respond to market forces in determining deposit interest rates. Exhibits 2.4 and 2.5 summarize the key elements of these two historic pieces of banking legislation.

DIDMCA provided for a six-year phaseout of Regulation Q. This phaseout plan was administered by a DIDMCA Committee composed of heads of each of the federal regulatory agencies involved. Unfortunately, the early administration of the price deregulation mandate resulted in considerable delay in totally abolishing Regulation Q. In particular, the committee was slow to lift rate ceilings on short-term deposit accounts. Accordingly, in the early 1980s, MMMFs continued to gain market share from banks. Finally, two years later, in October 1982, the Garn-St Germain Act mandated that banks be immediately provided with money-fund-equivalent powers.

Money market demand accounts (MMDA) and Super NOW accounts were conceived as interest-rate-paying transaction accounts to allow banks to compete with MMMFs. Many banks immediately and aggressively introduced these new accounts in an effort to regain lost market share. MMMFs' balances declined substantially, and banks recovered funds that had exited. Exhibit 2.1 indicates that MMMFs realized large, negative growth in

Exhibit 2.4

PROVISIONS OF DEPOSITORY INSTITUTIONS DEREGULATION AND MONETARY CONTROL ACT OF 1980 (DIDMCA)

1. Abolished Regulation Q ceilings in a six-year phaseout plan (1981–1986).

2. Allowed all depository institutions to offer interest-bearing checking accounts. Depository institutions were allowed to offer negotiable orders of withdrawal (NOW accounts) to individuals and nonprofit organizations. Credit unions were permitted to offer share draft accounts.

3. Mandated that all the depository institutions have access to the Federal Reserve System and its services including the discount window. Required that services of the Federal Reserve be offered on a cost basis.

4. Broadened the reserve requirements to include all federally insured depository institutions.

5. Eliminated state usury laws on residential mortgages. Usury limits on business and agriculture loans were also lifted, but limited to a cap of 5% above the discount rate. States were given a three-year period in which to reenact usury statutes.

6. Increased federal deposit insurance coverage to the $100,000 deposit level (from $40,000).

Source: Federal Reserve

Exhibit 2.5

PROVISIONS OF DEPOSITORY INSTITUTIONS ACT OF 1982 (GARN-ST GERMAIN)

1. Instructed regulatory authorities to provide depository institutions with money fund equivalent powers. This resulted in depository institutions being able to issue money market deposit accounts (MMDAs) and Super NOW accounts. Required accounts to have a minimum balance of $2,500 with no maturity date or interest rate ceiling. Initially, depositors were limited to three checks each month.

2. Eliminated the differences between the rate ceilings different depository institutions could charge. Previously, thrifts could offer a slightly higher saver rate.

3. Increased loan limit powers for national banks by permitting unsecured lending at 15% of capital and surplus monies with collateralized lending authorized at the 25% level.

4. Granted Savings and Loans both consumer and commercial lending powers.

5. Gave the FDIC broader failure resolution powers. The FDIC could arrange mergers across state lines for failed banks when no intrastate merger was viable.

Source: Federal Reserve

1983 (–18.38%). Of course, while there was aggressive pursuit of market share, little attention was paid to the profitability implications of the strategy.

At the time, the profitability impact of paying interest on deposits was really an unknown. Until Garn-St Germain, the only experience banks had with NOW accounts was the New England experiment in paying interest on transaction accounts. New England savings banks were not found to be adversely affected by payment of interest on transaction accounts. Nor did they seem to bid so aggressively that they had to invest larger sums in riskier or substandard loans. This early experiment led many bankers to believe that the removal of Regulation Q would not be problematic. However, the resultant skyrocketing of banks' interest expense proved to have immense profitability consequence. No single change has been more profound.

This early experiment led many bankers to believe that the removal of Regulation Q would not be problematic. However, the resultant skyrocketing of banks' interest expense proved to have immense profitability consequence. No single change has been more profound.

Product Deregulation:
Going Head-to-Head with the Nonbanks

The second competitive threat of the mutual fund challenge, which is much broader than that of the money funds alone, stems from the family of mutual funds concept. A mutual fund family typically includes a money fund, a bond fund, domestic equity funds, and perhaps a global fund. Fidelity Investments, for example, offers consumers literally hundreds of mutual fund options. The family of funds is a serious threat to commercial banks because money can be attracted away from banks through an equity fund, balanced fund, bond fund, or money fund. Then, as market conditions change, investors can shift their investment allocation among the family of funds without ever having to reintermediate back through a commercial bank.

Nearly $1.9 trillion of funds that were formerly lodged primarily within the commercial banking industry are today invested in mutual funds (Exhibit 2.1). The tremendous growth in mutual funds, as both a liquid and long-term investment alternative to bank products, continues to be a serious competitive threat to commercial banks. Beyond more competitive rates, mutual funds have a much broader product array, offered in a more integrated fashion. Banks presently lack this.

The product disadvantages of banks are spotlighted in the mutual funds and brokerage firms' aggressive marketing of asset management accounts. The original asset money management account formulated by Merrill Lynch was the Cash Management Account (CMA). CMAs allowed much of the financial activity traditionally associated with banks to be taken elsewhere. The Merrill Lynch CMA combined MMMF rates with check-writing ability; credit card access; and brokerage account privileges, including margin borrowing. The Merrill Lynch CMA initiative illustrates how, in a deregulated industry, more aggressive competitors can relegate banks to a much more limited financial role. Banks cannot allow themselves to be constrained by historical regulation in formulating their product/market strategies.

As a result of both pricing and product advantages, over the past three decades nonbanks have gained nearly a 70 percent share of the nation's financial assets. Moreover, nonbanks have emerged as the dominant providers of most traditional credit products. For example, nonbanks are the major providers of automobile credit, consumer installment credit, and commercial real estate and business leases. In the area of charge cards, although banks still have a narrow majority of the business, American Express, Sears, and AT&T are now among the largest providers. Nonbanks, particularly insurance companies, are realizing astounding growth in business lending. Exhibit 2.6 presents comparative market shares of banks and nonbanks.

Why the tremendous competitive success of nonbanks? What lessons can banks learn? Economies of scale sometimes provide nonbanks with a competitive edge. A contributing factor may also be the greater strategic and product focus of nonbanks. For example, nonbanks generally target their efforts to cherry-pick the most profitable customer segments of specific bank product lines. Nonbanks, arguably, have become more market oriented and innovative. They have devoted greater, more focused expenditures to marketing efforts than have commercial banks. Nonbanks also have been active in bringing new technology and automation to the delivery and servicing of traditional bank products. Finally, to the great dismay of commercial bankers, nonbanks are not subject to the same regulatory scrutiny as banks. The resulting unlevel playing field has been the focus of great debate.

Experts argue that further deregulation is necessary to ensure banks adequate opportunity to compete (see Harvey Rosenblum's sidebar, *Shrinking Profit Opportunities in Banking and the Credit Crunch: Where Do We Go From Here?*, page 34). In many respects, there exists a somewhat uncertain cause-and-effect relationship. Did the advantage of being less regulated create a real advantage for nonbanks, or did it merely provide an incentive for them to evolve in ways that prepared them to compete? For example, nonbanks gain some cost advantage from not being as regulated, but, from a cost perspective, their less regulated history may have made them much more prepared for intense price competition. Nonbanks do not undergo supervisory examinations, nor are they restricted by community reinvestment requirements. This is clearly a regulatory advantage. Further deregulation is essential to enable the management of banks to compete successfully, not so much because they require expanded powers, but more because they need to be more disciplined and bottomline-oriented.

Shrinking Profit Opportunities in Banking and the Credit Crunch: Where Do We Go From Here?

Harvey Rosenblum
Senior Vice President and Director of Research
Federal Reserve Bank of Dallas

In 1963, the U.S. Supreme Court ruled that the product market served by the commercial banks was the unique *cluster* of products that banks could offer— demand deposits, commercial and consumer loans, savings instruments, etc. In addition, the court decided that competition in these products typically took place within a small geographic area such as a city, a county, or a metropolitan area. For nearly three decades, legal and economic scholars have debated the wisdom of the Court's conclusions regarding the extent of the product and geographic markets.

We can give the Court the benefit of the doubt and say that its decision was correct in 1963. Ensuing events, however, render these conclusions almost ludicrous in the environment of the early 1990s. This notion of a unique cluster of products offered within a severely confined geographic area, together with a long-standing prohibition on interstate banking, have combined to restrict the ability of commercial banks to exploit any economies of scale or scope that might exist. As a result, the cost structure of banking has not been able to adapt as effectively as that of would-be competitors from outside the commercial banking industry. This mattered little when there were only a few such potential competitors; however, events since 1963 have changed the number of potential competitors dramatically. In addition, in 1992 and 1993 the level of short-term interest rates returned to levels not seen since 1963, thereby making the under-lying cost structure of the banking industry a relatively more important factor than during the 1980s.

Among the more important of the events that increased the number of potential competitors was the credit crunch of 1966. This period of credit stringency was a by-product of the disintermediation fostered by Regulation Q ceilings which set deposit rates below open market interest rates. During this first credit crunch, banks were forced to allocate the quantity of credit available to their loan customers because of their own inability to raise deposit funds in the market. As a result, the dependability of banks as a reliable source of credit was called into question, and borrowers began to find innovative means of securing credit from other sources. Informed observers of the linkage between macroeconomic policy and the microeconomics of banking labeled Regulation Q as "the cutting edge of monetary policy."

In 1969–1970 and again in 1973–1974, two similar monetary policy/dis-intermediation-related credit squeezes occurred. Each time, bank borrowers rose higher on the learning curve in their adaptations to finding alternative credit sources. During the 1973–1974 credit crunch, money market mutual funds (MMMFs) were born, giving rise to a new and potentially permanent source of competition on both the deposit and credit sides of commercial bank's balance sheets.

Another credit crunch followed in 1979–1982, but this time, owing to the de facto and de jure phaseout of Regulation Q, credit was allocated on the basis of price, rather than the quantity of funds available. Unfortunately, few borrowers anticipated, nor could they afford to pay on a sustained basis, the rates of interest that prevailed. As a result, interest rate risk was translated into credit risk. Again, the result was diminished profit opportunities for some banks as their best customers found ways to locate other sources of credit—either through direct market access or from other competitors.

What is common to each of these credit crunch cycles is that, in the aftermath of each cycle, there was a ratcheting down of commercial banks' market share, particularly if the market is defined in a way that reflects the relevant realities (i.e., products and competitors) of the time. Interestingly, these changing market realities were reflected in the Federal Reserve's redefinitions of the monetary aggregates in 1980, but not in the Fed's or other regulatory agencies' definition of the product market for bank merger or bank holding company application analysis, which remained bound by the Philadelphia National Bank decision.

The loss of market share stemmed directly from the growth of new (and in some cases, renewed) competitors. The mirror image of the reduced market share was the reduction in the set of profitable opportunities that confronted the commercial banking system. No longer was it possible for commercial banks to earn high and stable profits as the bulk of the industry did in the 1950s, 1960s, and 1970s. Under these circumstances, it is easy to understand why the commercial banking industry (narrowly defined) experienced capital flight during the 1980s. Further reducing the profitable opportunity set was the differential regulatory burden that banks faced (for example, the Community Reinvestment Act and other socially oriented legislation) vis a vis the nonbank competitors or nonbank banks, the twin oxymorons of the 1980s.

To stem the flight from the industry, the concept of risk-based capital was introduced in the late 1980s, to become fully effective in late 1992. However, the design of the risk-based capital system has several inherent flaws, the most notable of which is the way it allocates the flow of capital away from commercial lending by favoring the purchase of government securities and home-mortgage-related instruments.

Even though risk-based capital requirements did not take effect until year-end 1992, their influence and impact on bank behavior and decision making began to be felt as early as 1989, as banks began to anticipate the capital requirement implications of every new asset put on their books that might still be there in 1993. In effect, banks behaved as if the new capital requirements were already in place. The recession that began in the summer of 1990 further exacerbated the credit squeeze being felt by those businesses that relied primarily on banks as a source of working capital. The recession made banks even more cautious in their lending standards than they had been previously. This is confirmed by the Fed's quarterly survey of lending practices, which showed no abatement in the rising credit standards for business loans by banks until May 1993.

The credit squeeze pathology had begun before the 1990 recession. The recession was more like a secondary infection that zaps an already weakened patient whose long-term prognosis was not all that good in the first place. Additional stress was placed on the weak patient by the Too Big To Fail (TBTF) doctrine that was largely responsible for wiping out the FDIC's insurance reserves. This necessitated a more than tenfold increase in FDIC insurance premiums at a time when banks could least afford to pay them. Moreover, because the FDIC fund was so depleted, the FDIC was forced to handle its TBTF cases as de facto liquidations, at least as far as the treatment of borrowers from the resolved bank were concerned.

The ramifications of banks' reduced willingness to lend are: a) bank customers seek other sources of credit; b) bank customers learn how to run their businesses with reduced credit needs (often with a smaller business and a smaller economy as a result); and c) banks suffer a further erosion of market share and profit opportunities; thus d) reinforcing the industry's downward spiral.

This story need not have such a gloomy ending. There are public policy interventions could potentially arrest and reverse these negative trends. But, it is important and imperative that the right interventions be made; otherwise, the patient is unlikely to improve. This is why the diagnosis of the *root cause* of the perceived credit shortage is so critical. Attacking the symptoms or the secondary sources of the problem will provide some *temporary* relief, but no lasting solution.

The primary source of the credit crunch is the reduced profitability of providing credit in the new competitive environment that has evolved over the last 10–20 years. The risk-return calculus favors acquisition of assets other than bank loans, particularly commercial loans. Reducing capital requirements, easing monetary policy, and reducing regulatory burdens (including bank examiner scrutiny) will temporarily alter behavior and reduce some of the pain, but it will not reverse the underlying pathology whereby reduced profit opportunities produce a reallocation of capital available to that portion of American business enterprise that relies most heavily on banks. (It should be noted, however, that in response to supervisory pressures, the banking industry has raised its capitalization significantly over the 1991–93 period, thus temporarily stemming the long-term trend of capital flight from the industry.)

Where then does the solution lie? This essay began with a critical review of the mindset created by the Philadelphia National Bank case as the source of the beginning of the demise of the needs for banks. If each of the separate services provided by banks can be provided by other firms, often at lower cost and with more convenience, then the *cluster* ceases to have any market usefulness, particularly if law and regulation prohibit the addition of new products and services into the cluster. Of what use is a cluster of services to the market if service providers cannot add and delete services from the cluster in response to changing demand and cost conditions? This is the critical point.

Given this analysis, it would seem that the best way to deal with the credit crunch over the long term would be to eliminate the prohibition of interstate banking and the separation of commercial banking and investment banking. This would allow banks to become the department stores they need to be to meet the full range of business financial needs (and households' needs as well, particularly if the *sale*, but not necessarily the underwriting, of insurance products were permitted). Currently, banks can provide for the straight debt needs of businesses, but cannot provide for the equity needs or any of the hybrid products between straight debt and equity. As a result, banks do not offer the desired cluster of services to meet the full range of commercial financing needs of their customers. As such, their limited product mix relegates them to a status of irrelevancy to an increasing portion of their clientele. In addition, the circumscribed geographic area that banks have been allowed to serve has restrained their ability to provide their customers' desired cluster of products on an economically efficient basis because of the limited ability to capture whatever economies of scale or scope may exist. The irony is that commercial banks, which were once referred to as the department stores of finance because they offered a wider cluster of needed products relative to their competition, now find themselves in the position of offering a narrower range of relevant products than their competitors. Herein lies the answer to the credit availability problems that so many businesses perceive they confront. An additional advantage of broadening the cluster is that it will subject this cluster of services to passing the test of the marketplace, a test that has been largely absent since the early 1930s.

NONBANKS GAIN SIGNIFICANT MARKET SHARE

Supplier	1960–69	1970–79	1980–89	1990–92
Depository institutions	43	46	39	29
Commercial banks	27	29	24	20
Thrift institutions	16	17	15	9
Nondepository institutions	29	30	36	45
Insurance companies	15	12	10	11
Pension funds	5	5	7	7
Mutual funds (including money market mutual funds)	*	1	3	6
Mortgage pools and federally sponsored agencies	2	4	8	11
Other financial sectors[1]	7	8	8	10
Nonfinancial sectors[2]	28	24	25	26

* Less than 0.5 percent.
1 Monetary authority, finance companies, real estate investment trusts, security brokers and dealers, and issuers of securitized credit obligations.
2 Household sector, nonfinancial business, state and local government general funds, U.S. government, and the foreign sector.

Source: Flow of funds accounts, Z.1 statistical release, table L.6; Guide to the Flow of Funds Accounts, Federal Reserve; 1993 (p.26)

. . . nonbanks have worked to gain broad access to the industry's raw material, liquid funds. . . . It is no coincidence that many nonbank competitors are also extremely large money management firms.

It is the competitive heritage of mutual funds companies and other nonbanks that may be their greatest advantage.

From an economic structure perspective, the effective strategy of vertical integration is essential to the success of nonbanks. Vertical integration attempts to establish backward and forward management and control of a given product. For instance, were General Motors to own and control its raw materials, production mechanisms, and distribution network, it would be considered a fully vertically integrated company. In financial services, nonbanks have worked to gain broad access to the industry's raw material, liquid funds. MMMFs, for example, can access large amounts of money without geographic constraints. At the same time, they can intermediate those monies and place them in a wide spectrum of investment vehicles. Finally, similar to the Merrill Lynch CMA account, mutual funds can combine check-writing ability with fund investments. It is no coincidence that many nonbank competitors are also extremely large money management firms.

At the same time that economies of scale and vertical integration are becoming more important, marketing and branding are also rising as strategic factors. The mutual fund industry is a prime example of how, as a result of mass market and media advertising, savings funds can be gathered and later shifted among a family of funds. Advertising and branding, along with a competitive rate, are used to attract initial deposits or investments. The option of moving funds easily keeps the investor effectively within the individual mutual fund company. Fidelity is an example of a preeminent nonbank competitor. With assets under management approximating $250 billion, Fidelity offers one of the most highly developed families of funds. Fidelity makes extensive use of alternative delivery methods, including round-the-clock, toll-free phone lines and aggressive use of the mail and advanced technology, including automatic computer stock order and quotation systems. They also make an enormous investment in television, radio, and print media advertising. Great institutional pride is taken in the success of the company's efforts to build brand name recognition.

Fidelity's distribution and cost structure model, typical of many mutual fund companies, is central to the advantaged low-cost position of nonbank competitors. The absence of any regulatory history inspired the design of more cost-competitive approaches to the marketplace.

Competing When You Are Not Really Sure How

Marketplace forces and the emergence of nonbank competitors made deregulation inevitable. DIDMCA and Garn-St Germain recognized the reality of marketplace forces and the gathering competitive pressures. It must be recognized, however, that banking industry experience with hard-boiled competition was really somewhat limited. As a result, the ability to effectively and intelligently compete was not nearly as developed as was the recognition that the banks' market share was under attack. Not surprisingly, therefore, the early attempts at competing were not always successful.

In the transition to a more competitive financial services industry, the aggressive pricing tactics employed by poorly managed thrifts during the 1980s are the best example of the danger of competing before all the necessary capabilities are in place. In a typical case, a poorly run S&L with both negative net income and net worth would keep its doors open by employing aggressive deposit pricing and offering large premiums to attract both local and national CD funding. In spite of many S&Ls' being very weak institutions, consumers would disregard the thrifts' economic insolvency because all accounts were federally insured through the FSLIC, the S&L industry equivalent of FDIC. Indeed, savers became increasingly rate sensitive and sought out thrifts paying the highest rates, regardless of potential risk. Because regulation transferred only minimal direct risk to consumers, the taxpayer-funded and government-managed insurance system eventually had to deal with the results of these irrational pricing practices. A federal bailout of the industry's insolvent insurance corporation was the initial step. Subsequently, the cost of today's broader financial services restructuring has been borne by all.

Aggressive thrift pricing, on top of the effective competitive efforts of nonbanks, was quite problematic for the more traditional commercial banks. To maintain deposits, banks had to match these excessive rates, thereby creating further interest rate pressures and squeezed profitability margins. While MMMFs tended to match thrift rates, banks' higher cost structure did not allow them to offer the same rates without actually operating at a loss. As a result of the government closing the weak thrift institutions, either by letting them fail or merging them out, pricing has become far more rational, and banks have improved their interest margins. Market forces are again seeking equilibrium.

In parallel fashion, and in an effort to force the marketplace to seek a rational equilibrium, the government has restrained the brokered deposit market by tying brokered deposit authority to bank capital levels. If an institution's leverage capital ratio is less than 4 percent, or if its total risk-adjusted capital falls below 8 percent, that bank or thrift can no longer accept brokered deposits. Through this mechanism the government seeks to provide deposit insurance to those banks with adequate capital structures. Well-capitalized banks, that is, those with more than 10 percent total risk-adjusted capital and a 5 percent leverage capital ratio, face no such prohibitions. Banks in between these levels—those that are adequately capitalized—can appeal to the FDIC for the right to broker deposits on an individual bank basis. In addition to limiting brokered CD authority, the FDIC, in a June 1992 ruling, capped rates at 0.75 of a percentage point above the local market average, even when offered by an adequately capitalized bank. For nationally brokered CDs, rates are constrained by a 120 percent limit of a comparable Treasury security plus the 0.75 percent local price limit. These FDIC rules are a further attempt to forestall unsound practices similar to those that led to the thrift crisis of the 1980s. More subtly, they also represent the reintroduction of price regulations to channel competition for the purposes of achieving greater soundness of the financial system.

A Traditional Profitability Equation That No Longer Equilibrates

As noted, the most significant result of deregulation was the dramatic increase in the cost of funds. Banks no longer had a built-in, low-cost core deposit base because deregulation placed the price of those deposits at or near market. The traditional industry profit equation simply no longer held true. At the same time, the level of interest rates increasingly has important effects on the value of the core deposit franchise. High interest rates increase the value of the core deposit franchise, while low rates decrease the inherent value of a branch-sourced deposit base. Given the high fixed-cost nature of most banks' cost structures, this interest rate sensitivity has profound strategic importance.

With increased competition, banks were forced to seek ways to compensate for higher cost of funds and the resulting decline in interest margins. Raising prices on the loan side was one possible remedy. However, banks are limited in their ability to increase loan interest rates because loan products and asset markets are already very competitive. Banks face competition not just from within the industry, but are pressured in the loan market by nonbank providers. In response to asset margin pressures, many banks chose to raise their loan-to-asset ratios. The effectiveness of this strategy was constrained by the fact that as average loan risk increased, effective risk-adjusted loan spreads actually decreased. Over time, this led to greater loan losses and future earnings problems. In contrast, some banks attempted to reduce loan ratios and lower capital requirements by securitizing assets, a strategy that has become a major trend. However, one drawback of securitization is that banks tend to securitize the higher quality, standard credits, which often leaves behind substantial asset quality risk on the balance sheet. Again, with the traditional profit equation out of balance, many intuitive management responses only exacerbate the performance problem. The old paradigm simply was not holding true any longer.

Through the mid-1980s, the banking industry wrestled, first, with how to respond to net interest margin pressures produced by nonbank competition and, subsequently, with price deregulation that was seen as a requirement for leveling the playing field with nonbanks. As they competed aggressively for market share, it is not surprising that banks did not see any improvement in their eroding margins. Slowly at first, the earnings dilemma posed to the industry was recognized. With product volumes available to banks declining, banks had two alternative courses of action: introduce new products to increase revenues or aggressively reduce costs. Reflecting more a cultural bias than any strategic insight, the industry generally chose to pursue a further broadening of product powers rather than address the more complex task of reducing costs to fit the available market revenue.

Viewing Product Deregulation as a Siren Song

Many who view deregulation-induced price competition as the cause of the industry's profitability squeeze see product deregulation as the potential answer. Investment banking, securities, insurance, and real estate products have all been viewed as potential

Reflecting more a cultural bias than any strategic insight, the industry generally chose to pursue a further broadening of product powers, rather than address the more complex task of reducing costs to fit the available market revenue.

sources of new revenue for the banking industry. Each opportunity presents unique challenges. While product deregulation has been strongly championed by the industry, it is not clear what bottomline relief it will ultimately bring.

The most profound bank product constraints are contained in the Banking Act of 1933 (Glass-Steagall), which prohibited banks from engaging in both commercial and investment banking. Before Glass-Steagall, banks could perform and compete in both functions. Over the past two decades, the largest commercial banks have sought investment banking powers. Although no definitive action has taken place at the federal level, Congress has examined this debate and considered legislation a number of times. Nevertheless, through innovation, regulatory decrees, and the workings of the marketplace, the line between commercial and investment banking has become increasingly blurred. Today, for all practical purposes, banks can engage in many aspects of investment banking that had previously been prohibited.

Formal legislative relief from Glass-Steagall prohibitions most likely will continue to lag behind the reality of marketplace. It is worth noting, however, the creative ways competitors have found to get around the restrictions. For example, investment banks effectively participate in retail banking. They take deposits through money funds, which are technically considered securities. Many nonbanks, including securities firms, have also been able to establish banks and offer their customers FDIC insurance through various product-specific loopholes. Nonbanks accomplished this by acquiring commercial banks, and then divesting either the commercial loan portfolio or demand deposits. These divestitures played on the literal legal definition of a bank as an institution that provides both demand deposits and commercial loans.

Commercial banks have also found ways to participate in corporate finance. Commercial banks, for instance, today routinely syndicate private placements. Although in many ways a private placement is akin to a public debt security, it can also resemble a long-term loan. Similarly, while there have been debates concerning legal technicalities of whether commercial paper is a security or a loan, commercial banks participate in the underwriting of large amounts of commercial paper. Practically speaking, there are only a few product areas from which commercial banks are prohibited.

Securities Underwriting: A Potential Profit Source?

The most significant power sought by large banks is the ability to underwrite securities. Through Federal Reserve regulatory decree, some banks, such as Chase, Citicorp, J.P. Morgan, Bankers Trust, Chemical Bank, and NationsBank do underwrite debt securities. A newer frontier involves banks' ability to underwrite equity securities. Today the Federal Reserve decides the extension of this underwriting power on a case-by-case basis as individual commercial banks apply. After having been carefully scrutinized, J.P. Morgan and Bankers Trust have won the privilege of underwriting equity securities. In noting these changes in commercial banking powers, George Salem of Prudential Securities concluded in a 1991 study that J.P. Morgan has effectively transformed itself into an operation more like Goldman Sachs than a traditional commercial bank. In making the case for J.P. Morgan shares, Salem noted at the time, "In the United States we see only two publicly traded peers with which to compare P/Es—Bankers Trust and Morgan Stanley. Goldman Sachs—perhaps J.P. Morgan's closest rival—is a private company." J.P. Morgan, Bankers Trust, Chemical, Chase, Citicorp, and other large institutions actively use investment banking underwriting powers.

Underwriting, however, is not a function that most regional and community banks seek to perform. NationsBank is one superregional that has aggressively pursued investment banking and underwriting as well as built significant capabilities both to originate and distribute assets. Also, First Chicago has sought to build a corporate finance business through the wholesale recruitment of experienced Wall Street deal makers. A few other regional banks have hired former investment bankers and attempted to develop investment banking and capital market potential within the commercial bank. For the most part, the experiments of regional banks entering the capital markets and investment banking arena have not been successful. Given the modest profitability potential of underwriting and the limited skill sets most banks possess in this area, regional institutions cannot expect this function to contribute meaningfully to their profit objectives.

... George Salem of Prudential Securities concluded in a 1991 study that J.P. Morgan has effectively transformed itself into an operation more like Goldman Sachs than a traditional commercial bank.

Retail Investment Products—A Potential Panacea?

In retail markets, product deregulation efforts focus on mutual funds. While banks' ability to underwrite mutual funds is currently restricted, as agents they can distribute these products and earn fees derived from both the sales load and 12-1-b fees. Moreover, banks are not prohibited from managing mutual funds or owning discount brokerage subsidiaries. It is only the underwriting of mutual funds from which banks are explicitly excluded. However, banks do have some ability to run commingled funds through their trust powers. Through appropriate structures, when set up as agents, for instance, banks continue to aggressively move into mutual funds. Like other Glass-Steagall restrictions, market and competitive forces are demanding that banks pursue creative approaches to work around or overcome historical regulation.

For most banks, the key motive for emphasizing mutual funds revolves around the strategic need to acquire and retain customers on a relationship basis. Changing demographics and the maturing of the baby boomer generation will increasingly require banks to offer investment products. Exhibit 2.7 profiles the dramatic demographic shift in U.S. population toward those age groups that characteristically save and invest rather than borrow. The ultimate profitability of bank entrance into the retail mutual funds arena is the subject of some debate.

Insurance Battles: The Jury Is Still Out . . .

In the long run, insurance products will prove far more alluring to banks than securities products. The margins on whole life, annuities, and other mainstream insurance products are very attractive to commercial banks. The margin to a bank could be two to three times higher than that earned on a CD, even after splitting the fee 50–50 with an insurance company. Annuities allow bank customers to benefit from tax deferment and higher yields. Insurance and annuity products provide an opportunity for both the consumer and the bank. Only regulatory changes and strong lobby interests stand in the way.

The proposed U.S. Treasury banking industry reform bill of 1991 had strongly advocated extending broader insurance powers to banks, but this effort was effectively blocked by the insurance lobby. In fact, the insurance lobby flexed its muscle in attempting to roll back some of the existing insurance powers previously acquired by banks. As a result, the American Bankers Association (ABA) was forced to back off from their nationwide branching

---

Exhibit 2.7

DEMOGRAPHIC SHIFTS IN U.S. POPULATION

Dramatic demographic changes are driving growth of consumer savings and investments while depressing consumer loan demand.

| Age | Population (Millions) | | | Growth |
	1990	2000	2010	
< 25	90mm	91mm	90mm	0
25 – 34	44	37	38	–14%
35 –44	38	44	37	–2%
45 – 54	26	37	43	+69%
55 – 64	21	24	35	+65%
65 – 74	18	18	21	+14%
≥ 75	13	17	18	+39%
TOTAL	250	268	282	+13%

Baby Boomers

Source: First Manhattan Consulting Group

demand when the insurance industry threatened to roll back existing credit life and other insurance powers that banks enjoyed.

Independent Insurance Agents (IIA) have further attacked banks' efforts in federal appeals court. A February 1992 federal appeals panel ruling rocked the banking industry by barring U.S. Bancorp of Portland, Oregon, from insurance sales. Until that ruling, nationally chartered banks in towns with populations less than 5,000 were permitted by the Office of the Comptroller of the Currency (OCC) to sell insurance. The OCC successfully appealed the decision, and in July 1993 a federal appeals court upheld a lower court ruling permitting nationwide sale of insurance from small towns. Now the lobby for IIA is pushing Congress to restrict banks from selling insurance outside their small towns.

An unfortunate further ramification of this ruling could be the clouding of the interstate branching debate. In 1992, Congress seemed ready to embrace this ABA initiative. A bill put forth in the House, however, died before the summer recess. There is some speculation that the Independent Bankers Association of America (IBAA) could eventually end its opposition to interstate branch banking legislation in return for congressional action granting small town bank insurance sales.

As superregional and megabanks continue to merge and consolidate, two insurance scenarios could possibly appear on the horizon. Some large holding companies may purchase life insurance companies in order to better control the insurance product they offer. Other bank holding companies may opt to align themselves with insurance companies by putting distribution of insurance products to their customers up for bid. Unquestionably, there will ultimately be alliances between banks and the insurance industry.

In the interim, as in the investment banking and mutual fund cases, banks will continue to look for imaginative ways to obtain product powers and get around regulations. Banks can act as agents, lease office space to licensed brokers or agents, or take other actions by restructuring their legal relationships in order to purvey various products. Insurance is very attractive to most of the commercial banking industry. Large banks—Chase and Citicorp, for instance—would not only like to sell whole life policies, but may also seek to develop the underwriting side of insurance. All banks will continue to covet various revenue possibilities and define them as products critical to their future.

Real Estate Businesses—An Opportunity?

One of the more fertile areas in which banks might produce fee income is the real estate market. Despite the economic slowdown of the early 1990s, the population continues to have great geographic mobility, which tends to create increasing demand for real

. . . two insurance scenarios could possibly appear on the horizon. Some large holding companies may purchase life insurance companies in order to better control . . . Other bank holding companies may opt to align themselves with insurance companies by putting distribution of insurance products to their customers up for bid.

estate loans and services. As the thrift industry shrinks, banks are quickly becoming major providers of home mortgages. With dramatic advances in mortgage loan securitization, banks have increasingly become originators, as opposed to balance-sheet, mortgage investors.

Most depository institutions have found portfolio investment in mortgages to have low profitability. As mortgages are securitized, originators may retain servicing rights. With strong origination systems in place, banks are beginning to examine the potential for such complementary real estate products as title insurance or appraisals. Furthermore, in many cases, banks already have the existing infrastructure for successful entry into the real estate brokerage area. This activity has hefty fee income potential and should be attractive to bankers.

Despite both revenue potential and complementary activities, and in reaction to the S&L catastrophe and its close ties to real estate equity development risk, the 1991 FDIC Improvement Act (FDICIA) ordered all FDIC-insured institutions to divest real estate development activities within one year. While provisions were made to give regulators discretion in extending time frames for divestiture, the message was clear that the FDIC wants banks out of the real estate development business. For the near-term, therefore, this type of real estate business cannot be pursued as part of the industry's restructuring program. Doubtless, however, future opportunities will renew the debate.

Toward a Permanent, Yet Flexible, Solution

The savings and loan experience provided a rude awakening to the cost of federal deposit insurance. Various estimates place the ultimate total cost to taxpayers for S&L failures in the $500 billion or greater range, including bailout financing costs. In the wake of the S&L debacle, Congress has become more forceful in not allowing commercial banks to follow a similar route.

By enacting FDICIA in December 1991, Congress took steps to discourage forbearance (i.e., earlier closure) and to encourage closer examination and prompt corrective action regarding problems that surface in the commercial banking industry. The FDIC was ordered to implement a risk-based deposit insurance program. In order to replenish the depository insurance fund, the FDIC has increased insurance rates for banks and thrifts. Rates rose, on average, from the previous $0.23 per $100 of deposit insurance to $0.28 per $100. The effective date for the revised insurance rates was January 1, 1993.

The new system may provide a model of future regulatory reform. It divides banks and thrifts into nine risk-based classes based on capital strength and supervisory examinations (Exhibit 2.8). After a 1993–94 phase-in period, the FDIC will gradually

Exhibit 2.8

FDIC PREMIUM STRUCTURE: RISK CATEGORIES*

	Healthy	Supervisory Concern	Substantial Supervisory Concern
Well capitalized	25¢	28¢	30¢
Adequately capitalized	28	30	30
Other	30	30	31

* Bank insurance rates per $100.
Source: FDIC

discontinue subsidization of weak banks by further increasing their insurance rates. Ideally, a more market-oriented approach to pricing deposit risk will eventually prevail.

Ross Perot, during his 1992 bid for the presidency, inaccurately predicted a serious wave of bank failures would occur in December 1992, after the election. Fortunately, a crisis did not occur. In fact, the latest FDIC status estimates project the insurance fund becoming sufficiently replenished by 1998 to permit a substantial reduction of bank deposit insurance premiums.

The risk-based deposit insurance program is modeled after the recently implemented risk-based capital system. It considers not only asset riskiness but also capital levels, asset liability profiles, and other aspects of supervisory opinion.

Early intervention, or prompt corrective action, was a provision addressed by FDICIA. The Act allows regulators, who are now expected to be more vigilant and active within banks, to take earlier regulatory action when problems occur. For example, given certain specified problems, such as declines in capital ratios or increases in problem loans, regulators are expected to enter into specific agreements with individual commercial banks.

The handling of Southeast Bank in Florida, for example, involved an application of early closure prior to passage of FDICIA. Before the closure of Southeast, banks traditionally were not closed until their book value capital or solvency positions reached the zero point. Southeast was deemed to have failed and was merged into First Union when it actually had more than one percent of accounting book value capital. Nevertheless, because the bank had become reliant on the discount window, regulators were able to demand payment for borrowings. FDICIA explicitly mandates early closure for problem institutions. The handling of Southeast may serve as a model for the way similarly troubled institutions will be managed in the future.

Although some critics argue that closure rules should have remained in the subjective domain of the relevant regulators, the early closure mandate did eliminate any possibility of forbearance or other political interference serving to stall the closure of a failing bank. Prompt corrective action and early closure also can stem potential insurance losses by preserving the inherent franchise values of troubled institutions. The failed bank bid by First City (Texas) demonstrates how franchise values can be captured by regulatory authorities. In that case, auction bid premiums paid by Chemical Bank and others actually exceeded the insurance cost estimates.

Limiting Taxpayer Exposure via a Narrow Core Bank

The cost of industry restructuring has been enormous for taxpayers. Parallel with any further deregulation or restructuring, there is recognition of the need to limit such potential future costs. One new idea being considered would create limitations on deposit insurance. Under the proposal, banks would be required to set up narrow or core banks where FDIC-insured deposits could be invested only in limited-risk securities such as Treasury bills or specific eligible assets like consumer loans. It would prohibit risky assets such as commercial loans. Deposits funding core bank activities would be federally insured. Funding used to support non-core activities would not be insured, and would be priced at prevailing market rates.

If the proposal were to be adopted, banks would literally have to redesign their legal entities and restructure themselves into new core banks. Risky lending business would have to be conducted outside the core bank and funded separately. A theoretical model of the narrow bank concept was developed by Robert Litan of the Brookings Institute. Lowell Bryan, a McKinsey & Company consultant, has also strongly advocated the core bank model. Representative Charles Schumer (New York) has done a good job explaining the concept to other political leaders. Nevertheless, the odds of its being enacted remain low. Most banks and bank holding companies oppose the core bank concept because of concerns regarding its cost and implementation complexity.

One consequence of the core bank concept could be that further impetus is given to consolidation, since many banks would rationally choose to merge rather than restructure. Under a core banking scenario, most smaller banks and bank holding companies that meet certain guidelines would be exempt and not forced to legally reorganize and reengineer their banks. The principle adverse impact would be realized by middle-size and smaller regional bank holding companies. They would find the money and management resources required to restructure their entities so

Under a core banking scenario, . . . the principle adverse impact would be realized by middle-size and smaller regional bank holding companies. They would find the money and management resources required to restructure their entities so costly that they might choose not to comply and simply sell out.

costly that they might choose not to comply and simply sell out. In contrast, the largest banks could more easily shoulder greater administrative burdens along with the legal costs involved. As a result, the pace of industry consolidation might actually be further fueled.

If some form of new regulation does occur, could we come full circle and see Regulation Q reenacted? Legislation of this type is not likely. Looking forward, however, one can envision continuing adjustments to today's capital and product (insurance and securities, for example) frameworks. Regulatory adjustments should be expected to continue as the industry muddles toward a new paradigm. However, if banking industry losses mount and the taxpayer is again perceived to be at risk, a core bank framework could be enacted.

An Effective and Affordable Safety Net

Current federal banking protection consists essentially of two components: federal depository insurance and access to the Federal Reserve discount window. The concern of the Congress and regulators has been to keep general commerce and other speculative activities, such as securities underwriting, outside the safety net so that taxpayers do not become liable for losses occurring in these sectors.

Traditional separation of investment banking and commercial banking included the desire to keep securities firms away from the safety net. The idea that there would be no access to that protection, or ultimately to taxpayers' pockets, has been modified by the Federal Reserve as a result of experience with serious stock market decline. During the stock market crash of October 1987, securities firms became illiquid and approached banks for lines of credit. Initially, banks were cautious in extending such credit. Realizing the extreme urgency, the Fed stepped in to encourage banks to make their lines available. Had the Fed failed to act promptly, an already panicky circumstance could have reached crisis proportions. Recognition of that problem led to provisions in FDICIA that extended the safety net to securities firms. In effect, banks have become a necessary lender of next-to-last resort.

Recent Regulatory Focus: Capital Adequacy

The most recent changes in the regulatory arena involve the new capital adequacy requirements of the Basle Accord. Effective in the United States at the start of 1992, Basle was designed to set global leverage capital standards. Originally, the United States, whose regulators wished to make standards more rigorous, and the Bank of England began a higher capital standard initiative.

These two countries' central bankers successfully broadened the standard to be a worldwide one.

The thrust of the Basle Accord is to establish risk-adjusted capital requirements in which each asset category and off-balance-sheet item is given a specific risk weighting. For example, Treasury bills receive a zero rating, mortgages a 0.5 rating, and commercial loans a weight of 1.0. Based on the Basle Accord standards, a bank with $3 billion of assets, consisting of $1 billion in government bills, $1 billion in mortgages, and $1 billion in commercial loans, would be assessed to have $1.5 billion in risk-weighted assets. With a Tier I standard of 4 percent, the bank would require $60 million of equity capital. Total minimum capital standards including Tiers I and II are set at 8 percent.

A significant aspect of the capital requirement is the exclusion of goodwill as capital. Second, emphasis is focused on tangible or real capital. In addition, loan loss reserves no longer count as Tier I capital. Under the new provisions, some portion of loan loss reserves will still count, but only under Tier II standards. Likewise, only noncumulative preferred stock, which is not the type of preferred stock traditionally issued, is deemed Tier I. Cumulative preferred stock and subordinated debentures are regarded as Tier II. Thus, Basle provides a far more rigorous demarcation between Tier I and Tier II capital.

U.S. regulators generally impose stricter capital standards than those implied by Basle. The thrift debacle and subsequent efforts to protect against taxpayer liability led regulators to set higher requirements: U.S. banks normally need to have 4.5 percent to 5.5 percent in equity capital, generally referred to as the leverage ratio. Obviously, the higher the standard, the less funding available for loans. Indeed, it is often argued that higher-than-required equity standards imposed on domestic banks reduce the nation's available lending capacity and therefore undermine economic growth. Without funding available from banks, commercial activity and growth can be severely stifled. Banking companies could double commercial lending levels in some cases by lowering equity levels to the minimum of the Basle standard.

Regulatory Practices, Priorities, and Implications

The greatest portion of regulatory impact does not come in the form of planned regulation. It comes in the more imprecise and unpredictable arena of crisis and resolution. The 1990s auger well for a more benign, less interventionary, regulatory regime. Regardless of the continuation of capital as "King of Regulation" or more insightful approaches, such as the plans of the New York Fed and Chicago Fed (see Chapter 3, page 79), a few hard learned truths have been established in the thinking of the OCC, FDIC, and the Federal Reserve.

The first is that forbearance is a prescription for disaster. Hospitalizing financial institutions painfully delays, but does not alter, their inevitable destiny. Worse, it tends to infect other financial institutions in the process. Second, product and geographic integration can be managed, but not stopped. Third, prompt return to the private sector of assets seized in bank closures results in the highest regulatory return, both in asset yield and in minimization of disruptive costs and disincentives conveyed to private sector financial firms. Not unlike the experience of banks, these lessons were painful to learn and, therefore, will not be easily forgotten by bank regulators. One should expect continuing regulatory adherence to these principles throughout the decade.

The new capital rules can change the strategy of balance sheet management and the entire strategy regarding bank expansion. Capital has become an overriding consideration not only of regulators, but it also has become more important to investors. Some analysts, notably J. Richard Fredericks of Montgomery Securities, forecast the winners in the Darwinian banking world will be those with "fortress balance sheets." These banks would have high levels of real, tangible capital, high levels of asset quality, and other traditional measures of solid balance sheets.

From the perspective of acquisition strategy, if one does purchase accounting versus pooling accounting, it can create substantial goodwill, detracting from tangible capital. Accordingly, in the future most large mergers would be expected to be done on a stock pooling basis. More important, banks with strong capital position will be operating from a position of relative strength. (See Chapter 6 for further discussion of these ramifications.)

To gain regulatory approval, banks must enter merger agreements with a strong capital ratio. The merger should actually strengthen the capital position of the combined institution. As a result, merging institutions often need to issue additional equity capital before or shortly after a merger, to maintain acceptable capital ratios. The Chemical Bank-Manufacturers Hanover merger is a prominent example of this point. The new Chemical Bank raised a record amount of equity ($1.57 billion) shortly after it merged. Similarly, NationsBank and First Union have each consummated merger transactions where equity issues followed. In the stock market, banks that have stronger tangible equity levels have been accorded higher market-to-book value premiums. This valuation reality also puts strongly capitalized firms at a currency advantage when competing for mergers.

The Challenge of Managing Industry Restructuring

As the pressures of deregulation continue, cost reduction emerges as one of the principle elements of the banking and merger envi-

. . . a few hard learned truths have been established in the thinking of the OCC, FDIC, and the Federal Reserve.

The first is that forbearance is a prescription for disaster. Hospitalizing financial institutions painfully delays, but does not alter, their inevitable destiny. Second, product and geographic integration can be managed, but not stopped.

ronment. Consolidation is the vehicle that both the industry and regulators have selected to address the problem of excess industry cost and inadequate revenues. Through acquisition and consolidation, redundancies in the form of branches and employees are eliminated, and general corporate overhead and bank holding company expenses are typically cut.

Today, it is a generally accepted proposition that banking has too much capacity and suffers from the excessive costs that high capacity implies. While the 1980s saw asset growth and new product powers pursued as a means of generating sufficient revenue to address the excess capacity problem, a more pragmatic approach is being adopted in the 1990s.

More profoundly and explicitly, there are simply more costs in the banking system than there are available revenues in the marketplace. Pricing deregulation in the early 1980s exposed the problem. Initial industry responses focused on seeking expanded product powers as a means of increasing available revenues. At the same time, many banks went too far up the risk curve in seeking loan volume. Today many of these banks are burdened by the resources required to unwind the loan problems that their aggressive growth created. A new realism now marks industry thinking. Fundamental cost reduction, achieved through consolidations that eliminate excess capacity, and fundamental redesign of the operating process are necessary solutions.

Regulations had to be changed to allow consolidation to be pursued as a vehicle to address the industry's restructuring needs. For example, Garn-St Germain enabled banks to expand into other states even where no laws provided for interstate banking. Under its provisions, a bank can enter any state by purchasing a failed savings and loan or failed bank. Some notable acquisitions include Bank of America's 1983 purchase of Seafirst; Chase Manhattan's 1985 purchases of several privately insured Ohio S&Ls and Park Bank in Florida; and Citicorp's 1986 purchase of several failed S&Ls in California, Illinois, Florida, Maryland, and Nevada. Large banks in Texas, First Republic and MCorp, were purchased by NCNB (now NationsBank) and BANC ONE, respectively. Some—the BANC ONE and NationsBank transactions in Texas, for instance—have added exceptional franchise value. While many acquirers have had mixed success with their deals, these first interstate transactions represented important early steps toward nationwide restructuring.

To date, in-market mergers have already resulted in substantial elimination of redundant branches and personnel. The BankAmerica-Security Pacific, Chemical-Manufacturers Hanover, Society-Ameritrust, and First Union-Southeast deals were all accompanied by major reductions in branches, personnel, and correspondent operating expenses. The structural economic advantages of in-market consolidation have been well demonstrated in the

More profoundly and explicitly, there are simply more costs in the banking system than there are available revenues in the marketplace. Pricing deregulation in the early 1980s exposed the problem.

A new realism now marks industry thinking. Fundamental cost reduction, achieved through consolidations that eliminate excess capacity, and fundamental redesign of the operating process are necessary solutions.

early 1990s. The case for consolidation as part of the solution to the industry's restructuring needs has been documented. Accordingly, a critical hypothesis underlying the industry paradigm shift has been validated.

In this chapter, we have presented an overview of the industry's evolving regulatory framework and have put into context the pricing and product deregulatory movements of the past decade. Our goal was to present the industry as one facing a fundamental revenue shortfall relative to its expense base. Pricing and product changes are not capable of providing needed structural relief. The industry's ultimate health is dependent on building institutions with operating and managerial efficiencies that can only be achieved through consolidation and fundamental restructuring. Failure to do so will leave banks competitively disadvantaged and subject to further erosion of their traditional franchise.

3

Consolidation as Part of the Solution

It can be debated whether consolidation was or was not expected to follow earlier pricing and product deregulation. Whatever its cause, consolidation aims to solve one of the industry's greatest challenges. It is a critical response to the industry's having a cost structure that exceeds available marketplace revenue. It works to eliminate the industry's excess capacity and represents an important stage in a larger movement that promises to produce a restructured industry that is competitive within a much broader financial services arena. A consolidated and more competitive industry represents a key element of the new, emerging banking paradigm.

The Pace of Industry Consolidation

After remaining fairly stable for more than 20 years, the number of U.S. banking organizations declined more than 25 percent during the period 1980 to 1992 (Exhibit 3.1). There are clear trends of mergers and acquisitions, bank failures, intraholding company consolidations, and declining de novo bank formations. These trends are expected to continue through the current decade. Accordingly, we agree with forecasters who suggest that only 5,000 banking organizations may survive the 1990s.

Acquisition activity was heavy throughout most of the 1980s. Exhibit 3.2 indicates that more than 200 deals were consummated each year after 1983, with the exceptions of 1989 and 1990. At the same time, between 1984 and 1992, the number of bank failures ranged from 79 to 221 (Exhibit 3.3). The Federal Deposit Insurance Corporation (FDIC) indicates that at the end of 1992 there were 863 problem banks (Exhibit 3.4). Moreover, the amount of assets lodged in FDIC-insured problem banks rose from $335.5 billion in 1986 to $464.5 billion at year-end 1992 (Exhibit 3.5). Acquisitions and failed institutions both play critical roles in the consolidation movement.

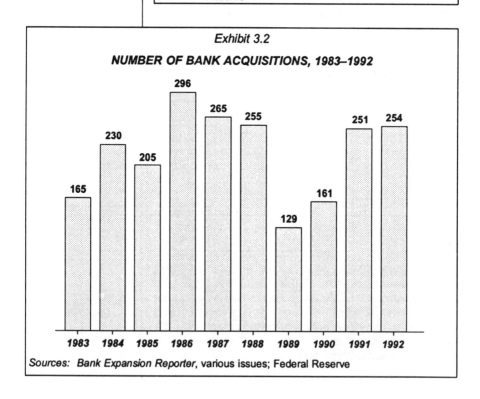

Exhibit 3.1

NUMBER OF INSURED U.S. COMMERCIAL BANKS, BANKING ORGANIZATIONS, AND BRANCH OFFICES 1980–1992

Year	Number of Insured U.S. Commercial Banks	Number of Banking Organizations*	Number of Branch Offices
1980	14,478	12,347	38,353
1985	14,290	11,008	43,239
1990	12,211	9,110	51,305
1991	11,806	9,004	53,000
1992	11,363	8,729	53,744

* Banking organizations are the sum of independent banks, one-bank holding companies, and individual multibank holding companies. In 1992 there were 867 multibank holding companies.

Note: Home offices are not included in branch data.

Sources: NIC Database, Bank-Branch Structure File, Federal Reserve

Exhibit 3.2

NUMBER OF BANK ACQUISITIONS, 1983–1992

Year	Acquisitions
1983	165
1984	230
1985	205
1986	296
1987	265
1988	255
1989	129
1990	161
1991	251
1992	254

Sources: Bank Expansion Reporter, various issues; Federal Reserve

Exhibit 3.3

ENTRY AND EXIT IN BANKING, 1980–1992

Year	New Banks	Failures of[1] FDIC-Insured Banks	All Mergers and Acquisitions*	Large Mergers and Acquisitions*
1980	267	10	188	0
1981	286	10	359	1
1982	378	42	422	2
1983	419	48	432	6
1984	489	79	553	14
1985	346	120	553	7
1986	283	145	625	20
1987	217	203	710	21
1988	234	221	569	18
1989	204	207	388	9
1990	165	169	442	20
1991	106	127	231p	23
1992	94	122	N/A	25
Total	3,488	1,503	5,472p	166

Key: p = preliminary data, 1991 merger data includes only Federal Reserve approved transactions.

[1] Bank failure data are from the *Annual Report of the Federal Deposit Insurance Corporation.*

* These numbers reflect the number of transactions; however, a merger may involve multiple banks.
Merger and acquisitions are from Stephen A. Rhoades, "Mergers and Acquisitions by Commercial Banks, 1960–1983," *Staff Studies,* No. 142 (Federal Reserve Board, January 1985) and annual updates supplied by the author. Larger mergers and acquisition data are for mergers in which both organizations have deposits in excess of $1 billion and exclude acquisitions of thrifts and failing banks.

Sources: Federal Reserve Board; New bank data are from the *Annual Statistical Digest.*

The initial wave of consolidation activity seemed to encourage de novo bank formations. Displaced bankers were eager to supply new local bank options to communities that had seen their independent banks sell out. De novo banks were often chartered with the eventual goal of a later sell-out for a healthy premium. Exhibit 3.3 indicates that the rate of de novo charters declined dramatically toward the end of the 1980s. This reflects several important prospects. First, the rising intensity of competition suggests that the time required for a new bank to break even is

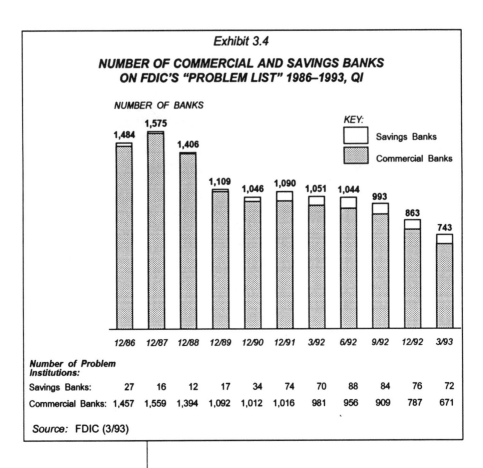

Exhibit 3.4

**NUMBER OF COMMERCIAL AND SAVINGS BANKS
ON FDIC'S "PROBLEM LIST" 1986–1993, QI**

NUMBER OF BANKS

KEY:
☐ Savings Banks
▨ Commercial Banks

Number of Problem Institutions:											
	12/86	12/87	12/88	12/89	12/90	12/91	3/92	6/92	9/92	12/92	3/93
Savings Banks:	27	16	12	17	34	74	70	88	84	76	72
Commercial Banks:	1,457	1,559	1,394	1,092	1,012	1,016	981	956	909	787	671

Source: FDIC (3/93)

becoming longer, and prospective profitability levels are not as favorable as in the past. Second, acquirers are increasingly seeking larger banks to buy, since they must expend a similar amount of resources regardless of the size of the deal. Also, larger capital investment costs and the increase in scale economies have also dampened the interest of new bank entrants.

Bank holding companies are increasingly consolidating, or folding in, the independent banks operating within their systems. Even banks such as BANC ONE, First of America, and Barnett Banks, which have strong strategic and philosophical commitments to keeping acquired banks autonomous and operating as networks of separate community banks, have increasingly consolidated their back offices to rationalize costs. As will be discussed in later chapters, cost rationalization has proved to be a critical part of bank acquisition strategy.

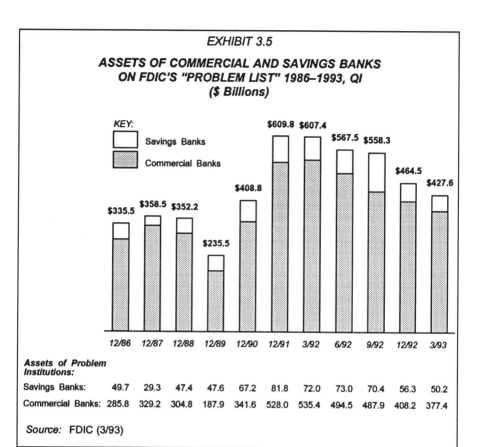

EXHIBIT 3.5

ASSETS OF COMMERCIAL AND SAVINGS BANKS
ON FDIC'S "PROBLEM LIST" 1986–1993, QI
($ Billions)

KEY:
☐ Savings Banks
▨ Commercial Banks

Assets of Problem Institutions:	12/86	12/87	12/88	12/89	12/90	12/91	3/92	6/92	9/92	12/92	3/93
Savings Banks:	49.7	29.3	47.4	47.6	67.2	81.8	72.0	73.0	70.4	56.3	50.2
Commercial Banks:	285.8	329.2	304.8	187.9	341.6	528.0	535.4	494.5	487.9	408.2	377.4

Source: FDIC (3/93)

It is not surprising that cost reduction is a critical element of successful bank acquisition efforts, particularly when viewing the consolidation wave as a systemic response to the industry's excess capacity problem. Moreover, the evidence from bank mergers-to-date suggests that those banks that pay relatively high prices for acquisitions, and fail to improve their productivity performance, destroy shareholder value. In many cases, these acquiring banks, themselves, have been taken over because they were not successful in implementing cost-effective merger strategies. On the other hand, banks such as Wells Fargo and Bank of New York that have moved aggressively to reduce costs as part of their merger strategy have improved their shareholder value and enhanced their capacity to do additional transactions. The positive capital market response to successful acquisition-based cost reduction further underscores its potential value.

A Short History of Geographic Deregulation

Traditionally, banks were subject to limitations of the geographic area in which they could operate. Historically, controversies surrounding geographic deregulation centered on intrastate branching. The decade of the 1980s saw this focus shift to interstate restrictions, with most states legislating some form of interstate banking. Meanwhile, individual states' branching laws continued to shift away from unit banking and toward statewide branching. The legislative elimination of restrictions on intrastate and interstate banking during the 1980s produced a changed industry landscape. Geographic deregulation caused increased competition, as well as increased consolidation pressure.

One point not to be overlooked concerning geographic deregulation is the impact of the proliferation of automated teller machines (ATMs). This technological innovation has allowed banks to provide greater service yet lessen their investment in branch infrastructure. Furthermore, by sharing their ATMs with other regional and national banks' networks, institutions use electronic banking both to take deposits and provide retail credit. This is de facto interstate banking. Despite this apparent breach of the McFadden Act, the Comptroller of the Currency in 1980 ruled that ATM-sharing and networking are permissible. Again, somewhat archaic regulations were not allowed to block marketplace forces of change.

The Evolving Nature of Interstate Banking

The pace of interstate banking quickened in the 1980s as many states passed laws allowing interstate expansion on either a regional or national basis. As discussed in the preceding chapter, a provision of the 1990 Garn-St Germain Act allowed for interstate takeovers of failed or failing institutions. In June 1985, the Supreme Court affirmed the legality of regional bank compacts established by state legislatures. Banks from states not named in a particular state's regional definition were prohibited from participating in that state's interstate mergers.

Ironically, even without these regional restrictions, banks from New York and Texas would probably not have become significant players in the consolidation game.

The establishment of regional pacts limited the number of bidders for indigenous institutions to banks located in similar geographic areas. Typically, regional pacts excluded New York, California, and Texas for fear that large banks from these states, if allowed entry, would gobble up all the smaller banks. Some argued that regional banks should have opportunity and time to gain size in order to eventually compete against large national banks. Ironically, even without these regional restrictions, banks from New York and Texas would probably not have become significant players in the consolidation game. Their troubled loan portfolios and weak capital positions during the latter half of the 1980s prevented them from undertaking significant acquisitions.

The timing of the deregulation and consolidation movement has had a profound influence regarding which banks have emerged as industry leaders.

From the early days of interstate banking, the Southeast Compact has been the best example of a regional banking zone. There, several large regional banks have been allowed to acquire and grow, while entry by banks outside the region is still prohibited. Only two states in the South—Louisiana and Tennessee—have elected to change their status to now allow national entry.

Other states selected a regional approach for only a short time period until their initial law triggered or changed to permit national entry. Many New England and Midwestern states fit this description—Connecticut, Massachusetts, Ohio, Michigan, and Illinois are examples.

As of this writing, 48 states (all except Hawaii and Montana) have enacted laws permitting interstate banking. Most states (34) provide for national entry, some with no restrictions. Others require that the acquirer's home state grant reciprocity, that is, permit out-of-state banks similar entry. Fifteen states maintain regional laws. Ten of these states are in the Southeastern Compact. Exhibit 3.6 summarizes state laws permitting interstate banking.

It is not clear whether regional banking compacts will ultimately achieve their objective of producing banking entities large enough to compete against large, national competitors. The regional zones in the South, New England, and Midwest did help create some relatively large banks: Fleet, Shawmut, and Bank of Boston in New England; PNC, BANC ONE, Norwest, and NBD in the Midwest; and NationsBank, First Union, SunTrust, and Wachovia in the Southeast. Some of these institutions may be able to complete their acquisition growth programs and survive. However, as the merger landscape discussion in Chapter 5 points out, some of these superregional banks, as well as a number of other relatively large regional banks, may not be able to remain independent because other larger, more successful banks may eventually view them as targets. In this light, the legacy of regional banking would be that of facilitating regional and national bank consolidation. Many of the state, regional, and superregional banks created in the process may eventually function as state or regional administrative centers for larger, perhaps national, banking companies. If the past is any indication, how the industry structure unfolds will be a function of environmental pressures, the boldness of management, and luck.

. . . the legacy of regional banking would be that of facilitating regional and national bank consolidation. Many of the state, regional, and superregional banks created in the process may eventually function as state or regional administrative centers for larger, perhaps national, banking companies.

Micro-Market Deregulation: Branching Liberalization

While interstate banking laws govern industry structure from a national perspective, branching laws strongly influence the com-

Exhibit 3.6

INTERSTATE BANKING LAWS

STATE LAWS ALLOWING INTERSTATE BANK HOLDING COMPANIES

Nationwide Entry without Reciprocity	Nationwide Entry with Reciprocity	Regional or Contiguous State Entry with Reciprocity	Entry Not Allowed
Alaska	California	Alabama	Hawaii
Arizona	Connecticut	Arkansas[2]	Montana
Colorado	Delaware	District of Columbia	
Idaho	Illinois	Florida	
Maine	Indiana	Georgia	
Nevada	Kentucky	Iowa	
New Hampshire	Louisiana	Kansas	
New Mexico	Massachusetts	Maryland	
Oklahoma[1]	Michigan	Minnesota	
Oregon	Nebraska	Mississippi	
Texas	New Jersey	Missouri	
Utah	New York	North Carolina	
Wyoming	North Dakota	South Carolina	
	Ohio	Virginia	
	Pennsylvania	Wisconsin	
	Rhode Island		
	South Dakota		
	Tennessee		
	Vermont		
	Washington		
	West Virginia		

1 Bank holding companies from states not granting reciprocal entry to Oklahoma banking organizations must wait four years before making additional acquisitions.
2 Entry into Arkansas is contingent on submission, approval, and compliance with an extensive plan guaranteeing certain levels of community service and investment.

Source: Financial Industry Trends, Annual 1992, Federal Reserve Bank of Kansas City

petitive structure of the industry on a micromarket basis. The McFadden Act requires state law determination of the ability of commercial banks to branch. There are essentially two types of state branching regimes. The first, unit banking, requires that banks be separately chartered and that all activity of a given bank take place in a single banking office. Branch banking, the second type, allows for a commercial bank to have numerous offices to the extent permitted by state law.

Unit banking regulations are based on the premise that locally controlled and managed banks can keep funds available on a more equitable basis, rather than allowing funds to be shifted to branched banks headquartered in urban commercial centers or other areas in a state. The mobility of funds, however, probably cannot be constrained by branching laws. Unit banks, nevertheless, tend to have higher operating expenses, and their lack of diversification creates greater risk. Interestingly, banks in states that have historically restricted branching practices tend to have realized the highest bank failures. Additionally, unit banks have tended to operate with higher liquidity and lower loan ratios. In many respects, unit banking restrictions represent an outdated approach to regulation.

The advent of securitization has also added to the incentive to consolidate by adding value to standardized lending terms.

Branching, on the other hand, results in banks' tending to have more diversified loan portfolios and more efficient operations which, in turn, lessen risk and expense. The advent of securitization has also added to the incentive to consolidate by adding value to standardized lending terms. Today, arguments against branching have been dispelled, and the trend is to liberalize branching laws.

While unit banking laws historically dominated, the number of states with unit banking statutes has seen significant reduction (Exhibit 3.7). From 1960 to 1992, the number of unit banking states declined from 18 to zero while branching states increased to 50, with the statewide branching classification increasing from 16 to 34. As the consolidation movement unfolds and a new industry paradigm is established, branching can be expected to become increasingly liberalized until full nationwide branching is in effect.

Comparative Analysis:
North Carolina versus Illinois

State branching laws have, to a certain extent, determined each state's role in the interstate banking arena. For example, North Carolina has permitted statewide branching for over 135 years. As a result, through intrastate consolidation, North Carolina banks became some of the South's largest. They learned how to operate large branching systems and developed substantial commercial lending organizations. The expertise and experience gained in the

Exhibit 3.7

BANK BRANCHING TRENDS

	1960	1977	1985	1990	1992
Unit Banking	18	12	8	3	0
Limited Branching	16	16	18	14	16
Statewide Branching	16	22	24	33	34

Source: Federal Reserve Bank of Kansas City; Authors.

One clear exception to this experience is Northern Trust, which has been very successful in the new competitive environment because it specializes in the less geographic-intense businesses of private banking, trust processing, and corporate services.

process have had an important impact on the ability of North Carolina banks to compete and expand in the present deregulation era. Today, NationsBank (formerly NCNB), First Union, and Wachovia are three of the major surviving banks in the nation and among the dominant banks in the Southeast. Critical to their acquisition success are the scale and management skills that their home state branching laws encouraged.

In contrast, Illinois is an example of a staunch unit banking state. Illinois still has about 1,000 independent commercial banks, and its banking system is very fragmented. Although it is a major state in terms of population and commercial activity, it will not be a major headquarters state in the interstate banking arena. Historically, Illinois did not allow its Chicago banks to branch statewide, grow, and develop the ability to manage larger multimarket, multibank entities. While First Chicago remains a large institution headquartered in Illinois, it has been unable to extend its franchise across the state. Only in the late 1980s were Chicago banks able to make acquisitions throughout Illinois. At the same time, First Chicago has not participated in interstate banking as well. From a national consolidation perspective, the Illinois banking community appears to have been somewhat shortsighted in its approach to regulation, ultimately shortchanging its banks' ability to grow.

One clear exception to this experience is Northern Trust, which has been very successful in the new competitive environment because it specializes in the less geographic-intense businesses of private banking, trust processing, and corporate services. Its strategy focuses on products that do not require large-scale geographic investment for growth.

Exhibit 3.8 illustrates the dramatic difference in the numbers of banks in these two states. Interestingly, their different structures seem to produce quite different financial performance, as measured by return on assets and return on equity.

Exhibit 3.8

**COMPARATIVE ANALYSIS OF BANK STRUCTURE
ILLINOIS VERSUS NORTH CAROLINA**

Year	Number of Banks		ROA		ROE	
	Illinois	North Carolina	Illinois	North Carolina	Illinois	North Carolina
1992	1006	78	0.72%	1.03%	9.32%	15.24%
1991	1061	81	0.67%	0.74%	9.40%	10.99%
1990	1087	78	0.68%	0.85%	10.05%	13.77%
1989	1119	78	0.88%	0.97%	13.53%	15.62%
1988	1149	71	0.99%	1.06%	15.66%	16.86%
1987	1209	68	−0.23%	0.92%	−3.88%	15.38%
1986	1218	65	0.71%	1.07%	10.70%	18.22%
1985	1233	63	0.63%	0.98%	9.55%	16.82%
1984	1240	63	−0.11%	0.97%	−1.76%	16.47%

Source: FDIC Division of Research and Statistics

Interstate Acquisition versus Interstate Branching

Although many observers refer to interstate banking as interstate branching, it is important to note that in a legal sense banks are still not doing interstate branching. Interstate branching is still illegal under the McFadden Act. What we are actually observing in terms of the formation of regional and superregional banks is interstate expansion through bank acquisition. Bank holding companies, operating under the Douglas Amendment of the Bank Holding Company Act, are expressly allowed by specific state statutes to acquire banks in other states. They are still prohibited, however, from branching into other states. Also, for the most part, they cannot acquire a bank and then convert it into a branch of an out-of-state bank.

What may on the surface appear to be a semantics issue, really is not. Moreover, the economic consequences of interstate branching are significant. Branching is now an important policy issue. Ironically, it is no longer viewed as important for geographic expansion but, rather, is viewed as essential to converting acquired banks into efficient operating units. NationsBank, later joined by other superregional banks, pushed for interstate branching reform in the Treasury Bank Reform Bill of 1991. The larger superregional banks are very desirous of gaining further branching authority in order to eliminate unnecessary costs and organizational impediments involved with having separate subsidiaries. NationsBank's Chairman, Hugh McColl, has personally led the charge to win interstate branching rights by giving numerous public speeches and testifying before Congress. It has been estimated that more than $10 billion could be saved by the commercial banking industry if wider branching were adopted.

Banks like NationsBank believe that tremendous cost savings could be obtained by eliminating separate filings, bank examinations, and boards of directors required to operate numerous individually chartered institutions. These duplicative administrative functions not only require additional expense, but also consume management time. Unnecessary repetitive requirements could be significantly reduced if branching were allowed.

Nevertheless, interstate branching is still a very controversial political issue. Banks, therefore, have begun to play political hardball on the issue. Some banks have announced they will no longer give financial support to the American Bankers Association (ABA) or any state trade organizations that oppose full branching powers. The ABA's decision to drop its request for branching as a political tradeoff to stop the insurance industry's initiative to roll back bank insurance powers provoked further controversy. NationsBank said that if this kind of decision were to happen again, it would drop out of the ABA. Such threats are no longer idle. Bank of Boston previously withdrew from the ABA, stating that it could no longer justify the expense. Since superregional banks also pay a large percentage of the dues of various state associations, it would seem that their political bargaining strength will be increasingly felt.

Branching prohibitions represent once well-intentioned legislation that is simply no longer relevant. For example, consider the consumer inconvenience resulting from branching restrictions in natural geographic markets. For a long time, it has been evident that there are numerous banking markets that are arbitrarily divided by state lines—Washington, D.C.-Maryland-Virginia; New Jersey-New York-Connecticut; TexArkana; and Kansas City, Kansas-Kansas City, Missouri. Where people live and work across state lines, their banking services are impeded by arbitrary boundaries. Branching restrictions not only impose unnecessary inefficiencies on competing banks, but on consumers as well. Eliminating such absurd restrictions, however, is often a politically complex endeavor. The old industry paradigm developed around these regulations and is somewhat dependent on them today. Bankers' initial resistance to regulatory change that will further increase competition in the marketplace is understandable.

In 1992, a federal court confirmed a rule that permits thrifts to branch across state lines. Stiff opposition was felt from banking groups who opposed the issue as unfair because, meanwhile, banks are not allowed to branch across state boundaries.

The ABA's decision to drop its request for branching as a political tradeoff to stop the insurance industry's initiative to roll back bank insurance powers provoked further controversy. NationsBank said that if this kind of decision were to happen again, it would drop out of the ABA. Such threats are no longer idle.

Further complicating the issue, the Senate only a day earlier had added an amendment to pending legislation prohibiting thrifts from branching across state lines for at least 15 months. Many sides in the debate hailed the court's decision as heading in the direction of reason but argued prohibition on bank branching also needed to be terminated.

The past decade has seen technology enhance the ability of banks to handle and process transactions on both a national and global basis. In this context, present restrictions seem outdated, and it is probably only a matter of time before nationwide branching will be permitted. Of course, the political wrestling and haggling will continue until this issue is finally laid to rest.

Orderly Dissolution of the Thrift Industry

The financial services industry's excess capacity is also being reduced greatly through the ongoing dissolution of the thrift industry. Exhibit 3.9 shows the dramatic decline in the number of thrifts and the thrift industry's aggregate assets since 1988. Currently, unhealthy thrifts are being aggressively closed through merger or put in the Resolution Trust Corporation (RTC) for liquidation. Other troubled S&Ls have been taken over and placed in conservatorship. The government is not permitted to practice forbearance as it once did, and thrift institutions can no longer keep themselves afloat by issuing nationally brokered CDs at irrational prices.

The thrift industry is being combined piecemeal into the commercial banking industry. Commercial banks have actively bid for RTC-controlled thrift deposits, branches, and assets. Banks are also purchasing healthy thrifts. Various thrift investments can be beneficial to banks in a number of ways. First, combining purchased thrift franchises with preexisting banking offices can result in substantial cost savings. Redundant branches, employees, and operating systems can be eliminated. Second, in some markets, thrifts can serve as valuable entry vehicles. In many key urban markets only a limited number of banks exist, and often many of them have already been purchased. Thrift acquisition may be the only market-entry mechanism. Finally, thrift consolidations in local markets can produce dominant market shares. With increasing market share positions, oligopolistic effects may permit stronger pricing on both the deposit and asset sides.

Another controversial twist in FDIC thrift strategy concerns the 1992 failure of Crossland Savings, a New York-based thrift with branches throughout the country. In the auction of Crossland, two interested bidders, Republic of New York and Chase Manhattan, had their offers rejected by the FDIC. The FDIC called the bids inadequate. In the hope of achieving a higher sale value later, the FDIC decided to retain and manage Crossland

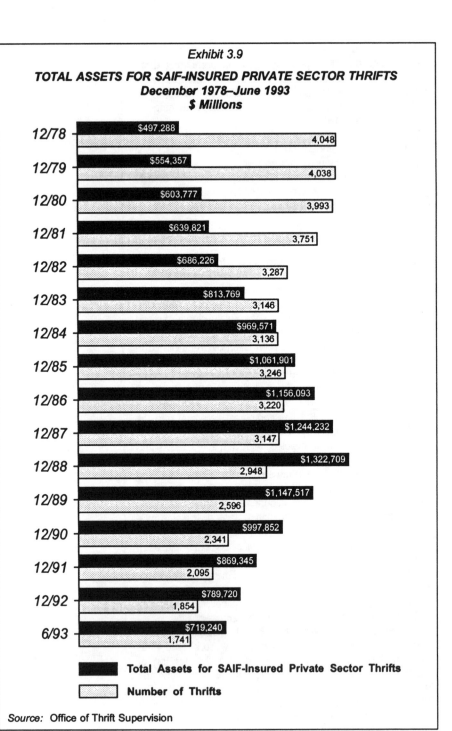

Exhibit 3.9

TOTAL ASSETS FOR SAIF-INSURED PRIVATE SECTOR THRIFTS
December 1978–June 1993
$ Millions

Date	Total Assets	Number of Thrifts
12/78	$497,288	4,048
12/79	$554,357	4,038
12/80	$603,777	3,993
12/81	$639,821	3,751
12/82	$686,226	3,287
12/83	$813,769	3,146
12/84	$969,571	3,136
12/85	$1,061,901	3,246
12/86	$1,156,093	3,220
12/87	$1,244,232	3,147
12/88	$1,322,709	2,948
12/89	$1,147,517	2,596
12/90	$997,852	2,341
12/91	$869,345	2,095
12/92	$789,720	1,854
6/93	$719,240	1,741

■ Total Assets for SAIF-Insured Private Sector Thrifts
▢ Number of Thrifts

Source: Office of Thrift Supervision

itself. The Crossland decision signaled a new way the FDIC could attempt to reduce taxpayer liability by not accepting bids that are deemed too low. This was an interesting change of direction and sent notice to bidders that if they bid too far below market value, the FDIC would retain the option of simply operating the franchise itself.

The inherent danger of the FDIC strategy lies in the possible further devaluation of a franchise once it is being operated by the government. Recently, the FDIC decided to auction off Crossland through a public offering. Undoubtedly, the postmortem analysis of its earlier decision to delay sale and operate the institution will remain controversial.

Emerging from the rubble of the S&L cataclysm are lessons that banks have learned from attempts to consolidate and integrate thrifts. One strategy often employed by banks is to make sure that a bank in the acquirer's holding company exists in the geographic location of the desired thrift. It is important to note that a competent bank management structure would already be in place. As previously mentioned, this approach allows the bank acquirer simply to merge the thrift into an existing bank, thus eliminating duplication of infrastructure costs. In this light, it is argued that thrift purchases for market share enhancement objectives are more defensible than those based on using thrifts for market entry vehicles.

In acquiring thrift franchises, banks cannot overlook the importance of doing their homework. Considerable time must be spent on the due diligence function in order to ensure there are no surprises in the quality of assets and deposit values being purchased. This is especially necessary in dealing with real estate, which accounts for a large percentage of thrift assets.

Another concern in thrift acquisition involves personnel. Because thrifts have generally offered limited product lines, their personnel are often not equipped to handle the complexity and number of products offered by banks. Consequently, in converting thrifts into banks, a large percentage of people generally must be replaced. As a result, the real value of the acquired thrift is inherent in its customer franchise. While branches may be closed and employees dismissed, there is hope that the customer base and market share will endure.

RTC Defies Comparison

The 1989 Financial Institutions Regulatory Reform and Enforcement Act (FIRREA) created the RTC to oversee resolution of troubled thrifts. After several years of congressional neglect, FIRREA provided $50 billion to be used by the RTC to sell, liquidate, or conserve ailing thrifts. Assuming available funding, merger assistance or liquidation options have been considered the least costly resolution approach. Unfortunately, the RTC quickly and easily used up initial funding and was forced to place several institutions under public conservatorship until additional funds were provided by Congress. Generally, conservatorships prove more costly to taxpayers. In a conservatorship, troubled institutions quickly lose their franchise value as depositors leave, assets deteriorate, and employees resign.

Observers will continue to debate the ultimate success of the RTC even after its October 1, 1993, extended sunset date. In truth, analysis of the RTC defies comparison. Almost overnight Congress created an entity with more than $390 billion in assets. A relatively small budget and professional staff were assigned to implement the intent of Congress. The government also discouraged the RTC from liquidating assets when their sale would have material effects on already weak or even nonexistent markets. RTC auctions have been well utilized by commercial banks as a low-cost vehicle to build franchise value. Many other bargain-hunting investors have sought RTC properties.

Whatever the pundit's final assessment of the RTC, it will leave a legacy as one of the largest government ownership programs to come and go in a relatively short time period.

Antitrust in the Consolidation Era?

The antitrust policy of the U.S. Justice Department has played a central role in shaping bank consolidation patterns. The initial quest for interstate banking authority derived from the fact that in the late 1970s many state multibank holding companies had reached market share limits—approximately 10 percent at that time—in their various local markets. Further growth, in that context, could be achieved only through cross-state expansion. Accordingly, political initiatives for interstate bank merger liberalization began.

Following the 1985 Supreme Court decision affirming the legality of regional banking, an interstate merger wave became a major factor on the banking landscape. Unfortunately, the economics of the majority of these early interstate transactions proved to be unacceptable from a shareholder's perspective. On the other hand, it became apparent that merger efficiencies were much greater in the case of in-market combinations. To capitalize on these potential merger efficiencies, however, would require relaxing historical market share constraints.

The Wells Fargo takeover of Crocker dramatically illustrated this point. (See Chapter 5 for a discussion of in-market merger cost savings.) The approval of the merger between these two larger California banks involved the formation of an institution with more than 30 percent deposit share in a market where the dominant bank, BankAmerica, had an even larger share. The

Wells Fargo-Crocker deal, and many others that followed, resembled textbook oligopolies. Regulators not only raised local market share limits to 30 percent, but allowed the inclusion of 20 to 50 percent of thrift deposits in the market share analysis.

In implementing a more relaxed antitrust policy, regulators were mindful of the large number of nonbank competitors that provided alternatives to banking customers. From one perspective, the historical deposit market share measures were simply no longer relevant. Additionally, the industry's excess capacity problem and regulators' case loads of troubled banks required mergers as a remedy. Mergers could provide prompt relief. In seeking to solve the fundamental industry structure problems, some local market, oligopolistic powers would be tolerated.

While the traditional antitrust reliance on measures of deposit concentration has become an increasingly less meaningful indicator, market dominance remains an appropriate concern of the regulators. The recent BankAmerica-Security Pacific and Society-Ameritrust transactions provide the best evidence that antitrust issues remain an important aspect of bank merger strategy. In each of these transactions, the Justice Department forced the acquirer to make divestitures in excess of $1 billion in banking assets over original proposals. Although antitrust rules may be loosened to facilitate consolidation, the regulators seek to create an industry with strong competitive rivalries, not just a small set of large players.

Reagan: Bigness Is Not Bad

To put the developments described above in proper context, it is useful to review the changes in the approach to bank antitrust policy that occurred in the 1980s under the Reagan and Bush administrations. The Department of Justice under President Reagan greatly liberalized antitrust enforcement. A 1982 Merger Guideline document enlarged the category of mergers that were presumptively valid based on market shares and set up an analytical framework that permitted justification for some mergers that had previously failed market share tests.

In February 1985, the Justice Department formally acknowledged that nonbank competition was not reflected in bank market share analysis. Justice announced that it would not challenge a bank merger unless the resulting Herfindahl-Hirschman Index (HHI) was above 1,800 and the increase from the merger was greater than 200. The 200 increase contrasted with the 50 used as the safe harbor point for mergers in general. The HHI was and is based upon market deposits, and Justice allowed thrift deposits a 20 percent weight. That is to say, one could include 20 percent of the market's thrift deposits in the market share computation. Bank regulatory agencies immediately adopted this new

> . . . market dominance remains an appropriate concern of the regulators. The recent BankAmerica-Security Pacific and Society-Ameritrust transactions provide the best evidence that antitrust issues remain an important aspect of bank merger strategy.

guideline and soon began giving thrifts a 50 percent weight. Broader market definition, which was appropriate, put the relative market share positions of banks in the proper perspective. It also facilitated the consolidation process aimed at building commercial banks sufficiently large to compete with nonbanks.

Evolution of Bush Policy

The Justice Department under the Bush Administration announced a policy of enforcing the 1982 Merger Guidelines as published. Strategies using mitigating factors to gain approval for mergers that were outside the original 1,800/50/0 delineated for industrial mergers were to be viewed with skepticism. Two 1991 cases involving First Hawaiian-First Interstate and Fleet-Bank of New England suggested this policy shift would be applied to the banking sector. In these two cases, the Justice Department settled with relatively small divestitures and easy concessions. However, the major transactions of 1991 demonstrated that Justice had the political will and support to enforce demands that were materially different from those it required in previous years.

In mid-1991 Chemical and Manufacturers Hanover as well as NCNB and C&S/Sovran announced megamergers. The Chemical deal resulted in only a 106 point increase on the HHI—to 537—in its primary market, New York. Similarly, the NCNB merger, really a geographic market extension, did not involve material overlap. Accordingly, both mergers gained relatively easy approval. Bankers believed, or at least hoped, that a broad signal for in-market consolidation had been given. Those who opposed bank mergers increased pressure on Justice's Antitrust Division to stop those mergers that it viewed as anticompetitive. Enough pressure eventually surfaced to motivate the Justice Department to take a much more careful look at subsequent large in-market transactions that were occurring more frequently as banks consolidated.

Looking back, one can see that the anti-merger political pressure seemed to intensify considerably after the BankAmerica-Security Pacific and Society-Ameritrust announcements. Congress held hearings on banking sector antitrust enforcement, and state legislative bills targeted to block the BankAmerica deal in Washington and Arizona were introduced. As mentioned previously, those two deals received approval only following billions of dollars of branch and deposit divestitures. Although Federal Reserve approval tends to be predicated on passing the 1,800/200/50 test, the Justice Department appears to use this test only for routine transactions. In the competitive impact statements accompanying the Society-Ameritrust consent decree, Justice asserted that when HHI is above 1,800, a bank "merger that increases the HHI by more than 50 points is of significant competitive concern and may be unlawful, depending upon an analysis of all other factors." Here, Justice has taken a stronger antitrust stance than previously.

From a conceptual perspective, Justice appears not to follow the Supreme Court precedent that the product market consists of a cluster of bank services. Rather, it separates the consumer and business markets. It generally views competition in the large business market as national and, thus, very competitive. Consumers are also viewed as having many alternative suppliers, in particular, nonbanks. The small business customer, however, is believed to be locally constrained and, therefore, receives critical review. In this regard, Justice notes that thrifts often either have not pursued small business lending or have not significantly built commercial portfolios. Accordingly, it is reluctant to allow thrifts to be included in the deposit market share test.

The market segment of locally constrained small business customers has received great attention and varied treatment by Justice. In analyzing this segment, a key question arises: What size business is large enough to protect itself against price increases by being able to access out-of-market banks? In the Society-Ameritrust merger, it concluded that Cleveland companies with sales exceeding $10 million could obtain loans from lenders in Detroit or Pittsburgh. In the First Hawaiian merger with First Interstate (of Hawaii), Justice concluded that Hawaii businesses, given their unique geography, must have sales greater than $50 million to gain alternative access to West Coast banks. The BankAmerica-Security Pacific case probably is the most controversial. Businesses with sales of less than $100 million were deemed locally limited. If a $10 million limit such as that applied to Cleveland had been used in the BankAmerica-Security Pacific case, there may have been little need for large scale divestitures.

Kenneth A. Letzler and Michael B. Mierzewski[1] have observed that the Antitrust Division "believes that the appropriate aim of divestitures is to introduce new and viable competitors whose presence will mean that the market is substantially as competitive as it was before the merger." In this regard, Justice may decide the type of assets and liabilities divested, approve buyers, decide the number of buyers, and select the branches to be included in the divestiture program. Letzler and Mierzewski note that Justice, in effect, is micromanaging the divestiture program. They point out that Justice, by ignoring the free market role in handling divestitures, tends to make divestitures more costly, complicated, and time consuming.

Overall, the Justice Department has been supportive of bank consolidations and the pursuit of potential operating efficiencies. Yet the political process requires thorough review of competitive effects. Many different regulatory authorities are allowed to participate in the process. For example, state attorneys general have joined the debate by adding a populist and parochial twist to

The BankAmerica-Security Pacific case probably is the most controversial. Businesses with sales of less than $100 million were deemed locally limited. If a $10 million limit such as that applied to Cleveland had been used in the BofA-SecPac case, there may have been little need for large scale divestitures.

the antitrust equation. States have raised issues related to community reinvestment, employment, and loan commitments. In this light, in-market mergers will play an important role in the consolidation strategy of individual banks. However, the burden of delay, legal costs, informational requirements, and divestiture will be significant in the future. As a result, the structural evolution of the industry may be at a slower pace than desired. There is no denying, however, the market and economic forces that press for change.

New Sources of Capital Opened Up to Strengthen Balance Sheets

Traditionally, the United States has not allowed commercial firms and banks to combine their business activities. There is long-standing opposition in this country to firms like Du Pont or General Motors owning commercial banks. At the same time, there are concerns about banks like Citicorp or Chase owning large industrial firms. In either case, it is argued that there is potential for undue political or economic influence. The merits of the case aside, it is one of the most basic tenets underlying the regulation of banking and commerce.

Today important debates surround the issue of commerce's involvement in banking. The proposed 1991 bank reform bill included provisions allowing limited commerce involvement. The rationale was that commerce represented the best source for additional capital required by the commercial banking industry. For perspective, it should be noted that other countries—notably, Germany and Japan—permit the mixing of banking and commerce. Germany has universal banks, which not only blend banking and commerce, but also have combined other aspects of financial services. From a global viewpoint, the trend is toward a universal bank model. The populist and local control aspects of U.S. regulatory policy run counter to this global trend.

Besides the argument of undue political and economic influence, other questions concerning the mixing of banks and commercial firms exist. For instance, if Sears or Ford owned banks, and those particular companies become troubled, would the pressure of problems in their nonfinancial business give rise to a need to drain monies from an affiliated depository institution? Fears persist, especially since the S&L crisis, that risks could expand and jeopardize the FDIC insurance fund, thereby creating an extreme taxpayer obligation. Given the performance of the S&L industry in the 1980s, these concerns are not unfounded.

Even without federal legislation, however, regulatory action and market pressures have brought nonbanking capital into the financial system. A prominent example of this involves the banking investments and maneuverings of investment/merchant bankers Kravis, Kohlberg, and Roberts (KKR). In 1990, KKR was allowed to buy a 9.9 percent interest in First Interstate as a portfolio investor. Subsequently, KKR provided significant capital for Fleet's purchase of the failed Bank of New England, allowing KKR to gain 24.9 percent ownership in 1991. In this sense, a nonfinancial firm investor (KKR) found an effective, substantial way into banking.

The question arises as to the extent to which this direct ownership of financial institutions should be permitted. At present, ownership of less than 25 percent is tolerated. Existing standards prevent the investing entity, as in the KKR-Fleet-Bank of New England case, from operating or actively participating in a bank's management. Irrespective of the current debate, the notion of mixture exists and will continue to evolve. As other experimental structures develop, the stage is set for proliferation of mixed entities. Exhibits 3.10 and 3.11 indicate the largest LBO funds and other entities or individuals that could potentially invest in depository institutions. Several of these investors have already made bank portfolio investments.

What Role Should Foreign Entities Play?

Significant change is underway in the banking landscape. Questions often arise regarding prospects and potential roles of foreign entities participating in the traditional brick-and-mortar retail branch banking arena. Interestingly, many foreign competitors have already been here, only to have sold their interests and returned to focus on their home markets. In parallel fashion, some U.S. banks have had various branch bank networks in different European countries as well as other areas around the globe, and they too, have sold those branches and returned home to focus on national consolidation. Logic as well as financial experience in retail banking seems to suggest marginal capital is better spent in implementing strategies on the home front.

Before consolidation activity really accelerated, enactment of the International Banking Act of 1978 may have discouraged some expansion-minded foreign banks. The Act specified that foreign entities would be subject to the same expansion laws that indigenous banks in their home states faced. This closed the possibility of foreign banks having wider freedom than U.S. banks to merge across the country. Perhaps some would-be acquirers stayed away.

There have been some conspicuous exceptions to the general exit of foreign competitors who had been geographic retail players. One, ABN-Amro, a Dutch-based institution, having purchased several banks and thrifts in the Illinois and New York markets, now has a large North American bank with extensive operations in those states and in Canada. Its focus spans several

Even without federal legislation, however, regulatory action and market pressures have brought nonbanking capital into the financial system. A prominent example of this involves the banking investments and maneuverings of investment/merchant bankers Kravis, Kohlberg, and Roberts (KKR).

Exhibit 3.10

LARGEST LBO INVESTORS
March 31, 1990

	Top 20 LBO Funds	Estimated Size of LBO Funds ($ Millions)
1	Kohlberg Kravis Roberts	$5,600
2	Forstmann Little	2,500
3	Morgan Stanley & Co., Inc.	2,250
4	Merrill Lynch Capital Partners, Inc.	1,900
5	Acadia Partners/Robert Bass (America S&L of CA)	1,600
6	Thomas H. Lee Equity Co.	1,600
7	Butler Capital	1,400
8	Shearson-Lehman Hutton, Inc.	1,300
9	Robinson-Humphrey Co. Inc.	1,250
10	Wasserstein Perella Group Inc.	1,060
11	Clayton & Dubilier	1,000
12	Continental Equity Corp	1,000
13	First Boston Corp.	1,000
14	Manufacturers Hanover Trust Co.	1,000
15	Welsh Carson Anderson & Stowe	910
16	Blackstone Capital Partners	850
17	Prudential-Bache Interfunding	800
18	Donaldson Lufkin & Jenrette	750
19	Charterhouse Group International	612
20	First Chicago Venture Capital	600

Exhibit 3.11

LIST OF POTENTIAL BANK INVESTORS
Potential Bank Investors

Prince Abdulaweed

Buffett, Warren

Corporate Partners

Crown Family

Jacobs, Irwin

Lindner, Carl

Perlman, Ronald O.

Pohlad, Carl

Pritzker Family

Rainwater, Richard

Simon, William

Tisch, Lawrence and Preston

areas: retail banking, small business, middle market, corporate and real estate lending, and trust banking. Despite having achieved some size and breadth, it has yet to emerge as a nationwide competitive force.

A second exception to the general absence of foreign bank activity in U.S. bank consolidation is a series of middle-sized California banks owned by Japanese parents. As part of a Pacific Rim strategy, the Japanese appear to have deemed it important to have outlets and distribution networks for participation in commercial banking activity within California. However, these banks, which include Sumitomo, Union Bank (Bank of Tokyo), and Bank of California (Mitsubishi), are not large and control only minor market shares in local California markets. Unlike many medium-sized U.S. banks that have tended to sell out, they remain independent. However, they have been, at best, mediocre performers.

Another rationale for the acquisition of a U.S. retail banking institution by foreign interests is the desire to build dollar-denominated investments as part of a portfolio strategy. Allied Irish, Royal Bank of Scotland, National Westminster, and the Bank of Ireland's ownership of U.S. banks are examples of this strategy. Allied Irish has long been an owner of First National Bank of Maryland and recently has made some adjacent acquisitions in contiguous states. Similarly, others appear to be limited geographic plays, such as the Royal Bank of Scotland's investment in Citizens Bank (Rhode Island) or the Bank of Ireland's acquisition of First New Hampshire. Exhibit 3.12 presents a list of major foreign bank U.S. subsidiaries.

To a certain extent, loan losses and the recent recessionary economy have soured foreign desires for U.S. expansion. From a strategic standpoint, foreign banks may be waiting for the United States to mature and consolidate as a banking market. In their home countries, however, foreign banks generally have less regulatory, product, and geographic restrictions with which to contend. The more consolidated markets from which they come allows them to engage more explicitly in classical, oligopolistic competition. From its perspective, the U.S. market may still be too fragmented and too competitive. Perhaps, when U.S. bank consolidation has reached a critical mass nationally, Japanese or other foreign competitors may choose to participate.

Foreign competitors may not wait, however. In order to position themselves for participation in the end game, foreign banks may soon begin to seek out buying opportunities before the final maturation of the consolidation process. As a possible example of this strategy, Banco Santander, a large Spanish institution, provided recapitalization funds to become a significant owner of First Fidelity, a large New Jersey-based regional bank. Thus, this Spanish investor is now positioned to participate in and benefit from the U.S. bank consolidation movement via First Fidelity.

One, ABN-Amro, a Dutch-based institution, having purchased several banks and thrifts in the Illinois and New York markets, now has a large North American bank with extensive operations in those states and in Canada. Its focus spans several areas: retail banking, small business, middle market, corporate and real estate lending, and trust banking.

Exhibit 3.12

TOP 25 FOREIGN OWNED U.S. BANK SUBSIDIARIES
Based on Total Assets as of December 31, 1992
($ Millions)

Rank	Bank Name	Total Assets
1	Union BK	$16,681.42
2	Marine Midland BK NA	15,795.95
3	National Westminster BK USA	15,574.23
4	Harris T&SB	8,674.34
5	Bank of Tokyo TC	7,622.63
6	Bank of California NA	7,209.51
7	La Salle NB (Chicago)	7,125.18
8	*First National Bank of MD	7,015.62
9	National Westminster BK NJ	6,651.91
10	Sanwa BK of California	6,534.91
11	Sumitomo BK of California	5,398.82
12	European American BK	5,360.23
13	Industrial BK Japan TC	5,046.94
14	Bank of the West (San Francisco)	3,608.58
15	IBJ Schroeder B&TC	3,297.06
16	Israel Discount Bank of NY	2,633.85
17	Fuji B&TC	2,351.23
18	Bank Leumi TC of NY	2,162.97
19	Daiwa BK TC	1,321.32
20	First Los Angeles	1,266.17
21	Tokai BK of California	1,264.03
22	LTCB TC	1,234.24
23	LaSalle NW NB (Chicago)	1,177.60
24	Barclays Bank of NY NA	1,141.59
25	Manufacturers BK	1,099.64

* Total Assets as of June 30, 1993

Source: Federal Reserve Bank Call Reports as of December 31, 1992

Still, nationalistic fervor and legislative concern over substantial foreign entry and ownership of major financial institutions remain ominous clouds above any foreign institution seeking expansion in the U.S. financial sector.

Similarly, Banc Nationale de Paris (BNP) has made a series of community bank acquisitions in northern California, creating Bank of the West. Banks from a few other countries may still be interested in acquiring into the U.S. market. Canadian and Australian banks are known to be shopping for entry vehicles. Still, nationalistic fervor and legislative concern over substantial foreign entry and ownership of major financial institutions remain ominous clouds above any foreign institution seeking expansion in the U.S. financial sector.

Consolidation Requires New Regulatory Paradigms; and Vice Versa

While it is difficult to forecast what could happen in regulatory design, two prominent models of regulatory restructuring have appeared. The alternative plans have been nurtured under the two regional Federal Reserve Banks that have been most active and visionary in working on regulatory framework redesign. The first is the New York Fed arrangement labeled the Functional Holding Company Plan, and the second is the Chicago Federal Reserve Bank plan referred to as the Chicago Plan. The New York Fed Plan, championed by its ex-president, Gerald Corrigan, advocates a functional holding company system as the financial service/commercial banking organizational regime of the future. Essentially, this would functionalize the holding company into the various components of finance: commercial banking, investment banking, real estate, and, perhaps, insurance activities. In the view of many, nonbank American Express exemplifies this model. The American Express business portfolio has included a commercial bank; credit card unit; travel and credit-related services; an insurance venture; a securities arm (Shearson Lehman, a retail and wholesale investment banking institution); and retail financial planning (IDS). This prototype could conceivably be a model of the future. Under its approach, each business unit or function would be regulated by its traditional regulator—functional regulation.

In contrast, the chief concern addressed by the Chicago Plan is that the present system does not foster proper market discipline in the behavior of financial firms. It argues that in an effective regulatory structure, the disciplining influence of financial markets should be fully utilized. Through vigilant observation of the debt and equity markets, unwise risky loans, expansion activities, or other ill-advised management initiatives would be quickly impounded into market prices and, thus, signals would be quickly sent to management. In effect, management would be disciplined by having to answer to the capital markets as well as to the regulators. The market would simply raise the cost of financing or not purchase the securities of a particular institution.

Key to the Chicago Plan is the creation of a mandatory role for subordinated debt in the capital structure of the bank. Subordinated debt has an advantage over equity capital because debt holders have an incentive structure more in line with prudent management than do equity holders. There is a difference between the disciplining influence of bank equity capital, which has limited downside risk and unlimited upside potential, and debt, which has neither upside potential nor deposit insurance protection. In addition, equity capital fosters access to deposit insurance and debt. To be effective, the Chicago Plan requires that banks approach the debt markets on a regular basis to roll over capital.

Key to the Chicago Plan is the creation of a mandatory role for subordinated debt in the capital structure of the bank. Subordinated debt has an advantage over equity capital because debt holders have an incentive structure more in line with prudent management than do equity holders.

Changes in debt prices or the inability to roll over the debt would serve to discipline the bank.

The Chicago Plan also provides for separately capitalized affiliates. The commercial bank in the holding company is separately financed from other risky activities, such as the securities unit. Firewalls would be placed around these affiliates so that losses in one area, such as underwriting, could not spread from the securities firm to the commercial bank. Some observers remain lukewarm and skeptical of the firewalls concept. They point to Continental Bank as an example of the practical limitations of firewalls. In a moment of crisis resulting from poor performance of an affiliate, First Options, funds were transferred from the bank to the troubled affiliate without proper approvals. On the other hand, the counterexample of too stringent firewalls renders liberalization ineffectual.

The Strong Banks Get Stronger

Stronger banks are favored under the new risk-based capital and insurance frameworks. These institutions receive more favorable treatment in their application for mergers and new product powers. Additionally, strong firms will face relatively less regulatory oversight and will be relatively free to price and/or broker deposits . . .

We have reviewed a number of important environmental and regulatory factors that have led to tremendous consolidation in the banking industry. It is now clear that the competitive environment will limit the number of banks that can achieve high performance. As discussed, this is the inevitable result of the industry cost structure exceeding current and prospective revenue available in the financial marketplace.

Regulators appear increasingly comfortable with both the ambition and pace of the consolidation movement. Even though the Justice Department will increasingly scrutinize in-market mergers, it will remain generally supportive of mergers that pursue prospective operating efficiencies. Bank consolidation, especially when viewed in the broader financial services marketplace, is not going to have a fundamental effect on the overall competitive environment. In this context, the net result of the myriad regulatory changes that have developed recently is the creation of a finer separation of the relative strength of banking institutions.

Strong, well-capitalized institutions can acquire. Those that are not, cannot. That is to say, strong banks will get stronger while weak banks get weaker. Increasingly, stronger banks will be able to make advantageous purchases of weak banks. This systematic consolidation of weak banks into strongly capitalized institutions provides regulators with some degree of comfort. It also bears dramatic witness to the mid-1980s Darwinian forecasts of noted bank analyst J. Richard Fredericks.

Increasingly, financial markets and regulators are favorably regarding those banks that have both high capital ratios and capital productivity. Stronger banks are favored under the new risk-based capital and insurance frameworks. These institutions receive more favorable treatment in their application for mergers and new product powers. Additionally, strong firms will face relatively less regulatory oversight and will be relatively free to price and/or broker deposits for funding. As some of these institutions act to exploit their strategic advantage, they may find it helpful to partner with commercial firms. Arrangements similar to that between Fleet and KKR may be the model. Of course, once the industry gets past the credit excesses of the 1980s, it is unclear whether capital will be a constraining resource.

Ultimately, geographic liberalization in the form of intrastate branching and interstate banking offers the prospect of relatively high market shares and concomitant potential market power and cost savings. Stronger institutions will be able to exploit these opportunities. Consolidation will not only be pursued as a means to an end, but also as part of a permanent structural solution.

What is the future of the superregional bank in an industry that is renowned for cycles? Will the consolidation era be a panacea for the banks that are able to survive the 1990s? The nonbank threat will still be present. The industry's cost structure problem will not disappear. Most important, the sustainable high performance required for long-term success will not yet have been achieved. Consolidation is part of the solution, and one important element of the broad paradigm shift currently under way. The next chapter further explores the issues involved in achieving and sustaining high performance.

4

Managing for Shareholder Value

Today there is general agreement among bank executives that the ultimate objective of bank strategy is to maximize shareholder value. Against the backdrop of deregulation, increased competition, and shifting market valuation parameters, leading commercial banks have been forced to rethink both their objectives and their strategies for achieving those objectives. Focus and energy now center on actively building shareholder value as both an element of consolidation strategy and as an end in and of itself.

To build shareholder value, banks must increase their return on equity (ROE). Unfortunately, strengthening ROE in the banking industry is difficult to achieve for several reasons. As reviewed earlier, price deregulation and nonbank competition have significantly reduced the industry's aggregate revenue potential. Product deregulation, in the form of new powers, has not yet proven to be an effective remedy to this revenue problem. Many banks, therefore, have pursued aggressive geographic expansion and consolidation strategies to achieve profitable growth. Growth through acquisition, however, has also proven it can be a problematic course to strengthen ROE.

Difficult industry conditions imply that, at least in the short run, meaningful ROE improvement may only be achieved by strengthening the profitability and value of existing business portfolios through restructuring or divestiture. Given that a bank's current stock price is the key enabler for participating in the consolidation process, and only those institutions with strong currency can take advantage of merger opportunities, it is critical that banks gain as much market value as possible through restructuring strategies if they are to stay in the consolidation game.

The Wall Street Journal's January 6, 1988-front-page story, "At First Chicago Corp., Some Think the Unthinkable: Splitting Up the Company," was considered very dramatic when it appeared. Until the mid-1980s, business line divestiture and restructurings were unthinkable strategic options for most banks. The debate at First Chicago was about what could be done to strengthen the bank's ROE and stock price. One bold suggestion was to break up the bank. Weak profitability in many business units had contributed to an overall market value that most likely was less than the sum of the values of individual business units. The challenge to senior management was to increase profitability either by improving business unit operating performance or divesting underperforming businesses. First Chicago management considered the extreme option of breaking up the bank. In the end, management chose a less dramatic course.

Today it is critical for bank management to better understand what drives market value and what set of levers are available to build shareholder value. Our first goal in this chapter is to develop some key fundamental concepts to guide our thinking through business portfolio value building. Next, we outline the steps involved in breakup-value analysis (BVA) and discuss some specific challenges related to that analysis. We then apply the breakup valuation techniques to four case study banks—Fifth Third, Wells Fargo, Bankers Trust, and State Street—interpreting the implications of our analyses. Finally, we highlight some of the more prominent restructuring examples in the banking industry.

Adopting a Shareholder Value Perspective

A bank's market capitalization and individual share price generally reflect investor expectations. Leaving aside special situations such as takeover bids, share prices are the starting point for estimating total shareholder return (dividend yield plus changes in stock price). Share prices are driven to a large extent by expected financial results. These results are dependent on the quality of management's strategic decisions and their implementation efforts. Anticipated results are usually discounted for perceived risks and management's track record and credibility. The Wall Street analysts' job, as will be discussed in Chapter 11, is to do the required strategic and financial analysis.

Ultimately, strategic and tactical decisions must focus on the basic ways of improving shareholder value: making and delivering products and services profitably; practicing strong credit risk management; and buying and implementing acquisitions that make financial sense. Later chapters address the basic operating levers in detail.

There are two types of strategic decisions that management continuously makes that have the greatest impact on value. Viewed within the strategic context of the firm as a whole, each requires a different perspective in using shareholder value methodologies: (1) the selection of business lines in which to compete or exit and (2) the choice of business line strategies. Effective implementation is always critical, but the right strategic decisions must be made in the first place. Accordingly, the focus of this chapter is on analyzing the strategic business portfolio of a bank.

In the past, increasing earnings per share was considered the key to increasing shareholder value. This is no longer viewed as true, if, indeed, it ever was. Earnings are subject to too many variable accounting adjustments. Also, they do not reflect required capital and its implied cost. Not surprisingly, therefore, the correlation between growth in earnings per share and share prices has been poor. Instead, the stock market is better understood as evaluating operating performance in an equity framework that emphasizes ROE and ROE relative to cost of equity. In the process, the following factors are usually considered:

1. Current and projected return on equity;

2. The bank's cost of equity;

3. The quality, stability, and dependability of future earnings;

4. Anticipated growth in earnings over time.

ROE: The Key to Building Shareholder Value

As mentioned, the key to a strong stock price is a high ROE relative to the return required by the stock market. Return on equity is commonly defined as net income divided by common equity. While we do not intend to burden this book with accounting methodologies and definitions, Exhibit 4.1 presents a simple framework of the decomposition of ROE.

This framework is often referred to as an ROE/DuPont analysis. It begins with a bank's overall goal, building shareholder value through maximizing long-term stock price. It decomposes stock value into its two essential drivers—ROE and growth. Next, the ROE components are identified—fully allocated, risk adjusted net income and the economic capital invested. Net income further breaks down into net interest income, risk adjustment provisions, fully allocated noninterest expense, taxes, and other balance sheet adjustments.

ROE and ROA are both sourced from the same bottomline net income. Both can be tracked at the business unit level. Many banks, however, have not yet rigorously implemented equity allocation methodologies to the business unit level. As a result it is important to note that a number of banks, including BANC ONE, use return on assets (ROA), not ROE, as their managerial focal point. Return on assets isolates the essential performance of bank managers from financial management policies involving the use of

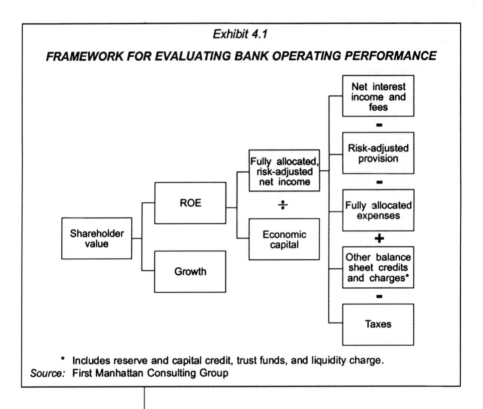

Exhibit 4.1

FRAMEWORK FOR EVALUATING BANK OPERATING PERFORMANCE

* Includes reserve and capital credit, trust funds, and liquidity charge.
Source: First Manhattan Consulting Group

financial leverage, which tends to magnify ROE. Of course, the two measures are highly related—ROE is the product of multiplying ROA by a bank's gearing ratio—assets divided by equity. Philosophically, or algebraically, operating performance can be translated into ROE.

The Performance Hurdle: A Bank's Cost of Equity

Banks' required "hurdle rate" return is most commonly referred to as the cost of equity (K_e). All banks should know their cost of equity because it is the standard by which the stock market ultimately evaluates their performance.

Cost of equity (K_e) is a theoretical measure. Unlike the average cost of debt or level of funding expense, which can be measured in the marketplace, a bank's cost of equity can only be estimated based on the bank's performance in the stock market. Estimating the cost of equity is necessary in order to determine the minimum rate of return that shareholders require on their investment in a bank's stock.

Returns that exceed a bank's cost of equity attract additional investors and lead to an increase in market value. Failure to generate returns that at least match a bank's cost of equity implies inadequate return to investors and a lack of market interest in a bank's stock.

Cost of Equity Estimation:
The Capital Asset Pricing Model

A sophisticated method for estimating the cost of equity is derived from the capital asset pricing model (CAPM). The CAPM approach assumes that a shareholder requires a specific level of return as determined by four different factors:

- The real time value of money, or the minimum compensation that all investors require for the use of their money (risk-free rate of return);

- The expected inflation for the period during which the investor's money will be tied up (inflation premium);

- The expected return on all equity compared to the risk-free rate (average stock market risk premium);

- The risk that investors incur by investing in a specific firm's equity (beta).

The first two factors are considered straightforward to evaluate. The return on U.S. Treasury bills is often used as a proxy for the risk-free rate of return. However, the Treasury bill rate does not always reflect investors' inflation expectations or their notion of the time value of money. To address this issue, the 10- or 20-year Treasury bond rate is also used as the risk-free proxy. Of course, using long-dated government bonds as a proxy for the risk-free rate implies other theoretical deficiencies. Namely, it ignores the interest rate risk inherent in long-term fixed income securities.

The difference between the expected returns on all equity and the risk-free rate is termed the average stock market risk premium. Estimates of the average stock market risk premium vary. A frequently cited study by Ibbotson and Sinquefield, which analyzed rates of return from 1926 to 1981, found that stocks have historically returned 5.9 percent in excess of Treasury bills. This historical average difference in returns is generally accepted as the average stock market risk premium.

Obviously, not all stocks have the same risk. As a result, the risk premium required by investors in corporate equities varies from one equity issue to another. The CAPM requires one to measure the riskiness of an individual stock by calculating the volatility of its returns relative to the volatility of the returns on all equity.

Beta is the regression coefficient that relates the volatility or movement in a specific stock's price to the movement of the stock market as a whole. Stocks that are less volatile and less risky than the market average have a beta of less than one; stocks that are more volatile than the market have a beta greater than one. Beta, in conjunction with the average stock market risk premium, is used to calculate the bank-specific risk premium:

$$\text{Bank Risk Premium} = \text{Beta} \times \frac{\text{Average Stock Market}}{\text{Risk Premium}}$$

Based on the market determined proxy for the risk-free rate and a bank's beta-derived risk premium, the cost of equity (K_e), or required rate of return, can be estimated:

$$\text{Cost of Equity } (K_e) = \text{Risk-Free Rate} + \text{Bank Risk Premium}$$

Having established a cost of equity, one can develop strategies aimed at outperforming this risk-adjusted hurdle rate. Recall ROE exceeding the cost of equity creates value; ROE underperforming the cost of equity destroys value.

Key to Performance: Beating the Cost of Equity

A bank's performance relative to its cost of equity, or its ROE/cost of equity ratio (ROE/K_e), is an important indicator of relative profitability. Measuring and tracking profitability relative to the cost of equity is a useful way to better understand how shareholders evaluate a bank's performance. Knowing what strategic and tactical options are available to improve performance relative to K_e is important.

Consider how the stock market evaluates a bank's ROE/K_e performance. An ROE/K_e equal to one means that the bank is merely satisfying investors' required rate of return. A ROE/K_e ratio greater than one means that the bank is outperforming investors' required rate of return. A ROE/K_e ratio of less than one means that the bank is failing to meet investors' required returns.

Profitability, Growth, and Shareholder Value

Ultimately, a bank's stock market performance can be explained by its profitability and growth performance. As discussed above, profitability is defined as ROE/K_e. Growth is defined as the expected growth rate of earnings.

A stock price equals the present value of the expected future returns to the shareholders. Growth plays an important role in stock valuation but is only a positive factor if the firm is earning in excess of its required return. If the firm is not meeting required profit levels, growth means that shareholders are being asked to invest rapidly in businesses that are not earning what they should.

The following formula derived from the "Constant Dividend Growth Model" expresses the key performance/growth interrelationships:

$$\frac{\text{Market Value}}{\text{Book Value}} = \frac{ROE - g}{K_e - g}$$

where:

ROE is the expected return on equity
g is the growth in earnings
K_e is the cost of equity

As a result of this relationship, generally an ROE/K_e ratio greater than one translates into a market-to-book ratio greater than one. Similarly, an ROE/K_e less than one results in a market to book ratio less than one. If ROE and K_e are equal; then the market-to-book would equal one. Growth acts to magnify these relationships, either positively or negatively.

By integrating the decomposition of ROE, the Capital Asset Pricing Model, and the Constant Dividend Growth Model, management is equipped with a powerful analytical framework for management decision making. Not only can strong focus be placed on the sources of shareholder value, but stock market performance can be reverse-engineered back to bank operating decisions.

Some concerns about misinterpretation

It is critical that the results of applying CAPM, the ROE/K_e framework, and market-to-book analysis, not be interpreted too mechanistically. There are innumerable factors that affect stock price. The model just described is a theoretical model that can be used for discussion of the interrelationship among stock price, profitability, risk, and growth. It is offered here to help explain the relationship between profitability, growth, and stock market performance, as well as provide a foundation for discussing strategies to build shareholder value.

We recognize the limitations of theoretical models, such as CAPM and the estimation of the beta coefficient, but, we also believe there is great merit in adopting a disciplined and structured approach to managing shareholder value, even if a slight leap of faith is required. The industry's track record suggests a formal performance framework could be invaluable in focusing management attention on shareholder value as a key performance objective.

Analyzing and Interpreting a Bank's Market Value

Proper analysis of a bank's market value provides insights about profitability, growth, and value contribution. Important implications for a company's portfolio strategy, at both the corporate and business levels, are often generated through careful assessment of historical, peer group, and business unit valuation analyses.

The ratio between the market price and book value of the firm's equity—market-to-book ratio—is a measure of the premium or discount that shareholders apply to the firm's equity.

A market-to-book ratio of one means the shareholder believes that one dollar of investment in the firm is worth one dollar. A ratio greater than one means that shareholders value every dollar invested in the firm more than a dollar. A ratio of less than one means that the market is discounting the value of the investment.

Instead of allowing every dollar invested to return less than a dollar, the market bids down the price of the stock in order to achieve the required return on investment. This phenomenon is analogous to that of the bond market, where a bond often trades at a price other than par value in order to give bondholders their required return.

Application of shareholder value analyses are intended to show the relationship among ROE, growth, and stock price. They are based on the assumption that a bank creates value for its shareholders, as reflected in higher stock market value, when it undertakes investments and strategies that produce returns in excess of the cost of equity.

Exhibit 4.2 presents comparative peer group data for 30 leading money-center and regional banks. The ROE data are normalized for nonrecurring gains and losses in 1992. The X axis plots each bank's ROE/Cost of equity ratio. The Y axis plots their market-to-book ratio. The graph represents an effective way to summarize the relative profitability and stock market performance of a bank and its peers. High profitability (ROE/K_e) banks include Fifth Third, State Street, Norwest, and BANC ONE. These banks all enjoy high market-to-book value ratios. Conversely, Citicorp, First Chicago, Chase, and Chemical Bank's weak 1992 profitability produced relatively low market-to-book value ratios. As these 1992 data demonstrate, profitability directly translates into market valuation.

In many ways, the fundamental dilemma facing all bank management is how to balance profitability and growth in order to build maximum shareholder value. Growth must be managed in the context of profitability, and vice versa. High ROE and low growth strategies can lead to a high market-to-book value ratio while failing to generate sufficient size and total market value.

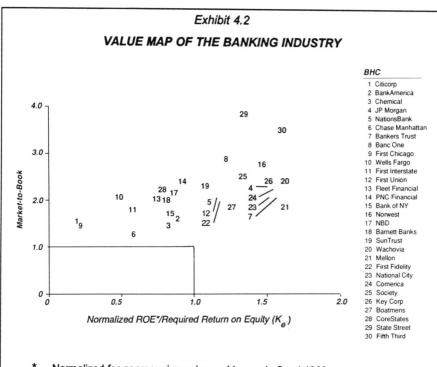

Exhibit 4.2

VALUE MAP OF THE BANKING INDUSTRY

BHC

1 Citicorp
2 BankAmerica
3 Chemical
4 JP Morgan
5 NationsBank
6 Chase Manhattan
7 Bankers Trust
8 Banc One
9 First Chicago
10 Wells Fargo
11 First Interstate
12 First Union
13 Fleet Financial
14 PNC Financial
15 Bank of NY
16 Norwest
17 NBD
18 Barnett Banks
19 SunTrust
20 Wachovia
21 Mellon
22 First Fidelity
23 National City
24 Comerica
25 Society
26 Key Corp
27 Boatmens
28 CoreStates
29 State Street
30 Fifth Third

Market-to-Book (y-axis: 0, 1.0, 2.0, 3.0, 4.0)

Normalized ROE*/Required Return on Equity (K_e) (x-axis: 0, 0.5, 1.0, 1.5, 2.0)

*   Normalized for nonrecurring gains and losses in fiscal 1992.
Source: Presentation to the Association of Reserve City Bankers, First Manhattan Consulting Group (April 3, 1993)

Conversely, weak ROE with high growth might generate adequate total asset size but fail to achieve a strong stock market performance. It is these tradeoffs between profitability and growth, between size and market value, that need to be managed more actively by top management.

The 1980s: A Decade of Value Destruction

In the 1980s, many banks chose to emphasize short-run asset growth at the expense of long-run profitability. There was a tendency for many banks to make important strategic decisions based on their desire to keep up with the competition. Bank of New England's acquisition spree and subsequent demise may have been the result of its desire to become the largest bank in New England. During the 1980s, many money center and superregional banks saw their growth ambitions lead to business portfolio strategies that ultimately destroyed shareholder value.

The rapid growth of real estate construction lending during the 1980s that forced many banks to the brink of failure was driven to a large extent by a fear of missing out on high up-front fees and high yields that otherwise would have gone to the competition. A similar logic influenced the aggressive growth of highly leveraged transaction lending. Both sources of growth were short-lived.

Cycles of credit expansion and contraction have been important hallmarks of financial history. The point is that over the long run banks that outperform the competition are able to resist the extremes of these cycles.

Credit quality variability is the most frequent reason for inconsistent performance. The banking industry's general failure to achieve true performance consistency is the most common explanation for bank stocks not obtaining a higher market multiple.

Aggressive growth through mergers and acquisitions was also a hallmark of the 1980s. The empirical evidence of the impact mergers have had on shareholder value is mixed at best (see Chapter 6). Many mergers, in the 1980s, failed to build value because the acquirer either paid too much to win, or did not achieve sufficient cost savings from, a transaction. In the past few years, the banking industry has improved its merger record by accepting far less dilution—that is, by not overpaying for acquisitions—and realizing much greater cost savings as a result of more aggressive implementation programs. Nevertheless, banks will continue to face strong pressure to win deals because their chances for survival rest on becoming too large and too highly valued to be acquired. There is the distinct likelihood that some banks will pay too much for some transactions just to survive.

While there may be some methodological debate, all banks must have an understanding of where their greatest value-building opportunities exist. Developing disciplined strategies for balancing profitability, growth, and market value is emerging as one of the most critical challenges facing commercial banks.

Credit quality variability is the most frequent reason for inconsistent performance. The banking industry's general failure to achieve true performance consistency is the most common explanation for bank stocks not obtaining a higher market multiple.

Managing as if Shareholders Mattered

The ability to improve operating performance and build shareholder value will determine the winners and losers in the 1990s. As has already played out for many institutions, the real opportunities to increase profitability and build shareholder value are not to be found in improving incremental profits in various business lines but in restructuring the bank's entire business portfolio—divesting low-profit, value-eroding businesses while investing in higher-margin, value-creating businesses.

All banks have such opportunities to build shareholder value. The opportunities, however, are buried in the bank's existing business portfolio. Management's challenge is first to identify and quantify the opportunities, and then to act on them with confidence.

It is healthy to debate the relative profitability, growth prospects, equity requirements, and value contribution of individual bank businesses. The larger the bank, the more active the debate about proper valuation of major businesses and which portfolio actions to take. In the effort to maximize shareholder value, it is important that a bank's management know the value contribution of each business within its portfolio. Similar to valuing the entire bank, one can analyze the ROE/K_e relationship of individual business lines.

Once bankers understand the variations among their business units' risk-adjusted ROEs, and develop a perspective on the potential ROE of each unit, they can better manage for value. Top management can explicitly allocate equity and other resources. That is the essence of portfolio strategy.

Defining the Bank's Portfolio Strategy

Management would do well to conduct a critical self-assessment in which each of its businesses is examined from the point of view of a stock market raider. Typically, a raider considers all portfolio characteristics, including present and potential performance of each business unit. An objective review of a bank's portfolio can identify the underlying sources of value creation and destruction.

Conceptually, evaluating a bank's business portfolio is quite straightforward. There are five parts to such an analysis: (1) define each of the business units; (2) assign equity capital to each unit; (3) estimate each unit's market value; (4) compare the relative market values to the book values of the business units to determine which units are increasing or decreasing shareholder value; (5) relate the financial values to the strategic outlook for each unit.

In defining each specific business (Step 1), either product or customer groups can be used. Proper analysis often requires that certain customer groups be broken down into subsegments and unbundled relationships; similarly, many products must be unbundled or disaggregated. Mortgages and credit cards are prime examples of businesses that could be disaggregated into origination, servicing, and investment. Exhibit 4.3 presents a useful categorization of business lines that we will use later in the chapter for illustrative purposes.

Allocating capital to each business is the next step (Step 2). Capital allocation should basically follow the regulatory risk-adjusted guidelines. Since these guidelines do not address all business lines, one must often determine the capital level subjectively or extrapolate it from those of stand-alone businesses. Ultimately, a determination must be made of a business' standalone capital requirements.

Step 3 involves determining the market value of each business unit, often by discounted cash flow (DCF) analysis. DCF

It is healthy to debate the relative profitability, growth prospects, equity requirements, and value contribution of individual bank businesses.

Exhibit 4.3

POTENTIAL LINE-OF-BUSINESS DEFINITIONS

Community Banking

1   Consumer (credit and deposit)
2   Affluent/private banking (credit and deposit)
3   Small business (credit and deposit)
4   Middle market (credit and deposit), including leasing
5   Middle market operating services

Corporate Banking

6   Large corporate credit, including leasing
7   Large corporate operating services
8   International trade finance/FX/foreign corporations

Real Estate

9   Commercial real estate
10   Residential developer financing
11   Mortgage origination

Credit

12   Credit cards
13   Consumer finance
14   Factoring

Operating Services

15   Cash management/non-borrowers (equals lines 5 + 7)
16   Mortgage servicing
17   Corporate trust
18   Custody/master trust/securities processing

Trading Investments

19   Balance sheet management/ALCO

Insurance

20   Life insurance

Advisory

21   Corporate finance/trading
22   Trust: Personal asset management (e.g., mutual funds, trust)
23   Institutional asset management (including trust)
24   Bad banks/special assets

Source: The MAC Group (now Gemini Consulting Group)

---

hinges on cash flow projections and the discount rate selected. Other methods that have also been used in this step include use of recent market transactions and pure-play public market values for a given line of business.

Step 4 is an assessment of the market value contribution of each unit of the book value equity assigned to it. For those units with disproportionate value contribution, their ROEs obviously exceed investors' required return. Conversely, if value appears to be destroyed, then the ROEs are not covering the cost of equity. Step 4 is a derivative of the analytical work completed for Steps 2 and 3.

Finally, Step 5 considers what conclusions are appropriate. Before reaching decisions, it is necessary to assess the future market potential, competitive environment, and sustainability of the bank's line of business strategy. If a business unit is currently not creating value but has great market potential, and a particular bank can build it into a valuable, sustainable position that will yield returns above the hurdle rate, it should not be discontinued.

It is important to note the steps outlined above greatly simplify the challenge and complexity of doing BVA. Each step involves somewhat technical analytical tasks. For example, it is not easy to get cash flow data for each defined business unit. Management reporting systems do not always match business line definitions. Transfer pricing can be both theoretically deficient and operationally difficult to ascertain. Additionally, shared costs must be allocated rationally. Finally, a usable discount rate may rest on ascertaining reliable betas for each business line. Break-up value analysis is not for the analytically timid.

Portfolio theory argues that investors prefer that corporations not diversify on their behalf since they can construct portfolios of individual pure plays on their own. A former senior bank executive, and now senior investment banker, S. Waite Rawls, sheds some valuable light on this key bank portfolio issue. Rawls questions the traditional rationale for banks being in both the retail and wholesale banking businesses (see S. Waite Rawls' sidebar, *Why Wholesale Banking and Retail Banking Don't Mix*, page 96). In making the case against banks being in these two vastly different businesses, he notes that diversification into different businesses does not enhance portfolio value.

Breaking up the business portfolio

The business portfolios of large banks are often considered to be too complex and diverse to manage for value maximization. Generally, the larger the bank, the more complexity and performance variability in its portfolio. Large portfolios generally can be improved by restructuring, which adds focus and capital to the more attractive units while downsizing or divesting the poor performers.

Management reporting systems do not always match business line definitions. Transfer pricing can be both theoretically deficient and operationally difficult to ascertain. Additionally, shared costs must be allocated rationally. Finally, a usable discount rate may rest on ascertaining reliable betas for each business line. Break-up value analysis is not for the analytically timid.

Why Wholesale Banking and Retail Banking Don't Mix

S. Waite Rawls
Executive Vice President
Chicago Corporation

Wholesale banking and retail banking have become fundamentally different businesses that are best pursued by different companies. Consider these three definitions: 1. Banking is a generic term that draws no distinction between commercial and investment banking. 2. Retail includes consumer and small or local business banking. 3. Wholesale is large corporate banking. The dividing line between wholesale and retail is admittedly fuzzy. I do not believe that this bit of fuzziness negates my argument at all, but it does allow institutions some flexibility as to where to draw their line.

Some History

Most banks believe wholesale and retail belong together because that is the way they are and that is the way they grew. They defined their products as loans or deposits or securities sales and provided those services to whoever demanded them. Along the way, probably in the late 1960s or early 1970s, they organized internally to separate wholesale from a growing branch system, but they continued to do both. And the standard model for a big bank today—Chemical, Chase, First Chicago, Merrill, Kidder—does both.

By the late 1970s, in fact, the trend (or fad) was to do even more, and the financial supermarket was a great catch phrase. Some tried to grow into that status, but most tried to acquire it. AMEX-IDS-Shearson-Fireman's Fund-Lehman was probably the most celebrated; but many others—Citicorp, Sears, Prudential, and others—also went in that direction. Only a few (Goldman or either of the Morgans or AIG) stuck to wholesale or retail (A.G. Edwards or many of the regional commercial banks). But today we are beginning to see a reversal as some institutions are opting to go one way or the other: for example, Bankers Trust's or Continental's exiting retail operations; the de-emphasis or exit of wholesale at Prudential, Dean Witter, or BankAmerica; or the split of Shearson Lehman. What is going on here?

Why Do Both?

There are three reasons usually given to do both wholesale and retail: history, synergy, and diversification.

The we've-always-done-it-that-way logic is admittedly powerful. Perhaps it is not right, but it should be accepted as being powerful.

The synergies argument has always been fascinating. There really are not many marketing synergies because the customer base is fairly distinct. But a lot of people talk about operating synergies or economies of scale: "We already have a (pick one: branch, deposit, securities) system. We might as well get the volume up." Some even sound like economists: "We want to be able to move money from those who have wealth (individuals) to those who need capital (corporations)."

Diversification of earnings gets a lot of mileage with discussions of countercyclicality of businesses carrying great weight. If these arguments are good ones, why is the trend going the other way? And why today, when we think of the players who are good or successful, do we include so many who have chosen to focus, and so few who do both?

Is There a Parallel in the Corporate World?

We certainly saw the creation of some of these supermarkets in the 1960s and 1970s in the nonfinancial world—we called them growth-oriented, diversified conglomerates. Arguments of synergies, economies of scale, and diversification held the day. I believe we are now in the process of rejecting those arguments for three major reasons.

First, there is a growing argument that the core competence of a manager or group of managers gets stretched and diluted when applied to too many groups of customers, products, or distribution channels. There is an old saying that a specialist knows more and more, about less and less, until he knows everything about nothing. Conversely, a generalist knows less and less, about more and more until he knows nothing about everything. This latter description can probably be applied to the management of many conglomerates.

In a rapidly changing world, conglomerates tend to lose the ability to stay on top of the fundamentals of products, customers, and competition and begin to manage more and more by the numbers, which are necessarily short-term and historical, not forward thinking. Competence is at the center of control, and they both get diluted.

Second, the corporation becomes a mutual fund—a portfolio of companies in different businesses. But each holding company is illiquid in such a corporation, because it is harder for corporate management to buy or sell securities or reallocate capital among the businesses than it is for the mutual fund manager to buy or sell stocks. And modern portfolio theory, preferring a series of pure plays, puts forth the strong argument that it is the role of the investor, not management, to diversify.

Third, investors are pretty smart folks, and they have raised the cost of capital for these companies by lowering their stock prices. This creates an all too familiar problem in which the whole is worth less than the sum of the parts—otherwise seen as an opportunity for a corporate raider or LBO deal firm.

What Does That Say About Banks?

It is a pity that it is hard to buy a bank. Otherwise we would have already seen a few bought to be broken up—along wholesale versus retail lines. The core competence of management has been tested and found wanting, and the stock prices of diversified financial firms have fared worse than focused firms. Yet inertia persists.

Wholesale banking and retail banking really are different businesses, and they offer few synergies. Retail banking is mass-marketing oriented and driven by technology and distribution systems. It is highly standardized, rewarding those that grow market share or provide the lowest cost of delivery or squeeze the highest revenues out of the delivery system. The product is not a deposit or a security but the delivery system itself.

Wholesale banking is a job shop as opposed to an assembly line. Its rewards go to those who develop skill-based communications networks both internally and externally. Internally, the organizations that mobilize cross-functional expertise and deliver ideas to sophisticated customers are the winners. Externally, they harness global information from syndicate partners, trading markets, and institutional investors to deliver liquidity and a lower cost of capital to customers. Like retail banking, the product is not a deposit or a security but a delivery system. The product and customers are fundamentally different.

What Does This Suggest?

To make the point, I offer four suggestions, any of which could be wrong:

1. Citicorp would be better as three separate companies: an emerging world wholesale firm, a developed world wholesale firm, and a retail firm.

2. The newly merged Chemical should split along wholesale/retail lines, similar to the Shearson split from Lehman.

3. Paine Webber should exit wholesale, not de-emphasize it.

4. Superregional banks as a group should put a cap on their corporate business and not attempt to service the skill-based needs of large corporation.

Breakup-value analysis (BVA) helps explain which businesses are value creating as opposed to value destroying. BVA will shed light on: (1) the market value of each business; (2) the relative performance and cross-subsidies between business units; and (3) where improvement in operating performance is required. While our perspective is that of bank management, it is important to note that BVA can generate important investor insights regarding potential acquisition targets and fundamental bank investment value.

Opportunities for Methodological Debate

The allocation of equity to each business unit is a similarly complex problem that has the potential to undermine the credibility of business unit ROE calculations used in BVA. Equity should be allocated to business units in a three-step process of successive approximations. First, the industry average amount of equity for the business unit should be estimated. Consultants, investment analysts, or other market sources can provide important input for this estimate. Second, this industry average should be adjusted for how much more or less risky the business unit is than the industry as a whole. Third, there will remain equity that will need to be allocated through a process of internal negotiation. All the while, management should be cognizant of the Federal Reserve capital allocation guidelines. From the standpoint of building management consensus around breakup-value analysis, a commitment to this process is essential to making the recommendations of the analysis realistic and actionable.

An additional issue that should be addressed in developing reasonably accurate financial statements for each business unit concerns how to transfer price deposits and funding sources. A common problem in many diversified banks is the accounting system treatment of a bank's retail business as a low-cost funding source for the commercial lending business units. As a result, the spreads on the commercial business may appear to be too wide and the spread on the retail business too narrow. In addition, there is a common problem of matching the maturity of loans to commercial and individual customers with bank liabilities. While this is a complex problem, an approximation may be made by finding a pure play financial institution and trying to transfer-price the funding for the business units in a manner consistent with these pure plays.

To the extent possible, overhead must be understood at a much finer level of detail. It is important for business units that use such shared resources as senior executive time, professional staff, and training to understand the extent of their use of these resources and to be charged a standard cost per unit of use.

Often management lacks confidence and resolve in the methods used to allocate equity and overhead to the various business units. Substantial amounts of management time and systems investment are required to overcome this problem. Commitment to the process is imperative.

Case Illustrations of Bank Value Sources

To illustrate both the fundamental concepts and the business portfolio analysis developed in this chapter, it is useful to consider some case examples. We have chosen to analyze 1990 data for four different banks—Fifth Third, Bankers Trust, Wells Fargo, and State Street—in order to remain focused on case illustration of our concepts and avoid any current market valuation debate.

The data displayed in Exhibits 4.4–4.7 are developed along the five-step process outlined earlier. Both business line equity allocation and profitability were estimated based on publicly available data and interviews with the case study banks' investor relations staffs.

Fifth Third

Exhibit 4.4 shows that Fifth Third's premium businesses are processing (custody, master trust) and consumer-oriented businesses. Other value creators, although small, are credit cards and trust/personal asset management.

Bankers Trust

Bankers Trust's strategy of favoring investment banking rather than traditional commercial banking has created value. In particular, corporate finance advisory and underwriting, along with proprietary (own account) investing, have proved to be a strategic success (see Exhibit 4.5). International investments have focused on fee generation as opposed to lending. The processing businesses, organized in a business unit called Profitco at Bankers Trust, also creates value.

Bankers Trust limits its lending in order to curb the potential risk of credit-problem-driven value destruction. Nevertheless, it appears to have a few large corporate lending and operating service groups that are negative contributors.

Wells Fargo

Consumer businesses, including credit card and affluent banking, contribute very heavily to the value of Wells Fargo (Exhibit 4.6). Additionally, institutional and personal asset management also contribute positively to Wells' premium.

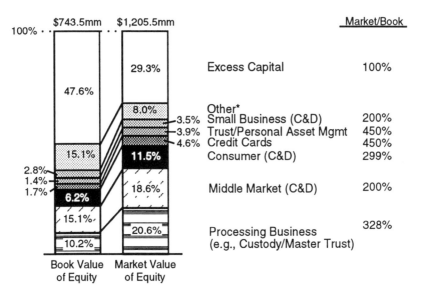

Exhibit 4.4

BREAKUP VALUE OF FIFTH THIRD (1990)

	Market/Book
Excess Capital	100%
Other*	
Small Business (C&D)	200%
Trust/Personal Asset Mgmt	450%
Credit Cards	450%
Consumer (C&D)	299%
Middle Market (C&D)	200%
Processing Business (e.g., Custody/Master Trust)	328%

* Other consists of: mortgage origination/warehousing, balance sheet management/ALCO, affluent/private banking (C&D), middle market operating services, trust/institutional asset management, residential developer financing, corporate trust/bond trusteeship, commercial real estate, large corporate credit, including leasing, and international trade/FX/foreign corporations.

Source: Proprietary MAC Group (now Gemini Consulting Group) Model of Industry Average Returns by Line-of-Business; estimated variations; MAC Group calculations.

Remaining regional businesses, chiefly middle market lending, are substantial but do not greatly detract from value. Real estate business lines absorb much equity and are valued quite low.

State Street

State Street's premium businesses are securities processing, fiduciary, and asset management (Exhibit 4.7). Significant equity is invested in high value processing (custody and master trust). Asset management also creates great value for State Street. Corporate skills developed in processing are related to asset management. The global nature of securities processing has been translated by State Street into impressive international reach.

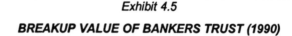

Exhibit 4.5

BREAKUP VALUE OF BANKERS TRUST (1990)

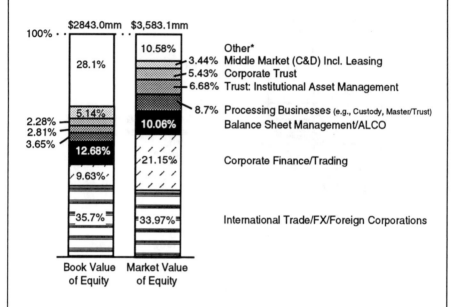

* Other consists of: middle market operating service, consumer (C&D), small business (C&D), international trade/FX/foreign, residential developer financing, large corporate operating service, mortgage origination, affluent/private banking (C&D), large corporate credit, including leasing, and corporate financing/trading.

Source: Proprietary MAC Group (now Gemini Consulting Group) Model of Industry Average Returns by Line-of-Business; estimated variations; MAC Group calculations.

State Street's strategy de-emphasizes general lending and real estate-related credit. However, since loans require more equity investment than processing or asset management, the proportion of investment in low-value lending is relatively substantial. Despite the value of their credit card portfolio, the bank sold this line of business. The sale raised funds to invest in the technological advancement of its core processing business.

Case Study Implications

Across the four case study banks, the business mix in a bank's portfolio clearly matters. The analyses suggest that the more equity that can be invested in attractive businesses, as opposed to being assigned to value-destroying segments, the higher the overall market value a given bank will realize. Business portfolio con-

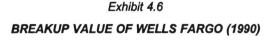

Exhibit 4.6

BREAKUP VALUE OF WELLS FARGO (1990)

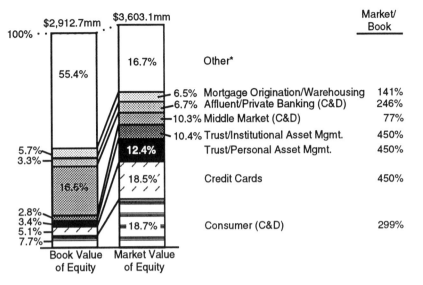

	Market/Book
Other*	
6.5% Mortgage Origination/Warehousing	141%
6.7% Affluent/Private Banking (C&D)	246%
10.3% Middle Market (C&D)	77%
10.4% Trust/Institutional Asset Mgmt.	450%
Trust/Personal Asset Mgmt.	450%
Credit Cards	450%
Consumer (C&D)	299%

$2,912.7mm $3,603.1mm

100%

55.4%   16.7%

5.7%   12.4%
3.3%
16.6%   18.5%

2.8%
3.4%
5.1%   18.7%
7.7%

Book Value of Equity   Market Value of Equity

*   Other consists of: middle market operating service, consumer (C&D), small business (C&D), international trade/FX/foreign, residential developer financing, large corporate operating service, mortgage origination, affluent/private banking (C&D), large corporate credit, including leasing, and corporate financing/trading.

Source: Proprietary MAC Group (now Gemini Consulting Group) Model of Industry Average Returns by Line-of-Business; estimated variations; MAC Group calculations.

---

struction, or reconstruction if required, is the most critical strategic management decision.

The case study banks tend to be high performers because they focus on high value-creating businesses. These include consumer and private/affluent banking; small business; processing; advisory (including asset management); and credit cards. Corporate lending, real estate-related credits, and corporate operating services appear to be of low value or value destroying.

These case study diagnostics are consistent with First Manhattan Consulting Group's studies of the banking industry's value creation and destruction (Exhibit 4.8). In terms of building shareholder value, their work has found that consumer and small business units were the most valuable. Trust, including personal and institutional advisory services, and credit card were also found to add high value.

Exhibit 4.7

BREAKUP VALUE OF STATE STREET (1990)

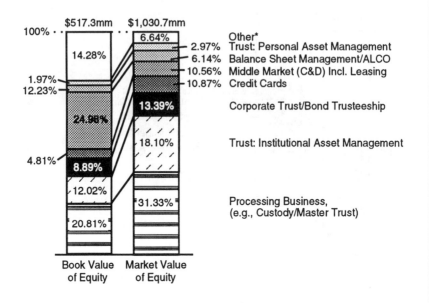

Other*	
2.97%	Trust: Personal Asset Management
6.14%	Balance Sheet Management/ALCO
10.56%	Middle Market (C&D) Incl. Leasing
10.87%	Credit Cards

Corporate Trust/Bond Trusteeship

Trust: Institutional Asset Management

Processing Business,
(e.g., Custody/Master Trust)

Book Value   Market Value
of Equity   of Equity

* Other consists of: Middle market operating service, consumer (C&D), small business (C&D), international trade/FX/foreign, residential developer financing, large corporate operating service, mortgage origination, affluent/private banking (C&D), large corporate credit, including leasing, and corporate finance/trading.

Source: Proprietary MAC Group (now Gemini Consulting Group) Model of Industry Average Returns by Line-of-Business; estimated variations; MAC Group calculations.

Is Portfolio Restructuring a Credible Strategy?

Despite the widely accepted hypothesis that all banks have some portion of their business portfolio in value-destroying businesses, the banks most aggressive in restructuring have been those that have been saddled with weak market-to-book ratios and marginal capital positions. Bank restructuring initiatives have most frequently been reactions by troubled institutions faced with capital pressures rather than systematic, forward-looking efforts to enhance value.

Examples of trouble-inspired restructurings include BankAmerica in the mid-1980s, Ameritrust before it merged with Society, MNC Financial prior to its merger with NationsBank, First Interstate, Continental Bank, and Midlantic Bank.

Exhibit 4.8

RELATIVE VALUE CONTRIBUTION/DESTRUCTION OF BUSINESS LINES

Business (Ranked by Value Created as of 12/31/89)	12/31/89 Estimate of Market Capital Attributable to the Business	12/31/89 Shareholder Value Created/ (Destroyed)*	11/30/90 Estimate of Market Capital Attributable to the Business	11/30/90 Shareholder Value Created/ (Destroyed)*
1 Branch delivery (consumer and small business)	$85 billion	$65 billion	$80 billion	$50 billion
2 Commercial real estate lending	40	20	(18)	(38)
3 Trust (personal and institutional services)	20	15	22	17
4 Credit card	18	12	16	9
5 Middle market	35	8	34	7
6 Cash management	10	6	11	7
7 Corporate finance	10	6	(3)	(10)
8 Other fee-based services	−10	4	11	5
9 Swaps, FX, securities trading	6	2	6	2
10 Other consumer lending	15	(5)	16	(6)
11 International banking	0	(15)	0	(13)
12 Residential mortgages (on balance sheet)	0	(15)	0	(17)
13 Large corporate (loans and lines)	0	(25)	0	(23)
14 Other (incudes LDC)	(9)	(33)	(5)	(30)
Total U.S. Banks	$240 billion	$35 billion	$170 billion	$(40) billion

* Value Created = Market capital value less invested common equity; variability by banks is high, with some creating—and some destroying—value in virtually every category.

In terms of enhancing shareholder value, branch operations focusing on consumers and small businesses was the single most valuable business, according to First Manhattan Consulting Group estimates. In this analysis, the difference between market capital attributable to a line of business and the amount of equity invested in the business is the shareholder value either created or destroyed. For example, bank branch delivery operations at the end of 1989 generated an estimated $85 billion in market capital on $30 billion of invested equity, creating an estimated $55 billion in shareholder value.

Source: First Manhattan Consulting Group. Reprinted in William Love and Christopher Svare, "Restructuring Intensifies," *Bank Management* (January 1991).

Weighed down by credit problems, Midlantic, Ameritrust, First Interstate, and Continental Bank were all forced to divest geographic franchises that they had acquired previously and to sell several nonbank subsidiaries. The international offices of BankAmerica and Continental were cut back significantly. First Interstate sold its commercial mortgage, leasing, and asset-based finance units. Continental Bank withdrew from retail banking and sold its credit card business. MNC Financial was forced to part with its crown jewel, an affinity credit card business, in order to address its capital challenge. This unit now exists as an independently traded public company, MBNA.

The New York money centers have also been forced to do considerable restructuring. Capital pressures have required management to divest both marginal and successful businesses to raise needed required capital. Chemical Bank sold its merchant credit and factoring businesses before it merged with Manufacturers Hanover. It had also closed branches in both New York and overseas. In 1991 Chemical Bank and Manufacturers Hanover used a whole-bank merger to effect a more comprehensive restructuring.

Chase Manhattan sold interstate branch offices and foreign businesses, such as its Dutch banking unit, and then restructured its New York City retail branch network. Citicorp has aggressively restructured in recent years. It chose to spin off its private mortgage insurance and student loan businesses. Additionally, it was forced to sell some of its technology-oriented businesses, including Quotron.

It is instructive to note that firms that restructure as a reaction to troubled circumstances often remain vulnerable to takeout. Ameritrust and MNC Financial met this fate. Others, such as BankAmerica and First Interstate, narrowly escaped the same fate. Midlantic remains a target. An article in the August 18, 1993, *American Banker* illustrates this point: reporting that UJB Financial Corp. was putting the final touches on a major restructuring of the bank's business portfolio, it noted that plans called for unprofitable businesses to be slimmed down or shuttered so that investments could be concentrated in healthy areas. However, the article continued, "Whether Mr. Semrod (UJB Chairman) will get to announce his plans before UJB is taken over is not clear. UJB was the subject of intense takeover rumors last week." Business portfolio restructuring and business line divestitures are logical approaches to raising equity capital in distressed situations. Far-sighted management should pursue restructurings to ensure that distressed situations are not allowed to deteriorate further.

Only a limited set of banks have proactively restructured to build shareholder value. Probably the industry's most shining example is Bankers Trust (BT).

Only a limited set of banks have proactively restructured to build shareholder value. Probably the industry's most shining example is Bankers Trust (BT). As a result of mediocre performance in the early 1970s and a careful strategic examination of future prospects, BT chose to embark on a radically different business strategy that called for widespread restructuring. The bank sold its traditional retail and commercial businesses in an effort to remake itself as an investment bank. Judging by its high ROE in recent years, it has been most successful. Since the move by Bankers Trust, no bank has pursued as dramatic a restructuring effort without either severe credit problems or the encouragement of regulators.

Aggressive Pursuit of Shareholder Value Needed

Many bank executives are familiar with the concepts of shareholder value that are discussed in this chapter. Yet many banks whose market valuations have lagged the industry have either rejected or only halfheartedly accepted the strategic implications of the stock market's appraisal of their performance. Why are so many banks unwilling to implement the lessons of shareholder value analysis?

Recently, in many well-known industrial companies, powerful outside directors have ousted their CEOs because of perceived inattention to shareholder value concerns—General Motors and Westinghouse are cases in point. It is difficult to cite many examples in the banking industry. In fact, several vulnerable bank CEOs have survived apparently similar situations.

Historical evidence would suggest that bank shareholders need more aggressive representation. A strong role for bank boards should be seen in the future. Self-interest is also a great motivator. It may be helpful for bank management to have a greater share of their personal wealth linked to the stock price performance of the banks they run. Recent SEC actions aimed at relating executive compensation more directly to stock price performance should assist in focusing some management.

In any case, however, management must understand the strategic value of all business units and have the will to take whatever actions may be necessary to ensure that the highest values are realized. The emerging industry paradigm includes a management that has the necessary analytical orientation and the resolve to act on the shareholder value implications of the analysis.

Summing Up

Maximization of shareholder wealth is the defined goal of all publicly traded banks. The relationship between ROE and a bank's cost of equity is the key determinant of a bank's stock valuation. The banks with the largest consistent spread between their ROE and K_e, as well as the highest profitable growth, enjoy the strongest stock price performance. It is imperative that banks

Recently, in many well-known industrial companies, powerful outside directors have ousted their CEOs because of perceived inattention to shareholder value concerns—General Motors and Westinghouse are cases in point.

use their cost of equity as a performance test for each line of business in their portfolio. The stronger the spread between the ROE of individual lines of business and their related equity cost, the greater the value of the business and its contribution to the overall value of the firm.

High earnings performance, in terms of ROA or ROE, will prove increasingly difficult to achieve. In today's consolidation environment, a strong stock price or currency is necessary to be able to pursue merger opportunities. In the short run, business portfolio restructuring may offer the quickest and most substantive method to strengthen profitability and market value.

Shareholder value analysis is useful in identifying which lines of business create, rather than destroy, value. Although the analytical work involved requires addressing such difficult issues as determining individual unit discounted cash flows, allocation of equity, and establishment of market valuation parameters, the results highlight the relative value added by various lines of business. The value contributions of individual businesses provide the necessary insight into how to restructure a bank portfolio to improve market value.

Too often, however, bank restructuring initiatives have been undertaken as reactions to troubled circumstances that place institutions in weak stock market and capital positions. Many troubled institutions have found themselves subject to takeover pressure. Others, such as BankAmerica, First Interstate, and Continental Bank, have used restructuring to materially raise their market value. Bankers Trust stands out as a bank that proactively restructured in order to enhance shareholder value.

As pointed out, mergers represent a major strategy the industry is using to restructure itself. In the next chapter, we will examine important issues that have determined the consolidation patterns that have occurred to date. Additionally, we will explore some future consolidation possibilities, including a crystal ball list of possible ultimate survivors.

5

The Consolidation Landscape: Separating the Winners from the Losers

Right or wrong, industry consolidation through mergers has quite colorfully taken center stage on the evolving banking landscape. This is probably appropriate. The banking industry is in need of serious restructuring to ensure the long-term viability and profitability of the players who remain. Mergers are helpful in reducing the industry's excess capacity. While they will not necessarily fully accomplish the broad-based restructuring required, they are a step in the right direction.

Origins of the Consolidation Movement

The impetus for interstate banking, and consolidation, occurred in the 1970s when several expansion-oriented bank holding companies (BHCs) gained significant market coverage within their home states, only to find their growth restricted by federal antitrust limits. At that time, for antitrust purposes, market share tolerance levels approximated 10 percent of bank deposits in a defined local market. Reflecting some frustration with this constraint on growth, attempts were made to get Congress to legislate interstate banking. In 1979, the Association of Bank Holding Companies lobbied for a bill that proposed to amend the Douglas Amendment and permit BHCs to acquire banks in contiguous states. The effort did not receive much political attention, but it did highlight the extreme difficulty of establishing a framework for achieving industry-wide political consensus.

Different segments of the banking community had different views on how to proceed on the interstate banking front. Money-center banks strongly advocated nationwide banking. Many regional institutions sought regional banking compacts to allow themselves expansion opportunity but, at the same time, not open their market to larger out-of-region competitors. Particular attention was paid to blocking what was believed to be the predatory expansion aspirations of the money-center banks.

In contrast, other regional institutions, less focused on the prospects for long-term survival, did not favor regional compacts. They preferred national or regional laws that would quickly trigger full national banking in order to gain the maximum bidders and highest sale price for their institutions. In contrast, U.S. small independent banks' official view, as expressed by the Independent Bankers Association of America (IBAA), opposed all forms of interstate banking. The debate was inherently negative in that it pitted big banks against small banks.

Because the prospects for passing federal legislation appeared completely doomed, a group of individual banks in Florida pushed an InterSouth Bill in 1979. Dubbed the Confederate Amendment, this bill's regional merger design included only those states, except for Texas, that were in the original Confederacy. Because Texas was thought to have too many large banks, it was excluded from the original compact design. The Florida bill failed, but it led to a 1981 commission of nine academics whose mission was to perform a comprehensive review of the public policy ramifications of interstate banking. This study, entitled *Interstate Bank Expansion: Market Forces and Competitive Realities*[1], strongly recommended geographic liberalization as procompetitive and deemed continuing the status quo inefficient and inadvisable. Its findings provided important support for further geographic deregulation, and ultimately interstate banking, as solutions to the industry's excess capacity and its corresponding profit and growth problems. Paralleling the product and pricing deregulation discussed in Chapters 2 and 3, these first steps toward geographic deregulation were enormously important in setting into motion changes in the traditional industry paradigm.

Evolution of Interstate Banking Laws

Despite the great potential for variations in interstate legislation, the approaches adopted or considered to date have tended to fit one of three basic modes: nationwide entry, regional entry, or regional entry with a phase-in to nationwide entry. Because phase-in legislation commits a state to nationwide interstate banking within a definite time frame, it frequently is categorized with nationwide legislation. The ramifications of the three major types of interstate banking laws, however, each need to be examined.

Nationwide Entry

Unlimited nationwide entry was designed to benefit bank acquisition targets and consumers. National bidding could increase stock prices for target banks. Additionally, the entry of larger, out-of-region banks would increase the product set available to consumers. Increased stock prices for target banks were achieved, however, at the potential perceived cost of allowing out-of-state or out-of-region banks to dominate local banking markets. Many observers feared such an outcome. No evidence yet exists, however, that such outside control negatively affects the banking industry's performance or conduct.

Regional Reciprocity

Many considered the regional reciprocity option to be an interim step or adjustment to nationwide banking. It was described generally as an alternative that afforded time to existing banks in a state or region an opportunity to adapt to the changing financial environment. Where regional reciprocity was in effect, the major beneficiaries were the leading in-state and regional banks that were expanding by acquisition within their regions. These regional banks grew and established networks at less expense than they would have incurred if they were forced to bid for local acquisitions against banks headquartered outside their regions.

Regional reciprocity created multistate regional bank organizations. The emergence of strong regional banks was thought to be important for various reasons. First, it was hoped that regional banks would be more responsive to middle market firms, municipalities, or regional industries. Second, the development of several larger regional banks was thought to foster competition in certain banking product and service categories, then limited only to the large money-center (regional and nationwide) institutions. Third, while regional industrial or commercial firms could expand their representation into natural markets that crossed state lines, their banks could not. Traditionally, banks were precluded from following the growth of the customers they had financed. Regional reciprocity arrangements allowed some regional banks to further develop, expand, or extend product expertise throughout the region. Those banks in states adopting regional reciprocity enjoyed greater geographic liberalization, without risking falling prey to out-of-region competitors in the early days of consolidation.

National Phase-in and Triggers

Once a state decided that it preferred some form of interstate banking to the status quo, it had to select a specific regional or nationwide approach to geographic liberalization. Because this choice often was controversial and sometimes politically difficult, a blending of the two alternative approaches often occurred. This approach called for authorizing regional interstate banking for a short time period, generally two to four years, after which time nationwide entry would be permitted. For example, Kentucky and Rhode Island had nationwide triggers after two years; Ohio had a three-year trigger.

In-state banks had considerable strategic flexibility under the regional-with-trigger option. Larger bank holding companies could choose an expansion strategy aimed at gaining size, growth, and multistate presence. Other companies could sell out and either become part of larger in-state or regional entities, or wait for nationwide bidders. Unit banks could remain independent, join regional entities, or wait for bids to come as a result of nationwide reciprocity. Small banks' fears of unfriendly takeovers by out-of-state bank holding companies were probably unfounded. Experience has demonstrated that interstate acquirers target larger banks and not small, independent banks.

Interstate Merger Provisions

Numerous and often inconsistent provisions accompany different states' interstate banking laws. The Southeast region's state laws have been the most uniform. Typical provisions include type of entry, design of region, anti-leapfrogging prohibitions, reciprocity, phase-in determination (triggers), type of institutions, opt-outs, and nonseverability clauses. Exhaustive discussion of these provisions is not within the scope of this book. However, two provisions—design of region and opt-outs—have great relevance to bank consolidation strategy. Each is discussed next.

Design of a region

At the outset, no formal method existed to determine which states should be included or excluded from different regional compacts. Regional proposals utilized a variety of different approaches to make these determinations.

States' selection of regional partners reflected a mix of different regional design approaches. For example, Georgia, North Carolina, and South Carolina allowed entry by Kentucky banks, but initially Kentucky allowed entry by banks only in states immediately adjacent to it. Other states, such as Maryland and Missouri, were included in more than one regional proposal. Each state's design was potentially unique.

Banks from three states—New York, California, and Texas—were principally excluded from participation in the regional interstate banking movements. Massachusetts and Connecticut excluded New York from the Northeastern zone. Utah excluded California from its 12-state Western region. Similarly, both the Southeastern and Western zones left out Texas. Again, these states were excluded out of the fear that their disproportionate size might bias developments in a particular region. In retrospect, since the Texas and New York banks were very troubled throughout the early phases of the consolidation period, their predatory roles never would have materialized.

Regions were formalized with overlapping geographies. Accordingly, states had to determine whether to allow an acquisition when the acquiring institution operated principally in a state included within the region, but controlled some banks (and deposits) in states outside the region. A strict rule would require all deposits of a regional bank holding company to be within the states in the region if it was to be allowed to make acquisitions. Even on this point, not all states adopted the same cross-region acquisition criteria.

Florida, Georgia, Tennessee, South Carolina, and North Carolina all established a more lenient test for determining the permissibility of acquisitions. Each of these five states requires the regional bank holding company to hold more than 80 percent of its total deposits (of bank subsidiaries) within the region. For example, suppose that a Georgia bank holding company has 19.9 percent of its deposits in a Kentucky bank subsidiary, and that Florida excludes Kentucky from its region. This Georgia bank holding company still could make an acquisition in Florida and not be forced to divest an earlier Florida bank acquisition. Recently, this regional deposit requirement was cited as a potential constraint on NationsBank's rumored pursuit of Rhode Island-headquartered Fleet Financial.

Opt-outs

Invariably, some parties—generally small banks—opposed interstate banking regardless of its form. In cases where the support for legislation was fragile and the political clout of small bank opposition was substantial, legislatures adopted opt-out provisions allowing any in-state bank to choose not to participate in interstate activity for a certain period—Indiana and Ohio are examples. Banks could opt out of interstate activity and participate solely in intrastate consolidation. If a particular institution opted out, it would neither be permitted to acquire other institutions nor be eligible to be acquired. Legal analysts have observed that bank boards of directors who opt out may be subject to lawsuits that allege perpetuation of control by directors and/or management. Additionally, some shareholders may object to losing the opportunity to be sold for a premium.

Legal analysts have observed that bank boards of directors who opt out may be subject to lawsuits that allege perpetuation of control by directors and/or management. Additionally, some shareholders may object to losing the opportunity to be sold for a premium.

Current Status of Interstate Laws

Interstate laws have continued to evolve. As Exhibit 3.6 indicated, all but two states, Hawaii and Montana, have now legislated some form of interstate banking. Thirty-four states are today open nationally. Only 14 states, plus the District of Columbia, still have more restrictive regional designs. These include 10 states in the Southeastern compact, as well as such major states as Minnesota, Wisconsin, and Missouri.

The Fate of Regional Compacts

The Southeast is the nation's best example of a regional banking zone. The region has seen an avalanche of mergers that has resulted in the formation of several superregional banks—NationsBank, First Union, Wachovia, and SunTrust. Now that most of the major banks in Florida, South Carolina, Georgia, Maryland, and the District of Columbia have been acquired, some would argue that it is time to open up the Southern zone. However, this fairly simple notion quickly becomes complex.

To end the highly unified Southeast compact requires that one of two difficult alternatives take effect. The first—legislated national banking—would require congressional action. At the time of this writing, however, national banking does not appear to be the highest-ranked initiative priority of the Clinton Administration. Even if it did become one, a new law would most likely allow for a one- or two-year transitional period. A second approach would involve most of the major states in the Southeast compact changing their state banking laws. This approach would obviously be complex and problematic. It would be very difficult to get all of the individual states to act at the same time on a somewhat controversial bill. If interstate banking proponents are successful in changing the laws in some of the states but not others, it could provide acquisition entry by out-of-region banks while still locking in the Southern superregionals. The 80-20 rule described earlier could force major divestiture if Southern banks elected to enter other regions.

Nevertheless, natural competitive pressures may work to resolve this problem. Two of the region's largest banks, NationsBank and First Union, most likely will need to gain approval to acquire outside the Southeast region because they soon will have exhausted most of their opportunities within the region. Additionally, these banks tend to promote aggressive branch consolidation as a preferred tactic for cost savings. As this book goes to the press, a law permitting interstate banking in 1996 for North Carolina has been passed. Similar changes in the laws of South Carolina, Georgia, and Florida are expected to be pursued shortly.

In another evolving region, the two largest Minneapolis-based banks, Norwest and First Bank System, may also be forced soon to push for a national law to enable them to continue expansion outside their defined region. Today, for example, if Norwest could recruit a large acquisition in California, it would have to get either federal or Minnesota legislation passed in order to consummate such a deal. In contrast, the largest banks in Wisconsin and Missouri seem content to expand within their region without acquisition competition from out-of-region banks, or the threat of their own takeout. Accordingly, the interstate laws in these states would not be expected to change in the near future.

Regional interests vary significantly, reflecting the relative competitive strengths and market capitalizations of the region's banks. As banks' strengths evolve, pressure to change regional banking laws will continue. The evolution of geographic deregulation in response to shifts in relative competitive strengths is a natural part of the ongoing industry paradigm shift. Against this legislative backdrop, we expect the economics of consolidation to remain compelling.

The Unfolding of Bank Consolidation: Antitrust Policy

With the liberal interpretation of antitrust law by the Justice Department and federal banking agencies during the Reagan and Bush Administrations, banks have aggressively pursued acquisitions seeking maximum market share limits. Unless limited by state law, the current antitrust-mandated limits approximate 30 percent of a defined market's deposit base. The market deposit base is defined to include various portions of thrift deposits. Unfortunately, antitrust law has yet to explicitly factor the nonbank product set into local definitions of market share and size. As a result, a truly level playing field is not yet in place.

Somewhat oligopolistic local bank market structures could potentially result from bank consolidation. Bank strategists would be terribly remiss if they were not carefully factoring into their acquisition program the liberal structure of the nation's antitrust laws. High local market shares should translate into both servicing economies and increased pricing discipline, and, therefore, ultimately higher profitability. Superficially, public policymakers could raise questions about competitive levels, but relevant out-of-market bank and intense nonbank competition ensures appropriate balance. One need only look at the dramatic erosion of bank market share to nonbank competitors that has marked the past decade. Of course, to assume a rational approach to bank regulation is itself a bit irrational, given historical events.

Thrifts Phase Out Under Control

Against this banking industry backdrop, the survival prospects for the thrift industry are bleak. Although a distinct minority of thrifts may, to remain independent, transform themselves into highly efficient mortgage and/or consumer banks, most thrifts will find it necessary to combine with commercial banks. This competitive reality stems from the inherent profitability limitations of their deposit profile and dominant asset—mortgages. The lack of significant interest-free demand accounts and predominance of market-priced deposits have resulted in a serious erosion of thrifts' historical funding advantage On the mortgage front, the increasing securitization and disaggregation of mortgages has almost eliminated their portfolio holding value. Moreover, evidence exists suggesting if one adjusts for the embedded prepayment option in a mortgage, its core yield would not be substantially different from that of a Treasury bond. As a result, from an economic perspective, the financial rationale for thrifts may have actually ceased to exist.

On the mortgage front, the increasing securitization and disaggregation of mortgages has almost eliminated their portfolio holding value.

Fortunately, now in the aftermath of the thrift taxpayer bailout and the various RTC liquidation programs, the thrift industry phaseout is under control. As pointed out earlier, thrifts have become a part of most banks' consolidation strategy for various reasons—market entry, market share, and cost savings. For this reason, we forecast an orderly dissolution of the industry.

Ultimate Status of Community Banks

The number of community banks is seriously declining. Smaller banks have constituted the largest percentage of failures and mergers in recent years. This derives from two key factors. First, community banks tend to be dependent on one local market, and if a particular local economy deteriorates, the local bank tends to weaken. Second, the operating and compliance scale economies in banking continues to rise. This leads to ongoing profitability and capital pressures, which, in turn, makes smaller banks more amenable to merger.

Today, there is a pronounced demographic skewness in the age of bank senior management, shareholders, and directors.

Another factor that has traditionally motivated independent-minded community banks to merge out revolves around management succession. Today, there is a pronounced demographic skewness in the age of bank senior management, shareholders, and directors. Characteristically, these groups must address their wealth liquification and succession position. Often, sale is the most attractive option.

Despite the real pressures on community banks, several hundred of these institutions can survive, if well run. The case can be made that these institutions should be able to offer better personal service than the larger regional and national banks who, by their very nature, may tend to be impersonal. There are distinct consumer and business segments that will value such personal service.

Successful community banks will have to exhibit many of the key success factors possessed by high-performing larger banks. Namely, expense control, credit quality, market share and distribution strength, sales culture, and acquisition capability.

Technological Considerations Raise the Consolidation Stakes

Throughout this period of industry consolidation, technological expenditures have continued to escalate. Salomon Brothers has done considerable investigation into this under-researched area. Experts estimate that banks spend between $15 billion and $20 billion per year on information technology. Research findings have shown a clear pattern of large banks accounting for ever increasing shares of technology spending while smaller banks—both community and regional—elect to make less discretionary expenditures in the technology area. In 1985, Salomon Brothers estimated that its 35 large-bank universe spent nearly $5 billion or 59 percent of the industry's total. It estimated that spending levels in 1990 would approach $12 billion, with its 35-bank universe spending 68 percent of the total. The 35 largest banks, led by Citicorp, should account for more than 80 percent of the $175 billion the banking industry is seen spending on technology in the 1990s. Scale would appear to be increasingly critical to support technological spending and development.

Noteworthy about the nature and magnitude of technology stakes, however, is that some very large banks have joined the ranks of those who have elected to buy, or outsource, technology. Led by CEO Tony Terracciano, First Fidelity, a $30 billion institution, elected to go to outside vendors in 1990 rather than work through the consolidation and rationalization of its numerous disparate systems that had resulted from earlier acquisitions. Another large bank, Continental, has also been an aggressive outsourcer in its attempt to reduce expense levels. Today outsourcing discussions are common, even among the largest superregional banks, as the industry wrestles with its cost structure.

Given the technological requirements of the industry, it is not surprising that technology has become an important part of the consolidation picture. Banks that likely could become targets over the short or intermediate run are reluctant to incur the expense of investing in or restructuring their technological infrastructure. On the other hand, acquirers have become aggressive in consolidating many of an acquiree's back-office requirements to obtain cost savings. Indeed, such cost savings are an important part of the industry's improving its acquisition record in terms of value creation and dilution (see Chapter 6).

Research findings have shown a clear pattern of large banks accounting for ever increasing shares of technology spending . . . The 35 largest banks, led by Citicorp, should account for more than 80 percent of the $175 billion the banking industry is seen spending on technology in the 1990s.

Banking companies' use of technology has created new services and higher productivity. Expansion-minded banks are actively seeking efficient system approaches (see John P. Singleton's sidebar, *The Technology Scene and the Role It Should Play*, page 120). One focus of consolidation is the elimination of both duplicative and disparate systems, with a general preference for as few systems as possible. Through this process, systems-based scale economies and technology are changing the industry's landscape and, in doing so, adding to the pressure for consolidation.

The Emerging Banking Landscape

Over the past decade, the face of U.S. banking has dramatically changed. A quick perusal of 1980's largest commercial banks' assets (Exhibit 5.1) reveals modest consolidation success in terms of the asset size and value rank achieved over the decade. Collectively, these banks controlled 34 percent of the nation's banking assets in 1980. By 1990, the figure had decreased to 22 percent. The only two banks on this list that could be deemed consistently successful are J.P. Morgan and Bankers Trust. With the exceptions of BankAmerica and Chemical Bank, the largest banks of 1980 were not able to use interstate banking to become highly valued multistate entities.

Exhibit 5.2 reflects a more current ranking (September 30, 1993) of the nation's largest banks in terms of market capitaliza-

Exhibit 5.1
LARGEST U.S. COMMERCIAL BANKS RANKED BY ASSETS (1980)

Bank		Assets 1980 ($ Billions)
1	Citicorp	$115
2	BankAmerica	112
3	Chase Manhattan	76
4	Manufacturers Hanover	56
5	J.P. Morgan	52
6	Continental Illionis	42
7	Chemical	41
8	Bankers Trust	34
9	First Interstate	32
10	First Chicago	29
	Average	$59

Source: Annual Reports

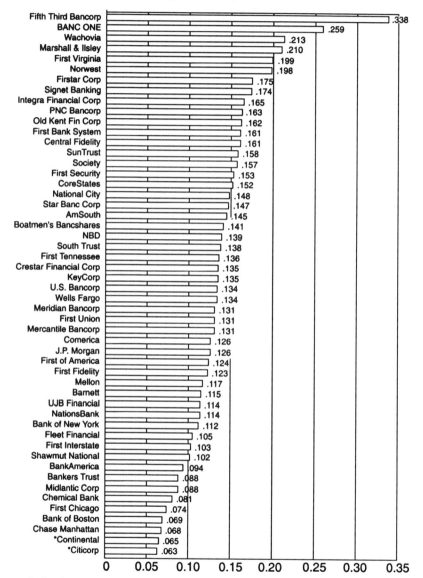

Exhibit 5.2

**TOP 50 BANKING ORGANIZATIONS
MARKET CAPITALIZATION TO TOTAL ASSETS
September 30, 1993**

Fifth Third Bancorp	.338
BANC ONE	.259
Wachovia	.213
Marshall & Ilsley	.210
First Virginia	.199
Norwest	.198
Firstar Corp	.175
Signet Banking	.174
Integra Financial Corp	.165
PNC Bancorp	.163
Old Kent Fin Corp	.162
First Bank System	.161
Central Fidelity	.161
SunTrust	.158
Society	.157
First Security	.153
CoreStates	.152
National City	.148
Star Banc Corp	.147
AmSouth	.145
Boatmen's Bancshares	.141
NBD	.139
South Trust	.138
First Tennessee	.136
Crestar Financial Corp	.135
KeyCorp	.135
U.S. Bancorp	.134
Wells Fargo	.134
Meridian Bancorp	.131
First Union	.131
Mercantile Bancorp	.131
Comerica	.126
J.P. Morgan	.126
First of America	.124
First Fidelity	.123
Mellon	.117
Barnett	.115
UJB Financial	.114
NationsBank	.114
Bank of New York	.112
Fleet Financial	.105
First Interstate	.103
Shawmut National	.102
BankAmerica	.094
Bankers Trust	.088
Midlantic Corp	.088
Chemical Bank	.081
First Chicago	.074
Bank of Boston	.069
Chase Manhattan	.068
*Continental	.065
*Citicorp	.063

* Continental and Citicorp were ranked 51 and 52, respectively as of 9/30/93.

Sources: The Wall Street Journal for share prices; company reports for total assets and shares outstanding as of 6/30/93.

The Technology Scene and the Role It Should Play

John P. Singleton
General Manager ISSC (a wholly owned subsidiary of IBM)
Former Vice Chairman and COO
Security Pacific Corporation

Current Environment

The current environment in the financial services industry is dynamic and challenging. Intense competition, partially due to overcapacity and commodity-deposit products, is sustaining a rapid pace of change. Most institutions are undergoing drastic expense reductions in their struggle to survive. Others are merging with competitors, thereby requiring vast consolidations of functions and systems on a scale and pace never seen before. This new environment has brought to light our existing shortage of the right type of leadership to manage this ever changing arena.

Role of Information Technology

In an environment in which the only constant is change, effective use of information technology is critical. When exploited to its fullest extent, information technology can be a strategic weapon: witness the powerful airline reservation systems. Development and implementation of systems should focus on moving and gaining market share for the institution. In the financial services industry, information technology is at the heart of supporting the strategic objectives of internal clients—the holding company, banks, and affiliated subsidiaries.

In light of these strategic objectives, information technology should be managed to support effective management of expenses and identification of cost savings opportunities through more efficient use of technology. Major decisions should be based on technology's impact to ROI or EPS, not just application size or transaction rates. Centralization should be employed when appropriate to minimize duplication and take advantage of economies of scale. Automation can contribute significantly to improving productivity, accuracy, and effectiveness. Innovative technologies such as image processing, when justified by sufficient volume, should be deployed to realize additional savings. When cost justified, image processing should attack every piece of paper in a bank. Banking and financial systems should be reengineered rather than just migrated to a new computer. We have lost the art of employing an industrial engineering approach. The reengineering of total functions should be a contagious process leading to positive bottomline results.

To enable the organization to manage its core business, selected MIS is critical. Currently, a lack of business-oriented people exists in the information systems environment. They do not know how to create partnerships with their internal clients. To be effective, systems must be implemented that provide these internal clients with needed information, such as the profitability of individual products, services, and customers. This enables managers to capitalize on profitable products, enhance the contribution of marginal products, and analyze the feasibility of terminating unprofitable products. The ability to conduct what-if analysis and to forecast capital is critical. Generic general ledger systems just cannot do the job today.

To enhance existing client relationships and obtain new customers, technological solutions should be focused on managing the total customer relationship. Solutions should support cross-selling opportunities and relationship marketing.

Information technology can be further used as a competitive weapon to move market share through product differentiation made possible by a quick turnaround of development efforts. This development time can be reduced significantly through the use of such tools as computer aided software engineering (CASE), which provides the ability to standardize the program development process. Code generators and self-documenting compilers are just two of the features that enhance overall quality and productivity.

To meet internal client needs effectively, not only is it critical to have a thorough understanding of the requirements, but the necessary level of quality must also be understood. When implementing systems solutions, there is always a tradeoff between cost and quality, and information systems professionals must work closely with their clients to determine the most effective mix for the situation at hand.

This increased requirement of business to be flexible and timely in responding to market needs is one of the critical factors driving outsourcing growth. The most common functions that are outsourced include data center management and planning, back office operations, high-volume transaction processing, networking, application development, application maintenance, application planning, and data base management. However, prior to outsourcing, there are several key questions to be answered:

- Do you understand the role of technology and the value it can add to the effectiveness of the organization?

- If technology is not playing an important role, will outsourcing help?

- What is motivating you to outsource?
  - Cost?
  - Poor management?
  - Lack of control?
  - Poor quality of service?
  - Lack of confidence?
  - Lack of quality people/expertise?

The decision to outsource requires a thorough evaluation of the potential benefits of outsourcing and the associated risks. The potential benefits include:

- Lower cost (even though the insourcer is making a profit on your business);

- New technology (not necessarily);

- Top-quality people (depends on the size of your account);

- Time to focus on real business rather than technology (although technology can be a strategic competitive weapon);

- Control (do you really gain control?);

- Contracted quality standards (can you really have partnerships with your clients when everything is under outside contracts?).

Prior to outsourcing, several critical steps should be taken:

1. Understand your level of performance relative to peer groups.

tion per dollar of assets. Fifth Third was selling for 33.8 percent per dollar of assets. And, BANC ONE sold for 25.9 percent. Note that the largest banks in 1980 do not presently rank high on the market capitalization per dollar of assets measure. None rank in the top 10 banks on this important shareholder value-oriented measure of performance. Of the largest banks in 1980, J.P. Morgan (#33) rated the highest on this shareholder value measure: it sold at 12.59 percent per dollar of assets. A market capitalization measure as compared to asset rank, better reflects a bank's strategic position and its correspondent currency strength to make strategic moves.

2. Determine existing direct expenses.

3. Identify costs of acquiring outsourcing services.

Only when a thorough analysis of both internal and external information systems alternatives is completed will it be possible to make an effective decision regarding outsourcing.

One of the greatest challenges in this dynamic environment is the effective integration of acquisitions, which requires bridging dissimilar configurations and consolidating systems and networks. Moving to common systems enhances product consistency, provides the foundation for common back office operations, and establishes a standard platform for future acquisitions. Reducing the number of redundant systems minimizes complexity and risk and eliminates the need to authorize multiple balances. Common systems also promote more timely implementation of product enhancements.

To provide uninterrupted superior service to clients, a smooth and flawless transition is required following a merger/acquisition. As experience is gained, the development of an acquisition template and proven conversion software can facilitate this process. Several banks—BANC ONE, NationsBank, and Norwest, for example—are beginning to realize competitive advantage as well as significant gains in market value as a result of their active and effective acquisition programs.

As can be seen, information technology provides a central role in the current environment of heavy competition and bank restructuring. To take full advantage of the power of information technology and its potential contribution to the success of the institution, information technology executives should be involved in the strategic planning process from its inception.

A New Set of Power Bankers

In any strategic context, the major superregionals are now the powerful banks. These institutions have combined value-enhancing mergers, both intra- and interstate, with effective operating tactics to achieve very strong market valuations. Exhibit 5.3 indicates relative market capitalization rankings as of September 30, 1993. Today's prominent megaregional banks—BankAmerica (#1), BANC ONE (#3), NationsBank (#5), Norwest (#7), First Union (#8), and PNC (#9)—all rate highly in terms of this important measure.

Exhibit 5.3

TOP FIFTY BANKING ORGANIZATIONS
MARKET CAPITALIZATION
September 30, 1993

	National	Market Capitalization
1	BankAmerica	15,653,352,000
2	J.P. Morgan	15,102,160,000
3	BANC ONE	15,097,810,667
4	Citicorp	14,326,612,500
5	NationsBank	13,107,574,000
6	Chemical Bank	11,354,490,000
7	Norwest	8,033,350,000
8	First Union	8,003,000,250
9	PNC Bancorp	7,286,397,000
10	Wells Fargo	7,019,373,000
11	Chase Manhattan	6,801,077,250
12	Wachovia	6,788,109,250
13	Bankers Trust	6,582,480,000
14	SunTrust	5,581,412,500
15	NBD	5,499,077,250
16	First Interstate	5,050,641,375
17	Fleet Financial	4,761,204,750
18	Bank of New York	4,702,762,875
19	Barnett	4,373,415,000
20	National City	4,224,253,000
21	First Chicago	4,056,877,500
22	KeyCorp	3,833,366,625
23	First Bank System	3,780,525,000
24	Society	3,743,328,000
25	First Fidelity	3,626,246,750
26	Mellon	3,483,590,000
27	CoreStates	3,391,022,259
28	Comerica	3,223,046,750
29	Fifth Third Bancorp	3,278,251,000
30	Boatmen's Bancshares	3,151,542,500
31	U.S. Bancorp	2,619,855,125
32	First of America	2,421,095,625
33	Shawmut National Corp	2,294,082,000
34	Bank of Boston	2,176,756,500
35	Firstar Corp	2,132,732,875
36	Signet Banking	1,941,522,000
37	Crestar Financial Corp	1,612,530,000
38	Integra Financial Corp	1,608,336,000
39	Marshall & Ilsley	1,567,701,000
40	UJB Financial	1,536,930,000
41	Meridian Bancorp	1,524,643,875
42	SouthTrust	1,523,554,000
43	Midlantic Corp	1,430,220,000
44	Continental	1,427,814,000
45	Old Kent Fin Corp	1,417,430,000
46	AmSouth	1,329,756,750
47	First Virginia	1,296,412,250
48	Central Fidelity	1,190,732,250
49	Mercantile Bancorp	1,188,164,000
50	First Tennessee	1,125,440,000

Sources: *The Wall Street Journal* for share prices; company reports for total assets and shares outstanding as of 6/30/93.

Again, looking at shareholder value as a key measure, comparative market-to-book value ratios of the 50 largest banks are presented in Exhibit 5.4. Superregional banks dominate the list. Only J.P. Morgan, from the 1980 list, is valued above 1.75X book value. On August 2, 1993, the top four banks—BANC ONE, Fifth Third, Huntington Bancshares, and Northern Trust—were all trading above 2.2X their tangible book value.

In contrast to the superregional banks, the money-center banks carry the lowest market valuations. Since consolidation strategies are dependent upon strong relative market valuations (currency) and capital strength, money-center banks will remain disadvantaged vis-a-vis superregional acquirers. With their acquisition prospects limited, these banks have selected strategies that emphasize scale-driven products—credit cards and mortgages, for example—that are delivered nationally, without branch support. In this light, one can project that money centers will continue to see their relative rank decline, while the continued geographic expansion by the superregionals, if properly managed, should propel them to even greater size in terms of market value.

Since consolidation strategies are dependent upon strong relative market valuations (currency) and capital strength, money center banks will remain disadvantaged vis-a-vis superregional acquirers.

Where Does It Go from Here?

Although many bankers maintain that they are firmly wedded to autonomy, and some investors question the wisdom of cross-regional acquisitions, there is no reason to believe that the pace of consolidation in the near future will be any different from the recent past. The annals of bank structure are quite clear about bankers' responses to county, statewide, regional, and national geographic liberalization. Each liberalization phase has been followed by mergers, creating a smaller number of larger banks.

In the future, the merger pace may even accelerate. Consider, for example, that although there are still many banking organizations in the United States, there is a declining number of desirable acquisition candidates. Some of the available targets are actually beginning to see the number of potential bidders decline. Moreover, the general level of stock prices supports more capital fund-raising for acquisition, and the relative valuations of acquirers versus acquirees make deals more feasible. Finally, and perhaps less obviously, banks such as BANC ONE, NationsBank, and BankAmerica have moved to a size and value level where they are positioned to do almost any deal. Their earnings dilution risk is not nearly as significant as that faced by smaller institutions.

The Threat of Hostile Bank Takeovers

Historically, there have not been very many hostile takeover attempts on banks. The past several years, however, have witnessed several significant attacks. Exhibit 5.5 indicates the hostile takeover attempts of the 1980s and early 1990s.

Exhibit 5.4

TOP FIFTY BANKING ORGANIZATIONS
PRICE RELATIVE TO BOOK VALUE
August 2, 1993

More than 200% Of Book Value	176–200% Of Book Value	151–175% Of Book Value	126–150% Of Book Value	101–125% Of Book Value	0–100% Of Book Value
BANC ONE Corporation	Barnett Banks, Inc.	Bankers Trust	AmSouth Bancorp	BankAmerica Corp.	Chase Manhattan
Fifth Third Bancorp	CoreStates Financial	Boatmen's Bancshares	Bancorp Hawaii	Bank of Boston	Continental Bank
Huntington Bancshares	Firstar Corp	Comerica, Inc.	Bank of New York	Chemical Banking	
Northern Trust	First Bank System	Crestar Financial	Citicorp	MNC Financial, Inc.	
Norwest Corporation	Integra Financial	First of America	First Chicago Corp.		
State Street Boston	J.P. Morgan	First Fidelity	Mellon Bank Corp.		
SunTrust Banks	KeyCorp	First Interstate	Midlantic		
Wachovia Corporation	Signet Banking Corp.	First Union Corp.	Republic New York		
	Society Corp.	Fleet Financial Group	United Jersey Banks		
	Wells Fargo	Meridian Bancorp			
		National City Corp			
		NationsBank			
		NBD Bancorp			
		PNC Bank			
		Shawmut National			
		SouthTrust Corp.			
		U.S. Bancorp			

Source: Montgomery Securities

Exhibit 5.5

UNILATERAL TAKEOVER ATTEMPTS OR INITIATIVES
(In Order of Proposed Transaction Size)

Target	Initiator	Date
Royal Bank of Scotland	*Hong Kong & Shanghai*	*1981*
Union Commerce	*Huntington*	*1981*
Florida National	Southeast	1982
First Bankshares of S.C.	Bankers Trust of S.C.	1983
Security New York	*Norstar*	*1983*
Florida Coast	*Barnett*	*1984*
BancOhio	*National City*	*1984*
Pontiac State	Comerica	1984
Statewide	Midlantic	1984
Michigan National	Comerica	1985
BankAmerica	First Interstate	1986
Madison Financial	Exchange International	1986
Standard Chartered	Lloyds	1986
The Conifer Group	Fleet Financial	1986
The Conifer Group	*Bank of New England*	*1986*
Irving Bank	*The Bank of New York*	*1987*
Marine	Marshall & Ilsley	1987
First Fulton	*Barnett*	*1987*
Centerre	United Missouri	1988
Centerre	*Boatmen's*	*1988*
Star Banc Corp.	Fifth Third	1992
Puget Sound	*KeyCorp*	*1992*
Sunwest Financial	Unnamed	1992
Sunwest	*Boatmen's*	*1992*
UJB Financial	Chilmark Capital[1]	1992
Peoples Westchester	Pohlad, Jacobs, and others	1993
Peoples Westchester	*First Fidelity*	*1993*
Rochester Community Savings Bank	First Empire State[2]	1993
Evergreen Bancorp	KeyCorp	1993

Successful takeovers indicated in **bold italic.**

1 Chilmark Capital led an effort to require UJB to find a buyer. The dissident group was defeated in a highly contested proxy vote.

2 First Empire State was the financial press guesstimate.

Source: Goldman Sachs

> *With the increasingly broad public trading of bank shares, and the relative ease with which a 10 percent shareholder can exert substantial pressure on a bank's destiny, one would expect continued pressure from uninvited suitors.*

Regulatory hurdles tend to discourage hostile bids. The regulatory process involves time delays that can allow targets a chance to construct a program of defensive measures to defeat a bid or recruit a higher or more friendly (white knight) offer. With the increasingly broad public trading of bank shares, and the relative ease with which a 10 percent shareholder can exert substantial pressure on a bank's destiny, one would expect continued pressure from uninvited suitors.

Exhibit 5.5 indicates that several uninvited attempts have succeeded. In other cases, the bid served to put the target in play, which resulted in a third-party takeout. Examples of this result are Conifer Group's merger with Bank of New England and Centerre's merger with Boatmen's. Other takeover resistance has resulted in the target's making an arrangement with a friendly white knight, in which an investment is made in the target with a view toward possible merging at a later date. Examples of this pattern are Chemical Bank's agreement with Florida National and Marine Midland's investment in Michigan National.

The Bank of New York's move on Irving Bank and Boatmen's offer for Centerre illustrate the circumstances that can motivate a hostile attempt. Both targets had been underperformers, and yet, as in-market propositions, they represented very valuable, if not critical, mergers to the acquirers. Simply put, the near- or intermediate-term survival of these two acquirers may have hinged on these deals.

More recent examples of poor performance motivating unilateral takeover attempts include NationsBank's 1991 uninvited bid for C&S/Sovran and Fifth Third's unsolicited offer to buy Star Banc. NationsBank was successful in acquiring C&S/Sovran and increased its asset size by more than 50 percent. Star Banc was able to successfully repel Fifth Third. Given the premier respect of investors for Fifth Third's equity, Star Banc's decision to not accept the offer will remain a controversial decision.

An Era of Cost Takeouts

A major dimension of mergers in recent years involves the cost savings that can be achieved. Expense controls, in general, and reduction of the target's noninterest expenses (NIE), specifically, have been critical to making mergers value-creating and nondilutive (see Chapter 6).

Through analysis of major merger and acquisition efforts, First Manhattan Consulting Group (FMCG) has compiled cost-saving benchmarks that measure the typical percentage reduction in the noninterest expense of the target (Exhibit 5.6). Clearly, the magnitude of cost saves is greatest in in-market deals, which can, on average, yield 35 percent cost reduction. The more distant mergers result in less, but still substantial, cost savings—25 and

Exhibit 5.6

ESTIMATED MERGER NONINTEREST EXPENSE SAVINGS

Cost saving potential varies by type of cost and proximity

Area of Bank	In-Market	Contiguous	Out-of-Market
Branches	20%	10%	5%
Operations	30%	25%	15%
Systems	55%	50%	40%
Trust	25%	20%	15%
Indirect OH	60%	40%	15%
Other	30%	25%	10%
Weighted Average	35%	25%	15%

Source: First Manhattan Consulting Group

15 percent of the acquiree's noninterest expense for contiguous and out-of-market deals, respectively.

The breakout of expense saves shown in Exhibit 5.6 indicates that systems consolidation and corporate (indirect) overhead are major sources of savings in all types of mergers. Depending on the degree of redundant delivery capacity or branch overlap resulting from an in-market merger, retail branch expenses can also be a major source of cost savings. Recently announced in-market acquisitions with high branch system overlap have the potential for even higher than 35 percent cost reduction. Shawmut's acquisition of People's of Worcester and Fleet's acquisition of Sterling Bancorp are both examples of transactions with cost reduction potential due to branch overlap exceeding 50 percent.

Exhibit 5.7 indicates the cost saving experience of several merging banks. Savings, in this case, are shown as a percentage of the combined NIE of the merged institutions. The savings range from 11 to 20 percent. Not surprisingly, contiguous market mergers, such as NationsBank–C&S/Sovran, tend to achieve the lower limit of this range.

Given the magnitude of potential savings from bank mergers, it is clear that some mergers have the capacity to almost pay for themselves. If capitalized at prevailing market values, FMCG estimates that cost savings could justify paying an additional 1.3X book value for in-market mergers, an additional .9X book value for contiguous market mergers, and an additional .5X book value for out-of-market mergers.

The Next Wave of Mergers

In-market mergers will continue to be popular as these deals result in significant cost savings and market share gains. Mergers

Given the magnitude of potential savings from bank mergers, it is clear that some mergers have the capacity to almost pay for themselves.

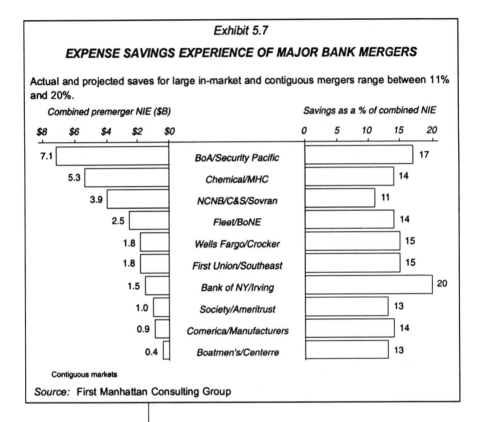

Exhibit 5.7

EXPENSE SAVINGS EXPERIENCE OF MAJOR BANK MERGERS

Actual and projected saves for large in-market and contiguous mergers range between 11% and 20%.

Combined premerger NIE ($B)	Merger	Savings as a % of combined NIE
7.1	BoA/Security Pacific	17
5.3	Chemical/MHC	14
3.9	NCNB/C&S/Sovran	11
2.5	Fleet/BoNE	14
1.8	Wells Fargo/Crocker	15
1.8	First Union/Southeast	15
1.5	Bank of NY/Irving	20
1.0	Society/Ameritrust	13
0.9	Comerica/Manufacturers	14
0.4	Boatmen's/Centerre	13

Contiguous markets

Source: First Manhattan Consulting Group

among banks in adjacent states will also continue at a brisk pace as medium-size targets become increasingly scarce. Each of the nation's regional markets is left with a small number of large banks and a large number of small banks but few of middle size.

The relative maturity of state and regional consolidation, as well as intermittent merger opportunities around the country, suggests that there will be an increasing number of cross-regional mergers in the future. The value maps and the survival lists developed later in this chapter will point out potential interregional deals.

Acquisitions as a Means of Loan Portfolio Diversification

A long-known reason for bank failures has been the inherent dependence of banks on local economies. When a serious recession hit a particular economy, the local bank often failed. Even statewide banking organizations have undergone serious trouble and sometimes failure when a severe state or regional recession unfolded. As the United States has experienced a series of rolling recessions, banks in the Southwest, New England, Mid-Atlantic region, and California have become quite troubled. In the case of Texas, most of the state's large banks failed—First Republic, First City, and MCorp. As a result of shifting regional economic outlooks, today banks more easily see the value of diversification.

The goal of loan portfolio diversification can be easily extended to interstate banking consolidation strategies. That is to say, perhaps the best way to ensure a truly diversified business mix is to do mergers between banks in regions whose core business activities are not highly correlated. The result would certainly be a more diversified asset portfolio.

A strategy based upon national or interregional mergers, however, raises legitimate questions regarding the difficulty of managing long-distance mergers. Thus far, NationsBank and BANC ONE have had great success with their long-distance Texas franchises. Minnesota banks, Norwest and First Bank System, are also doing well with their Colorado acquisitions. In reflecting upon long-distance managing, many executives point out that they can travel around the country as easily as they can drive or fly within their own headquarters state. So modern transportation and communications greatly facilitate long-distance management. Accordingly, interregional and national bank merger expansion will become more frequent in the future.

KeyCorp and Fleet Financial are examples of banks that have deliberately pursued acquisitions for the purpose of diversification. KeyCorp has pursued its "polar banking" or "snowbelt" strategy by buying banks in Maine, Oregon, Washington, and Alaska. Underlying this somewhat controversial strategy was a desire both to achieve greater geographic diversification and establish positions in less competitive banking markets. Fleet Financial has long been sensitive about its dependence on its New England roots. By merging with Norstar of upstate New York and developing national product-based businesses such as mortgage banking and student loans, it obtained some measure of diversification. Diversification is a very legitimate and important goal. Cross-region or cross-country mergers are an effective means of pursuing this goal.

The goal of loan portfolio diversification can be easily extended to interstate banking consolidation strategies. That is to say, perhaps the best way to ensure a truly diversified business mix is to do mergers between banks in regions whose core business activities are not highly correlated.

Merger of Equals:
The Good, the Bad, and the Nominal

One of the most interesting concepts to evolve out of the consolidation mania is that of the merger of equal (MOE). Throughout the merger era, MOEs have occurred periodically and most likely will continue to occur (see James J. McDermott-Richard I. Stillinge's sidebar, *Swift Merger Pace: More to Give Up the Ghost*, page 132). An MOE involves two similarly sized banks that com-

Swift Merger Pace: More to Give Up the Ghost

James J. McDermott, Jr., President
Richard I. Stillinger, Associate Director of Research
Keefe, Bruyette & Woods, Inc.

Ten years ago, a new environment for bank mergers and acquisitions was taking shape. Individual states had begun to enact statutes permitting cross-border deals for locally domiciled banks on either a nationwide or—more often—regional basis. Since then, interstate deals have mushroomed, and continuing consolidation of the banking industry has become almost a foregone conclusion. During the same period the approach of most banks to mergers and acquisitions, both within and outside their home states, has changed markedly.

In brief, that approach has grown more demanding and disciplined. Ten years ago some banks seemed to be pursuing acquisitions, at least in part, to enhance prestige or promote growth for its own sake; others had acquisition rationales that were more justifiable, but still not sharply defined. Now, on the other hand, most acquisition-minded banks seem to be applying much more stringent criteria with respect to return on investment and dilution of earnings or book value. The increased prevalence of in-market acquisitions reflects two aspects of this shift toward greater discipline: more emphasis on market share as an element widely considered essential to banking success; and the quest for cost savings, more readily attainable by eliminating duplication within a common market, in order to increase acquired banks' contribution to profit.

A hard-nosed approach is evident also in greatly intensified due diligence efforts before formal acquisition agreements are struck. Gone is a former tendency to give the benefit of the doubt to target banks of reputed high quality; those banks' portfolios often failed to withstand scrutiny after a deal was closed. Finally, the drive to maximize an acquiree's profitability—for both in-market and market-extension deals—has produced greater acquirer willingness to insist on layoffs and early retirements, despite wounded local community sensibilities and disruption in the lives of those affected.

In our view, three related developments account for this gradual evolution of stricter, more focused acquisition criteria. First, bankers themselves have had bitter experience of the pitfalls resulting from failure to approach acquisitions carefully and thoughtfully. Second, investors observing such pitfalls have paid increasing attention to acquisition policy, holding banks to higher standards and penalizing those that have neither applied sound policies nor—at least—learned the lessons of experience. Third, as industry consolidation continues apace, bankers wishing to remain independent have recognized that survival depends on profitability maintenance, which is difficult enough without ill-advised acquisitions.

Another result of these developments is increased involvement by outside bank directors in responding to the new merger-and-acquisition environment—not to mention the changed environment for banking in general. Given a recent history of poor credit decisions, and the continuing loss of market share to non-bank competition, a rising degree of difficulty inherent in the business has forced directors to take a more broadly active role. Their role will, if anything, expand further as the pressure on banks intensifies, driving the industry toward consolidation at an accelerating clip.

Thus a bank's ultimate fate will depend on what route it chooses to take: growth through acquisition and merger, pursuit of a purely independent course, or favorable reaction to overtures from potential acquirers. This crucial decision, even more than specific long-range planning or the immediate conduct of the business, requires the board's committed participation.

Relatively few of the combinations done since the advent of interstate banking could properly be described as mergers of equals; several of the most important of those have occurred within a single state, in order to derive maximum benefit from cost savings. The reason cited most often for the paucity of MOEs in general is the so-called "social" issue: neither of two potential partners is willing to cede definitive overall control to the other, although clear-cut lines of authority are essential to success. Even where arrangements for relatively equitable power-sharing can be worked out and such a merger occurs, those arrangements may result in stalemate rather than real cooperation; or if one bank's management does in fact accept a subordinate role, some of its retained executives may become disgruntled and perform poorly.

Other considerations also have militated against potential MOE agreements, e.g., the likely unwieldiness of integrating operations where neither partner dominates in size. Furthermore, even if integration goes reasonably smoothly after completion of a deal, any delay in the timetable for the process—as initially presented to investors by management—can hurt the combined company's stock.

Thus unqualified success in completed MOEs has been rare. Perhaps the most prominent positive example is the merger between Chemical New York and Manufacturers Hanover. Those two managements have been able to share authority in an apparently harmonious manner; the great cost savings available from two franchises with substantial overlap are being achieved on schedule; and their combined asset-quality problems are being reduced at an impressive pace.

Despite the difficulties associated with MOEs, talk has grown more prevalent about mergers between large institutions in entirely different regions—as opposed to what had occurred almost exclusively thus far, namely, MOEs within a region or state. It has been an intriguing question whether such talk would be substantiated by actual combinations or would prove to be only bold speculation, as potential partners ultimately balked at implementing their tentative conversations. Now we observe what seems the first major break in a wall of inaction, with the merger agreement between Society and KeyCorp. Their initial announcement laid out the rationale for interregional MOEs, emphasizing not so much prospective cost savings—which, inevitably, will be relatively small without geographical overlap—but rather greater opportunity both for revenue growth and for strategic acquisitions.

Bankers and analysts alike have highlighted maintenance of satisfactory revenue growth as a pivotal industry problem for the mid-nineties; and the prospective doubling in market capitalization of KeyCorp and Society, compared with what either company alone can muster, will permit consideration of acquisitions—both within and outside their combined territory—previously deemed prohibitively dilutive. This latter incentive is especially attractive at a time when prices demanded by—and paid to—acquirees have been rising.

KeyCorp and Society seem to have resolved the immediate social issues by agreeing to establish a board of directors and an executive management team split equally between the two present companies, to keep the KeyCorp name but locate the headquarters in Society's home city, and to have Society's chief executive officer succeed KeyCorp's older CEO as head of the new company in

bine in such a fashion that neither party receives a substantial gain or loss in market value, earnings per share, or book value. Upon announcement, the market renders a judgment about the MOE and assigns a price-earnings ratio that may or may not be different from those held by either of the two banks prior to merger. Upward price-earnings ratios (P/E) were initially given to Bank of New England (BNE), SunTrust, and C&S/Sovran Financial as larger institutions capable of doing larger value-added mergers.

SunTrust probably has been the most successful MOE to date. Unfortunately, BNE and C&S/Sovran did not prove to be successful. Besides getting caught in severe regional recessions, these banks succumbed to out-of-control credit problems and the failure to develop the organizational discipline necessary to excel in the rapidly changing environment.

1996. Once this deal is completed the progress of integrating its components and generating higher revenue growth, will be closely watched for clues to its ultimate success; but we believe that the die has been cast, and that KeyCorp-Society will encourage latent leanings within the banking industry toward interregional MOEs—in part because interested parties may wish to move early in order to maximize the choice of partners. Thus at least a few more blockbuster MOEs are likely to materialize in the not-too-distant future.

It seems almost inevitable that the onrushing trend toward consolidation of the banking industry, through both merger and acquisition, will feed upon itself. The prohibition against interstate branching, and the remaining state barriers to fully nationwide cross-border combinations, will fall; as part of that process, the "Southeastern compact" will be dissolved—either through gradual further erosion of individual states' participation or all at once, by federal legislation. The strong superregional banks will get even stronger, benefitting in the acquisition derby from high market capitalizations, and from advantages of size for absorbing the rising costs of both regulation and technology.

Those same costs will drive an increasing number of small and mid-sized banks to give up the ghost, accepting any reasonable offer to be acquired. As for mid-sized banks in particular, only well-managed, high-performance institutions will be able to survive indefinitely; and even some of those may eventually decide that survival is not worth the struggle. The banking industry will not be transformed overnight, any more than it has been already; however, the present trend toward sweeping change was set in motion years ago, and nothing seems likely to stop it.

Two recent MOEs that have attracted a lot of attention involve Comerica-Manufacturers National and Chemical-Manufacturers Hanover. As in-market transactions, both of these deals promise high cost savings as well as complementary business fits. Before merging, each of these banks was limited by its size and market valuation in terms of being able to participate in the acquisition game. With larger size, both banks are back in the consolidation game. Chemical Bank won a hotly contested bid for much of the failed First City franchise and has confirmed it is shopping for banks in New Jersey. Comerica has experienced considerable difficulty in wringing out its in-market cost saves. It recently announced a transaction with a California bank, Pacific Western.

Many mergers are announced as an MOE, but the designation is really only nominal. When BankAmerica acquired Security

Pacific, the official description was that of an MOE. Nevertheless, it was clear to all that, as is so often the case, one party (BofA) would dominate in terms of retaining its name, management, headquarters, and operating systems. Also, Security Pacific received a healthy premium for selling, whereas a true MOE involves very little, if any, premium. Other examples of MOEs that really were acquisitions are Fleet-Norstar and PNC-Provident. Fleet and PNC were clearly the dominant banks, and these deals more resembled acquisitions after consummation.

MOE transactions are difficult to execute. Because the parties essentially require shareholders to sell out for little or no premium, an MOE attempt may end up being an invitation for another acquirer to offer a low bid that could easily appeal to the shareholders. This is an inherent danger with banks that are widely held. As this book goes to press, Society and KeyCorp have announced their intention to merge as an MOE.

Who Will Ultimately Survive?

To understand which banks have the best chances of surviving the consolidation of the banking industry, it is helpful to consider the success determinants, or sources of strength, of those banks that have already achieved a great measure of self-determination. By doing so, we can address the most frequent question asked throughout the various merger waves: how large must an entity be to expect to survive?

Although there are numerous important determinants of bank survival, absolute size looms as one of the most important. The largest banks in terms of equity, assets, and earnings may possess relative and/or absolute advantage. Larger firms, as a general matter, have the resources to pursue more strategic options and withstand more risk. Perhaps more importantly, large size makes a bank increasingly difficult to digest as an acquisition, limiting the field of potential acquirers. With respect to size, however, analysts are quick to point out that goals aimed at being "the biggest" may be misguided. Absolute asset size is certainly no guarantee of creating shareholder value. Pursuit of size to the detriment of shareholder value will undermine efforts to perform against other key criteria.

Better indicators or determinants of survivability are a bank's market capitalization and market-to-book ratio. These measures reflect the shareholder's perspective—the market's valuation of an institution and the strength of its currency. Ultimately, a bank's stock price defines its ability to execute value-creating acquisitions. Since successful mergers are a critical dimension of the industry's restructuring, absolute and relative market capitalization are both very important. The value maps for various regions, to be discussed later in this chapter, illustrate the importance of relative and absolute market capitalization, as well as market to book value relationships.

In the merger environment, capital strength has also proved to be strategically important. Strong equity positions are often necessary to gain regulatory approval for desired combinations, particularly when the acquiree has a deficient capital position or a cash purchase is being attempted.

In addition to financial strength, it almost goes without saying that management and corporate integration skills are important. Although a wide range of management and corporate skills is relevant, as long as consolidation remains the industry's central focal point, those banks with advanced merger integration templates have a decided advantage. As consolidation matures, managements' restructuring strategies and execution will become paramount.

The relative strength of a bank's franchise also will determine an entity's ultimate chance of survival. In the beginning of the industry's consolidation, an institution's initial size and location defined its strategic position. Today, local market share, measured town-by-town, is a critical measure. Being among the top three competitors in priority markets is imperative. The breadth of product offerings is an equally important franchise consideration.

As consolidation began to unfold, banks in many states, such as Florida, South Carolina, Kentucky, Arizona, and Indiana, were quickly identified as sellers. In the 1990s, banks must continue to analyze their relative size and market coverage to assess their positions realistically. In a broad sense, many of the nation's major states or urban markets have been already captured (Exhibit 5.8). With fewer markets available to be bought, many acquirers will be forced to reconsider their basic options. Some may involve larger mergers than those seen to date; some may be hostile. Others may consider an MOE. Finally, some banks will find their greatest value in simply selling out.

In summing up, there is a great disparity in the ranking of various banks with respect to the key survival determinants identified: (1) institutional size; (2) market capitalization and market-to-book value (currency); (3) capital strength; (4) internal management skills; and (5) value and strength of existing franchise positions. Now that the consolidation process has matured, remaining banks must continually reassess their strategic positions to determine their highest value alternatives. Today, to hope to be a survivor, one must aggressively be planning and executing to do so.

Although a wide range of management and corporate skills is relevant, as long as consolidation remains the industry's central focal point, those banks with advanced merger integration templates have a decided advantage. As consolidation matures, managements' restructuring strategies and execution will become paramount.

Exhibit 5.8

TOP 15 STATES BY ASSETS WITH OTHER DATA
December 31, 1992 ($ Millions)

State	Bank Assets	GSP*	Population**	No. Banks
NY	$760,171	$441,068	18,002,100	229
CA	324,115	697,381	29,955,700	410
IL	201,659	256,478	11,443,300	1,018
PA	192,910	227,898	11,892,900	314
TX	175,475	340,057	17,055,000	1,089
FL	147,382	226,964	13,044,500	397
MA	130,945	144,791	6,019,800	259
OH	122,681	211,545	10,858,600	271
NJ	107,722	203,375	7,735,500	119
MI	100,280	181,827	9,314,000	218
NC	93,173	130,085	6,653,100	122
GA	74,767	129,776	6,503,900	397
VA	71,613	136,497	6,212,900	170
MD	67,622	99,074	4,801,900	510
CT	63,619	89,000	3,287,116	99

* Data for 1989
** Data for 1990
Source: Federal Reserve Bank; U.S. Statistical Abstract

Surveying Today's Banking Consolidation Landscape

Among a variety of performance characteristics, market value strength will determine the ultimate position of an institution during this period of industry consolidation and restructuring. Understanding relative market value strength is critical to developing consolidation strategy. Market value maps provide a graphic depiction of the financial strengths of competing banks. One can visualize a bank's buying power—or vulnerability—relative to other institutions.

Market value strength is most frequently thought of in terms of total market value, that is, the number of shares of outstanding stock multiplied by the price per share. Total market value is a critical dimension, one that defines the universe of competitors that can afford to acquire a particular bank. However, equal consideration should be given to market-to-book value ratios. As a rule, an acquiring bank needs a market-to-book value ratio equal to or greater than its target if it is to forestall dilution.

On the other hand, potential targets that have a strong market-to-book ratio (or similarly a strong price-earnings ratio) are more difficult to acquire.

Understanding relative market value strength is vital in examining either independence options or the financial viability of potential mergers. Banks with low market-to-book value ratios and small market values have the fewest options; they fall in the lower left-hand corner of a market value map. On the other hand, banks with high market-to-book value ratios and large market capitalization sizes have the most options. They can more readily remain independent and have the most flexibility in choosing which consolidation strategy to pursue: acquiring other institutions, merging to become equal partners with another institution, or becoming a separate subsidiary of a larger bank. These banks fall in the upper right-hand corner of the value map.

In assessing market value strength, it can be useful to map graphically the total market value and market-to-book ratios of major competitors in a particular region. Exhibits 5.9–5.12 present a series of market value maps for each major region. The vertical axis indicates total market value, as measured in absolute dollars. The horizontal axis presents the market-to-ratio book value ratio, as relative market value. For example, Exhibit 5.9 indicates that, at this time, NationsBank had a total market value of $13.33 billion and a market-to-book value ratio of 1.54X. Each region's market value map is presented and interpreted below.

The Southeastern Region

Exhibit 5.9 depicts the present value map for the Southeastern region. A review of this map reveals several important points:

1. There are five dominant banks in the Southeast—NationsBank, First Union, Wachovia, SunTrust, and Barnett. Each of these banks has valuable franchises and many options. However, at this point only NationsBank projects an ambition and has the capacity to become a truly nationwide institution.

2. Now that most banks in Florida, Georgia, and South Carolina have sold out, acquirers will start to increase their focus on Virginia, Alabama, and Tennessee. Virginia has the geographic location and demographic qualities that may cause its banks to hold out for national banking legislation and a wider sell-out auction.

3. Some of the most vulnerable targets in the region include Hibernia, Union Planters, and Riggs. These banks possess meaningful franchises but do not have the market value strength to continue adding signifi-

Exhibit 5.9

SOUTHEAST VALUE MAP

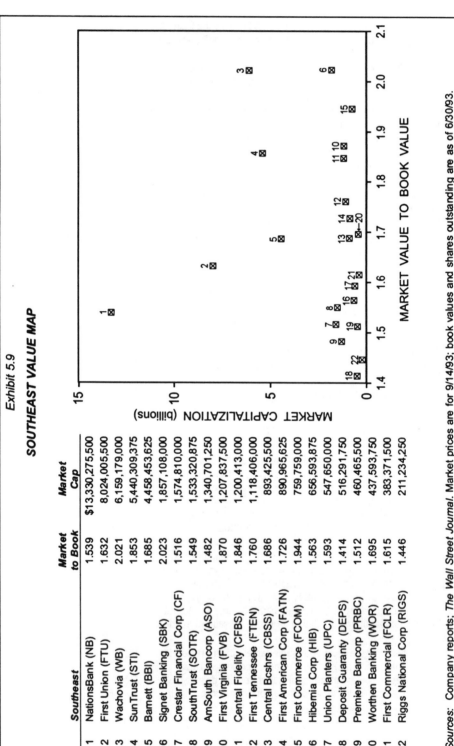

Southeast		Market to Book	Market Cap
1	NationsBank (NB)	1.539	$13,330,275,500
2	First Union (FTU)	1.632	8,024,005,500
3	Wachovia (WB)	2.021	6,159,179,000
4	SunTrust (STI)	1.853	5,440,309,375
5	Barnett (BBI)	1.685	4,458,453,625
6	Signet Banking (SBK)	2.023	1,857,108,000
7	Crestar Financial Corp (CF)	1.516	1,574,810,000
8	SouthTrust (SOTR)	1.549	1,533,320,875
9	AmSouth Bancorp (ASO)	1.482	1,340,701,250
10	First Virginia (FVB)	1.870	1,207,837,500
11	Central Fidelity (CFBS)	1.846	1,200,413,000
12	First Tennessee (FTEN)	1.760	1,118,406,000
13	Central Bcshrs (CBSS)	1.686	893,425,500
14	First American Corp (FATN)	1.726	890,965,625
15	First Commerce (FCOM)	1.944	759,759,000
16	Hibernia Corp (HIB)	1.563	656,593,875
17	Union Planters (UPC)	1.593	547,650,000
18	Deposit Guaranty (DEPS)	1.414	516,291,750
19	Premiere Bancorp (PRBC)	1.512	460,465,500
20	Worthen Banking (WOR)	1.695	437,593,750
21	First Commercial (FCLR)	1.615	383,371,500
22	Riggs National Corp (RIGS)	1.446	211,234,250

Sources: Company reports; *The Wall Street Journal.* Market prices are for 9/14/93; book values and shares outstanding are as of 6/30/93.

cant size or resist an offer by any one of the several larger banks in the region.

The Northeastern Region

Like the Southeastern region, the Northeastern consolidation is quite mature. Several large superregional banks have been created—PNC, Fleet Financial, Bank of New York, and First Fidelity. Most of these banks are actively seeking acquisitions in the region. The money centers continue to be valued at much lower premiums to book but still are among the largest banks in terms of the sheer size of their asset and equity bases. The Northeastern Value Map (Exhibit 5.10) reveals the following:

1. Money-center institutions by and large are shut out of the consolidation game. Chemical Bank, as a result of its merger with Manufacturers Hanover, has a chance to get back into the game, but at the present time it cannot compete for large deals against the more highly valued superregionals. For example, Chemical could not successfully bid for First Interstate or CoreStates (see Chapter 6).

2. Most of the superregionals in the region have market capitalizations that are sufficiently strong to avoid being bought by each other or attacked by a money-center bank. At the large-bank level, only an MOE structure would provide for combinations of the region's larger banks.

3. The two large New England banks, Bank of Boston and Shawmut, have avoided medium-term vulnerability as their market values are improving at a rate that should allow them time to further restructure and grow via in-market mergers. Bank of Boston and Shawmut have both announced expansion plans and are currently in the midst of transactions. Bank of Boston has just consummated deals with Multibank and Society for Savings. Shawmut has definitive agreements to buy New Dartmouth in New Hampshire, People's Bank in Worcester, and Gateway Financial.

4. BayBanks remains New England's most attractive target. In a July 1993 *American Banker* interview, its chairman, William M. Crozier, Jr., noted how coveted his bank has become to would-be acquirers. Although selling out was deemed a distinct possibility, Crozier indicated that he had a range of options and terms he could negotiate, such as with whom he would partner, when he would merge, and what price would be

Money center institutions by and large are shut out of the consolidation game. Chemical Bank, as a result of its merger with Manufacturers Hanover, has a chance to get back into the game, but at the present time it cannot compete for large deals against the more highly valued superregionals.

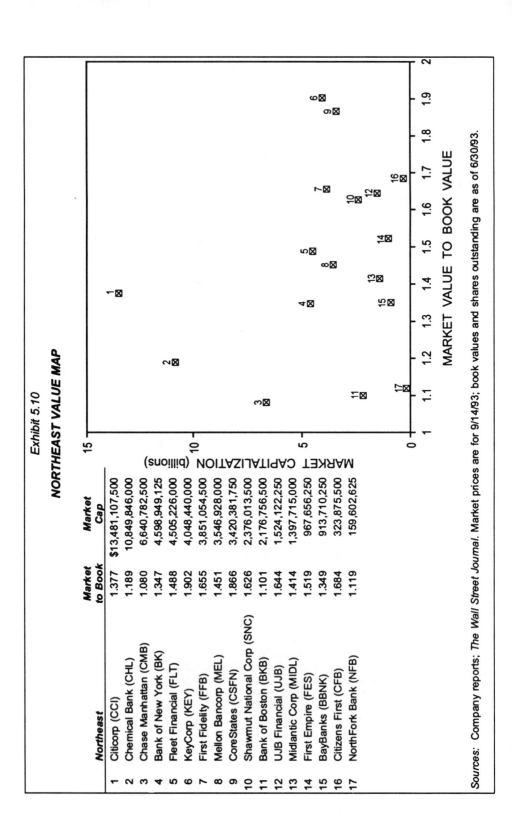

Exhibit 5.10

NORTHEAST VALUE MAP

Northeast		Market to Book	Market Cap
1	Citicorp (CCI)	1.377	$13,481,107,500
2	Chemical Bank (CHL)	1.189	10,849,846,000
3	Chase Manhattan (CMB)	1.080	6,640,782,500
4	Bank of New York (BK)	1.347	4,598,949,125
5	Fleet Financial (FLT)	1.488	4,505,226,000
6	KeyCorp (KEY)	1.902	4,048,440,000
7	First Fidelity (FFB)	1.655	3,851,054,500
8	Mellon Bancorp (MEL)	1.451	3,546,928,000
9	CoreStates (CSFN)	1.866	3,420,381,750
10	Shawmut National Corp (SNC)	1.626	2,376,013,500
11	Bank of Boston (BKB)	1.101	2,176,756,500
12	UJB Financial (UJB)	1.644	1,524,122,250
13	Midlantic Corp (MIDL)	1.414	1,397,715,000
14	First Empire (FES)	1.519	967,656,250
15	BayBanks (BBNK)	1.349	913,710,250
16	Citizens First (CFB)	1.684	323,875,500
17	NorthFork Bank (NFB)	1.119	159,602,625

Sources: Company reports; *The Wall Street Journal.* Market prices are for 9/14/93; book values and shares outstanding are as of 6/30/93.

appropriate. Crozier clearly has a strong hand to play out.

The Midwest Region

The Midwestern region is one of the most interesting geographic areas to examine. Structural and regulatory constraints have severely limited the acquisition opportunities available to midwestern banks. First, restrictive banking laws in Illinois prevented large Chicago banks from becoming even larger, widely branched institutions that could evolve into superregional and national institutions. In Chapter 3, it was noted that the relative restrictions in state banking laws had a great deal to do with the current size and strength of North Carolina banks versus banks from Illinois. Also, the relative size and market value gains of some banks from the other midwestern states owe to these same restrictions. In the Midwest, BANC ONE, Norwest, PNC, and NBD are all stronger acquirers than First Chicago, Illinois' largest bank.

At the outset of interstate consolidation in the Midwest, many midwestern banks were of similar size. In 1986 the largest banks in Michigan, Ohio, and Wisconsin ranged in size between $7 billion to $9 billion in total assets. Few dominant banks in either size or operating performance existed. The MOE concept was suggested, but at the time, few midwest banks found this option appealing.

To compound regulatory problems, the midwestern states all defined their banking regions somewhat differently. In short, no two midwestern states agreed on which states constituted the Midwest. This structural reality prevented acquirers from developing regionwide expansion programs. This situation strongly contrasts with the common regional definition established in the Southeast that underpinned its managed bank consolidation.

To illustrate how regional definitions impeded cross-state merger strategies, consider Illinois law. By initially recognizing only those states that are contiguous to its borders as being in its region, Ohio and Minnesota were left out. Some Michigan banks that feared being taken over by Ohio banks bought Illinois banks, which in effect gave them a poison pill against Ohio acquirers. As a result, Illinois law not only undercut the growth ambitions of some Illinois banks, but somewhat warped the evolution of the Midwest region.

Given this backdrop, the Midwestern Value Map (Exhibit 5.11) suggests several ideas:

1. Chicago will not be the focal point of Midwest banking. At this time, First Chicago and Continental can only be considered long shots to be regional or national leaders in the consolidation game. First Chicago has a very valuable metropolitan Chicago franchise

Exhibit 5.11

MIDWEST VALUE MAP

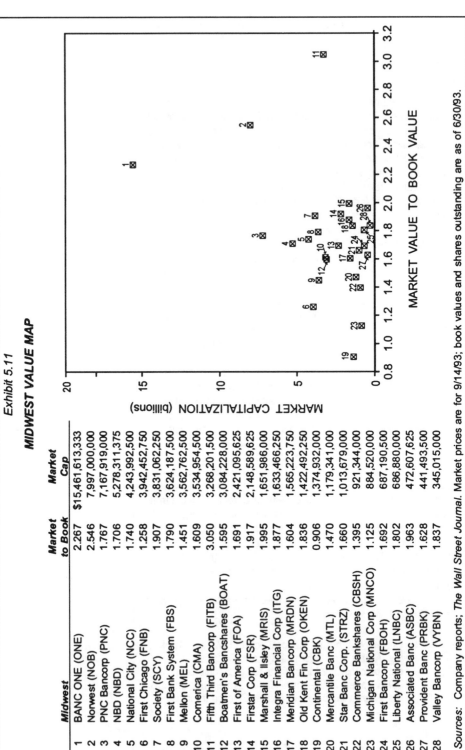

Midwest	Market to Book	Market Cap
1 BANC ONE (ONE)	2.267	$15,461,613,333
2 Norwest (NOB)	2.546	7,997,000,000
3 PNC Bancorp (PNC)	1.767	7,167,919,000
4 NBD (NBD)	1.706	5,278,311,375
5 National City (NCC)	1.740	4,243,992,500
6 First Chicago (FNB)	1.258	3,942,452,750
7 Society (SCY)	1.907	3,831,062,250
8 First Bank System (FBS)	1.790	3,624,187,500
9 Mellon (MEL)	1.451	3,562,762,500
10 Comerica (CMA)	1.609	3,534,954,500
11 Fifth Third Bancorp (FITB)	3.050	3,268,201,500
12 Boatmen's Bancshares (BOAT)	1.595	3,084,228,000
13 First of America (FOA)	1.691	2,421,095,625
14 Firstar Corp (FSR)	1.917	2,148,589,625
15 Marshall & Ilsley (MRIS)	1.995	1,651,986,000
16 Integra Financial Corp (ITG)	1.877	1,633,466,250
17 Meridian Bancorp (MRDN)	1.604	1,565,223,750
18 Old Kent Fin Corp (OKEN)	1.836	1,422,492,250
19 Continental (CBK)	0.906	1,374,932,000
20 Mercantile Banc (MTL)	1.470	1,179,341,000
21 Star Banc Corp. (STRZ)	1.660	1,013,679,000
22 Commerce Bankshares (CBSH)	1.395	921,344,000
23 Michigan National Corp (MNCO)	1.125	884,520,000
24 First Bancorp (FBOH)	1.692	687,190,500
25 Liberty National (LNBC)	1.802	686,880,000
26 Associated Banc (ASBC)	1.963	472,607,625
27 Provident Banc (PRBK)	1.628	441,493,500
28 Valley Bancorp (VYBN)	1.837	345,015,000

Sources: Company reports; *The Wall Street Journal.* Market prices are for 9/14/93; book values and shares outstanding are as of 6/30/93.

but has not been in a position to successfully acquire banks. Throughout the interstate consolidation waves, it has not had a strong enough stock price (currency) to purchase banks in neighboring states. Its only retail branch mergers to date have been small and defensive in nature.

Continental Bank has exited retail banking altogether and has a specialized business banking focus. Moreover, because it does not have a retail banking network, it is difficult to surmise who might view Continental as a target. Neither the geographic expansion of the retail banking business nor elimination of redundant retail delivery systems can be motivating factors for an acquirer. Nevertheless, it does possess a great middle-market commercial banking clientele and other high value units such as private equity and private banking. Additionally, it would greatly enhance the size of whoever acquired it.

2. BANC ONE, Norwest, PNC, and NBD are the strongest players in the region. BANC ONE and Norwest appear to have broken away in terms of market value. Although Norwest is smaller than BANC ONE in asset size, they both enjoy superior market-to-book value ratios.

3. Other banks attempting to become superregional survivors include National City, Comerica, Society, First of America, First Bank System, and Boatmen's. To survive, some of these banks may have to merge among themselves. Alternatively, some may be forced to accept offers too good to refuse.

4. Several banks in the Midwest will be increasingly coveted as targets. Potential targets could include Michigan National, Old Kent, First Bancorp of Ohio, Huntington, Provident, Star Banc, Firstar, Marshall and Ilsley, Associated, Liberty National, and Mercantile. However, because most of these banks are presently performing very well, each would be expensive to acquire.

5. ABN Amro, a Netherlands bank, continues to make large investments in Chicago. Its most recent acquisitions have involved large thrifts, Talman Federal and Cragin Federal. Although ABN has holdings in Canada and New York, it is clear that Chicago is its top focus. To date it has not ventured away from Chicago into other midwestern states.

6. Harris Bancorp is another foreign-owned bank in Chicago. Its Canadian owner, Bank of Montreal, has not aggressively expanded to date. However, recently it has appointed a new CEO and announced a modest, in-market expansion plan. Given Harris Bank's large parent and strong Chicago franchise, it could play a wild card role.

The Western Region

The West Coast is today already highly consolidated. The lack of many sizable California banks to buy will force some acquirers to enter the state via a thrift purchase and build out a core banking franchise with primarily thrift acquisitions. Although California is mired in a recession, several banks with national banking designs will be expected to leap for the opportunity to gain entry into the nation's largest state. The Western Value Map (Exhibit 5.12) suggests the following points:

1. BankAmerica is the only Western bank that has reached a size and market value that projects a clear chance of ultimate survival. It has successfully extended itself into the Northwest as well as the Southwest. Additionally, it has shown serious interest in entering the Midwest and New England.

2. Wells Fargo is generally considered a well-managed institution with the second best market share in California. However, Wells has not been successful in launching an interstate banking strategy and is beginning to lose relative market value strength. Additionally, Wells Fargo's strategic position has been impaired by its vast commercial real estate portfolio. Obviously, Wells Fargo would be an attractive target for some of the nation's largest, most highly valued banks. However, only the highest valued banks could afford Wells if it decided to sell out.

3. The only other California banks that have assets exceeding $10 billion are First Interstate (FI) and Union Bank. With nearly $50 billion in assets, FI is often mentioned as the leading California bank target. However, current management has greatly improved FI's earnings and has indicated that it would like to remain independent with a view of being an acquirer. Because of the size of its Western franchise and the importance, as well as paucity, of California bank entry vehicles, FI will probably remain one of the most visible targets in the country. For this reason, we chose to analyze a hypothetical purchase of FI by sev-

Exhibit 5.12

WEST VALUE MAP

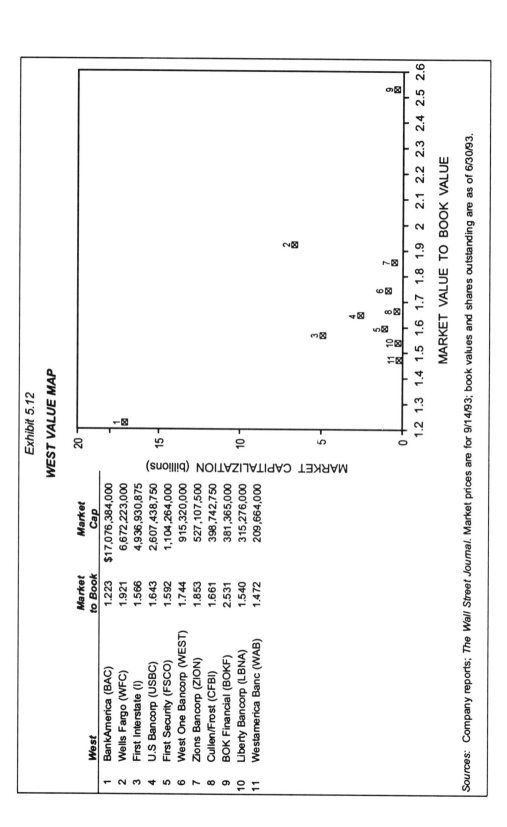

West		Market to Book	Market Cap
1	BankAmerica (BAC)	1.223	$17,076,384,000
2	Wells Fargo (WFC)	1.921	6,672,223,000
3	First Interstate (I)	1.566	4,936,930,875
4	U.S Bancorp (USBC)	1.643	2,607,438,750
5	First Security (FSCO)	1.592	1,104,264,000
6	West One Bancorp (WEST)	1.744	915,320,000
7	Zions Bancorp (ZION)	1.853	527,107,500
8	Cullen/Frost (CFBI)	1.661	398,742,750
9	BOK Financial (BOKF)	2.531	381,365,000
10	Liberty Bancorp (LBNA)	1.540	315,276,000
11	Westamerica Banc (WAB)	1.472	209,664,000

Sources: Company reports; *The Wall Street Journal.* Market prices are for 9/14/93; book values and shares outstanding are as of 6/30/93.

eral potential acquirers (see Chapter 6). Interestingly, Wells Fargo surfaces as a strong buyer candidate, if such a transaction were to be considered.

The Bank of Tokyo owns the majority of Union Bank. At its size ($16.7 billion), Union would normally be a takeover target. However, its Japanese owners most likely purchased it for strategic purposes. Specifically, many Japanese banks deem California bank ownership an important part of their Pacific Rim trading programs. Accordingly, the sale of this bank, in the short run, is not likely.

4. Other Western states also have some attractive targets. The most prominent one is U.S. Bancorp. With approximately $21 billion in assets and a dominant market share in Oregon, U.S. Bancorp should receive increasing attention. Other potential targets in the West include: First Security (Utah), Zions (Utah), and West One (Idaho).

A National Value Map

The region-by-region value map analysis presented above ignores the fact that the consolidation movement will become increasingly interregional and national in scope. Many of the large superregional banks are really now considering mergers that would essentially create coast-to-coast competitors. A national value map is necessary to address inter-region consolidation from the proper perspective.

Exhibit 5.13 indicates who some of the potential national players might be: BankAmerica, BANC ONE, Norwest, PNC, NationsBank, First Union, and Chemical Bank. As discussed earlier, NationsBank and First Union are still today somewhat confined by the Southern regional compact, but have ambitions that are national in scope. Examples of banks that could become cross-country merger targets for this group of national players include: First Interstate, U.S. Bancorp, Old Kent, CoreStates, and Mercantile. Each of these banks faces an uphill battle to survive in the long run yet would provide their acquirer with a meaningful market presence in a new or contiguous geography.

Looking Into Our Crystal Ball: Strategic Survivors List

Banks' survivability prospects can be analyzed by breaking out their relative position against the key strategic survival determinants. The expected survivors landscape is displayed here in four basic categories (Exhibit 5.14):

Exhibit 5.13

NATIONAL VALUE MAP

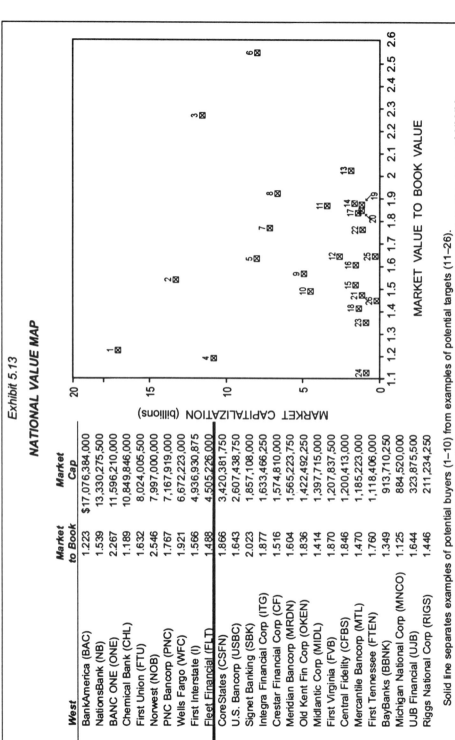

	West	Market to Book	Market Cap
1	BankAmerica (BAC)	1.223	$17,076,384,000
2	NationsBank (NB)	1.539	13,330,275,500
3	BANC ONE (ONE)	2.267	11,596,210,000
4	Chemical Bank (CHL)	1.189	10,849,846,000
5	First Union (FTU)	1.632	8,024,005,500
6	Norwest (NOB)	2.546	7,997,000,000
7	PNC Bancorp (PNC)	1.767	7,167,919,000
8	Wells Fargo (WFC)	1.921	6,672,223,000
9	First Interstate (I)	1.566	4,936,930,875
10	Fleet Financial (FLT)	1.488	4,505,226,000
11	CoreStates (CSFN)	1.866	3,420,381,750
12	U.S. Bancorp (USBC)	1.643	2,607,438,750
13	Signet Banking (SBK)	2.023	1,857,108,000
14	Integra Financial Corp (ITG)	1.877	1,633,466,250
15	Crestar Financial Corp (CF)	1.516	1,574,810,000
16	Meridian Bancorp (MRDN)	1.604	1,565,223,750
17	Old Kent Fin Corp (OKEN)	1.836	1,422,492,250
18	Midlantic Corp (MIDL)	1.414	1,397,715,000
19	First Virginia (FVB)	1.870	1,207,837,500
20	Central Fidelity (CFBS)	1.846	1,200,413,000
21	Mercantile Bancorp (MTL)	1.470	1,185,223,000
22	First Tennessee (FTEN)	1.760	1,118,406,000
23	BayBanks (BBNK)	1.349	913,710,250
24	Michigan National Corp (MNCO)	1.125	884,520,000
25	UJB Financial (UJB)	1.644	323,875,500
26	Riggs National Corp (RIGS)	1.446	211,234,250

Solid line separates examples of potential buyers (1–10) from examples of potential targets (11–26).

Sources: Company reports; *The Wall Street Journal.* Market prices are for 9/14/93; book values and shares outstanding are as of 6/30/93.

I   Strong: High-Probability Survivors

II   Strong, but May Not Stay Independent

III   Perhaps at a Decision Point

IV   Probable Takeovers

We will discuss the four categories presented in Exhibit 5.14 in reverse order.

Probable Takeovers

In reviewing Category IV, Probable Takeovers, we note two fundamental types of banks that we expect to ultimately be taken over. The first includes institutions that have become quite weak in terms of capital strength, and improving operating performance cannot help fast enough. Midlantic (New Jersey), Michigan National, Hibernia, and MNC Financial (Maryland) fit this description. Capital-weak institutions tend to attract buyout offers and often find such offers attractive. Only recently, MNC merged with NationsBank. Other larger institutions that were taken out as a result of weak capital and operating positions include Ameritrust (by Society) and Bank of New England (by Fleet Financial).

A second type of institution that tends to be a probable takeover target includes those banks that have become too small to remain independent. Among the banks listed in column four of Exhibit 5.14 are: AmSouth, Central Fidelity, First Tennessee, and Star Banc. Note that banks in this category may be quite large by traditional terms, and many are high performers. *Most of these banks are in the $10 billion range in asset size. However, their small relative size makes it difficult for them to make significant acquisitions of sufficient size to change their long-term prospects. On the other hand, their financial health and significant local market shares make them very attractive targets.* Those with high performance do not, however, feel immediate pressure to sell and, to a certain extent, can decide when and to whom they will sell.

Perhaps at a Decision Point

Banks in Category III, Perhaps at a Decision Point, have an approximate size range of $10 billion to $35 billion in assets and $1.4 billion to $4.2 billion in market capitalization. The largest include National City, KeyCorp, Society, and First Fidelity. Although the banks on this list are quite large, they face the same difficulty in acquiring large target banks as banks in Category IV.

The largest and strongest superregionals enjoy greater size in terms of market capitalization and/or market-to-book value. This gives them great advantage when attractive smaller banks are

Exhibit 5.14

THE SURVIVOR LANDSCAPE CONTINUES TO EVOLVE WITH SEVERAL POWERFUL LEADERS

(Market Capitalization in $ Millions)
Prices as of 9/30/93

I — Strong: High-Probability Survivors		II — Strong but May Not Stay Independent[2]		III — Perhaps at a Decision Point		IV — Probable Takeovers[3]	
BankAmerica	$15,653	SunTrust	$5,581	National City	$4,224	MNC Financial	$1,617
BANC ONE	$15,098	NBD	$5,499	Key Corp	$3,833	Midlantic	$1,430
NationsBank[1]	$13,108	First Interstate	$5,051	Society	$3,743	Michigan National	$890
Norwest[1]	$8,033	Bank of New York	$4,703	First Fidelity	$3,626	Hibernia	$698
First Union[1]	$8,003	Barnett Banks	$4,373	Comerica	$3,223	Signet	$1,942
PNC[1]	$7,286	First Chicago	$4,057	Boatmen's	$3,152	Marshall & Ilsley	$1,568
Wachovia	$6,788	Mellon	$3,484	First Bank System	$3,781	Integra Financial	$1,608
Wells Fargo	$7,019	CoreStates	$3,391	Republic	$2,776	Crestar	$1,613
Fleet Financial	$4,761	Fifth Third	$3,278	U.S. Bancorp	$2,620	SouthTrust	$1,524
Citicorp	$14,327	State Street	$2,710	First of America	$2,421	Meridian	$1,525
Chemical Bank	$11,354	Northern Trust	$2,200	Shawmut	$2,294	AmSouth	$1,330
JP Morgan	$15,102			Bank of Boston	$2,177	Old Kent	$1,417
Bankers Trust	$6,583			Huntington	$2,485	Bancorp of Hawaii	$1,149
Chase Manhattan	$6,801			Firstar	$2,133	First Alabama	$1,291
				Continental Bank	$1,428	UJB	$1,537
						Mercantile	$1,188
						Central Fidelity	$1,191
						First Tennessee	$1,125
						First Security	$1,104
						Star Banc	$1,058
						Wilmington Trust	$1,126
						Commerce Bancshares	$968
						BayBanks	$923
						West One	$964
						First American	$875
						Liberty National	$700
						Bank South	$687
						First Bancorp of Ohio	$534
						Valley Bancorp	$492

1 Could be larger than Citicorp in market capitalization before end of decade.
2 Takeover possibility, but would be very expensive.
3 Too small, weak, and/or low market valuation.
  Solid line separates banks that are targets due to weak performance (above the line) and banks that are targets due to small size (below the line).

Source: Larry A. Frieder, Florida A and M University, Tallahassee, FL.

sold or auctioned. There is risk that these Category III institutions will have to dangerously stretch and potentially dilute excessively to win significant deals. However, at the same time, getting bigger is critical to improving their long-term prospects. Careful strategic navigation is required. There is evidence (see Chapter 6) that when pursuing acquisitions, paying too much often results in acquirers subsequently becoming acquirees as a result of ill-advised transactions.

Many of the banks in this "At a Decision Point" category can do fill-in mergers aggressively. They are able to compete for smaller transactions and can create a lot of value in doing so. To these banks' advantage, many of the largest superregionals have lost interest in collecting small franchises.

Many banks on this list are strong or aggressively rebounding performers. Although it is doubtful that they can become national competitors, they do have a number of strategic options. The first tests the limits for survival as a high-performing regional bank. Opinions vary on the ultimate feasibility of this option. History will be written by those institutions that achieve the required performance levels. Wachovia appears to have selected this option. We expect to see a few more. To succeed, effective execution will be key.

A second option is to attempt to bulk up to move to the next size level (Category II) through a merger of equals. Two banks in this category that find themselves shut out of the acquisition game could use the size and potential synergies of a large merger to be able once again to compete for deals on a national basis. One must be mindful, however, of the limitations of an MOE discussed earlier in this chapter. That is, one party may end up in control, which means one party sold out for little or no premium. Also, merger integration efficiency may be impeded by the social terms of such deals.

The recently announced interregional MOE between Society and KeyCorp well exemplifies the "At a Decision Point" MOE (see James J. McDermott-Richard I. Stillinger's sidebar, *Swift Merger Pace: More to Give Up the Ghost*, page 132). The initial Society-KeyCorp MOE announcement was greeted by great skepticism by the stock market. Analysts reacted differently to the merits of this deal. The MOE debate aside, the banking community will closely examine the New KeyCorp for lessons applicable to their own strategic cases. This deal could set off several other MOEs in that many other banks may fear that the range of potential partners may narrow quickly.

Another recent MOE example of two firms that were in this category, Comerica and Manufacturers National of Detroit, illustrates the applicability of the MOE concept. These firms were also struggling from a strategic standpoint. Continuing their acquisition growth was proving difficult. Management of both institutions believed that the efficiencies available through an in-market merger would allow them to compete and perform better. The resulting merged bank hopes its size, capital strength, and operating prospects can enhance its chances for long-term survival.

All banks in Category III retain an option to sell out. However, they must be careful that their growth and size do not reduce their selling options or, more importantly, the magnitude of their potential sale premium to the disadvantage of their shareholders.

Strong Banks That May Not Choose to Remain Independent

The second category listed in Exhibit 5.14 identifies some very large banks that nevertheless may not choose, or be able to stay, independent. This list also includes three high-performance banks (Northern Trust, State Street, and Fifth Third), which are not as large as the other banks on the list, but enjoy very high market valuation.

Excluding these high-performing banks, the approximate size range in this category is $35 billion to $50 billion in assets and market capitalizations ranging from approximately $3.3 billion to $5.6 billion. These include: Wells Fargo, Barnett, Sun-Trust, NBD, Bank of New York, First Chicago, Mellon, Core-States, and First Interstate.

The banks in this category have built impressive and valuable franchises. However, their size in terms of market capitalization and valuation, as well as their existing franchise positions, are a significant notch below banks that have broken away to the next level, that is, the Category I institutions.

The options of these banks are somewhat similar to those available to the middle-positioned banks. Given their size and performance trends, these institutions can pursue long-run survival and should encounter much less outside takeover pressure vis-a-vis the middle-ranked firms. At the same time, an available strategic option would be to pursue an MOE. The other alternative would be to simply sell out. These banks should have considerable negotiation strength on the sale option. They can basically determine many of the particulars of any proposed transaction. To be sure, from the would-be acquirers' perspective, the takeover of any one of these institutions would be very expensive.

One can only speculate as to the end game of the two high-performing trust banks, State Street and Northern Trust, on this list. In doing so, one should note that the investment management and processing businesses in which each is engaged are subject to increasing scale economies. Additionally, these business lines are becoming highly global. These observations may suggest combinations between these institutions. Alternatively, combina-

Generally, these banks have not been as aggressive or successful in their merger strategies as those in Category I.

tions with other domestic or international competitors may be considered.

Fifth Third: The performance champion

With approximately $10.7 billion in assets, Fifth Third is relatively small compared to the other large banks listed in Category II. Nevertheless, Fifth Third's return on assets over the years has been the highest among regional banks. As pointed out earlier in this chapter, the market values its assets at an astounding 33.8 percent per dollar. Fifth Third's outstanding record can best be understood in terms of the success factors outlined in Chapter 1. Whereas most high performing banks excel at one or two of the key success factors listed, Fifth Third excels at most of them: strategic business portfolio mix; acquisition templates; cost discipline; innovative retail distribution and marketing; relationship banking; and credit quality. In recognition of this excellence, Salomon Brothers, for the third time in four years, has listed Fifth Third as overall individual performance champion in its *Bank Annual Edition.*

> *Whereas most high performing banks excel at one or two of the key success factors listed, Fifth Third excels at most of them . . .*

High Probability Survivors

The first column of Exhibit 5.14 identifies those institutions that currently seem best positioned for ultimate survival. Their market capitalization ranges from $4.7 billion to $15.6 billion. Seven banks on the list—BankAmerica, BANC ONE, NationsBank, Norwest, First Union, PNC, and Fleet—are classified as megaregionals that, to varying degrees, appear to have nationwide strategies. Wachovia and Wells Fargo seem content to be large and highly valued superregionals.

The large New York banks on this list have altogether different strategies. J.P. Morgan and Bankers Trust have essentially transformed themselves into investment banks. Retail deposit taking and portfolio lending are of no interest to them. In contrast, Chemical Bank is attempting to transform itself into a superregional bank with selected wholesale focus. Chemical's immediate challenge is to wring cost efficiencies from its recent merger. Strong results in this area may provide it with a higher market-to-book ratio, or currency, to compete better for large bank deals as they arise. In Chapter 6, we find that Chemical Bank, at its present valuation, most likely could not win the hypothetical deals that we analyzed. Although Citicorp still is the largest bank in terms of asset size, some megaregional banks have passed it in market capitalization rank. Citicorp's series of credit problems during the past eight years has limited its ability to establish an effective nationwide branching network. For the foreseeable future, Citicorp is not expected to be a factor on the national acquisition scene.

The strategic initiatives of the seven leading contenders for nationwide banking survival status have become the prime focus of bank analysts. Consider the status of Fleet. After nursing its credit problems for nearly three years, Fleet hopes to return to acquisition activity. Regulatory constraints may, however, restrict the bank's degrees of freedom. Recently, its chairperson, Terrence Murray, spoke of the prospect of an MOE. Rumors have been published regarding MOE discussions with both CoreStates and NationsBank. Perhaps this is a sign that the size of some of the largest superregional bank franchises is still not large enough to ensure permanent autonomy. The case of Fleet highlights the fact that even the nation's largest banks are not assured survival.

After nursing its credit problems for nearly three years, Fleet hopes to return to acquisition activity.

Like Fleet Financial, PNC has recovered from serious credit problems and has reentered the acquisition game with the purchase of an eastern Ohio bank holding company and Sears' mortgage subsidiary. Similarly, NationsBank has also made some selected nonbank purchases—consumer assets from Chrysler Financial and a Chicago options firm, Chicago Research and Trading (CRT).

BANC ONE, First Union, and Norwest are all actively filling in their existing regional franchises. On the West Coast, BankAmerica has been busy implementing its megamerger with Security Pacific in a difficult California economy. One would expect its acquisition strategy will reactivate soon and lead to new regions.

Our discussion, thus far, is based on current situations. Several times during the various consolidation waves, however, banks' relative strategic positions or category specifications have shifted. For example, at the trough of regional recessions, banks such as First Fidelity, Shawmut, and First Bank System were quite weak and vulnerable to takeout. Each of these banks subsequently strengthened and no longer should be classified as vulnerable. In fact, First Fidelity, under the leadership of CEO Tony Terracciano, may leverage (through value-additive acquisitions) its investor partnership with Banco Santander enough to be able to jump to Category II. Shawmut and First Bank System are each pursuing their own unique turnaround stories and now have good reasons to believe they can build strong, independent regional franchises. The proper strategic decisions, coupled with effective execution, provide the opportunity to write industry history.

Summing Up

The forces of consolidation will be relentless. The number of thrifts, community banks, and single-state bank holding companies will continue their serious decline. Most of the superregional bank holding companies are poised to cover their regions completely, either through contiguous state mergers or by filling in their existing franchises. Gridlock, or checkmate as the case may be, will eventually result. In some regions, it is already beginning to set in.

Those banks that have successfully completed their regional expansion must now establish a posture on interregional mergers. In the case of the Southeastern superregionals, the Southern regional banking compact will eventually be opened to facilitate cross-regional consolidation. Whether in state or federal government hands, this advancement of interstate legislation promises to be complex and difficult.

Although there are still numerous banks, there are far fewer desirable acquisition candidates. The merger pace is expected to quicken as targets begin to see the number of available and attractive bidders decline. In cases where a target is deemed to be critical to the survival of an acquirer, hostile takeovers may occur.

Besides the cost savings and revenue enhancements that acquirers seek from acquisitions, benefits from loan diversification are increasingly being sought. Interregional and cross-country mergers could join institutions whose loans have much lower correlations than mergers within a state or region. Given the paramount role of credit risk in a bank's profit equation, many argue that banks that fail to rid themselves of diversifiable risk are naive. Under any scenario, the benefits of consolidation are numerous, though the exact course it will take is uncertain. Critical to the new, emerging industry paradigm is a more concentrated industry structure.

Having explored the broad bank consolidation landscape, in the next chapter we turn to the financial mechanics that underlie bank mergers and examine the fundamentals of merger valuation. In doing so, we explore the tactics of successful merger strategies, and gain perspective of the alchemy of value creation through acquisitions. If there is one key skill for succeeding in this period of industry transition, it is creating shareholder value through acquisitions.

6

Doing Deals and Merger Mechanics

Although bank mergers are not a new phenomena, the merger waves of the past 10 years significantly differ from those of previous eras. In today's consolidating environment, mergers have become one of the most critical tools available for use by banks (as either acquirers or acquirees) to achieve their strategic objectives.

One lesson learned early on is that not all sellers are losers, and not all buyers are winners. In fact, there is evidence that indicates selling shareholders have gained wealth transfers from acquirers who often destroyed their shareholders' value in the process of paying large premiums. Often acquirers themselves became doomed targets as a result of doing value-destroying acquisitions.

In Chapter 5, the ongoing arena of industry consolidation was reviewed. Because mergers have played and will continue to play a central role in the restructuring of the banking industry, and the margin of error from the shareholders' perspective is so small, it is important to examine the mechanics of mergers and the experience gleaned thus far in the consolidation movement. While this chapter will not qualify the reader to negotiate a merger on behalf of their institution, it will provide an understanding of what is involved in doing a bank deal.

Merger Fundamentals

The ultimate objective of corporate finance, hence merger mechanics, is to maximize shareholder value. Bank corporate finance is no different in theory from general corporate finance applied to other industries.

Discounted Cash Flow

The core model for valuation is based on discounted cash flow (DCF). Sometimes earnings are used as a proxy for cash flow. Unfortunately, the financial press and other industry observers often discuss price to book value multiples instead of discounted cash flow in their critique of deals. Other gauges that sometimes come into play include respective premiums over existing market price, magnitude of earnings dilution, premiums paid for core deposits, price to assets, and price to hard book value. A whole set of valuation proxies have developed, but they cannot substitute for DCF analysis. While those most intimate with the mechanics of mergers insist on the discipline of DCF analysis, the popular press' discussion can lead to a misunderstanding regarding how merger valuation works in practice.

There are two components that drive pricing considerations in the market: economic values and strategic values. Economic value, also referred to as fundamental value, is based on discounted cash flow. Strategic value encompasses fundamental value and, based upon strategic advantages it might provide, the additional amount a buyer is willing to pay for a franchise. This can be quantified as the premium of acquisition price over fundamental value. Strategic value incorporates the notion that a buyer may gain a particular strategic position and operating advantage, within its long-term consolidation strategy, as a result of a purchase.

The fair or fundamental value of a bank is determined by computing its discounted future earnings. Although determination of fair market value may involve the use of several methodologies, calculation of the present value of future earnings is an effective initial indicator. It is often assumed that earnings per share (EPS) estimates for a financial entity constitute an adequate approximation of cash flow. Deal-specific adjustments, however, are usually made. For example, unusually large amortization of intangibles after a purchase acquisition, or highly conservative loan loss provisions that effectively distort true earnings and cash flow, would require adjustment in DCF analysis.

The analytical process involves estimation of future earnings based upon a comprehensive review of historical performance over a relevant period, generally five years. Next, an appropriate discount rate for computing the present value of future year's earnings must be determined. The discount rate assumption is an estimation of the rate of return required by an investor to compensate for the risk assumption applicable to the target entity. We discussed the cost of equity concept earlier in Chapter 4. Finally, each future year's earnings is then discounted back to the present. The sum of the present values constitutes fair market value. To cure imperfections and address the potential biases of subjectivity, analysts often conduct sensitivity analyses of the key variables to ascertain alternative values that, in effect, establish the boundaries of fair market value. Because there is never an analytically derived definitive value, understanding the nature of the important variables tested for sensitivity is critical.

Another extension of fair market valuation involves breakup value. This analysis, made popular during the leveraged buyout-intensive 1980s, involves analyzing the sum of the parts versus the whole. It was clear that the conglomerate movement and diversification led to decreases in inherent shareholder value when earnings efficiencies were not achieved and managements were unable to capture the competitive value of each separate business unit. The market imposed a valuation penalty on the conglomerate whole. The comparison of market prices against breakup values launched a new era that alerted management to the importance of shareholder value in the nonfinancial sector. The same concept is applicable to banking. As discussed in Chapter 4, when management evaluates its composite business mix and computes breakup values, it is often clear which lines of business should be divested. In the case of mergers and acquisitions, it is sometimes important to look at individual business line valuations.

Book Value: Its Role in Valuation

The principal accounting concepts used most in the valuation of banks are earnings per share and book value. Although stated book value is often referred to in bank stock market and merger discussions, it is clearly less important to value determination vis-a-vis the earnings variable. Nevertheless, aspects of a bank's book value deserve attention.

Book value often becomes the valuation basis when analyzing banks and thrifts with suppressed earnings. If earnings are not normalized or are nonexistent, a financial institution must trade or be sold on a book-value basis. Wall Street's use of book values in these situations explains the frequent payment of either high EPS multiples or takeout premiums much greater than existing market prices for many thrift acquisitions, even when their earnings are negligible or even negative.

To establish a basis for valuation, bank analysts often adjust stated book value by eliminating goodwill and other intangible values; the result is tangible book value. Computing hard book value is often the next step. This calculation adjusts for several other balance sheet components that do not represent true values. For example, asset quality adjustments are made by discounting the value of specific assets as shown on the balance sheet (e.g., "haircutting" the loan portfolio) to make an assessment of realizable value. Alternatively, a bank with a conservative loan loss reserve policy may show a net loan value below reasonable expectations of realizable value. In this case, a portion of the loan loss reserve may be appropriately added back to compute a higher hard book. These analyses are separate from the accounting treatment of reserves and loss provision.

Often a bank's investment account may also possess unrealized gains or losses that would need to be marked to market and included in a hard book value. Other hidden assets or franchise values such as undervalued real estate or excess pension funding would require detailed analysis that could lead to other book value adjustments.

The book value approach essentially sets a floor for merger pricing so that even an institution without earnings has a liquidation value. Takeout values at a significant discount to hard book value are rare. Frequently, takeout price floors will also include a premium for core deposits in addition to the established book value.

Dilution: The Focal Point of Bank Deals

In practice, upon the announcement of a deal or an offer, the stock market assesses the potential impact of the merger on the financial statements of the acquirer and imposes an immediate price adjustment to account for any implied earnings and book value dilution. Ordinarily, EPS dilution is the basis of the market's reaction. A transaction is dilutive if it reduces future expected EPS. Conversely, if future implied earnings are expected to increase, the transaction is termed accretive.

The critical decision criterion used in evaluating an announced transaction is the assessment of whether the deal is permanently dilutive. Permanent dilution results from the payment of a market premium for an institution and subsequently failing to realize sufficient earnings to earn back the premium. Investors make this type of assessment whenever a deal is announced. The key element in such an analysis is determination of potential cost savings and earnings efficiencies to be initially and ultimately realized by the merged entity. Although more difficult to factor in, the potential strategic value of the deal should also be assessed.

There are two principal methods that analysts use to measure dilution. One requires a comparison of the buyer's published 12-month EPS estimate with the pro forma (postmerger) consolidated EPS for the same period. This is the traditional approach. Well-known bank analyst David Cates emphasizes another method called dilution at the margin. This involves a comparison of premerger EPS against the computed price paid for earnings of the acquired entity. The importance of this method is its ability to isolate individual transaction effects that may be lost in transactions between institutions that are widely disparate in size. Cates points out that when a very large bank acquires a very small bank, the marginal dilution, however great, will be masked because the blended dilution is so small. However, a series of small dilutive mergers can adversely affect cumulative blended EPS of the acquirer.

The book value approach essentially sets a floor for merger pricing so that even an institution without earnings has a liquidation value. Takeout values at a significant discount to hard book value are rare.

A review of merger pricing evidence later in this chapter will show that three bank merger waves occurred in the 1980s. In the first wave (1985–86), acquirers frequently undertook double digit dilution, previously unprecedented and considered very questionable. In the next wave (1987–88), dilution standards moderated to single digits. Soon, however, the standard was again lowered, this time to the present standard, which is essentially intolerant of dilution; i.e., the implied dilution target is zero. This standard has been operative from 1989 to 1993 although many banks have met it through aggressive cost-saving programs that are considered part and parcel of the deal. The market has come of age with respect to dilution. Analysts and merger participants have developed a more synchronized understanding of the proper role of dilution in a consolidation strategy.

Different types of transactions, in-market versus contiguous, warrant different cost takeout assumptions and dilution parameters. While it may have been considered adequate to rely on cost takeout rules of thumb in the past, a much higher degree of analytical precision is emerging today. Accounting concepts are increasingly taking a back seat to operating decisions. The market looks very closely at the core nature of each deal, evaluating both fundamental and strategic values. The market accepts no dilution unless significant potential cost savings are realizable. If cost-savings estimates are reasonable and probable, and significant strategic importance can be assigned to the target, then moderate dilution may be tolerable.

In assessing dilution, market analysts attempt to quantify its threat by determining the earnings growth rate required to overcome any initial dilution resulting from a merger. Many bank holding companies hold out 15 percent as their target rate of EPS growth. Using this growth rate goal for acquirers, it is possible to calculate the required growth rate to equalize the EPS of the acquired and acquiring banks by some target date. Generally, the market expects the consolidated entity to earn back dilution within one or two years. If cost savings are not to be realized very early, adverse market response is a normal and expected reaction. Obviously, if 15 percent is deemed inappropriate, the analyst can incorporate a more realistic growth rate for the acquirer into his or her sensitivity analysis.

A presumption that the acquired bank will realize the required growth rate is dependent upon carefully prepared historical performance analyses and postmerger projections. In some cases, it may be necessary to incorporate strategic considerations and operating adjustments in order to overcome dilution based on the hurdle growth rates. The bottom line, of course, is that dilution is permanent if it cannot be shown that required growth is achievable. Permanent dilution is obviously not desirable. However, if

In the first wave (1985–86), acquirers frequently undertook double digit dilution . . . In the next wave (1987–88) dilution standards moderated to single digits. Soon, however, the standard was again lowered, this time to the present standard, which is essentially intolerant of dilution . . .

the target contributes disproportional capital, or strategic consid-erations exist that are critical to the consolidated bank's grand strategy, it may be viewed as questionable, but acceptable. For example, a bank may engage in one or two dilutive mergers if those transactions will enable it to establish certain franchise thresholds and subsequently allow it to complete a large, high-value added transaction. Significant business mix or loan diversifi-cation improvement may also rationalize some dilution.

A comparison of equity-to-assets ratios of the acquirer and acquiree can provide a relative capital contribution assessment. Assuming that leveraging can occur at the acquirer's same level, then the contributed capital of an acquiree may provide asset growth benefits to the combined entity. Regulatory capital ratio considerations should be evaluated in such instances as well.

In the final analysis, the ultimate test of the merger is its effect on shareholder value. If the market perceives that the dilu-tion, whether temporary or permanent, is acceptable, then share-holder value should increase as the market rewards prospective success through share price enhancements. An increase in an acquirer's share price and price-earnings (P/E) ratio is reflective of the market's positive affirmation of a deal. Analysts and boards alike should respect market reactions to deals. We reiterate our continued emphasis on the fundamental earnings power of the combined enterprise. Deal valuation, pricing, structure, and nego-tiation should theoretically be based on discounted future cash flow, not on book value or near-term dilution.

Dilution Framework: Anomaly or Fallacy?

Another corporate finance-based decision methodology useful in determining the advisability of a particular transaction is a com-parison of the estimated deal return against a hurdle rate that is equivalent to the acquirer's cost of capital. Financial theory sug-gests that investments should be made whenever the project's internal rate of return exceeds a specified hurdle rate. Interest-ingly, even if a deal appears to have too much dilution, it should, in theory, be consummated if the projected internal rate of return exceeds the cost of capital hurdle rate. If such conditions exist, the deal would enhance the net present value (NPV) of the bank acquirer. It is at the same time clear, though, that when the deal is announced, the market may penalize the acquirer's stock price if any dilution is indicated, even though the deal has a positive NPV. This valuation anomaly can only be resolved if the perceived earnings dilution proves to be temporary. If earnings dilution ap-pears to be permanent in the eyes of the market, only delivering on premerger return assumptions and cost-saving realization can eventually reverse an initial negative market reaction.

This valuation anomaly is important to understand. While the NPV may be positive, EPS dilution remains the binding constraint. Over time, the analyst community's standards are evolving toward the more theoretical NPV approach, but only slowly. Nevertheless, dilution should be viewed as a binding constraint that must be managed.

The purchase versus pooling decision, which is discussed next, provides management with a technique that can potentially address binding constraints they must overcome in pursuing a value-creating acquisition program. Purchase transactions reduce the requirement to issue shares and expose the acquirer to less EPS dilution. Which is the greater risk—EPS dilution or burdening the available Tier 1 capital with acquisition-generated goodwill? The answer to this question will vary by the acquirer's strategic position, balance sheet strength, and management risk profile.

Pooling versus Purchase—
Buyer's Acquisition Accounting

A critical decision a buyer must make in conjunction with determining the appropriate strategy for an acquisition is the method of accounting treatment to be used. The accounting treatment used in undertaking individual transactions that are part of a multi-staged acquisition plan can be key to a successful merger program. Stringent regulatory capital guidelines and equity market pricing behavior are important parameters that influence the purchase-versus-pooling accounting decision.

Under a pooling, the assets and liabilities of both entities are combined line-by-line with no resulting intangible assets. A purchase involves the absorption of one bank by another, in which case the premium paid over book value creates intangible assets. There are restrictions governing the use of pooling, and there may be benefits or costs implied by either method, depending upon strategic considerations such as the buyer's anticipated merger and funding plans.

Poolings are said to be kind to balance sheets, but brutal to income statements because of pooling-induced dilution of earnings per share. Pooling, however, is usually preferred in bank acquisitions because it leaves the capital position free of the goodwill associated with purchase accounting. Banks must qualify to use pooling accounting treatment. Among the restrictive conditions required to use pooling are the following:

- At least 90 percent of the value of the transaction must consist of newly issued stock.

- Ten percent of the transaction value can include cash paid to dissenting shareholders, cash paid for fractional shares, and tainted shares.

This valuation anomaly is important to understand. While the NPV may be positive, EPS dilution remains the binding constraint. Over time, the analyst community's standards are evolving toward the more theoretical NPV approach, but only slowly.

- Tainted shares are treasury shares that remain on the books of either the acquirer or acquiree for a period of two years.

Therefore, it is clear that a share repurchase program can undermine an acquisition that is reliant on pooling treatment. Tainted shares can only be cured through reissuance or following a two-year waiting period. Certain exceptions that apply in the determination of tainted shares include shares repurchased for a specific and approved future use, such as an employee stock purchase plan or a dividend reinvestment plan.

Most large bank transactions tend to be structured as poolings. The new capital rules, adopted as part of the Basle Accord, influence this because they require any goodwill from purchases to be subtracted from Tier 1 capital. The funding requirements of large deals also lead to poolings. It is much easier to issue new shares than to pay cash. Use of a stock (pooling) exchange also limits the effect that a cash-out would trigger on the tax rate of a target's shareholders. Pooling usually occurs when deals involve large premiums over book value or when the buyer is near its leverage limit. Exhibit 6.1, a management note on intangible assets published by Wells Fargo in their 1992 third quarter report, details the accounting ramifications of pooling versus purchase.

The premise that deal success relies on value creation, or recapture of lost dilution value, is often obscured when accounting for transactions as poolings. A deal is only feasible if investors believe that a realistic expense reduction and/or revenue enhancement plan exists, and that whatever value is to be realized exceeds the price premium paid over book value. If acquirers develop overly optimistic benefit scenarios and focus too much attention on their efforts to win the deal, they risk not only undermining the interests of their shareholders, but perhaps sinking the deal through raising future value concerns on the part of the target bank's shareholders.

Applicability of Purchase Accounting

In contrast to poolings, purchases are said to be kind to income statements, but brutal to balance sheets because of the substantial intangibles that derive from the premium paid over book value. Under the purchase method, the value of the assets on the acquiree's balance sheet must be adjusted to reflect goodwill; that is to say, the premium paid over fair market value of the acquired assets represents identifiable intangibles or goodwill. The Internal Revenue Service requires the amortization of goodwill over some reasonable period that is equated to the useful life of the franchise benefits; it may range from 15 to 20 years for bank assets. As a result, purchase accounting can be problematic because any goodwill created affects Tier 1 capital ratios in two ways: goodwill is

Exhibit 6.1

MANAGEMENT NOTE: INTANGIBLE ASSETS

WELLS FARGO & COMPANY AND SUBSIDIARIES

Wells Fargo's balance sheet shows both *tangible assets* (such as loans, buildings, and investments) and *intangible assets* (such as goodwill). Wells Fargo now carries $532 million of goodwill and $467 million of identifiable intangible assets on its balance sheet. Most came from its purchase of 130 branches of Great American Bank in 1990 and 1991, and Crocker National Bank in 1986.

These intangibles represent real value to Wells Fargo. For example, when Wells Fargo purchased the Great American branches, we paid a $465 million premium above the book value of the assets acquired in the transaction. We paid the price because Great American's Southern California franchise, with its excellent branch locations, strong customer base, and $6.2 billion in stable, low-cost core deposits, presented an important opportunity to strengthen our presence in Southern California and moved us to a number one market share in San Diego.

Wells Fargo's income statement is also affected by the level of intangibles. For example, for the first nine months of 1992, we incurred approximately $85 million of intangible amortization that appears as an expense on our income statement.

Intangible assets are typically created when companies pay a premium over book value to make acquisitions of businesses and use the "purchase" method of accounting. This is different from the "pooling" method in which the balance sheets of the two companies are added together on a line-by-line basis, thereby creating no intangible assets.

There are two types of intangibles. *Identifiable intangibles* are those that relate to the fair market value of specific customer relationships. Acquisitions of such items as core deposit liabilities, credit card relationships, and mortgage servicing rights create this type of intangible. We estimate the current value of future revenues attributable to such relationships in order to establish the amount of identifiable intangibles.

Core deposits, for example, might be worth 2 to 7 percent more than the actual amount on deposit with the bank, depending upon the relative costs of other borrowing sources. This premium is the core deposit intangible. The identifiable intangibles created when purchasing other lines of business, such as credit card and mortgage servicing rights, reflect the present value of expected benefit from those relationships.

The value of these intangibles is reassessed regularly. If we determine that the value of an asset is impaired, we make an adjustment to that asset on our books.

A second category of intangibles is *goodwill*. Goodwill represents the excess of the purchase price (premium) over the fair market value of the assets (including identifiable intangibles) and liabilities acquired.

Under accounting rules, intangibles are written off over a period of time and eventually disappear as an asset on the balance sheet. Some of the intangible amortization expense is deductible for tax purposes.

The following simplified example illustrates the difference in balance sheet and income statement treatment of an acquisition under the purchase and pooling methods of accounting.

Assume Bank A, with $1,000 of loans, $950 of deposits, and $50 of equity on its balance sheet, acquires Bank B, an identical bank. The purchase price is two times book value, using all stock and no cash: that is, Bank A issues $100 of equity for the purchase. If each bank earns $10, they both look like this before the acquisition:

ASSETS	LIABILITIES	INCOME
Loans $1,000	Deposits $950	Earnings = $10
	Equity 50	ROA = 1%
		ROE = 20%

In purchase accounting, the newly issued equity of $100 is added to the equity of the acquiring bank, and the purchase premium of $50 is counted as an intangible asset on Bank A's balance sheet. (For purposes of illustration, the fair value of Bank B's loans and deposits is assumed to equal book value.) Earnings are reduced by the amortization of the intangible assets, which we have assumed to be straight line over 10 years ($5 per year) and not tax-deductible.

The resulting balance sheet and income statement would be:

ASSETS	LIABILITIES	INCOME
Loans $2,000	Deposits $1,900	Earnings = $15
Intangibles 50	Equity 150	ROA = .73%
		ROE = 10%

Under the more restrictive pooling method, the balance sheet and income statement of the combined company would appear as indicated below, with the balance sheets of the two banks added line by line with no resulting intangible assets.

ASSETS	LIABILITIES	INCOME
Loans $2,000	Deposits $1,900	Earnings = $20
	Equity 100	ROA = 1%
		ROE = 20%

Although Bank A issued $100 of equity to acquire Bank B, there is only a $50 increase in equity representing the addition of the book value of Bank B. It is as though the other $50 in equity issued to shareholders of the acquired bank was "written off" on the acquisition date without ever flowing through the income statement as amortization.

At first glance, two identical acquisitions would give dramatically different results based on the accounting method used, which depends on the particulars of each individual acquisition and how the accounting rules fit the specific circumstances. Earnings are higher under the pooling method because there is no amortization of intangibles. ROA and ROE are also higher because of both the difference in income and the lower equity base.

However, when considering cash flow and tangible net worth, the two companies are identical. Since intangible amortization expense is not a cash flow, the cash earnings for companies using either accounting method are $20 after the acquisition is completed. Tangible net worth (equity less intangibles) is also the same for both companies.

Source: 1992 Third Quarter Report, Wells Fargo & Company and subsidiaries.

both deducted from the numerator and fully weighted (included) in the denominator. Thus, goodwill becomes an asset burden. A well-capitalized acquirer may be able to absorb accelerated amortization.

Purchase accounting is generally used when the prospect of creating significant goodwill is low. Two sets of deals qualify: smaller deals—filler acquisitions, for instance—or for larger transactions that involve relatively small premium prices paid on the seller's book value. Some purchase deals may reflect low premiums to stated book value at the time of the deal announcement. These low premiums, however, can prove to be illusive. When write-downs to book value may be required to bring an acquiree's asset quality profile to an acceptable level—typically up to the standard of the acquirer—by the time the deal closes, the implied premium to book value may become significant. Thus, the apparent economy of the deal is effectively eliminated as the increased goodwill levels must be subsequently amortized. In view of the potential book value write-downs, it is important that deal structuring incorporate sufficient protection to prevent a cheap deal from becoming an expensive deal and negating the appropriateness of using the purchase accounting method.

Tax benefits may accrue under purchase transactions. Amortization of goodwill tied to core deposits or other identifiable intangibles provides an income shelter unavailable under pooling.

Goodwill write-offs, even on an accelerated basis, can be offset by cost savings and other enhancements generated from a deal. An acquirer should realize an immediate positive market impact and improved valuation from enhanced cash flows. Poolings, on the other hand, involve the earn-back of dilution, which often produces a short-term hit to market value. Also, any tax benefits of purchase accounting could result in cash flow benefits that the market may value highly in the short run. While the accounting treatment selected for large bank acquisitions has tended to favor poolings, there are indications that different strategies may be successful in the future. In its 1992 acquisition of Security Pacific, BankAmerica elected to structure the acquisition as a purchase even though the transaction was a 100 percent stock exchange.

An advantage of purchase accounting is the ease of divestment of nonstrategic or undesirable subsidiaries that are marked to market as part of a purchase transaction. A leading bank analyst, Thomas Hanley of First Boston, has noted that future deals may be structured as purchases in order to allow the carve-out and sale of undesirable assets. Such asset sales would make acquisition success less dependent upon cost savings. This may be a more desirable strategy than pooling in situations where postacquisition profitability is questionable. It might be easier to achieve performance improvements by divesting under purchase accounting rather than trying to cut expenses to earn back dilution from a pooling or paying down goodwill. Moreover, poolings prohibit wholesale asset liquidations after the acquisition.

In the Real World . . .

For in-market mergers, analysts' cost takeout percentage standards have increased from a 10–25 percent range to a 30–50 percent

While the accounting treatment for large-bank acquisitions has tended to favor poolings, there are indications that different strategies may be successful in the future. In its 1992 acquisition of Security Pacific, BankAmerica elected to structure the acquisition as a purchase even though the transaction was a 100 percent stock exchange.

range over the past five years. While dilution tolerance has been reduced, cost takeout modeling by analysts is now less theoretical and more in line with what bank managements plan and pledge to pursue. While the historical tolerance for dilution has moved lower, there is now much greater consideration of how management intends to pull the available operating levers to strengthen performance of the combined entities to assure mergers are ultimately value additive. Analysts seek to accurately model management's integration plans and are relatively unforgiving in their subsequent financial analysis.

We are seeing a convergence of the theoretical accounting world of the analyst community with the operating world of the bank management team. This convergence of thinking is critical to the industry paradigm shift. While market scrutiny may reduce management's ability to outperform analysts' expectations, we are seeing an alignment of the analyst's perspective, bank management's perspective, and what is required to address the industry's structural challenges.

While dilution tolerance has been reduced, cost takeout modeling by analysts is now less theoretical, and more in line with what bank managements plan and pledge to pursue.

Perspectives in Doing Bank Deals

The parameters of a successful deal depend largely upon the particular context of each of the transacting banks; a merger becomes an exercise in negotiation between two entities with differing objectives. In this light, it is useful to consider the unique perspective of buyers and sellers in structuring deals that meet each party's respective objectives.

Acquirer Point of View

As suggested earlier, acquirers are particularly interested in limiting the potential earnings dilution of a merger since the dilution criterion is the binding constraint imposed by the stock market. Although relative price, earnings, and book value considerations weigh heavily in negotiation, earnings and cash flow implications are paramount to an acquirer.

When considering specific mergers, acquirers should assess the benefits that an individual deal may provide relative to the overall strategy of the bank. Analysts, for example, could have very easily criticized the high premiums First Union paid to gain entry into Florida and Georgia. Such criticism would have failed to appreciate the value of establishing statewide beachheads for dozens of lucrative in-state filler acquisitions and their accompanying major cost savings. For example, in Florida, First Union achieved hundreds of millions of dollars in cost savings from its in-market purchases of Florida National and Southeast. The latter purchase's cost savings were so substantial that First Union received a phenomenal one-year payback on its investment. Nevertheless, under conventional accounting measures, the original deal was considered a transaction of borderline quality.

Society's 1990 purchase of Trustcorp generated a lot of questions. Critics alleged that management may have destroyed shareholder wealth by accepting potentially permanent dilution. However, one could argue that building a better statewide franchise and defensively preempting an out-of-state competitor (NBD) added enough value to offset the small, potentially permanent dilution. In retrospect, the acquisition templates and market coverage developed as a result of the Trustcorp merger were crucial to Society's ability to exploit the in-market opportunity that Ameritrust subsequently presented. Also, because of the Trustcorp experience, management knew how to aggressively consolidate an acquisition to maximize shareholder value, and the investment community viewed the Ameritrust transaction as more credible. This increased credibility with Wall Street was important given that the deal structure implied double digit dilution without the consideration of the large in-market cost savings.

In retrospect, the acquisition templates and market coverage developed as a result of the Trustcorp merger were crucial to Society's ability to exploit the in-market opportunity that Ameritrust subsequently presented.

Seller Point of View

The benefits to the shareholders of an acquired bank (the seller) can be categorized along two dimensions: (1) the market price premium, or amount above the existing market price, that the sellers receive from the transaction and (2) the effective enhancements that may accrue to the sellers as a result of their owning new shares.

Shareholders exchange shares in the acquired company for a compensation package consisting of some combination of cash, notes, restricted securities, or common shares of the acquirer. In the case of a stock exchange, the benefit or enhancements to the seller consist of increased earnings per share, dividends per share, and book value per share of the new shares in the combined entity. Further benefits may include heightened marketability of shares, management team efficiencies, greater long-term valuation, and potential sell-out prospects of the acquirer—the latter referred to as a "double dip." Buyers absorb sellers' shareholder enhancements in exchange for greater potential core earnings of the consolidated entity as well as an improvement in the P/E ratios of the shares of the combined entity.

The true measure of market price premium paid to the seller's shareholders is generally calculated as the transaction value less the normalized stock market value of the acquired company. Normalized market value is considered to be current market value free of deal impacts (e.g., leaks). Usually the stock price one month before the announcement is free of leaks. In recent years, premiums to market have ranged between 25 and 35 percent for larger bank transactions.

Sellers think of enhancements in terms of incremental earnings, dividends, and book value that they gain as a result of exchanging each share of stock in the acquired company. Bank analysts frequently calculate and express such measures in absolute dollar terms and also as an incremental percentage. For example, a shareholder may exchange shares resulting from a transaction in which the acquirer offered 1.5 shares of its common shares in exchange for each of the acquiree's shares. Thus, the exchange ratio is 1.5 to 1. Using the exchange ratio, sellers may determine that their old shares, which reflect a recent EPS of $3.00, may be tendered for an equivalent pro forma EPS of $4.50, a 50 percent enhancement. Similarly, sellers may discover that their old shares, which reflect a recent $.75 dividend per share, may be tendered for an equivalent pro forma dividend per share of $1.00, a 33 percent enhancement. Finally, under pooling-of-interests combinations, it may also be possible to calculate a book-value-per-share enhancement that would accrue to sellers on a pro forma basis.

Obviously, sellers must make the critical judgment of whether indicated enhancements can be realized in light of the merger plan. Postmerger performance projections are reliant on cost savings and earnings improvements that may not materialize on schedule, if at all. Dividend policy is likely to be a sacred cow, remaining quite predictable post merger. An important conclusion is that seller enhancements are as solid as buyer performance projections. Sellers must be satisfied that the shareholder value of the combined entity will be enhanced over the long term.

Board of Director Framework

One of the most challenging tasks facing bank board members today is the evaluation of buyout offers. In effect, the task can be stated as a simple question: "When should we say yes, and when should we say no to offers?" Often, bank boards have opted for the quick solution, simply saying no to offers without applying an exhaustive and independent evaluation to such proposals. Clearly, fiduciary responsibility demands that boards determine whether shareholders' value can be maximized with the highest expected probability through continued operations or consolidation. The math is not simple because myriad issues cloud any evaluation process. A variety of methodologies exist to be used to conduct this analysis. Here we apply a Keefe, Bruyette & Woods framework as a starting point to construct a sound analysis.

In its basic form, the evaluation process attempts to determine whether shareholders are better off accepting an offer at the moment, or whether they should wait for equivalent future valuation gains from continued independent operating growth. Another way to express this relationship is to quantify how many years would be required for a bank to yield valuation gains through continued operations equivalent to a current premium offered by a potential suitor.

Exhibit 6.2 illustrates Keefe's board decision matrix that summarizes potential tradeoffs. Two primary variables are assumed as the basis for analysis: the bank's reinvestment rate and the premium over market value of the offer. This methodology makes the following reasonable assumptions, which could be evaluated under alternative scenarios and circumstances: (1) the bank's stock price is fairly valued by the market and is not likely to adjust significantly in the near future in any predictable way; (2) the bank's capital structure and dividend policies remain constant; (3) the bank's earnings (capital) growth rate remains constant; and (4) the market's valuation of the bank's performance remains constant, that is, the P/E multiple reflects normal market multiples for earnings and perceived risk, and increased earnings in the future will be proportionately valued.

In addition, shareholders will presumably evaluate a sell or hold decision on a present-value basis. In effect, investors ask how long it will take for the values of the two alternative strategic courses to cross over.

As indicated in the exhibit, banks with strong performance and high internal capital growth rates can achieve buyout offer cross-over points in relatively short periods. If such strong internally generated performance is possible, the bank will be less inclined to accept offers, even at significant premiums to market. In contrast, banks with weak performance and low internal capital growth rates may take a decade or longer to achieve investment cross-over with attractive buy-out offers. Thus, the framework enables a board to make the analysis a more definable task. That is, which avenue—independence or sale—offers the highest capital growth rates. Once quantified, the answer may become clearer, or at least more defensible.

If the board can argue that capital growth is strong and improving, then it is reasonable to reject a high premium offer because shareholders would conceivably achieve similar or greater benefits in a relatively short period of time. In such situations, the board should reject a premium offer. On the other hand, if a bank has a low capital growth rate and no objective or realistic prospect for a significant change in this regard, it is imprudent for the board not to accept a premium offer. It is unrealistic to expect shareholders to wait seven to ten years to achieve a valuation level that could be achieved almost immediately under an available buyout offer.

An example of how this decision process can be applied in the bank merger market is the first offer that Bank of New York made in 1987 to acquire Irving Bank Corporation at 60.8 percent over the then-market price. Irving had a substandard internal capi-

Exhibit 6.2

BOARD DECISION MATRIX
(Years required to earn back acquisition premium over market value)

DEAL PREMIUM	INTERNAL CAPITAL GENERATION RATE (1)										
	2%	4%	6%	8%	10%	12%	14%	16%	18%	20%	25%
20%	9.2	4.6	3.1	2.4	1.9	1.6	1.4	1.2	1.1	1.0	0.8
25%	11.3	5.7	3.8	2.9	2.3	2.0	1.7	1.5	1.3	1.2	1.0
30%	13.2	6.7	4.5	3.4	2.8	2.3	2.0	1.8	1.6	1.4	1.2
35%	15.2	7.7	5.2	3.9	3.1	2.6	2.3	2.0	1.8	1.6	1.3
40%	17.0	8.6	5.8	4.4	3.5	3.0	2.6	2.3	2.0	1.8	1.5
60%	23.7	12.0	8.1	6.1	4.9	4.1	3.6	3.2	2.8	2.6	2.1
80%	29.7	15.0	10.1	7.6	6.2	5.2	4.5	4.0	3.6	3.2	2.6
100%	35.0	17.7	11.9	9.0	7.3	6.1	5.3	4.7	4.2	3.8	3.1
120%	39.8	20.1	13.5	10.2	8.3	7.0	6.0	5.3	4.8	4.3	3.5
140%	44.2	22.3	15.0	11.4	9.2	7.7	6.7	5.9	5.3	4.8	3.9
160%	48.3	24.4	16.4	12.4	10.0	8.4	7.3	6.4	5.8	5.2	4.3
200%	55.5	28.0	18.9	14.3	11.5	9.7	8.4	7.4	6.6	6.0	4.9
220%	58.7	29.7	20.0	15.1	12.2	10.3	8.9	7.8	7.0	6.4	5.2
240%	61.8	31.2	21.0	15.9	12.8	10.8	9.3	8.2	7.4	6.7	5.5
260%	64.7	32.7	22.0	16.6	13.4	11.3	9.8	8.6	7.7	7.0	5.7
280%	67.4	34.0	22.9	17.3	14.0	11.8	10.2	9.0	8.1	7.3	6.0
300%	70.0	35.3	23.8	18.0	14.5	12.2	10.6	9.3	8.4	7.6	6.2

1 The internal capital generation rate is also referred to as the growth rate or the reinvestment rate. It is computed by multiplying a firm's specific rate of return on equity by the firm's retention ratio (1–dividend payout ratio).

Source: Adapted from Keefe, Bruyette & Woods "Bank Industry Issues," February 15, 1989.

tal growth ranging from 6.5 to 8.5 percent over the previous five years and faced somewhat difficult future growth prospects. The Bank of New York offer had a cross-over point of 6.5 years. In other words, stockholders would have to wait 6.5 years to get the same value offered by the suitor today. Ironically, after rejecting the initial offer, the Irving board eventually agreed to sell for a revised, lower, post-1987 stock market crash price. While Irving had failed to land any better value-enhancing bids, the cross-over point analysis was too compelling. The bottom line is that it would have been improper to force shareholders to wait several years to realize a value immediately available from a buyout offer.

On the other hand, in the fall of 1986, BankAmerica (BAC) received an offer from First Interstate that represented an 85 percent premium over market and was subsequently increased to 120 percent over market. At the time, BAC was quite troubled and its earnings growth was negative. According to management's internal ROE projections, however, the offer was not believed to be attractive enough to justify a decision to sell. It could be convincingly argued that BAC's shareholders would achieve growth equal to the offered premium in a relatively short period of time. Significant turnaround progress had already been made and rewards to shareholders would follow shortly.

Hindsight has proven BAC's board correct. However, it should be noted that the presumption was that enhanced growth prospects were reasonable and obtainable. BankAmerica correctly argued that it had new management, asset quality improvements would occur, and strategic operating changes would add market value.

If a board is able to show shareholders a reasonable expectation of achieving valuation levels equivalent to an offer within a short period of time, say, two to four years, then the decision to say no may make sense. This was the case of First Interstate/BankAmerica. If, however, the board cannot demonstrate that shareholder value can be internally generated to match an offer within a short period, then the opposite decision is indicated. Irving Trust's board found itself in this situation. The essential question, of course, is whether bank boards have reasonable expectations, as evidenced by a coherent strategy that justifies not accepting an attractive offer. As a result, in today's consolidation environment, working with the board to keep it abreast of strategic developments and future performance prospects, is a critical role for the CEO of the bank that seeks to remain independent.

Is the Bank Merger Market Rational? Examining the Evidence

In examining bank merger transactions during the past 10 years, we will draw upon the following sources: (1) a comprehensive

compilation of the most recent transactions that occurred between 1989 and the first quarter of 1993, as derived from SNL
Securities and First Manhattan Consulting Group (FMCG); (2) a
data base of select interstate banking deals that occurred between
1985 and 1968, as constructed by Kidder, Peabody Bank Equity
Research; (3) a 1990 study of bank acquisitions performed by
FMCG for the Bank Administration Institute; and (4) a bank
merger study by bank stock analyst David Cates.

The Early Experience

Clearly, the June 10, 1985, Supreme Court decision permitting
regional interstate banking sparked a strong interstate merger
wave. Exhibit 6.3 displays a broad array of merger detail including
the premiums paid for earn' ןs, book value, deposits, and assets
for interstate deals occurring in the 1985–1988 period. Exhibit
6.4 indicates the premiums paid for the same measures on all
mergers (both intrastate and interstate) during 1989–1992. The
premium paid in the early years, 1985 and 1986, are the highest.

Although there were a few significant interstate deals in
New England, the Southeast was the center of activity. Exhibit
6.5 summarizes the major Southeastern transactions in 1985 and
1986. Consistent with the high premiums paid, dilution undertaken by acquirers was substantial. Exhibit 6.6 indicates that several banks took double digit earnings dilution in 1985 and 1986.
Initially, the stock market rebounded from declines following
merger announcements and assigned improved price-earnings ratios to offset the dilution taken. The market conclusion seemed to
be that investors would accept near-term dilution if acquirers
were building strong regional franchises.

The Second and Third Merger Waves

Investor tolerance of dilution soon began to deteriorate. In the
second merger wave, dilution levels on transactions were lowered
substantially to the 5 to 8 percent range. The premiums paid for
book value, assets, and core deposits dropped in 1987 and 1988
(see Exhibit 6.3).

This trend toward reduced tolerance for dilution continued
through the late 1980s and early 1990s, when the dilution standard in a third merger wave was set close to zero. As a general
rule, banks were expected to wipe out any minimal dilution taken
on a deal within one year. In earlier years, banks had taken three,
and sometimes five, years to earn back dilution. Exhibit 6.4 reflects the estimated minimal dilution involved in all bank deals
made between 1989 and 1992.

As the data suggest, the stock market has had an increasingly binding effect on bank merger pricing and has tended to
focus acquirers on the imperative of cost reduction. That is, the
only way to pay target banks their required premiums and limit

Exhibit 6.3

INTERSTATE MERGERS AND ACQUISITIONS: 1985–1988
($ Millions)

	Number of Deals	Total Price	Average Trans-action Values	Value Standard Deviation	Premium to Earnings (x)	Premium to Equity (X)	Average Premium to Market (%)	Average Premium to Deposits (%)	Average Price to Assets (%)	Acquiree Total Deposits	Acquiree Total Assets
Total data base	231	36,542.8	158.2	279.2	16.6	1.79	32.7	13.9		262,729	336,903
Adjusted (a, b, c)		33,538.1	149.7	270.6	13.8	1.91	–	14.8		226,920	290,779
1988 Deals	36	3,925.8	109.1	180.5	31.8	1.58	40.3	13.0	10.05	30,243	39,047
Adjusted (a)		2,957.4	92.4	152.0	16.0	1.78	–	14.6	11.14	20,310	26,546
1987 Deals	58	10,988.2	189.5	339.8	16.0	1.85	47.3	13.0	9.99	84,448	109,967
Adjusted (b)		10,581.9	185.6	341.6	14.3	1.98	–	13.8	10.50	76,849	100,813
1986 Deals	73	9,130.8	125.1	231.6	17.8	1.87	30.2	16.2	12.53	56,293	72,881
Adjusted (c)		7,940.8	110.3	196.0	16.1	2.13	–	18.5	14.79	42,815	53,689
1985 Deals	36	6,176.3	171.6	193.7	11.7	2.15	20.7	17.3	13.61	35,753	45,389

(a) Excluding First Bank System/Central Bancorp, Comerica/Grand Bancshares, Bank of Tokyo/Union Bancorp, and Northern Trust/Concorde Bank.
(b) Excluding First Interstate/Allied Bancshares.
(c) Excluding Chemical Banking/Texas Commerce.

Source: Adapted from Kidder Peabody Equity Research, "Interstate Banking Mergers and Acquisitions," November 20, 1990, page 3.

Exhibit 6.4

BANK MERGER TRANSACTION PRICING
1989–1992 (Median Values)

	No. of Deals	Total Value ($mm)	Sellers' Total Assets ($mm)	Price/LTM Earnings[1]	Price/Tangible Book	Core Deposit Premium[2]	Price/Total Assets	Estimated Accretion or (Dilution) per Common Share[3]
1992	302	$11,865	$104,240	13.5x	1.51	4.6%	11.7%	–.3%
1991	251	21,016	274,689	12.7x	1.40	3.2%	11.0%	.1%
1990	162	2,929	35,871	13.6x	1.47	4.6%	12.3%	.3%
1989	129	9,177	79,879	14.5x	1.80	7.4%	14.7%	–.5%

1 Latest twelve months reported earnings prior to the M&A announcement.
2 (Price minus tangible book value) divided by core deposits; core deposits defined as total deposits less brokered and jumbo time deposits.
3 Positive number indicates accretion; negative number indicates dilution.

Source: First Manhattan Consulting Group and SNL Securities.

Exhibit 6.5

MAJOR ACQUISITIONS IN THE SOUTHEAST

Announcement Date	Company	Assets (millions)	Value of Transaction (millions)	Premium over Market (a)	Price As a Multiple of Earnings	Book	As a % of Assets	Accounting Treatment
	Citizens & Southern Corp.							
February 22, 1985	Landmark	$3,759	$516	48%	15.0x	1.98x	13.7%	Pooling
September 17, 1985	C&S Corp. (S.C.)	2,532	417	24	14.5	2.36	16.4	Purchase
	First Union							
March 4, 1985	Northwestern	2,635	306	40	13.4	2.03	11.6	Pooling
June 17, 1985	Atlantic	3,558	495	37	14.8	2.21	13.9	Pooling
September 20, 1985	Southern	1,022	216	37	19.1	2.29	21.1	Purchase
November 14, 1985	First Bankers	1,158	218	20	17.0	2.65	18.8	Purchase
June 11, 1986	First Railroad	3,631	779	32	17.9	2.42	21.4	Pooling
	First Wachovia							
June 17, 1985	First Atlanta	7,056	831	36	12.0	2.11	11.8	Pooling
	NCNB							
July 5, 1985	Bankers Trust (S.C.)	1,859	307	29	13.5	2.31	16.5	Purchase
July 25, 1985	Pan American	1,679	210	35	13.1	1.97	12.5	Pooling
	Bank of Virginia							
July 16, 1985	Union Trust	2,153	302	74	14.7	2.22	14.0	Pooling
	Sovran							
September 24, 1985	Suburban	3,093	408	18	12.1	2.02	13.2	Pooling
	Dominion							
May 16, 1986	Nashville City	596	103	—	20.5	2.51	17.3	Pooling
	SunTrust							
September 2, 1986	Third National	4,963	758	18	13.8	2.29	15.3	Pooling

Source: Weiant, William M. and Frank Suozzo. "Merger and Acquisition Activity in the Southeast," First Boston Equity Research (Sept. 30, 1986), vol. 12, No. 37.

		Estimated Dilution	
	Assets Acquired	Earnings Per Share	Book Value
First Union	$9.0	15%	11%
First Wachovia	7.1	7	4
NCNB	4.1	10–12	0
Citizens & Southern	7.0	16	6
Sovran Financial	3.8	15	15
Bank of Virginia	2.2	13	13
Dominion	0.6	9	7

Exhibit 6.6

MAJOR SOUTHEAST ACQUISITIONS: ESTIMATED DILUTION (1985) ($ in Billions)

Source: Weiant, William M. and Frank Suozzo. "Merger and Acquisition Activity in the Southeast," First Boston Equity Research (Sept. 30, 1986), vol. 12, No. 37.

dilution was to aggressively reduce the expense base of the proposed combined institution. To be fair, in some ways, the analyst community was simply trying to catch up with where leading regional banks were already headed. Deal pricing based on the value created through cost reductions would appear dilutive to analysts, if Wall Street failed to allow for any earnings improvement through cost takeout. As analysts adjusted their models to incorporate higher and higher cost takeout percentages, they more accurately forecasted future earnings, and also reduced the level of tolerable dilution.

In this light, in-market, in-state, and contiguous market mergers became fashionable. Banks that were slow to pick up on the tremendous success of the Wells Fargo-Crocker in-market merger in 1986 began to focus on in-market deals within their geographic areas. Examples of large in-market deals include: MNC-Equitable (Baltimore); CoreStates-First Pennsylvania (Philadelphia); Society-Ameritrust (Cleveland); Chemical-Manufacturers Hanover (New York); BankAmerica-Security Pacific (California); Comerica-Manufacturers National (Detroit); and First Union-Florida National-Southeast (Florida).

After a lot of activity in the late 1980s, merger pricing in the early 1990s became quite weak. Exhibit 6.7 indicates premiums paid for tangible book values in 1990 and 1991 ranged from 1.38X to 1.41X with respect to median values on all transactions. Premiums paid for earnings, ranged from 12.7X to 13.6X (median values). Similarly, premiums paid for core deposits had a low range of 3.2 to 4.6 percent. In 1992 and 1993 the premiums paid for mergers rebounded. Recently, several deals have been priced at multiples exceeding 2X book value, 16X to 18X earnings and $.20 per dollar of asset acquired. Of course, Dow Jones and NASDAQ stock market levels are at record highs, and overall bank valuations are healthy.

Interstate versus Intrastate Bank Deals

An interesting question that periodically crops up in the bank merger scene concerns whether intrastate or interstate deals justify and/or obtain higher premiums. Interstate acquiring banks apparently pay significant premiums for market entry even though prospects for immediate cost reduction are limited. On the other hand, intrastate deals offer substantial potential for cost saves and synergies and, accordingly, justify substantial premiums. One of the authors examined this question some time ago and found in a study of 164 bank mergers occurring across the United States between 1984 and 1986 that interstate bids commanded higher premiums vis-a-vis intrastate deals.[1] Even though the latter provide greater cost savings, the premium paid for an intrastate deal was found to be lower by one eighth of the target's value than was the interstate price. One might have expected that the market's skepticism of interstate banking benefits, as well as a steadfast position against dilution, would have changed this earlier pricing pattern toward the payment of relatively greater premiums for intramarket deals. Yet, in a more recent period (1989–92), the same measure as used in the earlier study—price paid to tangible book—indicates that out-of-state deals, for the most part, still command larger premiums (Exhibit 6.7). However, the data related to the median premiums paid for trailing 12 months' earnings are more ambiguous. In 1989 and 1991, the median interstate deals were priced higher, while intrastate deals involved larger premiums for earnings in 1990 and 1992.

Exhibit 6.7 TRANSACTION PREMIUMS: INTERSTATE VERSUS INTRA-STATE BANK MERGERS (Median Values)				
	Price/LTM Earnings*		Price/Tangible Book	
	Interstate	In-State	Interstate	In-State
1992	13.1x	13.4x	1.74	1.38
1991	14.8x	12.1x	1.53	1.31
1990	12.3x	14.2x	1.40	1.41
1989	14.4x	14.3x	1.85	1.75

* Latest twelve months reported earnings prior announcement.
Sources: First Manhattan Consulting Group and SNL Securities.

Does the Size of the Deal Matter?

As a general matter, larger deals tend to be valued more highly than smaller deals. Exhibit 6.8 uses the $1 billion level to distinguish large versus small deals. For every year from 1989 through 1992 (except 1990), the larger deals commanded a higher median premium for earnings and tangible book value. Several factors account for this pricing pattern. First, as the merger game matures, many large banks become less interested in bidding for smaller deals because they must do almost as much planning, regulatory filings, and other detail work on small deals as they would on large deals. Second, although not always the case, bigger deals involve larger franchise additions. Either greater market share or coverage of more markets may be imbedded in larger transactions. The regulatory, strategic, and operating economies available in larger bank acquisitions are clearly reflected in deal pricing.

Exhibit 6.8

MERGER PRICING BY DEAL SIZE
(Median Values)

	Price/LTM Earnings*		Price/Tangible Book	
	Over $1B	Under $1B	Over $1B	Under $1B
1992	17.0	13.4	1.73	1.50
1991	15.3	12.5	1.84	1.33
1990	12.3	13.7	1.29	1.44
1989	14.7	14.4	2.04	1.69

* Latest twelve months reported earnings prior announcement.

Source: First Manhattan Consulting Group and SNL Securities.

Method of Payment

As a general matter, stock exchange deals resulting from pooling of interest have involved payments of higher median premiums for earnings and tangible book value (Exhibit 6.9). Sellers accepting bank equity for payment normally charge for the perceived riskiness of receiving stock rather than cash. Of course, cash payment in purchased deals involves immediate tax liability. Moreover, paying cash may reflect some constraint on EPS dilution. As a net result, poolings tend to be priced higher.

Exhibit 6.9

MERGER PRICING BY METHOD OF PAYMENT
(Median Values)

	Price/LTM Earnings*		Price/Tangible Book	
	Pooling	Purchase	Pooling	Purchase
1992	16.1	11.7	1.87	1.35
1991	16.6	12.2	1.62	1.32
1990	14.6	13.0	1.73	1.33
1989	14.3	14.6	1.94	1.62

* Latest twelve months reported earnings prior announcement.

Source: First Manhattan Consulting Group and SNL Securities.

Evidence on Thrift Transactions

Exhibit 6.10 summarizes the evidence related to thrift mergers occurring between 1989 and the first quarter of 1993. Premiums paid for book value, core deposits, and assets were substantially below the levels paid for banks (Exhibit 6.4). This reflects the fact that, qualitatively, core deposits and assets purchased from thrifts are inferior to those purchased from banks. Thrifts tend to have only a minor percentage of interest-free demand deposit accounts, and a higher percentage of their savings deposits are priced at near-market rates. This eliminates much of their funding cost advantage. Moreover, thrift deposits tend to run off when re-

Exhibit 6.10

THRIFT MERGER PRICING
1989–1993, QI
(Median Values)

	Price/LTM Earnings*	Price/Tangible Book	Core Deposit	
			Premium**	Price/Total Asset
1993, Q1	14.4	1.38	2.14%	9.9%
1992	11.9	1.25	1.64%	7.9%
1991	12.2	1.05	0.87%	5.4%
1990	15.0	1.06	1.68%	9.4%
1989	14.5	1.30	2.91%	8.4%

* Latest twelve months reported earnings prior announcement.

** Price minus tangible book value divided by core deposits.

Sources: First Manhattan Consulting Group and SNL Securities.

priced downward by a bank acquirer. Similarly, assets purchased from thrifts are inferior to those acquired from banks. Mortgages are the major type of loan purchased. In an age of widespread securitization and intense competition, the inherent profit spread of mortgages is minimal.

The low deposit premiums paid during the period from 1989 to 1993 also reflects the vast amount of RTC deposits and branches auctioned at very low prices during this time period. Similar to bank merger transactions, prices were quite weak in 1990 and 1991. The median premiums paid for tangible book were 1.06X and 1.05X, respectively. These prices reflect the fact that thrifts do retain their hard book value as a floor liquidation value even in the worst of times. Similar to banks, there has recently been a remarkable rebound in the pricing of thrifts. In the first quarter of 1993, the median price paid for tangible book was 1.38X (Exhibit 6.10).

Can Acquisition-Based Growth Create Value?

The FMCG/BAI Study of Bank Acquisitions

In 1990, the First Manhattan Consulting Group (FMCG), under the auspices of the Bank Administration Institute (BAI), analyzed all acquisitions through the 1980s (1982–88) in which banks with assets greater than $1 billion spent at least 10 percent of their capital on the acquisition. The study, entitled *Analyzing Success and Failure In Banking Consolidation*, shows that 80 percent of the acquirers failed to create value for their shareholders. The impact of these acquisitions on the buyer's stock price—for the 80 percent that were ineffective acquirers—ranged from mildly negative to dismal when compared to stock prices of peer banks that made no acquisitions. The FMCG study represented a stern warning to an industry pursuing acquisitions as a source of growth.

FMCG colorfully labeled the acquirers they studied. Only six acquiring banks were found to be successful by achieving stock prices higher than the bank peer group. They earned an eagle designation. Twelve banks, called turkeys, had stock prices that by 1984 were an average of 15 percent lower than those of a peer group of banks. Eight banks that had stock prices that averaged more than 25 percent below the peer group were dubbed dead ducks. Nearly one half (46 percent) of the original (1982) 26 acquiring banks were themselves acquired within six years. Most vultures were not acquired immediately. However, after four years the probability of their being purchased was high. Going forward, poor stock price performance resulting from an ineffective merger strategy will likely become a root cause of the loss of independence.

The FMCG/BAI study identified the reasons why many acquisitions failed, while only a few achieved success. Four key preconditions needed for successful acquisitions were cited: (1) the acquirer must be diligent in controlling noninterest expense in its own operations; (2) the acquisition must not be too expensive; (3) the acquirer must target certain types of business mix that are more likely to permit recapture of the premium; and (4) the acquirer should seek geographical proximity to the acquiree, particularly intramarket mergers.

The study cast doubt on some traditional methodologies used to predict financial success in an acquisition. For example, the level of earnings-per-share dilution was shown to have no bearing on subsequent stock price behavior. The only valid measure for predicting future stock performance was the ratio between expected discounted cash flow value and price paid. The study found that the long-term impact of an acquisition on the acquiring bank's stock price will be positive if, and only if, the discounted cash flow value of the acquired bank, after the acquisition has been completed and all benefits and synergies have been realized, is near to, or higher than, the price paid for stock of the acquired bank. This FMCG study is frequently cited as an important catalyst to bank analysts' updating their traditional merger valuation methodologies to be more consistent with bank executives' view of the world.

Cates Bank Merger Review

David C. Cates, Chairman of Ferguson and Company studied two dozen mergers that had targets whose assets exceeded $3 billion.[2] These deals occurred between 1983 and 1988. Cates found only four of the 24 deals created value for the acquirer's shareholders, a finding similar to the FMCG/BAI results. Two other deals marginally added value. The majority of the deals, 18 in total, destroyed value.

Cates's methodology focused on the growth rate from the premerger base year that would enable the target's earnings to catch up to the acquirer's net income five years later, assuming the acquirer had an acceptable 8 percent growth prospect for its premerger earnings base. Exhibit 6.11 summarizes his findings. The four successful deals included two by BANC ONE (American Fletcher and Marine of Wisconsin); BankAmerica (Seafirst); and Trust Company (SunBanks). The last two deals involved little premium payment because Seafirst was a troubled bank acquisition and Trust Company-SunBanks was a merger of equals.

In summarizing his findings, Cates noted that the average postmerger growth rate of the 23 deals he studied (excluding Seafirst, which was in a strong recovery from a deficit position) was −8.6 percent. The average required growth to overcome dilu-

Exhibit 6.11

BANK MERGERS 1983–1988: WHICH WERE SUCCESSFUL?

Acquirer/ Target	Agreement Date	Deal Price to: Prior Stock Price	Book Value	Required Growth Rate	Actual Growth Rate*	Value Creative?
BankAmerica/ Seafirst	4/83	1.10x	.80x	NA	*	Yes
First Chicago/ American National	8/83	NA	1.57x	NA	-5.72%	No
Mitsubishi/Bank Cal Tristate	8/83	1.47x	1.18x	NA	6.02	No
Bank of Montreal/Harris	10/83	1.82x	1.38x	NA	10.6%	No**
Chase Manhattan/ Lincoln First	12/83	1.28x	1.14x	NA	5.72%	No
Trust Company of Georgia/SunBanks (FL)	7.84	1.13x	1.11x	14.8%	20.5%	Yes
Wachovia/First Atlanta	6/85	1.25x	1.91x	8.5%	5.8%	Almost
Security Pacific/Arizona Bankwest	8/85	1.44x	2.68x	NA	-17.0%	No
Sovran/Suburban (MD)	9/85	1.19x	2.03x	17.9%	-21.1%	No
BancOne/American Fletcher	5/86	1.59x	2.25x	9.5%	17.1%	Yes
Chemical/Horizon (NJ)	5/86	1.32x	2.50x	NA	-39.9	No
First Union/First Railroad (GA)	6/86	1.32x	2.54x	15.9%	Flat	No
PNC/Citizens Fidelity (KY)	7/86	1.10x	2.52x	14.7%	-7.3%	No
Maryland National/American Security	8/86	.93x	1.70x	16.9%	-48.2%	No
Sun Trust/Third National Nashville	9/86	1.17x	2.29x	9.4%	-14.72%	No
Chemical/Texas Commerce	12/86	1.25x	1.01x	20.8%	14.5%	Almost
Security Pacific/Rainier	2/87	1.39x	1.94x	22.6%	22.02%	No**
Hong Kong Shanghai/Marine Midland	7/87	0.67x	1.49x	NA	-32.0%	No
BancOne/Marine Milwaukee	7/87	0.97x	1.68x	14.2%	17.9%	Yes
First Fidelity/Fidelcor	7/87	1.21x	1.64x	NA	-44.0%	No
NatWest/First Jersey	8/87	1.55x	2.44x	NA	-61.2%	No
Shawmut//Hartford National	8/87	1.21x	1.39x	29.9%	-19.1%	No
National City/First Kentucky	1/88	1.29x	1.97x	20.1%	5.75%	No
Allied Irish/First Maryland	9/88	1.44x	1.69x	NA	-1.3%	No

* Through 1990
** Security Pacific Washington (old Rainier) was on target in 1990 but only because of nonrecurring gains; 1991 earnings revert to low level.

Source: David C. Cates, "Can Bank Mergers Build Shareholder Value?" *Journal of Bank Accounting & Finance*, pages 6–7.

tion effects was 15.5 percent. The average premium to predeal book was 1.78X, and the average premium paid to preannouncement stock price was 27 percent. This evidence caused Cates to conclude that the shareholder value creation record of U.S. bank mergers is "demonstrably disappointing."

From a shareholder value perspective, banks have become increasingly responsible in their deal making. The record of the industry during the first two merger waves (1985–88) was quite negative in the sense that too much dilution was assumed and shareholder value was destroyed. Both the FMCG/BAI and the Cates studies document this assessment. These studies also suggested the roots of the problem and the potential solutions. Namely, banks had to refrain from overpaying for deals and become far more expense-reduction oriented in their integration efforts.

Recent evidence (1989–92) suggests banks have eliminated the dilution criticism, with most recent deals being accretive within one year, if not immediately, after the merger. Most current deals are entered into with explicit cost save assumptions that eliminate problematic dilution and rationalize the economic underpinning of various mergers. Social bases for mergers that serve to protect both a target's senior management and rank-and-file employees, as well as maintain redundant overhead structures, have become increasingly rare. Although we reference dilution performance as an indicator of improvement by industry merger participants, we stress the theoretical superiority of discounted cash flow over dilution as the appropriate framework for merger valuation. Deals should be done because they create value for shareholders. EPS dilution is a Wall Street driven binding constraint that must be managed in price negotiations. Having discussed the analytics and issues in doing deals, as well as the industry's track record in creating value through acquisitions, we now turn to merger mechanics. Several specific merger analytics are discussed next—violation of the proportionality rule, collars and arbitrage, escape clauses, due diligence, lock-up arrangements, and repurchase strategies.

Most current deals are entered into with explicit cost save assumptions that eliminate problematic dilution and rationalize the economic underpinning of various mergers. Social bases for mergers that serve to protect both a target's senior management and rank-and-file employees, as well as maintain redundant overhead structures, have become increasingly rare.

Violation of the Proportionality Rule

Assuming that banks generally shift away from their traditional concentration on book value and dilution levels to focus on discounted cash flow as the key basis for merger valuation, there remains one serious flaw in the ongoing bank merger marketplace: potential sellers routinely violate the merger rule of proportionality.

The rule of proportionality concept suggests that sellers' evaluations of offers should focus strictly on the proportionality involved in a proposed deal. That is, the key concern of a seller should be the relative percentage ownership of the combined entity as a result of an exchange. This change in relative percentage ownership should provide the seller with significant enhancements, such as increased earnings, dividends, and book value. Often, in periods of low bank stock price levels, however, sellers are mistakenly absorbed with the absolute transaction value or the offer value in relationship to book value. For this reason, there tends to be a large number of deals in periods of high bank stock market levels and relatively few when prices are low. Properly conceived, there would be a more normal distribution of deal flow.

This viewpoint is supported by the fact that seller behavior is basically predicated on relative bank prices at the time of the deal announcement. The more relevant bank prices are those that exist at the deal consummation date because those are the actual values or prices received by the seller.

Exhibits 6.12 and 6.13 illustrate these points. First, the BANC ONE-Marine fixed exchange rate deal was struck in a period of low or modest bank stock price levels. As the data reveal (Exhibit 6.12), the aggregate transaction value increased nearly 58 percent, and the premium paid to tangible book value jumped from nearly 2X to 3X over the course of the consummation period. It is noteworthy that the exchange ratio and enhancements to the seller remained unchanged.

In the BankAmerica-Security Pacific deal, the seller, Security Pacific, also realized a substantially greater transaction value (about a 25 percent increase) and premium to tangible book (2.13X versus 1.21X) at the deal completion date (Exhibit 6.13).

Often, in periods of low bank stock price levels, however, sellers are mistakenly absorbed with the absolute transaction value or the offer value in relationship to book value. For this reason, there tends to be a large number of deals in periods of high bank stock market levels and relatively few when prices are low.

Exhibit 6.12		
BANC ONE CORPORATION–MARINE TRANSACTION		
	Announcement 3/25/91	*Completion 1/1/92*
Deal value ($M)	183.1	288.7
Price per share	28.335	44.679
Price/Book (%)	177.32	263.28
Price/tangible book (%)	198.70	291.83
Workout period (years)	22	
Price/LTM EPS (X)	14.91	22.45
Price/Deposits (%)	17.89	27.65
Price/Assets (%)	15.59	24.02
Premium/Core deposits (%)	10.34	20.60

Source: SNL Securities

Exhibit 6.13

BANKAMERICA—SECURITY PACIFIC TRANSACTION

	Announcement 8/12/91	Completion 4/22/92
Deal value ($M)	4,666.9	5,832.9
Price per share	32.890	41.360
Price/Book (%)	101.51	167.18
Price/tangible book (%)	121.19	213.42
Workout period (years)	3	
Price/LTM EPS (X)	NM	NM
Price/Deposits (%)	8.39	10.32
Price/Assets (%)	5.80	7.53
Premium/Core deposits (%)	1.55	5.38

Source: SNL Securities

Again, the exchange ratio and relative ownership percentages remained unchanged.

Ironically, one could argue that potential sellers who consider offers only when the financial markets are strong may face high probabilities that actual prices received at consummation will be lower. Conversely, those banks that sell out in times of lower stock prices may likely enjoy higher prices at deal closing, similar to the Marine and Security Pacific cases.

Collars and Arbitrage

Although each transaction is unique, there are common aspects that can facilitate the assessment of risk and determination of value. The capitalistic nature of the market inherently attempts to close short-term misevaluation gaps created as information is absorbed. The risk arbitrage community is a specific segment of the market that focuses exclusively on valuation gaps or inequities and attempts to make transaction plays (deal-specific investments) in order to capture profits that accrue as the markets adjust to the announcement of a deal and its implications, subsequent operating events, and final regulatory steps. In bank and thrift mergers, there is normally a six- to nine-month lag between deal announcement and closing because of the time required for additional due diligence, approval by each bank's shareholders, approval by federal regulatory bodies and the Justice Department. It is this time required before deal consummation that becomes the period of arbitrage in which investors (arbs) reevaluate the inherent merits of the deal and decide whether the initial relative valuations are appropriate.

There are some standard arb strategies that are applied to bank stocks and are worth mentioning. Arbs are quick to participate in announced deals that utilize collars. The objective is to second-guess the deal valuation and anticipate market adjustments in response to subsequent information related to the deal. The arbs also could position themselves to benefit from stock price adjustments that would occur upon a renegotiation of the transaction price that may derive from a deal's escape clause (discussed below).

Often in the case of collars, an arbitrageur can lock in and earn the highest premium spread indicated by the exchange ratios by shorting the acquirer, thereby driving its price down to the price floor of the collar and simultaneously going long on the seller's stock. This hedge locks in the arb's compensation for the time value of money during the period between announcement and consummation as well as the risk for delays, approvals, or modification required by deal participants or regulators. The existence of a collar and arbitrage tends to result in the maximum exchange ratio when deals close. Consequently, some acquirers have become thoroughly disillusioned by arbs milking their deals, and have started to insist on fixed transaction exchange ratios without collars.

The existence of a collar and arbitrage tends to result in the maximum exchange ratio when deals close. Consequently, some acquirers have become thoroughly disillusioned by arbs milking their deals, and have started to insist on fixed transaction exchange ratios without collars.

Escape Clauses

In the wake of failed consolidations during the 1980s, merger participants have reemphasized deal structure in protecting self-interests. The Summcorp-Trustcorp transaction referred to below is one example of the type of escape clause that a seller may include in a deal structure.

Since most larger transactions today are structured as stock deals, deal participants are exposed to adverse announcement changes throughout the six- to nine-month period from initial valuation through deal closing. During this interim period, deal participants and the market scrutinize both merger entities more closely in an effort to confirm the valuation assumptions that were used to negotiate price. Should these assumptions reveal excess or deficient value, the stock price of these firms could shift dramatically and destroy the merits of the deal. There is an increasing use of escape clauses in merger agreements to protect both sides from some heretofore undiscovered asset quality or other problem that could destroy the attractiveness of a deal. If an escape clause is needed, either deal participant could renegotiate price or call off the deal. The market, led by arbitrageurs, would adjust stock prices to incorporate any new information.

Bank deal structures are increasingly incorporating escape clauses as a means of mitigating operating and market risks. Acquirees want to ensure that acquirers are financially strong and stable enough to complete the deal and, most important, ensure that the ultimate exchange price and value of the underlying equity remain intact. The escape clause provisions of the agreement permit sellers to end the merger if the acquirer's price plunges below a specific level. The focus of the provision is to protect against specific risk of the acquirer, not market or industry risk. Therefore, the escape clauses now in use can only be exercised if the acquirer's stock declines considerably more than that of its peers. In practice, escape clauses establish a loss of value percentage, say, 10 to 20 percent, compared to losses of a specifically defined peer group index, and a specific valuation period.

Application of the provision could call for a renegotiation of the price and structure. For example, in 1992, Barnett Banks of Florida initiated a bid for Tampa-based First Florida Banks that incorporated an escape clause permitting First Florida to walk away if Barnett's stock price declined 20 percent before the deal closed. However, the escape provision protected Barnett from adverse macroeconomic developments—it could only be triggered if Barnett's price during a specifically defined valuation period declined more than 20 percentage points in comparison to an industry peer group, defined in this case as the Standard & Poor's regional bank index.

A collar is a form of escape clause that provides protection to both parties. A collar includes floor and cap prices, either of which may be used independently. A price floor protects the seller from erosions in the value of the stock price of the buyer's stock, that is, if the buyer's stock price moves below a certain level, the seller can terminate the deal. In contrast, a cap limits the effective price that the buyer must pay to the seller in terms of the value of the buyer's stock to be exchanged. If the buyer's stock price jumps dramatically prior to closing, the exchange price is limited by the cap stock price. The objective of caps, floors, and collars is to ensure that the relative valuation assumptions made by merger participants remain consistent and equitable.

Due Diligence

Due diligence, for the most part, is emphasized from the perspective of the buyer. The buyer attempts to determine the value of the acquired bank and, in doing so, evaluates all assets and liabilities. However, it is also essential that sellers perform exhaustive reverse due diligence on the buyer to assure shareholder value for the seller is maximized or enhanced by selling. Just as a buyer would not want to be surprised, or stuffed, a seller must also be careful. This is critical in stock deals in which sellers are to receive stock or paper with an imputed value. The risk is that the buyer's strength and market value could erode after deal closing, which would translate, in effect, to a less valuable price for the

However, it is also essential that sellers perform exhaustive reverse due diligence on the buyer when determining whether shareholder value for the seller is maximized or enhanced by selling. Just as a buyer would not want to be surprised, or stuffed, a seller must also be careful.

acquisition. An example of a careful reverse due diligence application is illustrated by Summcorp's (Fort Wayne, Indiana) 1988 deal to sell out to Trustcorp of Toledo, Ohio. Summcorp canceled that deal after reverse due diligence revealed that Trustcorp had severe asset quality problems and embedded operating difficulties. Since the deal was structured so that Summcorp's shareholders were to receive Trustcorp's stock, it became apparent that the premium offered was illusory.

Lock-Up Arrangements

Once a merger agreement is reached, buyers seek protection from the possibility that the deal does not serve merely to attract additional offers for the seller from third parties. This protection is provided in what is generally termed a lock-up arrangement. Accordingly, sellers are asked to give warrants to the buyer to purchase up to 20 percent (typically 19.9 percent) of the stock at a relatively low price. The substantial position that would be established at a low price tends to make third-party offers price prohibitive.

Repurchase Strategies

The turbulent capital market environment of the 1980s stirred substantial interest in share repurchase programs by all of corporate America, including banks. The 1987 crash as well as the extended economic recession during the late 1980s pressured bank earnings significantly and resulted in low stock prices within the banking industry, even among the stronger players.

Managements were quick to recognize the immediate opportunity to boost earnings per share by compacting the shareholder base through share repurchase. The true value effect of a share repurchase strategy in the banking industry can be quite complex.

A share repurchase program can be a two-edged sword for bank management. On the one hand, banks that have excess capital and a significantly undervalued stock may benefit greatly. On the other hand, the accounting treatment of a share repurchase can result in the obstruction of a planned or proposed merger as well as create capital adequacy problems that could inhibit growth and limit financial flexibility. The SEC considers the existence of tainted shares of both parties of a potential merger in its evaluation of the denial of pooling-of-interests accounting treatment.

Much has been written about the potential benefits and costs of share repurchase programs. Share repurchases can provide the following potential benefits to the company:

1. Reported earnings per share are enhanced, provided assets are not proportionately reduced (contraction of

A share repurchase program can be a two-edged sword . . . On the one hand, banks that have excess capital and a significantly undervalued stock may benefit greatly. On the other hand, . . . share repurchase can result in the obstruction of a planned or proposed merger as well as create capital adequacy problems that could inhibit growth and limit financial flexibility.

balance sheet) after the repurchase. The cash flow implications depend on the actual implementation.

2. Management sends a positive message to the market regarding management's outlook for the company's prospects.

3. The stock is supported in the face of bearish market conditions.

4. The company can acquire shares inexpensively for other uses, such as stock option plans, conversion of convertible securities, and dividend reinvestment plans.

5. Future equity issuance when share prices are higher will reflect the success of the program and the efficiency of the capital formation process. This is particularly the focus of banks that will utilize purchase accounting instead of pooling in completing acquisitions.

Share repurchase programs can involve the following hazards:

1. Future acquisition plans that rely on pooling accounting will likely be undermined. The net effect is that future acquisitions must use purchase accounting and, therefore, goodwill is created as well as a reduced regulatory capital position for the acquirer.

2. Weak banks' ability to grow will be further hampered in times of distress if needed capital cannot be replaced in the future.

Strategically, therefore, management should assess the amount of tainted treasury shares on its own books and the books of acquisition targets. If the level of Treasury shares is too great, a plan to cure the taint must be developed and executed if pooling accounting treatment is desired. If capital is adequate, asset quality is good, the current stock price is very low, and anticipated growth plans during the succeeding two years do not necessitate pooling accounting, an aggressive repurchase program may be beneficial. At issue is the level of future financial flexibility available after the repurchase.

The long-term strategy of the bank should drive the acquisition program, which, in turn, should drive a plan for how such growth is to be funded. For example, a regional bank may decide to emphasize three growth areas and formulate a plan to buy two banks in the future that will provide strategic value over a three-to five-year period. The plan should attempt initially to characterize the relative size of banks to buy; the potential dilution impact; the deal structure (stock and/or cash); the accounting method to be used; and an estimate of the post-deal market value of the bank's shares. If a short-term, attractive opportunity to repurchase shares exists, the entire merger strategy should be reevaluated for soundness and reasonableness. Among other factors, failure to do so may render a later merger plan impotent for lack of powder, that is, satisfactory regulatory capital, or the ability to use pooling accounting.

Playing Out the Consolidation Drama: Three Hypothetical Merger Case Studies

At this stage of the merger movement, with the pick of available targets getting smaller, it is interesting to consider a few hypothetical mergers involving some of the nation's leading potential bank targets. From the strategic perspective of a bank CEO and board of directors, industry consolidation poses challenges like that of a chess game. Great thought is involved in consideration of each move. As the game unfolds, opportunities are opened and options foreclosed.

The hypothetical analysis presented here highlights a number of merger analytics developed earlier in this chapter. We have selected First Interstate, CoreStates, and Barnett Bank as example targets. Although large, profitable, and substantial banks in their own right, each of them is greatly coveted by larger banks seeking to enter their markets. Our discussion will illustrate the desirability of each of these potential targets, as well as likely acquisition prices and potential acquirers.

In working through this exercise, the reader must be mindful that these case studies concern purely hypothetical buyers or sellers. Further, some numbers and assumptions made to pursue the analyses may vary somewhat from the current underlying economic facts. All stock market prices used in the analysis are from June 18, 1993. Again, our primary purpose is to illustrate the principles and merger mechanics involved in the acquisition process, not to predict actual events or values.

Shootout in the West: Wanted—First Interstate

As a starting point in assessing the feasibility of a bank merger, banks often calculate the potential earnings per share (EPS) dilution, independent of prospective cost saves, that a particular transaction implies. Generally, the offer price level or limit of an acquirer is indicated by the maximum offer price that would produce minimal or no dilution. Exhibit 6.14A illustrates this

Exhibit 6.14A

DILUTION ANALYSIS WITH NO COST SAVINGS

First Interstate Bancorp
Dilution Analysis (No cost Savings)
Date of Analysis, June 18, 1993
POOLING TRANSACTION: (100% Stock)

		Potential Acquirers of First Interstate Bancorp ($58.25, closing price of FI on June 18, 1993)						
Price:		50.00	38.63	47.63	53.13	100.13		
		NOB	CHL	NB	ONE	WFC	P.E	Price
First Year								
Postmerger	I	−1.76%	12.58%	8.49%	−2.97%	−5.49%	12.0	$70.17
Earnings	II	1.70%	15.08%	10.75%	−0.64%	−1.37%	13.0	$76.02
Dilution	III	4.93%	17.44%	12.91%	1.59%	2.45%	14.0	$81.86
	IV	7.95%	19.67%	14.97%	3.73%	5.98%	15.0	$87.71
	V	10.78%	21.78%	16.93%	5.77%	9.27%	16.0	$93.56
							BV%	Price
Immediate								
Book Value	I	−29.46%	6.23%	0.42%	−14.63%	−21.98%	198%	$70.17
Dilution	II	−25.07%	8.91%	2.89%	−12.03%	−17.21%	214%	$76.02
	III	−20.96%	11.44%	5.23%	−9.55%	−12.80%	231%	$81.86
	IV	−17.11%	13.83%	7.47%	−7.17%	−8.71%	247%	$87.71
	V	−13.51%	16.10%	9.60%	−4.90%	−4.91%	264%	$93.56
% Assets Acquired:		108.00%	34.06%	40.36%	69.47%	95.32%		
% Market Cap Paid:								
	I	72.93%	54.58%	43.84%	38.56%	95.45%		
	II	79.00%	59.12%	47.50%	41.78%	103.40%		
	III	85.08%	63.67%	51.15%	44.99%	111.36%		
	IV	91.16%	68.22%	54.80%	48.20%	119.31%		
	V	97.23%	72.77%	58.46%	51.42%	127.27%		

PURCHASE TRANSACTION: (100% cash)

Tangible Cap.								
Pre-Acq:		5.60%	4.87%	6.00%	7.59%	4.43%		
Post-Acq:	I	0.36%	2.49%	2.98%	2.64%	0.08%		
	II	−0.11%	2.26%	2.72%	2.26%	−0.37%		
	III	−0.58%	2.03%	2.46%	1.89%	−0.81%		
	IV	−1.05%	1.80%	2.20%	1.52%	−1.26%		
	V	−1.53%	1.57%	1.94%	1.15%	−1.70%		

point with respect to First Interstate (FI) as a hypothetical target and Wells Fargo (WFC), BANC ONE (ONE), NationsBank (NB), Chemical Bank (CHL), and Norwest (NOB) as hypothetical acquirers. In this case, ONE and WFC could pay $81.86, a 40.5 percent premium to market (Level III in Exhibit 6.14A), 14 times FI's 1993 estimated earnings, while undergoing only small dilution.

At this price, the book value effect on ONE (–9.55 percent), WFC (–12.80 percent), and NOB (–20.96 percent) would be antidilutive, or accretive. For NationsBank (5.23 percent) and Chemical (11.44 percent), the deal dilutes book value. Analysts and acquirers generally do not put much weight on book value dilution; earnings per share (EPS) dilution effects are more likely to dominate their perspective. The target bank, however, will consider the relative enhancement of its book value along with enhancements of earnings, dividends, and market value. In this regard, it is important to note that the data pertaining to the acquirer have a flip side. That is, the fact that this deal would be highly accretive to Norwest's book value (–20.96 percent) means that it would be, conversely, highly dilutive to the seller's book value position.

At nearly $50 billion, FI constitutes a major transaction. Exhibit 6.14A indicates that its purchase in terms of acquired assets compared with the asset size of Norwest and Wells Fargo is 108 percent and 95.32 percent, respectively. The percentage of an acquirer's market capitalization compared to what is offered to the seller is an even better indicator of size in terms of deal feasibility. In this context (the $81.86 level), Norwest and Wells Fargo would have to pay 85.08 percent and 111.36 percent of their respective market capitalizations. Transactions of this magnitude are atypical in that they represent too big a bet. The 44.99 percent relative market capitalization for BANC ONE, for example, may signal a problem. ONE's publicly announced policy is not to acquire targets that are valued greater than one third of the combined assets of ONE and the target.

Exhibit 6.14A also explores the feasibility of a 100 percent cash purchase. At level III ($81.86), it is clear that regulators would not see such a large cash purchase as feasible. In the NOB and WFC cases, tangible capital ratios would be driven to negative levels, –.58 percent and –.81 percent, respectively. Given the size of this transaction, it is unlikely that even a mixed deal—50 percent stock and 50 percent cash, for example—could work.

Exhibit 6.14B displays the dilution analysis with hypothetical cost saves included. The cost save assumptions (indicated in Exhibit 6.14B), although approximate, do attempt to reflect the relative nature of the merger in terms of in-market versus contiguous versus out-of-market (see Chapter 5 for merger cost savings discussion). For example, a deal with FI would be an in-market

Exhibit 6.14B

DILUTION ANALYSIS WITH COST SAVINGS

First Interstate Bancorp
Dilution Analysis (Cost Savings)
Date of Analysis: June 18, 1993
POOLING TRANSACTION: (100% Stock)

				Potential Acquirers of First Interstate Bancorp				
Cost Save:		15.00%	15.00%	15.00%	25.00%	35.00%		
		NOB	CHL	NB	ONE	WFC	P.E	Price
First Year								
Postmerger	I	–5.18%	10.81%	6.77%	–6.98%	–15.38%	12.0	$70.17
Earnings	II	–1.61%	13.35%	9.08%	–4.55%	–10.87%	13.0	$76.02
Dilution	III	1.72%	15.76%	11.28%	–2.23%	–6.70%	14.0	$81.86
	IV	4.85%	18.04%	13.37%	–0.02%	–2.83%	15.0	$87.71
	V	7.78%	20.20%	15.37%	2.11%	0.77%	16.0	$93.56

Exhibit 6.14C

MODIFIED DISCOUNTED CASH FLOW

Year	Fully Diluted Earnings[1]	Earnings Discount[2]
1	5.85	5.13
2	6.26	4.81
3	6.69	4.52
4	7.16	4.24
5	7.66	3.98
6	8.20	3.74
7	8.78	3.51
8	9.39	3.29
9	10.05	3.09
10	10.75	2.90
		$78.42[3]

1 Earnings growth of 7% assumed
2 Discount rate is 14%
3 Assumes takeout in year five at 14X EPS

merger for WFC, which could generate cost saves approximating 35 percent of FI's NIE. Because transactions with NOB, CHL, and NB are for the most part out-of-market, only 15 percent cost saves are estimated. ONE has significant overlaps with FI in several states including Texas and Arizona. Cost saves are estimated to 25 percent of FI's NIE. At the $81.86 price level, it is clear that two of the nation's largest banks, Chemical and NationsBank, could not compete because of the indicated double digit dilution impact of 15.76 percent (CHL) and 11.28 percent (NB). On the other hand, the more highly valued banks, ONE (−2.23 percent) and WFC (−6.70 percent), would enjoy immediate earnings accretion. NOB could bid, but it would have to accept some dilution (1.72 percent) initially; it could possibly earn it back in the second or third years.

These hypothetical results seem to indicate that BANC ONE's top-rated currency valuation and position for cost saves give it a strong ability to bid. However, WFC's larger in-market cost savings prospects suggest it would realize even greater earnings accretion at $81.86. Because both banks could deem such a transaction critical, an auction could become intense. Perhaps a final decision in such a situation could ride on qualitative factors important to FI's board of directors.

Another useful exercise involves a variation of discounted cash flow (DCF) analysis. Exhibit 6.14C projects FI's consensus EPS estimate at 7 percent compounded. Next, five years earnings are discounted to present values using a discount rate of 14 percent. To this, the present value of an assumed takeout in the fifth year at 14 times is added to arrive at $78.42. This price has a useful interpretation to the acquirer, acquiree, and the analyst.

Assuming 14 percent is the correct discount rate and the takeout levels still command 14 times EPS five years out, $78.42 indicates an intrinsic worth. That is, it may become the lower boundary for the seller or the upper boundary for the buyer.

CoreStates: A Northeastern Target?

Following the steps outlined above for the FI case, we now consider CoreStates (CSFN) as a hypothetical target, with Chase Manhattan (CMB), Chemical (CHL), Bank of New York (BK), BANC ONE (ONE), PNC Financial (PNC), and First Fidelity (FFB) as potential acquirers. Exhibit 6.15A indicates that $71.65, Level III, is the most likely price range. This price would give a premium to CSFN shareholders of 34.2 percent over the market. CSFN, like FI, would represent a major transaction. On a market capitalization basis, $71.65 would constitute about 113 percent, 91 percent, 87 percent, 59 percent, 44 percent, and 31 percent of the market capitalization, respectively, of FFB, CMB, BK, PNC, CHL, and ONE. Again, this deal would be a big strategic and financial

Exhibit 6.15A

DILUTION ANALYSIS WITH NO COST SAVINGS

CoreStates Financial Corp
Dilution Analysis (No cost Savings)
Date of Analysis: June 18, 1993
POOLING TRANSACTION: (100% Stock)

		Potential Acquirers of CoreStates Financial Corp ($53.38, closing price of CSFN on June 18, 1993)							
Price:		$29.88	$39.25	$56.25	$53.00	$30.50	$45.50		
		CMB	CHL	BK	ONE	PNC	FFB	P.E	Price
First Year									
Postmerger	I	19.99%	9.11%	4.08%	−2.47%	2.15%	6.72%	11.9	$62.15
Earnings	II	22.57%	10.94%	7.09%	−0.85%	4.58%	10.09%	12.8	$66.90
Dilution	III	24.99%	12.71%	9.92%	0.71%	6.89%	13.21%	13.7	$71.65
	IV	27.27%	14.40%	12.58%	2.23%	9.10%	16.13%	14.6	$76.40
	V	29.41%	16.03%	15.09%	3.71%	11.20%	16.86%	15.5	$81.85
								BV%	Price
Immediate									
Book Value	I	17.74%	5.79%	−0.58%	−8.99%	−2.20%	−2.41%	214%	$62.15
Dilution	II	20.39%	7.69%	2.58%	−7.27%	0.34%	1.28%	230%	$66.90
	III	22.88%	9.52%	5.54%	−5.60%	2.76%	4.72%	246%	$71.65
	IV	25.22%	11.27%	8.33%	−3.99%	5.06%	7.92%	263%	$76.40
	V	27.42%	12.96%	10.96%	−2.42%	7.26%	10.92%	279%	$81.15
% Assets									
Acquired:		22.69%	15.86%	53.22%	32.35%	47.33%	74.95%		
% Market Cap Paid:									
	I	78.38%	37.37%	74.52%	26.89%	50.65%	96.91%		
	II	84.91%	40.48%	80.73%	29.14%	54.87%	104.98%		
	III	91.44%	43.60%	86.94%	31.38%	59.09%	113.06%		
	IV	97.98%	46.71%	90.15%	33.62%	63.31%	121.13%		
	V	104.51%	49.83%	99.36%	35.86%	67.53%	129.21%		

PURCHASE TRANSACTION: (100% cash)

Tangible Cap.								
Pre-Acq:		4.39%	4.87%	6.35%	7.59%	7.90%	6.64%	
Post-Acq:	I	2.25%	3.22%	1.64%	3.97%	3.05%	0.71%	
	II	2.02%	3.05%	1.21%	3.67%	2.65%	0.18%	
	III	1.79%	2.88%	0.78%	3.37%	2.25%	−0.35%	
	IV	1.57%	2.71%	0.36%	3.07%	1.86%	−0.87%	
	V	1.34%	2.54%	−0.07%	2.77%	1.46%	−1.40%	

bet. Similar to FI, a transaction with CSFN for cash is not feasible from a tangible capital perspective (Exhibit 6.15A).

A review of Exhibit 6.15B indicates that a $71.65 price for CSFN would probably only be feasible for two of the list of acquirers, ONE and PNC. ONE would enjoy immediate accretion (–.89 percent) and PNC, even though gaining large in-market cost savings, would realize 2.02 percent initial dilution. Similar to the case of FI, CSFN's board of directors would face a difficult choice. In the CSFN case, it is interesting that the two potential money-center bidders, Chase (22.39 percent) and Chemical (10.69 percent), would have to take very large dilution to do an important deal in their backyard, Philadelphia.

Exhibit 6.15C shows the same variation of DCF discussed earlier in the FI merger case. Again, we assume 7 percent EPS growth from 1993's consensus estimate, 14 percent discount rate, and a 14X takeout price in year five. The indicated intrinsic worth is $78.42, or 46.9 percent above market price (June 18, 1993). This value is close to the offer price for CSFN analyzed earlier.

The NationsBank-Barnett Rumor

The procedures outlined earlier were applied to the hypothetical case of Barnett as a target. In this example, possible buyers in the region include NationsBank (NB), SunTrust (STI), and Wachovia (WB). If national banking were legal for Florida, then one could include BANC ONE (ONE) and BankAmerica (BAC).

Exhibit 6.16A shows that a $55.91 price, Level I, would result in 3.18 percent dilution to ONE and much higher dilution for all other potential acquirers.

Considering cost savings (Exhibit 6.16B), a $55.91 offer would be mildly dilutive to ONE and STI. The dilution levels implied for NB (8.41 percent), BAC (8.57 percent), and WB (4.77 percent) probably would make such a deal not feasible. Since the offer price would only be 20.2 percent over market, it is doubtful that BBI's board would seriously consider an offer this low.

Exhibit 6.16C displays the same DCF approach used with FI and CSFN. The indicated intrinsic worth is $57.90, or 25.2 percent above its June 18, 1993, market price. This value is greater than the offer value for BBI analyzed earlier.

What about the recent loud rumors that NB may take out BBI?

What about the recent loud rumors that NB may take out BBI? Because a 25 percent premium to market offer (approaching $60) would suggest more than 10 percent dilution for NB, even with large potential cost saves (30 percent of the target's NIE), a transaction between these two banks is not likely at this time.

In tracing the relative stock prices of NB and BBI over the rumor period, one finds that BBI's stock has experienced stronger relative gains vis-a-vis NB. It appears that effective cost saves from the First Florida merger, significant credit cost recovery, and Flor-

Exhibit 6.15B

DILUTION ANALYSIS WITH COST SAVINGS

CoreStates Financial Corp
Dilution Analysis (Cost Savings)
Date of Analysis: June 18, 1993
POOLING TRANSACTION: (100% Stock)

		Potential Acquirers of CoreStates Financial Corp						
Cost Save:		25.00%	25.00%	25.00%	15.00%	35.00%	25.00%	
		CMB	CHL	BK	ONE	PNC	FFB	P.E	Price
First Year									
Postmerger	I	17.21%	7.01%	−0.42%	−4.12%	−2.98%	1.77%	11.9	$62.15
Earnings	II	19.89%	8.89%	2.73%	−2.48%	−0.42%	5.31%	12.8	$66.90
Dilution	III	22.39%	10.69%	5.69%	−0.89%	2.02%	8.61%	13.7	$71.65
	IV	24.74%	12.43%	8.48%	0.66%	4.34%	11.68%	14.6	$76.40
	V	26.96%	14.09%	11.11%	2.16%	6.55%	14.55%	15.5	$81.15

Exhibit 6.15C

MODIFIED DISCOUNTED CASH FLOW

Year	Fully Diluted Earnings[1]	Earnings Discount[2]
1	5.24	4.60
2	5.61	4.32
3	6.00	4.05
4	6.42	3.80
5	6.87	3.57
6	7.35	3.35
7	7.87	3.14
8	8.42	2.95
9	9.01	2.77
10	9.64	2.60
		78.42[3]

1 Earnings growth of 7% assumed
2 Discount rate is 14%
3 Assumes takeout in year five at 14X EPS

Exhibit 6.16A

DILUTION ANALYSIS WITH NO COST SAVINGS

Barnett Banks, Inc.
Dilution Analysis (No Cost Savings)
Date of Analysis: June 18, 1993
POOLING TRANSACTION: (100% Stock)

		Potential Acquirers of Barnett Banks, Inc. ($46.25, closing price of BBI on June 18, 1993)						
Price:		$43.75	$33.88	$50.00	$53.00	$44.63		
		BAC	WB	NB	ONE	STI	P.E	Price
First Year								
Postmerger	I	9.98%	8.31%	11.70%	3.18%	9.37%	14.9	$55.91
Earnings	II	11.54%	11.22%	13.48%	5.03%	12.31%	15.9	$59.75
Dilution	III	13.04%	13.95%	15.18%	6.81%	15.07%	17.0	$63.60
	IV	14.50%	16.51%	16.83%	8.52%	17.66%	18.0	$67.44
	V	15.90%	18.93%	18.41%	10.17%	20.10%	19.0	$71.28
							BV%	Price
Immediate								
Book Value	I	−2.54%	1.46%	5.77%	−5.29%	−0.29%	255%	$55.91
Dilution	II	−0.76%	4.59%	7.67%	−3.28%	2.97%	273%	$59.75
	III	0.95%	7.52%	9.49%	−1.34%	6.02%	290%	$63.60
	IV	2.61%	10.28%	11.25%	0.53%	8.89%	308%	$67.44
	V	4.21%	12.87%	12.93%	2.32%	11.58%	325%	$71.28
% Assets Acquired:		20.60%	117.48%	31.69%	54.55%	103.85%		
% Market Cap Paid:								
	I	34.64%	91.42%	42.92%	39.73%	96.00%		
	II	36.95%	97.51%	45.78%	42.38%	102.40%		
	III	39.26%	103.61%	48.65%	45.03%	108.80%		
	IV	41.57%	109.70%	51.51%	47.68%	115.20%		
	V	43.88%	115.80%	54.37%	50.32%	121.60%		

PURCHASE TRANSACTION: (100% cash)

Tangible Cap.								
Pre-Acq:		3.55%	8.69%	6.00%	7.59%	7.05%		
Post-Acq:	I	1.63%	−0.16%	2.70%	2.19%	−0.46%		
	II	1.46%	−0.68%	2.47%	1.85%	−0.96%		
	III	1.29%	−1.21%	2.23%	1.51%	−1.45%		
	IV	1.13%	−1.74%	2.00%	1.16%	−1.95%		
	V	0.96%	−2.27%	1.76%	0.82%	−2.45%		

Exhibit 6.16B

DILUTION ANALYSIS WITH COST SAVINGS

Barnett Banks, Inc.
Dilution Analysis (Cost Savings)
Date of Analysis: June 18, 1993
POOLING TRANSACTION: (100% Stock)

Potential Acquirers of Barnett Banks, Inc.

Cost Save:		15.00%	15.00%	30.00%	15.00%	30.00%		
		BAC	WB	NB	ONE	STI	P.E	Price
First Year								
Postmerger	I	8.57%	4.77%	8.41%	0.91%	2.26%	14.9	$55.91
Earnings	II	10.15%	7.79%	10.26%	2.80%	5.43%	15.9	$59.75
Dilution	III	11.68%	10.63%	12.03%	4.62%	8.41%	17.0	$63.60
	IV	13.16%	13.29%	13.73%	6.38%	11.20%	18.0	$67.44
	V	14.59%	15.80%	15.37%	8.07%	13.83%	19.0	$71.28

Exhibit 6.16C

MODIFIED DISCOUNTED CASH FLOW

Year	Fully Diluted Earnings[1]	Earnings Discount[2]
1	3.75	3.29
2	4.01*	3.08
3	4.29	2.90
4	4.59	2.72
5	4.91	2.55
6	5.25	2.39
7	5.62	2.25
8	6.02	2.11
9	6.44	1.98
10	6.89	1.86
		$57.90[3]

* Analysts' estimates for Barnett materially changed after June 18, 1993 (date of analysis). Several estimates exceed $4.50 for Year 2 (1994).

1 Earnings growth of 7% assumed
2 Assumes takeout rate is 14%
3 Assumes takeout in year five at 14X EPS

ida's economic recovery have pushed BBI's stock price materially out of the range of regional buyers. Barring an unforeseen stumble by BBI, it appears that its independence is assured until Florida opens to national banking. Even then BBI still may retain its option of when, if, or with whom it merges.

The BBI case study also underscores the underlying complexity of the risk arbitrage game. That is, those arbitrageurs who circled BBI's shares wrongly estimated BBI's earnings strength versus NB's. However, this very strength and BBI's strong stock price performance limited the losses of those who bet on the rumor.

Merger Valuation:
It Comes Back to Management

The traditional investment banking standards related to mergers appear to be in the process of changing. Guidelines are helpful in that they allow you to efficiently replicate past logic. For example, investment banking logic has priced in-market acquisitions based on assumptions of 30 percent cost takeout and zero dilution. Such rules of thumb, however, can be a hindrance if they restrict one's thinking and make it difficult to address actual problems and opportunities in a changing environment. As mentioned earlier, changing industry standards is one signal of a paradigm shift.

Bank merger and acquisition price trends appear to suggest that transactions are being fully priced. Even assuming the full attainment of all cost reductions promised by management (upwards to 60 percent on in-market deals), many may only be break-even dilutive. This represents a dramatic shift in valuation economics since 1985, when the consolidation process began. This new approach to valuation and deal pricing could have a profound impact on how consolidation unfolds. Reducing costs and redundant delivery capacity is to be expected. Even with acquirers adopting more aggressive consolidation programs, the provision of significant returns to the acquirer's shareholders will continue to be very difficult.

Despite all the valuation methodologies and analytics, the mechanics of doing deals are best understood as simply trappings of the negotiation process. Discounted cash flow and dilution analyses can suggest a price to be offered, but at the end of the day, a high-stakes management judgment must be made. And the judgment is not about what discount rate to use, but rather the determination as to whether shareholder value can be as aggressively created as projected. Management must make an implementation assessment—can the bank's operating levers be pulled as hard as the spreadsheet wizards would like them to be?

After the valuation modeling is complete, it comes back to management, and the question of whether change can be managed fast enough so as to create value. Overcoming dilution is becoming less about merger pricing, and more about the aggressiveness with which management consolidates acquisitions and manages costs.

Summing Up

Competitive markets lead to rational pricing of deals. As more information has been developed about creating value through acquisitions, more rational pricing has emerged. While would-be acquirers may like to keep the benefits of cost savings from mergers with their own shareholders, competitive markets have evolved in such a way that this will not always be so. Despite the economies of consolidation, the acquired bank's shareholders often appear to benefit disproportionately.

Clearly, merger strategies have played a major role in determining the successful banks to date. Smart application of the numerous merger tools identified in this chapter are critical to a bank's survival chances. A perilous equilibrium, however, may be besetting the market for bank acquisitions. As a result, the stakes involved have become higher, the direction of the paradigm shift clearer, and the responsibilities of management greater. The current decade will reveal who is best prepared to compete in this end game.

Having examined the external landscape of commercial banks to determine the implications of consolidation scenarios and strategies, we next turn our focus to the internal operating levers that banks may pull to achieve success. Different approaches to meet the challenges of cost management, distribution management, relationship management, and credit management must be developed in order to truly transform the long-term potential of a bank. The first challenge we examine is cost management.

7

Working the Cost Lever

Although expense management is critical to both short-term performance and long-term competitive advantage, the evidence indicates that most banks do not manage their expense bases well. Ineffectiveness, despite claims of superior performance, is widespread. The availability of alternative conceptual approaches to expense management has not brought success. Reality is that there is no one cost management approach that is superior to all others. Effectiveness varies with the current strategic position and objectives of the bank. Without any doubt, effective expense management is a critical element of the new industry paradigm. Faced with thinning margins and slow revenue growth, management's only available response may be the aggressive working of a bank's cost levers.

Given the criticality of earnings to drive the stock price needed to facilitate acquisitions, the focus on cost management is both appropriate and prudent. In selecting a particular cost management approach, managers must be flexible and choose a strategy that best meets the current needs of their bank, while fostering a culture that promotes aggressive expense management as a key element of managerial competence.

While cost reduction can provide near-term earnings, it is a mistake to only address cost issues as a short-term concern. Because simplistic cost reduction can do as much harm as good, cost management within a longer-term strategic context is what is needed. The difference between the two is subtle, but profound. Short-term cost reduction moves, by definition, do not take into account such key factors as impact on quality, expectations for growth, or competitive positioning of the bank. Cost management, on the other hand, integrates the management of noninterest expense into a broader strategic framework. The objective of cost management is not to minimize costs, but to maximize revenue or perceived customer value relative to the cost base, and thereby, ultimately, maximize shareholder value. Indeed, bank

Because simplistic cost reduction does as much harm as good, cost management within a longer-term strategic context is what is needed.

executives should keep uppermost in their minds the pursuit of profitable revenue streams.

One of the most difficult aspects of evaluating alternative expense control performance is the lack of a comparative fact base. Analyses of expense ratios at the 50 largest bank holding companies over the past five years shows that only about 20 to 30 percent of them have been able to maintain consistent, low-cost positions. It is also instructive to examine the strengths and weaknesses of different approaches to expense management and the situations in which it makes sense to use them. By categorizing the different approaches, an overall approach to expense management can be developed. Lacking a strong expense orientation in the past, there is not a long industry history of success in the cost management dimension.

Reviewing Recent Industry Experience

Effectiveness of expense management is difficult to evaluate simply because banks differ so significantly in their underlying situations. Differences in banks' business mix can be expected to translate into substantial differences in the composition and sensitivity of their cost structures. Likewise, banks in different regions or markets face distinct competitive environments that can affect both revenue and expenses. For example, competition from failing thrifts in Texas and New England in the 1980s affected net interest margins adversely in those regions and produced upward-biased (weak) bank efficiency ratios. Moreover, when comparing expense ratios, regional differences in compensation and real estate costs can cause significant differences in expense ratios between banks in cities like New York, San Francisco, Pittsburgh, St. Louis, and Salt Lake City. Similarly, banks face a variety of opportunities for profitable investment and place different priorities on current and future earnings. Also, accounting policies can vary widely due to differences in reporting philosophy as much as for inherent conservatism. Since much bank investment is expensed rather than capitalized, a bank perceived as high cost may be making well thought-out strategic investments that will result in lower efficiency ratios and higher profits in later years.

Given these sorts of issues, any analysis that uses a single measure of efficiency to compare a large group of disparate banks must be qualified. However, such an examination provides useful insights about banks, in general, even if it has use only for individual banks. Exhibit 7.1 shows 1988 and 1992 efficiency ratios, or comparisons of noninterest expense to net operating revenues, for the 50 money-center, superregional, and regional banks that make up the Salomon Brothers bank universe. The banks in Exhibit 7.1 have been placed somewhat arbitrarily into three groups according to their 1988 performance: 20 high-cost banks with efficiency

	Exhibit 7.1		

EFFICIENCY RATIOS AT 50 LARGE BANKS

Low-Cost Banks	1988	1992	Change
Fifth Third Bancorp	.4963	.4731	(.0232)
J.P. Morgan	.5038	.5922	.0884
PNC Bank Corp	.5319	.5576	.0257
Wilmington Trust	.5369	.5347	(.0022)
Bancorp Hawaii	.5478	.5649	.0171
BANC ONE CORP	.5623	.6040	.0417
Wells Fargo	.5648	.5417	(.0231)
Republic New York	.5674	.5264	(.0410)
Signet Banking	.5737	.6853	.1116
Chemical	.5811	.6440	.0629
First Chicago	.5867	.7228	.1461
Group Mean	.5502	.5860	.0358

Average-Cost Banks	1988	1992	Change
National City	.6017	.6731	.0714
Bank of New York	.6030	.5668	(.0362)
Bankers Trust	.6051	.6649	.0598
Chase Manhattan	.6057	.6540	.0483
Wachovia	.6091	.5796	(.0295)
Fleet Financial	.6138	.5636	(.0502)
SunTrust Banks	.6166	.6091	(.0075)
Old Kent	.6167	.5595	(.0582)
NationsBank	.6204	.6532	.0328
NBD Bancorp	.6208	.6312	.0104
Continental Bank	.6224	.6123	(.0101)
Comerica	.6240	.6959	(.0719)
AmSouth	.6297	.6411	.0114
Crestar	.6346	.7003	.0657
CoreStates	.6347	.6710	.0363
Bank of Boston	.6351	.7441	.1090
Huntington	.6417	.6646	.0229
First American	.6463	.6947	.0484
U.S. Bancorp	.6496	.6481	(.0015)
Group Mean	.6230	.6435	.0205

Exhibit 7.1 Continued

High-Cost Banks	1988	1992	Change
First Union	.6554	.6389	(.0165)
First Tennessee National	.6555	.6488	(.0067)
Society Corp	.6588	.6303	(.0285)
Barnett Banks	.6607	.7390	.0783
Marshall & Ilsley	.6654	.6571	(.0083)
First Fidelity	.6732	.5801	(.0931)
West One Bancorp	.6827	.6458	(.0369)
Mercantile Bancorp	.6830	.6277	(.0553)
Citicorp	.6851	.6430	(.0421)
First of America	.6870	.6858	(.0012)
Northern Trust	.6896	.6823	(.0073)
KeyCorp	.6979	.6165	(.0814)
Boatmen's	.7051	.6379	(.0672)
BankAmerica Corp.	.7059	.6444	(.0615)
First Security	.7100	.6208	(.0892)
Norwest	.7101	.7192	.0090
State Street	.7126	.7172	.0046
First Interstate	.7365	.7503	.0138
Mellon Bank	.7924	.6777	(.1147)
First Bank System	.8000*	.7120	(.0880)
Group Mean	.6983	.6637	(.0346)
Universe Mean	.6371	.6435	.0064

* Estimated on normalized basis.

Note: The efficiency ratio is defined as the ratio of noninterest expense to net operating revenue.

Source: Bank Annual: 1993 Edition, Salomon Brothers, Inc.

ratios greater than .65, 19 medium-cost banks with efficiency ratios between .60 and .65, and 11 low-cost banks with efficiency ratios less than .60.

An examination of Exhibit 7.1 reveals several interesting insights. First, when taken as a group, the 50 banks showed almost no trend in their average expense ratio over the five-year period, with the 50-bank average increasing by less than one percentage point—only .0064—moving from .6371 in 1988 to .6435 in 1992. This lack of trend for the overall group average, however, is contradicted by results for the three subgroups. The 11 low-cost banks showed a significant increase in average efficiency ratio—from .5502 in 1988 to .5860 in 1992. Of the 11 low-cost banks, seven showed an increase over the period. In contrast, the high-cost banks as a group showed an improved efficiency ratio over the period—from .6983 in 1988 to .6637 in 1992. Of 20 banks in the group, 17 showed decreases. The medium-cost banks showed a slight increase in the average efficiency ratio—from .6230 in 1988 to .6435 in 1992. Of 19 banks in the medium-cost group, 12 experienced increases and seven decreases in their efficiency ratios. During a period when the popular press and agenda on the industry conference circuit would have suggested a tremendous focus on cost management, the results are mixed at best.

The significantly different trends experienced by the subgroups, and the lack of a trend for the group as a whole, spotlight the difficulty of making meaningful progress on the productivity front. Overall, banks appear to be subject to a reversion to the mean, with low-cost banks tending to increased efficiency ratios and high-cost banks tending to decreased efficiency ratios over time. The existence of the "reversion to the mean" phenomenon underscores that most banks find it difficult to achieve and sustain a low-cost position. Rather, banks tend to cycle around some average cost position depending upon the priorities and effectiveness of management. This conclusion is borne out by data from 1988 through 1992. We will have to watch and wait to see if future performance suggests any real progress. We know it needs to.

Consider the track record of the low-cost group. Of the 11 banks in the low-cost group in 1988, only seven were still in that group in 1992: Fifth Third, J.P. Morgan, PNC, Wilmington Trust, Bancorp Hawaii, Wells Fargo, and Republic New York. Of these seven, only four showed productivity gains over the five-year period—Republic New York, Fifth Third, Wells Fargo, and Wilmington Trust. Of these four, Wells Fargo is alone in being a "typical" commercial bank. In this case, their superlative performance sets them apart.

Cycling, however, is the dominant behavior. The four banks that dropped from the low-cost group were replaced by five additional banks that had substantially improved efficiency ratios

The existence of the "reversion to the mean" phenomenon underscores that most banks find it difficult to achieve and sustain a low-cost position. Rather, banks tend to cycle around some average cost position depending upon the priorities and effectiveness of management. This conclusion is borne out by data from 1988 through 1992.

over the five-year period. The same pattern is presented by the high-cost banks: of the 19 banks in the group in 1988, 11 had improved sufficiently to no longer fall into the high-cost category in 1992, only to be replaced by 11 new members whose efficiency ratios had deteriorated during that period.

The hypothesis that banks find it difficult to maintain a consistent low-cost position over time is further supported by the fact that of the 27 banks with 1988 efficiency ratios below the 50-bank average, only 15 still had below-average efficiency ratios in 1992. And of that group of 15, an elite 10 actually improved their competitive position during the period by further reducing their expense ratios. Beyond the four banks mentioned earlier, other banks making significant progress included First Fidelity, KeyCorp, Comerica, Fleet Financial, Bank of New York, and Wachovia. Thus, it would appear that only about 20 to 30 percent of banks have been successful in sustaining a low-cost position.

While analytically comforting, embracing "the reversion to the mean" hypothesis, however, would shortchange what we believe is the key overriding variable—management.

While analytically comforting, embracing "the reversion to the mean" hypothesis, however, would shortchange what we believe is the key overriding variable—management. Efficiency ratios will revert to the mean, if management allows it. We believe this behavior underscores the difference in short-term vs. long-term perspective discussed in the beginning of this chapter. In the short-run, strong cost performance can be achieved through basic cost reduction measures. Longer term, while continuous pressure and action is required to improve efficiencies, making productivity gains stick requires an equivalent commitment to a more permanent cost discipline. Moreover, long-term progress can only be made if the source of short-term gains are real, and not simply the temporary deferment of strategic investments.

Reflecting on the data presented in Exhibit 7.1, only 10 banks started the five-year period under our analysis in a good relative cost position, made efficiency gains, and ended in 1992 still among the elite. Looking ahead, continuing productivity progress in the second half of the 1990s will be critical to all banks' success. The successful management approaches of the 10 banks making real progress are worthy of emulation.

The comparative efficiency ratio analysis presented here is not without limitations. The major bank stock analysts and consulting firms do extensive trend and productivity analyses of banks' cost performance. FMCG has a proprietary bank efficiency ratio model that makes adjustments for potential sources of anomalies including workout and OREO expenses, differences in business mix, and extraordinary one-time expense and revenue items. Useful insights can be gained from this type of detailed analysis. At the end of the day, however, either a bank elects to take a proactive stance relative to costs or not. Analysis is not the issue. Management commitment is.

Approaches to Expense Management

Although the record of banks with respect to expense management has been less than stellar, this does not indicate either a lack of interest or resources devoted to the issue. Beginning in the late 1980s, major banking publications began to devote a great deal of attention to expense management. Unfortunately, most of those articles were published by either bankers or consultants and tended to be self-congratulatory case studies in the case of the former, or promotionally oriented descriptions of a particular technique or methodology in the case of the latter. Given the limited success of most banks with respect to expense management, despite all the available written material, it would appear that either significant barriers to effective expense management must exist or that the various methodological approaches are limited in their effectiveness, or both. The most commonly discussed cost management approaches are discussed below.

Mandated Cost Reductions: Across-the-Board and Gut Feel

In this simplest of all approaches, each profit or cost center is required to reduce its operating budget by the same percentage amount. At first glance this across-the-board approach is attractive because it requires little supporting analysis and appears superficially equitable. The approach can be commended. Implementation progress can be easily tracked.

Needless to say, there are many limitations and risks associated with an across-the-board approach. It is a poor way to address redundancies since it is based on an implicit assumption that all cost centers have the same proportion of unnecessary expense. This is a highly unrealistic assumption and does not differentiate between those cost centers that are well managed and operate efficiently and those with excessive or redundant levels of expense. Second, this approach can best be characterized as "antistrategic" because it once again assumes implicitly that all business units and functions are equally important. The drawbacks associated with an across-the-board approach often lead to some form of differentiated, mandated cost reductions. Cost centers are required to submit a menu of possible cost reductions with some subjective measure of priority attached to each entry. Senior management, usually on the basis of gut feel, then selects some subset of reductions from the aggregated menus, taking into account different levels of perceived redundancies and strategic priorities. For example, the consumer deposit banking business may be required to reduce expenditures by six percent while the mortgage banking business is required to reduce its expenses by only four percent. While this differentiated gut feel approach is usually viewed as superior to undifferentiated across-the-board cuts, it can be equally arbitrary and random in implementation. Effectiveness depends on senior management's ability to work together to identify excess expense and make strategic tradeoffs. Once again, management strength becomes a critical variable, even when you are trying to be expeditious and pragmatic.

Even if senior management should have the needed information to implement a differentiated approach, the approach suffers from a fundamental weakness: lack of a normative expense model. Failing to articulate what expenses should be, expense reductions are experienced by line managers as short-term deviations from what is viewed as normal or fair. As a result, even if expenses are reduced in the current period, they tend to creep back in succeeding budget periods as managers strive to return to what are perceived to be normal levels.

Internal Benchmarking

Through internal benchmarking, the bank looks inward across different organizational units, or across similar functions in different lines of business, to identify its most efficient business, operations, or staff units. The business processes and staffing practices of these "benchmark" units are then adopted by the less efficient units. In effect, the bank learns from itself by replicating innovative practices developed in one part of the bank within other parts. Internal benchmarking, as a technique, has proven particularly helpful to multibank holding companies that have acquired multiple banks and thereby have multiple different approaches and practices to examine.

Internal benchmarking has one major drawback and several requirements for success. The drawback is that potential gains are limited to the practices of the most efficient internal unit. One can easily imagine a situation where the practices of a bank's most efficient internal unit are nowhere near as efficient as those of external competitors.

The requirements for successful implementation of internal benchmarking have to do with sufficient size and a supportive corporate culture. The bank must be sufficiently large and operate on a decentralized basis so that improvements to existing business processes may be continually introduced and evaluated. Moreover, banks that offer no discretion to line managers are unlikely to find those managers experimenting with innovative improvements to business processes. A second requirement is that the bank must actively support the sharing and adoption of "best practices" among independent units by encouraging communication and providing incentives. Conditions such as these often are found in bank holding companies operating on a decentralized basis, where each bank is free to adopt whatever practices it chooses. In particular, BANC ONE, whose approach to internal benchmarking is discussed in Chapter 12, has found it to be extremely useful as a way to manage expenses. Beyond the expense discipline benefits, internal benchmarking also helps foster a performance-oriented management culture.

External Benchmarking

In external benchmarking efforts, data on staffing levels and productivity measures are gathered from peer banks and nonbanks in order to establish a reasonable set of performance standards. These benchmark standards can be used both to identify areas needing improvement, as well as to establish performance targets for those areas. While differences in organizational structure and business mix can create problems in obtaining comparable data, many banks have found external benchmarking to be an extremely valuable tool in identifying areas for improvement.

Despite the opportunity to gain real insights into comparative cost structures, some banks have found benchmarking to be less effective than they hoped. Differing experiences are often due to the way banks implement the benchmarking concept. Many banks, particularly smaller ones, benchmark against industry averages and view benchmarking as a source of information concerning staffing levels rather than a model for restructuring their business process.

Benchmarking to industry averages rather than to the bank or banks with the best existing practices creates many problems. One being if the bank is successful, it will end up as an average competitor with average returns. Benchmarks, improperly implemented, could actually contribute to the "reversion to the mean" behavior discussed earlier. By focusing on the average, rather than the above-average competitor, the bank misses many opportunities to achieve competitive advantage. This is especially true for banks that already possess an average level of efficiency.

A second mistake is to view benchmarking primarily as a staffing model rather than a business process model. For example, the number of tellers in a branch may be determined by a benchmark standard that assigns them on the basis of accounts housed in that branch. Many banks make the mistake of adjusting staff to match external benchmarks without realizing that the benchmark standard is inappropriate because the strategy business process, and supporting operating systems, as well as technology, may all be fundamentally different.

Using benchmarking as a staffing model can have two detrimental effects. First, the integrity of the business process can be degraded, and second, this degradation can result in erosion of core competencies that are the bank's basis for competitive advantage. For example, a retail bank following a relationship strategy may need to provide above-average levels of service as part of that strategy. In such a case, implementing a benchmarking standard that reduces the number of tellers to an industry average will reduce perceived service levels and be detrimental to the bank's chosen strategy. External benchmarking provides opportunities for significant self-insight. Management, however, must provide the judgment necessary for effective implementation.

Enlightened management can use benchmarking to push internal thinking and generate new ideas and options for productivity improvement. For example, instead of benchmarking and using the results as a staffing model, banks should instead use benchmarking as a way of identifying superior business processes. By benchmarking against the most efficient competitors rather than average ones, potential savings from restructurings are increased. Moreover, once an area has been identified where substantial contrasts in costs and staffing exist, the real question is why? What are the differences in the business process at the more efficient bank that lead to its apparent cost or productivity advantage? What changes should be made to the business process, not just the staffing levels, at the less efficient bank to make it comparable to the most efficient bank? By demanding answers to these questions, rather than being satisfied by short-term expense savings, long-term productivity gains can be made.

External benchmarking is perhaps the most difficult, but also potentially the most valuable, for those banks already considered very efficient. These banks often neglect external benchmarking because they have little to gain by benchmarking against banks that in most cases are less efficient than they are. To make the most of benchmarking, these best-practice banks must go outside the industry to nonbanks and industrial firms to identify possible business process improvements. The danger that benchmarking will be used in an unthinking way to drive staffing is lessened, since exactly comparable activities usually do not exist. Instead, banks must identify and benchmark against service or industrial firms that perform many of the same functions that they do, such as customer service, data entry, or collections.

Ultimately benchmarking is about goal setting. The more ambitious the goal setting, the more likely high levels of performance will ultimately be achieved. In the early 1990s, Tom O'Brien, CEO of PNC, began to publicly aspire to an efficiency ratio under .50. It is no coincidence that PNC is already considered to be among the better-performing cost-management banks.

Zero-Based Budgeting

Going back to a clean sheet of paper is what zero-based budgeting is about. Zero-based budgeting starts with the assumption that all cost-center budgets are erased to zero. Line managers must then

> *Enlightened management can use benchmarking to push internal thinking and generate new ideas and options for productivity improvement. . . . By benchmarking against the most efficient competitors rather than average ones, potential savings from restructurings are increased.*

> *External benchmarking is perhaps the most difficult, but also potentially the most valuable, for those banks already considered very efficient.*

justify every budget request and establish its need. Psychologically, zero-based budgeting shifts the basic assumption of the budget process from one that continues or incrementally changes current levels of activity to one that forces managers to articulate the basic underlying need for each individual activity. Proponents of zero-based budgeting argue that it leads not only to the elimination of redundancies, but also to a basic restructuring of business processes.

While zero-based budgeting is conceptually attractive, in practice it has principally been employed to pursue incremental cost reductions. Because zero-based budgeting is inherently a budgeting process, being non-incremental is difficult. Fundamental restructuring of a business process requires substantial data gathering and technical expertise in operations and systems, and is unlikely to be accomplished by financial staff under the time constraints associated with a budget process. Moreover, a zero-based budget's foundation is the way business processes are defined today, rather than some alternative. As a result, zero-based budgeting has been most successful in eliminating redundancies rather than driving major restructurings.

Zero-based budgeting also appears to lose its effectiveness if repeated. While the psychological shift in basic assumptions that is the core of the zero-based budgeting approach is often extremely useful in identifying expense reduction opportunities, the fact is that the vast majority of business activities must and will be continued from one budget period to another. If managers are continually forced to defend continuing these basic activities, soon they simply repeat past arguments and come to view the zero-based budgeting process as a paper-intensive bureaucratic process without real content.

Leveraging Scale and Scope

Scale economies in selected lines of business allow unit costs to decline as volumes increases. The existence of fixed investments and centrally driven costs allows banks to exploit the possibilities of economies of scale. Banks can aggressively seek to leverage these fixed investments by seeking additional volumes. The existence of scale economies allows unit costs to be managed downward through active management of the number of units rather than expense line items.

Processing-intensive businesses, such as mortgage servicing, credit cards, corporate trust, and corporate cash management, all exhibit large economies of scale. However, the existence of expense leverage points is not limited to processing-driven businesses. For example, in the traditional retail banking business, economies of scale exist at the account level, with larger accounts being more profitable than smaller ones; at the branch level,

While the psychological shift in basic assumptions that is the core of the zero-based budgeting approach is often extremely useful in identifying expense reduction opportunities, the fact is that the vast majority of business activities must and will be continued from one budget period to another.

where branches with many accounts are more profitable than those with only a few; and at the line-of-business level, with retail networks with more branches are more profitable than smaller networks. Economies of scale can provide important opportunities to lever a bank's cost structure. They should not be allowed, however, to be offered as the reason to grow a business rather than exercise appropriate cost discipline.

Indeed, a key success factor for those banks seeking to exploit economies of scale as part of their expense management strategy is learning enough about their business's cost dynamics to identify how leverage points should be exploited. For example, much marketing expense, such as local advertising, can be leveraged by increases in market share. The emergence of new leverage points is often driven by the availability of new technology or increased volume. In the former case, the new technology makes it possible to automate a previously labor-intensive function and thus change the ratio of fixed to variable expense. In the latter case, increased volumes often justify substantial fixed investments that create leverage for additional volumes and lower unit cost. For example, the introduction of automated dialing systems into collections areas of consumer lending businesses in the 1980s permitted either a reduction in collectors at current volume levels or a greatly increased volume of collections by the current collectors. In either case, a favorable productivity gain.

Many banks also seek opportunities to take advantage of economies of scope, defined as the ability to produce joint products together at a lower total cost than if the products were produced separately. For example, the unit costs associated with operation of a revolving credit system may be reduced if both credit cards and home equity products use the same, rather than uniquely dedicated, systems.

While those banks that have aggressively exploited scale and scope leverage points have often been extremely successful, there are a number of drawbacks to this strategy. First, timing is critical. The first bank to identify a leverage point and exploit it has a competitive advantage, since it can use its wider profit margins to increase marketing expenditures and further increase volumes or make additional fixed investments to create additional leverage points. Citicorp's aggressive 1980s growth in the credit card business is an example of such a scale-based strategy. In extreme cases, however, late entrants may find that the early entrants have attracted sufficient market share that the former stand little chance of attracting enough volume ever to become scale-efficient competitors. Such is the case in mutual funds processing and recordkeeping, where early entrants such as State Street and Northern Trust have used their scale and technological advantages to block the later entry by a wide set of would-be competitors, including U.S. Trust of New York, Bank of New England, and Bradford Trust to name just a few.

Second, achievement of economies of scale or scope is usually associated with high levels of fixed investment, a high ratio of fixed to variable cost, and a relatively high breakeven point. Thus while a scale competitor may have a significant unit cost advantage if volumes are sufficient, fluctuations or a permanent falloff in volumes can result in substantial excess capacity and operating losses. In recent years this situation has arisen in the mortgage servicing merchant processing, and various trading businesses. Accordingly, a scale-driven strategy is a risky one in businesses that are cyclical in their volumes. One need only look at the regular pattern of mortgage company divestitures at the end of any cycle of origination activity.

Business Process Reengineering

Like zero-based budgeting, business process reengineering begins with the psychological abandonment of the current expense structure. But where zero-based budgeting takes place within the annual budgeting process and focuses on current organizational and cost structures, business process reengineering takes place outside those processes and structures, focuses on key strategic processes that add value to the customer, and emphasizes a complete restructuring of work flows and supporting systems. As a result, while reengineering is not going to deliver short-term gains, it offers much greater potential for overhauling a business' cost structure.

Reengineering begins with the identification of the key business processes that are believed to add significant value to the customer. For example, in the case of mortgage banking, these processes might include loan origination and servicing. The work flows associated with the existing process are carefully documented from beginning to end with respect to key functions, outputs, volumes, elapsed times, and issues of quality. The existing process is examined for activities that add value from the customer's perspective. Those activities are retained, but may be restructured to improve efficiency. Activities not perceived as adding value to customers are de-emphasized or abandoned. The resulting "reengineered" process is not only more efficient from a cost perspective, but also more effective from the customers' perspective.

Process reengineering not only addresses the technical structure of work flows; it also examines supporting organizational and management issues to ensure that the new process performs as expected. For example, issues such as training, incentives, and career paths may require restructuring to improve performance. In some cases, where restructuring of the work process

. . . where zero-based budgeting takes place within the annual budgeting process and focuses on current organizational and cost structures, business process reengineering takes place outside those processes and structures, focuses on key strategic processes that add value to the customer, and emphasizes a complete restructuring of work flows and supporting systems.

flow is substantial, or where coordination among key activities is critical, the organization itself may be restructured to support the new process. By design, reengineering seeks to be radical in nature.

Reengineering has a unique set of strengths and weaknesses. By freeing itself from current practices, the bank is able to adopt "best practice" processes regardless of existing structures. However, such far-reaching change involves considerable costs, both explicit and implicit, in the short and long term. Technology investments, retraining of staff, and the potential need to "train" customers all contribute to the common perception that reengineering efforts are high-risk/high-return endeavors. A more constructive perspective is to consider reengineering a permanent, continuous improvement process. While there will be major, perhaps even revolutionary, steps forward from time to time, all efforts are part of the reengineering discipline being ingrained into the organization's culture.

Because reengineering projects cut across existing organizational and functional lines, they often require that staff be assigned on a dedicated basis from the affected areas to participate in the reengineering and to be a liaison with line areas. To be effective, members of this dedicated working group must be perceived as outstanding performers, and their withdrawal from day-to-day management for an extended period will adversely affect organizational performance in the transition period. The stress involved for the members of the group cannot be overestimated, as they will be forced to deal with conflicting personal allegiances and may become visible targets for resentment as the implications of a reengineering effort become understood by the broader organization.

In the longer run, the radical nature of reengineering and its far-reaching implications for every aspect of the bank will create uncertainty, anxiety, and stress on a large scale. Resistance at all levels is likely to occur and can be overcome only by persistent and forceful pressure from senior management. Indeed, implementation of the new processes will require substantial top management attention over a sustained period of time. As a result, the most radical of cost reduction strategies—reengineering—requires a constant management commitment to succeed. Like so many of the aspects of the profound paradigm shift currently underway in banking, management vision and leadership can be the critical limiting factor.

The Cost Reduction Opportunity in Acquisitions and Divestitures

Acquisitions in themselves do not generate cost savings, but they do present management with two types of opportunities that can be aggressively managed to achieve cost reductions. The first is similar to the benchmarking approaches discussed earlier and arises because the combined organization now possesses two approaches to every function. By choosing the more efficient, whether possessed by the acquirer or acquiree, significant cost reductions can be captured. In particular, mergers sometimes provide opportunities to adopt entirely new, or more effective, information or processing systems possessed by the acquiree.

The second opportunity arises because most mergers, particularly in-market mergers, create redundancies in fixed and overhead expenses. Eliminating these redundancies can lever the remaining fixed expense base and overhead, and result in economies of scale. For example, where two merging banks each maintained strategic planning functions before the acquisition, only one is required afterward. In addition to corporate staff, other redundancies often occur in the systems and operations areas and in overlapping distribution systems (Chapter 6 discusses merger cost savings).

In recent years, much attention has been focused on acquisitions, but divestitures often offer equally valuable ways to manage the expense base. The divestment of lines of business that do not leverage the existing expense structure, or that do not have sufficient market share to justify the investment required to remain competitive, can often generate funds to bolster the remaining core businesses and simultaneously resolve current performance issues. Timely divestiture of nonstrategic business lines is preferable to slow, but inevitable, erosion of shareholder value as the competitive position deteriorates over time.

While opportunities for cost savings through consolidation and divestiture are substantial, achievement is not automatic or even straightforward. Considerable effort is required to pursue acquisition- or divestiture-based cost savings. Considerable organizational risk is inherently involved with respect to perceived quality and customer relationships as well as in terms of stress and anxiety among employees.

The Banker/Consultant versus Regulator/Academic Debate

Cost reductions associated with consolidation are viewed by many observers as hypothetical and illusive. An interesting debate—between academic and regulatory economists on the one hand and bankers and consultants on the other—has broken out over whether such consolidation gains even exist. The economists argue that numerous empirical studies have failed to establish the existence of economies of scale in banking and that, therefore, mergers cannot be justified on such a basis. Bankers and consultants, on the other hand, point to the growing list of specific instances where efficiencies have been achieved.

To a great extent the findings of the academics have been based on defective methodologies and flawed or incomplete data sets. For example, the economists have formed their conclusions from two types of studies. The first tries to estimate the relationship between costs and bank size, usually using a sample of small banks participating in the Federal Reserve's Functional Cost Study (FCS). Almost all of the banks in the functional cost sample are under $300 million in size, and many use third-party outside processors to support their back-office operations. Extrapolation of results from these banks to much larger banks involves assumptions of homogeneity with respect to business mix and size that are completely unjustified. A $200 million community bank replicated a thousand times over does not equal a Citicorp!

The other type of study involves a before-and-after comparison of aggregate efficiency and expense ratios for large banks engaged in significant mergers. Once again these studies fail to identify consistent cost savings resulting from mergers. Some mergers produce cost savings; others do not. However, these studies do not explicitly take into account the variable focus and effectiveness of some management teams in achieving potential savings. Once again, management can play a siginficant role in achieving any hoped for normative cost structure behavior.

Bank expenses are necessarily measured on an aggregate level. As a result, they fail to capture or reflect changes in the allocation or structure of expenses. Significant cost restructuring can be pursued and not show up in aggregate statistics. For example, merger-related expense reductions can either be taken as higher earnings or redirected into investments elsewhere in the bank. One study of large bank mergers found that while aggregate expense ratios were not significantly reduced, the combined entities increased marketing expenditures after the merger. Such redirection of noninterest expense toward achieving market share makes strategic sense if previously unexploited economies of scale exist.

Regulatory economist Stephen A. Rhoades, in summarizing the work of three of his colleagues at the Federal Reserve Board, has addressed this cost efficiency debate.[1] Although hesitant to draw conclusions regarding the preliminary findings of three merger case studies (Wells Fargo-Crocker, Bank of New York-Irving, and First Union-Florida National), he notes that all three acquisitions have resulted in efficiency improvement relative to peer cost ratios.

Ultimately, the academic work in this area is of little value or relevance for management decision making because it focuses on banks at too aggregated a level. Large banks are really collections of different lines of businesses that, to a greater or lesser

extent, share a common infrastructure and management organization. It is at the level of the line of business, not at the bank level,
that economies of scale occur. And it is at the line of business
level that bankers are increasingly focusing their efforts and making decisions concerning expense structure. In this context, over
time, the Darwinian process of eliminating weak banks through
consolidation and allowing stronger banks to pursue restructuring
should result in a higher industry standard of cost management in
the future.

Can Management Make a Difference?

At the end of the day, managers are left with three unpalatable
facts. First, very few banks are able to achieve a consistent, long-
term cost advantage. The few banks that do are exceptional when
measured against either financial ratios or management commitment. Second, while there is no normative cost structure that
underlies all banks, the noted "reversion to the mean" phenomenon does exist. Most banks struggle to maintain cost discipline,
perhaps because it is simply not the nature of either humans, or
large organizations to be disciplined. And third, while a large
number of different approaches to expense management exist,
none appears to be effective under all conditions, and many of the
more effective are themselves extremely costly in terms of the
demands they place on the organization. Most importantly, all
these different techniques are available to any bank whenever
they might elect to employ one. Management effort and judgment
will inevitably play the critical role in allowing some banks, and
not others, to join that elite group of banks that has a cost-related
advantage.

From a management perspective, strategic cost management requires balancing and blending two competing perspectives
to cost reduction—incremental and radical. The incremental approaches include mandated cost reductions, internal and external
benchmarking, and use of economies of scale and scope. These
incremental approaches focus on continual improvement to existing processes and view expense management as a large number of
small steps taking place over a long period of time. In contrast, the
radical approaches, such as zero-based budgeting and business
process reengineering, and acquisitions as well as the opportunities available through divestitures, focus on one-time events that
create opportunity for substantial change in existing processes
within a short period of time. To achieve competitive advantage
with respect to expense management, managers need to employ
both incremental and radical approaches.

Incremental approaches are valuable because they use the
talents and considerable business knowledge of the in-place managers. Incremental approaches are also attractive because they can

be implemented within the existing organizational structure. They also require less senior management attention than required by the more radical approaches. However, incremental approaches are most effective when they are applied in a culture that views expense management as a basic business competency required of managers at all levels rather than as an unpleasant, intermittent requirement imposed from outside. Creating a culture that places a high value on aggressive cost management should be a key objective of senior management. If such a culture does not yet exist, a more radical approach to cost management may not only be necessary, but also represent the opportunity to begin the needed cultural change.

Often the most promising opportunities for cost reduction involve obtaining at least the assent, and more often the cooperation, of managers and staff across functional and organizational lines. Such a realignment of resources often cannot be obtained in the course of day-to-day operation, but can only occur in a crisis mode. Such a situation is created, sometimes purposefully, in the radical approaches. Unfortunately, creation of a crisis has heavy organizational and human costs and can consume great amounts of senior management time. Radical approaches, therefore, by definition, can be undertaken only in an institution where the necessary management leadership is provided.

In the final analysis, banks need to pragmatically alternate between incremental and radical approaches. Both incremental and radical approaches to cost management need to be used if a bank is to achieve cost management excellence. And the efforts must be tireless in the pursuit of continuous improvement. Through sustained effort, not only will productivity gains accrue, but a management culture will evolve that makes working the cost levers a source of institutional pride.

In the next chapter, we turn to the subject of distribution management. This, of course, involves one of the largest cost components of regional banks. In our discussion, we suggest that the entire industry distribution profit model needs major restructuring.

8

Retail Delivery Strategy: Systematic Schizophrenia

For as long as anyone can remember, distribution decisions in retail banking were essentially branching decisions. Governed by considerations of local market attractiveness and regulatory constraints, delivery strategy was really about site location decision making. Because most retail customers made buying decisions based on physical proximity, a distribution system of conveniently located branches became an incredibly valuable asset for the bank, a major source of real advantage, and a sustainable barrier to competitive entry.

When bankers talked about retail delivery strategy, they focused on how to achieve the most effective and productive use of this brick-and-mortar distribution system, as well as maintaining, tuning, and enhancing it to manage for profitability and growth. The forces of deregulation, new and changing technologies, and shifting customer buying behavior have all contributed to a new and intensely challenging environment. The branch-oriented distribution systems of the past can no longer be assumed to be effective, from either an economic or market perspective.

Rapidly changing profit dynamics of consumer banking have necessitated a thorough reevaluation of distribution strategy. Exhibit 8.1 presents how environmental pressures have required a rethinking of delivery strategy. Since 1980, deregulation and increased competition has significantly reduced industry profitability. Using 1980 as a baseline, the profits of retail banking could be estimated to approximate $12 billion or 137 basis points on pretax deposits. Over the course of the decade, as depicted in Exhibit 8.1, profit-reducing factors drove down profitability by approximately 124 basis points, principally through deregulation and competition-induced changes in the industry's deposit mix.

The industry did make strides in reaction to these adverse environmental events. Deposit repricing, increased fee income, and productivity gains all contributed to 80 basis points of progress to offset the revenue loss. Nevertheless, over the course of the decade, retail branch profitability declined to an average 93 basis points on pre-tax deposits. Over the ten-year period depicted in Exhibit 8.1, profitability declined 44 basis points or 32 percent, despite rather dramatic, at the time, repricing and cost-reduction moves. The trends that created this 1980s profit pressure will continue in the 1990s. The retail branch system is becoming a focal point of how the industry responds.

Financial service firms that fail to rethink their distribution strategies will not only miss chances to capitalize on marketplace opportunities, but may leave themselves dangerously exposed to competitors, not to mention the perils of a weak income statement. If the overall banking industry is going through a change

Exhibit 8.1

THE 1980'S TRANSFORMATION OF RETAIL BRANCH BANKING

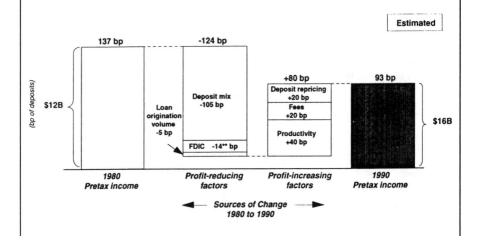

Note: Profitability of U.S. branch banking, 1980 versus 1990.
  * As used here the term "branch banking" refers to activities where balances or revenue are customarily booked in a branch. This includes consumer deposit taking, branch-oriented consumer loans, and services to small business (loans, deposits, and fees).
  ** Includes only FDIC charges between old rate and current "well-capitalized" rate.
Sources: FDIC Call Report data; First Manhattan Consulting Group analysis.

process politely termed a paradigm shift, retail banking today is a world in which its process could be termed rather rudely as being turned upside down.

Nonbanks have by competitive necessity learned to develop and implement effective non-branch distribution systems. In recent years such nonbank competitors as GMAC, AT&T Universal Card, and Countrywide Mortgage have enjoyed great success in taking market share from banks. Banks, on the other hand, have been reluctant to address their distribution shortcomings. Both the complexity of delivery system and fears of branch/non-branch customer cannibalization have contributed to this reluctance. The major contributing factor to banks' generally slow response to delivery system issues, however, is that bank managements have focused too much of their attention on the potentially adverse customer run-off associated with branch consolidations, and not enough on the potential market share gains from non-branch delivery and the accompanying profit gains from cost savings.

As we reflect on current distribution challenges, it becomes immediately apparent that successful distribution management will require schizophrenic, yet systematic, approaches. From a market segment perspective, banks must simultaneously serve preboomers and boomers who place different weights on the importance of the branch. Today, branches are, at the same time, both an important competitive advantage and a costly albatross. Management must balance short-term profit requirements with the need to build a franchise that has future value. However, if banks focus only on gains from consolidation, they run the risk of becoming involved in a game of musical chairs from hell, where a steadily decreasing number of branches seeks to serve an even faster decreasing revenue stream.

The overwhelming industry need is to shift away from the traditional branch approach to a new distribution paradigm. Lower cost delivery approaches are required to ensure profitability in the face of ever shrinking profit margins. Banks must continue to meet current consumer needs as they develop more microsegmented approaches for changing consumer behavior and preferences. Successful response to complex and often diametrically different forces will be one key test of survivability. To succeed, a fresh look at retail banking distribution is required.

. . . if banks focus only on gains from consolidation, they run the risk of becoming involved in a game of musical chairs from hell, where a steadily decreasing number of branches seeks to serve an even faster decreasing revenue stream.

Complex Challenges to Traditional Thinking

Ambiguity is never the friend of easy decisions; this is as true for retail banking as it is for other businesses. Uncertainty in retail banking arises from two sources: (1) a lack of full knowledge about the current business as a potential source and driver of growth and profitability and (2) uncertainty about future developments in customer buying behavior, technology, and regulatory actions. The resulting Gordian knot makes addressing an already difficult issue more difficult. To begin to wrestle with the topic, however, one must begin by examining the underlying retail banking profit model.

Wrestling with Retail Banking Profitability

Although bank cost accounting has made great strides in the past 10 years, in many respects it is still deficient. This inadequacy arises from an inability to differentiate profitability across customers, products, and distribution systems because existing cost systems have been built on a shared, aggregated basis. For example, customer segments may vary dramatically in their delivery needs with some demanding high levels of personal service and physical branch contact and others wishing to avoid it. Segments may also differ in sales and service needs. An upscale customer buying an equity mutual fund or variable annuity obviously requires a much different selling process than a student buying lifeline checking. The cost to sell and service these different customers is going to be very different. Today, however, the MIS capability to begin to address these issues is very limited.

Segment behavior differences cause profitability to vary widely across customers. Unfortunately, most bank profitability reporting systems cannot discriminate across customer segments. A variety of antiquated accounting practices and systems limitations make gaining access to the information sought for meaningful analysis difficult. For example, deposit products are usually accounted for at the branch that opened the account, regardless of where the customer's activity and servicing takes place. With revenues credited to one branch and servicing costs actually being incurred in another, true branch performance is masked. Similarly, the relative profitability of customers using traditional branches, as opposed to those using alternative, non-branch delivery systems, is unknown. While it is intuitively clear that a "self-service" customer who relies on ATMs and telephone delivery should be lower cost-to-serve than the customer who regularly and routinely visits a branch for the same service, no MIS exists to translate this cost reality into the management process and strategic resource allocation decisions.

Finally, allocating service costs to individual customers is imprecise simply because no one has devised a way of tracking and charging service costs to individual customers. How does one allocate the five minutes that the platform representative spends discussing a customer's grandchildren? While such precision is probably not required for strategic decision making, the inability to be precise inhibits the incorporation of such measures into bank MIS.

At the highest executive levels, there is concern about tinkering with a way of doing business that appears to work. If it ain't broke, don't fix it. Because the dynamics of customer profitability are not well understood, there is reluctance on the part of most banks to attack the existing cost structure for fear of fumbling away a profitable franchise. This understandable hesitancy is reinforced by the fact that retail banking's fixed costs are high and usually shared across customer segments, products, and even multiple lines of business. Thus, what appears to be a cost savings at the customer or product level may not result in a cost savings for the bank. This is particularly true with respect to systems where maintenance must be performed no matter what volumes are generated. Of course, if already reluctant to change, the complexity of the required changes allows one to find many alternative rationales to resist change.

From an analytical perspective, however, the problem is that existing performance measurement systems are just not up to the task. What MIS is available may actually make matters worse by misrepresenting performance and miscasting key issues. As an example, one bank used its revolving loan system to support both bank cards and home equity loans. The costs of the system were allocated to different products based on number of accounts serviced. The decision to move bank card servicing to an outside processor resulted in a reallocation of the entire system costs to the home equity business and created an impression that this product was no longer profitable. In reality, the only change had been in allocation methodology. Bankers reading this chapter can certainly generate their own long list of accounting and allocation absurdities that they have encountered. Not only are the accounting obstacles real, but the underlying economic problems also are crucial. Strong leadership in addressing accounting and financial systems constraints that are allowed to block the evolution of delivery system approaches is imperative for successful changes to be made.

Given today's intense pressures on institutions to achieve financial performance goals, it is vitally important that banks take whatever steps are necessary to understand and address the profit dynamics of their retail business. This will require the development of creative and flexible profitability models. Perhaps more importantly, it will require accepting some imprecision for the purposes of getting on with it.

Where Will the Retail Growth Come From?

Retail banking, like food retailing, is a mature industry with almost universal penetration. Accordingly, it is likely that overall industry revenue will only approximate the growth of GDP. Exhibit 8.2 presents an assessment of the growth prospects for retail

Because the dynamics of customer profitability are not well understood, there is reluctance on the part of most banks to attack the existing cost structure for fear of fumbling away a profitable franchise.

Bankers reading this chapter can certainly generate their own long list of accounting and allocation absurdities that they have encountered.

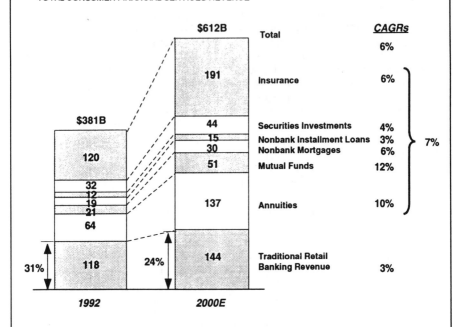

Exhibit 8.2

FORECASTED GROWTH OF RETAIL BANKING REVENUES

TOTAL CONSUMER FINANCIAL SERVICES REVENUE

		CAGRs
	Total	6%
191	Insurance	6%
44	Securities Investments	4%
15	Nonbank Installment Loans	3%
30	Nonbank Mortgages	6%
51	Mutual Funds	12%
137	Annuities	10%
144	Traditional Retail Banking Revenue	3%

$612B

$381B

1992 — 31%   2000E — 24%

Source: Presentation to the Association of Reserve City Bankers, First Manhattan Consulting Group (April 13, 1993).

banking revenues. It is clear that the revenue growth from traditional retail banking is limited.

The mature nature of the business is highlighted by the commodity-like nature of retail banking products. New products are easily duplicated by competitors. Competitive advantages generated through aggressive product development are ephemeral at best. The situation is further complicated by demographic and life-cycle changes among cost-attractive customer segments, and so the market for many banking products is actually shrinking. As more and more baby boomers enter middle age, their needs shift from financing their acquisition of real assets, an area where banks hold a competitive advantage, to complex non-deposit investment vehicles, an arena where banks are only a recent entrant.

At the same time revenue growth has slowed, costs have continued to grow well above the rate of inflation. Obviously, such trends cannot continue indefinitely, and one is led inevitably to the most fundamental question of whether it is even possible to maintain current service levels. If banking's future products cannot generate sufficient incremental revenue, then banks must seek out product, market, or service extensions that permit greater revenue generation from nontraditional sources. Alternatively, the large historical cost investment made in retail distribution systems will face even greater scrutiny. In the early 1990s, branch systems have come under tremendous downsizing pressure. As presented in Exhibit 8.3, it is expected that almost 10,000 bank branches will close by the end of the decade. In

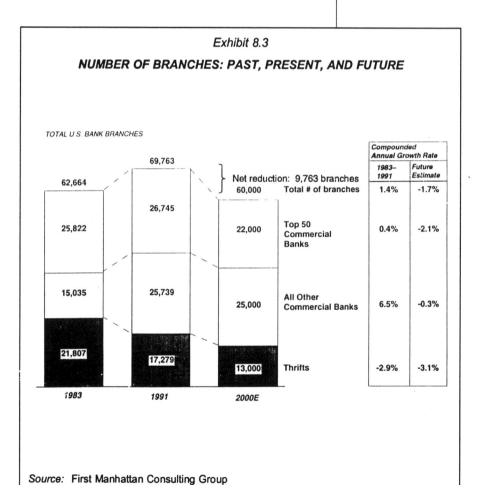

Exhibit 8.3

NUMBER OF BRANCHES: PAST, PRESENT, AND FUTURE

Source: First Manhattan Consulting Group

Chapter 7, we discussed incremental versus radical cost management approaches. In retail delivery, unless the revenue picture changes dramatically, the approach will necessarily have to be radical.

Consumer Inertia: Friend and Foe

The significant transaction costs connected with account closure and opening make most consumers extremely reluctant to change banking relationships. Similarly, they are reluctant to experiment with new products, which are perceived to be risky or to have significant up-front costs, and they often resist investing the effort to learn otherwise. Risk is an especially important consideration in payments system products because customers are unwilling to try new products for fear the product will not perform as promised. Customer reluctance to make ATM deposits is an example of this.

Bank marketers talk a lot about providing value, and how this "value-added" helps to develop a loyal bank customer base. Reality is that what is observed as loyalty may be more correctly termed consumer inertness. This inertness contributes to the stability of consumer deposits and revenues. It is the double-edged sword that makes moving market share difficult on one hand, but acquiring banks to gain market share work on the other. Changing or transitioning existing approaches to retail sales and customer service runs directly into this challenge of consumer inertness.

Consumers' innate conservatism has caused many well-publicized experiments in new distribution systems to fail. The sizable amounts squandered in home banking programs and the slow penetration of automatic teller machines (ATMs) lead to the conclusion that an overwhelming number of consumers still prefer the traditional branch and that any significant change in buying behavior will come slowly. At times, even potentially obvious consumer resistance has not deterred technological development efforts reaching beyond reasonable consumer interest. A good case in point is Texas Commerce's mid-1980s development of discount brokerage services delivered through the ATM.

While such evidence would have served a bank well in the 1980s, it is much more dangerous in the 1990s. There have been many unsuccessful experiments with alternative distribution systems, but there have also been some remarkable successes. Ironically, perhaps, reflecting the rise of superregional banks, much of the successful pioneering is being done by institutions not historically noted for having a high-risk profile. Examples of pioneering efforts include Seafirst in the use of video booth technology, National Commerce Bank, Memphis, in the introduction of supermarket banking, BayBanks' commitment to off-site ATM deployment, Shawmut's promotion of 24-hour telephone banking

Examples of pioneering efforts include Seafirst in the use of video booth technology, National Commerce Bank, Memphis, in the introduction of supermarket banking, BayBanks' commitment to off-site ATM deployment, Shawmut's promotion of 24-hour telephone banking service, and NationsBank's bank at work programs.

service, and NationsBank's bank at work programs. These successes create a toolkit of marketing techniques that can be transferred to other segments, products, and channels and positively affect future customer behavior. A customer who has an initial positive experience with a non-branch channel is much more likely to return for subsequent transactions. Given the investment and time required to bring on new capabilities, one cannot gingerly pilot the new channels, one must be prepared to make an early commitment.

Although customer inertia may have been an immovable force in the 1980s, it may erode much more quickly in the 1990s. Understanding and dimensioning the rate at which customer inertia decays is important to banks. Exhibit 8.4 presents a framework for developing a retail delivery strategy. If banks move too fast in the development of alternative channels, they may risk a series of expensive and potentially embarrassing marketing debacles. If they move too slowly, they will see an irreversible erosion of market share go to more innovative competitors.

At the same time, P&L pressures will increase, raising the stakes of the bet for, or against, continued consumer inertia.

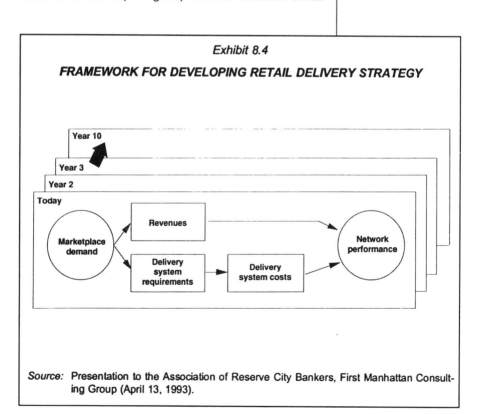

Exhibit 8.4

FRAMEWORK FOR DEVELOPING RETAIL DELIVERY STRATEGY

Source: Presentation to the Association of Reserve City Bankers, First Manhattan Consulting Group (April 13, 1993).

Banks must be aggressively proactive in developing new customer acquisition vehicles aimed at a less branch-intensive marketplace. As managers understand their customers and their profit dynamics better, opportunities for action will increase.

Regulatory Constraints on the Ability to Respond to Marketplace Change

Regulated industries often assume the characteristics of public utilities, providing service to all regardless of the costs involved. Often such utilities are required to provide service to unprofitable customers or market segments, in effect necessitating more attractive segments to subsidize less attractive ones. Of course, public utilities receive compensation for this redistributive function through rate relief, or a guaranteed rate of return on their investment. But, while government policy may sometimes treat banks as public utilities because of the financial services they offer, it provides no countervailing guarantee of profitability.

Regulatory constraints exist on such strategic actions as branch closings, segment withdrawals, and product pruning when such actions are seen to disproportionately affect protected groups. If all financial service providers were equally affected, one could view such regulatory constraints and their accompanying costs as simply a hidden tax. But significant differences exist between banks—and between banks and nonbanks—in their exposure to protected groups. Banks serving low-income areas are much more likely than suburban banks to bear such costs. In this respect, competitors utilizing non-branch distribution enjoy a significant competitive advantage because they enjoy much greater latitude in defining their market area and are less likely to require regulatory approval for acquisitions.

While it is clear that compliance with the Community Reinvestment Act (CRA) is both a source of significant ongoing costs and a constraint on market-driven decision making, it is also clear that it is politically unlikely that any administration will reverse, or even significantly modify, current requirements. CRA is a regulatory obligation that the industry must effectively learn to fulfill. Banks, however, should continue to aggressively push for the opportunity to pursue new sources of revenue as a quid pro quo for their quasi-public utility status. During the 1960s, thrift institutions received special regulatory treatment in return for financing housing; banks serving protected groups or economic areas deserve equivalent treatment.

Facing the Reality of Banks' Fading Competitive Advantage

Given considerable customer inertia, lack of reliable performance-oriented MIS, slow revenue growth, and regulatory constraints on key strategic actions, many banks have been reluctant to make major investments in revamping their distribution strategy. However, as banks face a variety of forces, such as changing consumer preferences, new technological options, and continued competitive pressure and profitability pressures, they can no longer ignore the need for proactive and forward-looking decisions about their distribution systems. Banks' consumer franchises have been built over many years and represent a major source of value for their shareholders. The failure to take action in the 1990s, runs the risk of fumbling away the franchise.

Consumer Behavior Is Changing

Anyone who enters a branch bank at noontime or on a Friday afternoon is bound to conclude that in-person service is still preferred by many consumer and commercial customers. But high levels of traffic may disguise the fact that branch-based service is no longer the dominant form of delivery for most customers. Studies show that for some segments, such as those under age 35, any channel but the branch is preferred.

A new wave of market research and related analysis on usage patterns is revealing new facts about consumer behavior and its implications for retail delivery channels. A barbell-like distribution of customer behavior exists between two major segments of consumers—those that are dependent on branches and those that prefer self-service. Exhibit 8.5 presents the typical usage distribution. Branch-dependent customers highly value the in-person service and social interaction. At the same time, focus

---

Exhibit 8.5
DELIVERY CHANNEL USAGE ESTIMATE

	In Person Teller/ Inside Branch		24-Hour ATM		Telephone Delivery	
	Number of Visits/Mo.	% of Total Usage	Number of Visits/Mo.	% of Total Usage	Number of Visits/Mo.	% of Total Usage
Branch dependent	4.7	70%	1.0	15%	1.0	15%
Mixed channel user	3.5	30%	6.0	52%	2.0	18%
Self-service oriented	1.5	11%	8.5	60%	4.0	29%

group research by banks has had self-service oriented consumers compare going to a branch with going to the dentist, clearly not an analogy that retail bankers should find comforting. With two somewhat polar extremes in consumer preferences emerging, a segmented approach will ultimately be required.

Market research reveals that delivery system preferences differ significantly by segment and geography. As a result, bankers must develop a detailed understanding of their existing customer base and the markets in which they operate if they expect to build an effective distribution strategy for the future. Understanding current and future segment-specific distribution priorities is critical to this task. As mentioned earlier, a bank cannot afford to be either too far ahead or behind its customers' preferences. For most institutions, this will require a major investment in market research and analyzing customer delivery usage patterns.

A 1993 landmark industry-wide study of market demand and usage patterns entitled "The Future of Retail Banking Delivery Systems" by BAI/FMCG, emphasizes the need for this investment. Exhibit 8.6 presents the BAI/FMCG study forecast of future delivery usage patterns. For the branch-oriented consumer, there will be some modest increase in the role of the telephone, but otherwise, their behavior patterns will remain stable. In contrast, the mixed-channel user will somewhat dramatically abandon the branch in favor of the telephone. And finally, according to this recent study, the self-service-oriented segment will conduct 95 percent of its retail banking activity through a non-branch channel. Coupling this customer behavior forecast with already anticipated shifts in marketplace demographics, significant change is ahead. It is essential that individual banks develop their own perspectives on the future and what delivery opportunities are appropriate.

New Channel Opportunities

Consumer acceptance and use of technology continues to expand. Automated teller machines (ATMs) were essentially unknown prior to the mid-1970s. Today, ATMs have become an essential element of how most people conduct their personal financial affairs. Similar trends exist for telephone-based sales and service delivery. This increased acceptance of technology has been driven, in part, by the aging of the population as boomers move into middle age. Preboomer segments have, for the most part, resisted new technologies. For them, the perceived reduction in personal service represents a significant discontinuity. In contrast, boomers and postboomers are much more likely to prefer technology-driven distribution over other options because they view them as extensions of more familiar behaviors and practices. In any event, as the population ages, preboomer cohorts are becoming a

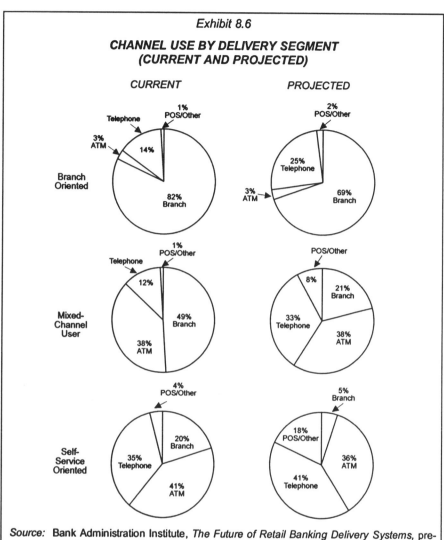

Exhibit 8.6

CHANNEL USE BY DELIVERY SEGMENT
(CURRENT AND PROJECTED)

CURRENT   PROJECTED

Branch Oriented

Current: Telephone 14%, 3% ATM, 1% POS/Other, 82% Branch

Projected: 2% POS/Other, 25% Telephone, 3% ATM, 69% Branch

Mixed-Channel User

Current: Telephone 12%, 1% POS/Other, 49% Branch, 38% ATM

Projected: 8% POS/Other, 21% Branch, 33% Telephone, 38% ATM

Self-Service Oriented

Current: 4% POS/Other, 20% Branch, 35% Telephone, 41% ATM

Projected: 5% Branch, 18% POS/Other, 36% ATM, 41% Telephone

Source: Bank Administration Institute, *The Future of Retail Banking Delivery Systems*, prepared by First Manhattan Consulting Group (October, 1993).

smaller proportion of the population, while boomers and post-boomers increase in relative importance.

A second major impetus to the widespread introduction of alternative distribution channels is the declining cost of technology (see John Russell's sidebar, *Trends in Retail Bank Distribution*, page 234). Both hardware and telecommunications costs have dropped precipitously, permitting banks to experiment with new approaches without major investment. For example, the cost

Trends in Retail Bank Distribution

John Russell
Chief Communication Officer
BANC ONE

Pick any point in time throughout the next decade, and you will be able to make this prediction about banking delivery systems: Radical developments in technology will increase access and reduce costs for all customers. Three factors continue to drive this evolution. First, customers are demanding more convenient access and are willing to pay for expanded service. Second, nonbank competition, unshackled by capital invested in bricks and mortar, is free to develop advanced products and delivery systems from a much lower cost base. And third, a blizzard of new technology will provide an array of access devices and systems that are mind boggling by any of today's standards.

Even so, it is unlikely that technology itself will be the primary driver that generates radical new product development or delivery system capabilities—as it did in the 1970s and 1980s. ATMs, point-of-sale, and home banking represented technological breakthroughs and expanded access points for customers. Advanced technology will allow us to refine delivery systems and communications capabilities in major ways through the decade. These capabilities will make it much easier to identify a customer, process a transaction, and deliver information back at lower and lower costs. The challenge in the 1990s will be to use this technology to develop a perceptible product difference and add value in what must now be a commodity business.

Based on current momentum, delivery systems are likely to advance on at least three broad fronts:

1. Advanced software used to develop a perceptible product and pricing difference;

2. Physical facilities designed to expand lines of business offered in a banking office;

3. Customer access from any point, any time, for almost any type of transaction.

Advanced software introduced in the early 1990s took a radically different approach to processing banking transactions. Previously most software was designed to process streams of accounts by account number. New systems focus on individual customers rather than account numbers. They are structured so that specific elements in each account, such as interest rate, monthly fee, or frequency of statementing, can vary by customer within an account structure. This capability provides every conceivable option in product structuring and pricing at the individual customer level. The software permits differentiation not only from competitors, but also among customers within the bank. These advanced systems also drive platform automation far beyond the capabilities of the late 1980s. They permit bankers to make instant decisions for customers, and, in fact, permit customers to design accounts. The objective is to tie customers as tightly as possible to the institution by providing exceptional service that, in turn, warrants premium pricing. Banks not operating on these new systems will have a difficult time competing with those that do.

The evolution of new operating systems is already transforming brick-and-mortar facilities. With an increasing number of transactions being handled electronically, fewer customers visit the lobby. Those who do will seek an expanded service offering and a higher caliber of employee to provide consultation and advice. Expanded services include financial planning, investment insurance, tax advice, legal guidance, and more. Services that banks are not permitted to offer will be contracted out until regulations change. Selling those services will require smarter, better trained, and motivated people. Therefore, the human factor in the delivery system will likely be a college graduate who is licensed in one or more areas to sell specialized, financially related products and who is being constantly retrained.

Customer access points will also continue to expand. While automated tellers are currently as common as mailboxes, their cost has fallen to the point where they are almost disposable items. Many more will be installed in a wide range of locations. They will dispense much more than cash. Airline tickets, travelers checks, insurance, bank statements, and several other documents and products can already be dispensed through ATMs. In addition, machines that can recharge cash cards are under development. These cash cards will actually replace cash in many vending, communication, and other cash intensive businesses.

Most households will have information centers that will become the focal point for communications, entertainment, education, medical services, and security. Communications companies are currently installing new technologies that use millions of miles of fiber optics, advanced digital networks, and satellite systems in order to carry data from many sources to your home and office.

The next generation of access devices will be hybrids of both computers and high definition television. These devices will provide a full range of communications and processing functions with extraordinarily clear audio and video capabilities.

These advanced systems will have as great an impact on education, entertainment, and shopping as they do on banking. In fact, banking alone will never be able to support these systems financially. The delivery systems will be used by a wide range of providers to truly revolutionize the financial services industry.

of an ATM is roughly half of what it was 10 years ago. Experts predict that it will decline another 50 percent in the 1990s. Similarly, specialized software that greatly increases the effectiveness of direct response and other alternative channels is now readily available. Not too long ago, many of these capabilities were viewed as both too futuristic and prohibitively expensive.

The increased effectiveness and decreased costs of new channels will have three effects. First, a bank's growth rate is no longer determined by the economic vitality of its local market or its ability to acquire a brick-and-mortar distribution system in a fast-growing geographic market. Instead, banks in slower-growing areas are developing alternative distribution channels that permit them to operate nationwide. As a result, growth is no longer constrained by the size and growth of their local markets, but only by the marketing effectiveness of the new channel and their willingness to assume the implied marketing and potential credit risks. Second, new niche marketing opportunities are becoming attractive, as products that were either too specialized or too expensive for a local bank branch to provide now become feasible. Indeed, the most successful regional banks are not those that merely enjoy a healthy and defensible branch franchise, but those that also possess an alternative distribution channel that permits them to generate growth beyond the boundaries of their branches' geography. Finally, new, lower cost channels provide the opportunity to both respond to and proactively reengineer consumer behavior to achieve lower sales and service costs. Exhibit 8.7 presents the most commonly employed approaches to reducing branch system operating expenses. When branches were the only channel available to serve customers, there were real constraints on banks' ability to evolve consumer behavior to reduce the cost to serve different market segments. With today's channel options offering varying service functionality and cost characteristics, more fundamental cost reductions through shifting customer behavior is a real strategic option.

The ability to define, develop, and manage new distribution channels effectively will be a critical competence for banks in the 1990s. New delivery channels will need to both be a source of growth and provide the capacity to serve the increasing proportion of consumers who prefer branch-independent service. These new channels will be strategically critical from both a revenue and cost perspective. And like many of the strategic issues addressed thus far, the constraints are not financial, technological, or consumer acceptance, but management vision.

Thinking About the Future Transition

It is ironic that 10 years ago the absence of branch networks was seen as a strategic disadvantage that doomed nonbanks to being

Both hardware and telecommunications costs have dropped precipitously, permitting banks to experiment with new approaches without major investment. . . .Not too long ago, many of these capabilities were viewed as both too futuristic and prohibitively expensive.

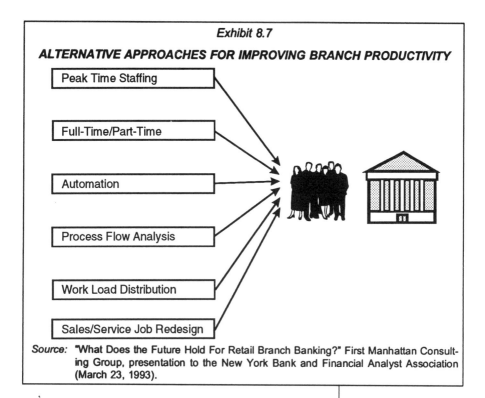

Exhibit 8.7

ALTERNATIVE APPROACHES FOR IMPROVING BRANCH PRODUCTIVITY

Peak Time Staffing

Full-Time/Part-Time

Automation

Process Flow Analysis

Work Load Distribution

Sales/Service Job Redesign

Source: "What Does the Future Hold For Retail Branch Banking?" First Manhattan Consulting Group, presentation to the New York Bank and Financial Analyst Association (March 23, 1993).

niche players. Forced by necessity to compete without branches, nonbanks have made great strides in delivering nonbranch service. The successes of USAA, AT&T Universal Card, Countrywide Mortgage, and Fidelity Investments can no longer be viewed as isolated exceptions. Innovative marketing, combined with electronic and telephone delivery, means that nonbanks now either dominate or have the potential to dominate many key product markets such as charge cards, mortgage banking, and investment products. Over time, one should anticipate nonbank penetration across the full bank product array.

Banks must move quickly, but carefully, to meet this real and present threat by competing on more than locational convenience. The challenge is to develop a concept of convenience that encompasses and exceeds the traditional one. A broader, more universal concept of convenience will enable banks to compete on a more equal basis with nonbanks, and also allow those within the same market to adopt a variety of alternative postionings. By doing so, each bank may truly differentiate itself from local competitors and create a sustainable competitive advantage in the minds of consumers.

At the same time the declining importance of in-person, personal service to a growing proportion of consumers means that banks must develop innovative non-branch delivery approaches if they are to avoid a share-of-wallet loss among younger consumers to nonbanks. Simultaneously, however, branches will remain critical to the retention of priority consumer and commercial segments that prefer traditional branch service. But even with those segments, banks will be challenged to develop new sources of revenues and cost structures that will make the operation of the branches financially attractive.

These two conflicting demands dictate that banks defend and reposition their traditional branch-driven franchises while simultaneously accelerating development of alternative channels aimed at customers who are not branch-oriented. To achieve both these objectives may require banks to adopt a systematically schizophrenic approach to the marketplace. Such an approach would require aggressive defense of its geographic franchise by finding ways to economically deliver in-person branch service to consumers who prefer it, while at the same time developing new delivery channels to attack market segments that are not branch-oriented, and prefer to have their banking needs met through non-branch channels. Either course—focusing and rationalizing the existing branch system or expanding non-branch capabilities—by itself would be a significant undertaking. To pursue both dimensions simultaneously represents a major management challenge. Exhibit 8.8 presents how the economics of serving consumer segments with these two different approaches may evolve over time. Noteworthy are the expected losses projected for branch users.

These two conflicting demands dictate that banks defend and reposition their traditional branch-driven franchises while simultaneously accelerating development of alternative channels aimed at customers who are not branch-oriented. To achieve both these objectives may require banks to adopt a systematically schizophrenic approach to the marketplace.

While development and successful implementation of delivery system restructuring is absolutely critical to long-term survival of the bank, to date many have taken an ad hoc approach to this issue. In part, this is because much management attention and energy have focused on significant short-run cost reductions available from in-market mergers. Also, however, it is not yet politically acceptable in many retail banking organizations to talk boldly about the change required. As a result, at most banks, management has not yet fully wrestled with the fundamental changes occurring in the marketplace. Ignoring these troubling marketplace changes jeopardizes the bank's basic franchise.

Becoming an efficient, low-cost producer is of little advantage if customers wander off while consolidation is played out. By ignoring fundamental and far-reaching changes in consumer preferences, banks risk initiating a death spiral of consolidation and market share erosion, leading to further consolidation, where eventually, the music stops with no chair left being available. Inventing new and improved approaches to sales, service, and delivery is as critical to success as achieving cost reductions

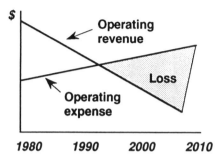
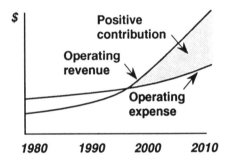
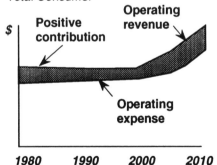
Retail Delivery Strategy **239**

through consolidation. If banks do not address the distribution issue quickly, irrelevance—from consumers' perspective—will be the industry's fate.

Adopting a Market-Based Approach to Meeting Customer Delivery Needs

If banks are to be effective in reacting to the fundamental changes in consumer preferences and behavior taking place today, they must use market-based approaches in their problem solving.

Market-based refers to the character of the market as it actually is today rather than a management assessment founded on historical experience. Historically based conclusions about consumer behavior and the traditional business profit model, no matter how useful they once were, must be aggressively scrutinized for relevance. Managers must build a new set of business and marketing assumptions based on current customer research and analysis. The ultimate competitive advantage does not lie with technology or economies of scale, but with superior knowledge of the consumer, a corresponding business profit model, and the ability to keep both up-to-date.

Historically-based conclusions about consumer behavior and the traditional business profit model, no matter how useful they once were, must be aggressively scrutinized for relevance.

New Approaches to Segmentation

A key element in developing a market-based approach is establishing appropriate segmentation. Traditionally, in consumer banking most approaches to segmentation have been based on age and income; they have generally worked well, as long as delivery preferences remained homogenous across segments. But consumers are beginning to differentiate themselves by delivery preferences. As a result, new approaches to segmentation must be developed, especially ones based on delivery channel preferences and profitability to the bank.

Segmenting consumers by delivery channel preferences and profitability means that distribution-related strategic issues can be addressed using a fact base that addresses the needs of both the customer and the bank. Examining revenue-cost relationships by segment allows the bank to establish appropriate strategic priorities and avoid costly and embarrassing errors. Identifying service and functionality requirements by segment ensures meeting customer needs and allows the bank to engineer delivery channels to meet profitability targets. In addition, the buying behavior of distribution-related segments is often driven by key life events, such as relocation or retirement. Identification and exploitation of these key events is often critical to marketing success.

A market segment-based approach to delivery strategy does not require understanding rocket science, but it does require change More homogeneous marketing approaches have long been preferred for their communication and implementation ease. Of course, today, one must be increasingly focused on impact.

While new segmentation approaches will be valuable in identifying opportunities for adding new channels, they will be equally helpful in generating insights about how to reconfigure old ones. Once again, the emphasis should be on meeting customer needs. Those services that are perceived by the customer as adding value should be emphasized; all others should be discontinued, or at least de-emphasized.

Convenience will continue to play a key role in determining customer preferences, but instead of restricting the definition of convenience to geographical proximity only, it should be expanded to include convenience of time, place, and mode. Once customers define what convenience means to them, managers then need to establish how much they value each form of convenience. Consumer evaluation will then determine whether the convenience can be packaged and delivered in a way that meets the bank's economic goals. Products can be designed around consumers' delivery needs that also make sense from a delivery economics perspective. BankAmerica's Versateller checking, an ATM-oriented checking account, is an example of such a product.

Addressing Customer Channel Economics

The ability to align delivery costs with customer preferences and actual usage is key to both developing new channels and defending old ones. As customer preferences and delivery costs change over time, banks must continually adapt their channels to be cost-efficient and service-effective. To do so, they must establish a clear understanding of the cost of serving different customer segments through different channels.

The imperative of designing delivery channels to be responsive to customer needs does not mean that banks should neglect a key lever that they have available. Banks have the potential, through the use of appropriate incentives, to manage consumer behavior and service costs. In designing new channels or reconfiguring old ones, banks need to manage customer behavior proactively. To do so successfully, banks need to understand what changes in behavior will have the greatest impact on costs and the least on perceived benefits; they also have to understand what leverage points are available to secure desired behavior. Incentives are often the most visible leverage points, but others, such as bundling a perceived high value attribute with a desired change in behavior, are also possible.

The Future of Retail Banking Distribution Systems

As retail banking becomes more complex and differentiated, management will have to alter the way it thinks about distribution. In the past, when all banks used similar, homogenous, branch-based distribution channels, good management could be defined as efficient and effective operation of the branch system. Because competitors managed their own branch systems, performance was easily measured in terms of relative performance, with benchmarking studies versus peer competitors used as the principal vehicle to measure relative performance. Market penetration was most easily measured as the proportion of households served in a geographic market. Efficiency was commonly measured as cost per account, operating expense per dollar of deposits, or average branch deposit size. As retail banking becomes more heterogenous, both in customer preferences and the delivery channels used to satisfy them, these gross measures of managerial performance fail to reflect either the reality of market dynamics or managerial performance.

Future market penetration studies may still use households as the basic unit of measurement but will focus on discrete customer segments. Market segments will be defined in terms of their preference for particular delivery channels instead of by gross geographical aggregate. In addition, as banks become more credible competitors for other products besides insured deposits, the concept of share-of-wallet, or proportion of total household revenue expended on financial services, will increasingly become a key measure of marketing and delivery performance. Similarly, cost-per-account becomes a less valid measure of efficiency than total cost-to-serve, which distinguishes between segments that use similar products but different distribution channels.

The Need for New Channels

Over the past 10 years the consumer goods industry has learned that effective product management requires brands, no matter how well established, to undergo constant reinvigoration and repositioning through addition of new features and extensions. Retail banking requires a similar process of continual reinvigoration if it is to preserve its consumer franchise. In banking, however, the process of repositioning and innovation must encompass not only product features but delivery channels as well.

Demographic and psychological changes will require new channels to satisfy new definitions of convenience. Indeed, the ability to conceive, implement, and manage new distribution channels will be a key competitive weapon. Successful exploitation of new distribution channels will enable banks to achieve

Market segments will be defined in terms of their preference for particular delivery channels instead of by gross geographical aggregate. . . . the concept of share-of-wallet, or proportion of total household revenue expended on financial services, will increasingly become a key measure of marketing and delivery performance.

significant one-time gains in market share, similar to those experienced by Citibank and BayBanks during the 1980s when they aggressively introduced ATM networks in New York and Boston, respectively. Such innovative approaches to distribution truly differentiate banks from their competitors.

In some cases new distribution channels may use much of the infrastructure and processes that support existing channels and require only marginal incremental resources, such as those incurred when adding a branch phone for loan applications. Others may require a quantum leap in terms of resources and support. While multiple channels will be a major drain on bank resources, they offer the opportunity, if properly designed, for banks to achieve significant cost reductions compared to traditional channels.

Multiple channels will require the development of both new managerial skills and a new organizational paradigm. Just as consumer goods companies developed product managers, banks must develop managers who are experts in distribution management. These distribution managers will be experts in designing, developing, and managing distribution systems. Much of their time will be spent in developing organizational structures and incentives to support new distribution initiatives, which, in turn, will involve training, incentives, MIS, and defining managerial roles and responsibilities. Exhibit 8.9 summarizes the challenges and management priorities in evolving the retail delivery system.

Given the complexity of the issues, the resources required, and the undeniable risks involved, it is tempting for management to defer addressing delivery system issues until the industry consolidation now under way is completed. But to refrain from addressing these issues would be a major mistake. First, delaying implementation risks losing both marketing and cost advantages to nonbanks who are already moving aggressively. Second, distribution strategy should become a major part of consolidation strategy. For example, a potential acquisition is worth more if it possesses a new channel or marketing advantage that can be levered through consolidation.

Managing the Implementation Process

Too often banks address delivery system issues on an ad hoc basis, conducting small-scale experiments with new approaches but failing to either put them into a conceptual framework or back the successful ones with substantial resources. Instead, they need to develop explicit management processes to support effective, large-scale change: for instance, one that would include a strategic blueprint for delivery system development. Such a strategic plan would not only set out priorities for direction but also identify integrative mechanisms across different channels. This is particularly important where channels share systems, facilities, or marketing endpoints.

. . . it is tempting for management to defer addressing delivery system issues until the industry consolidation now under way is completed. But to refrain from addressing delivery system issues would be a major mistake.

	Exhibit 8.9		

**MANAGEMENT PRIORITIES FOR MANAGING
THE RETAIL DELIVERY SYSTEM**

	Historical	*Today*	*By 2000*
Facilities investment	High	Moderate	Low, significant charge-offs
Platform/teller automation	Moderate	High	Low
Sales training	Low	High, aimed at branches	Moderate, aimed at central sales force
Customer information systems	Low	Moderate, decentralized	High, centralized
ATMs	Moderate	Moderate, on-site	High, off-site
Interactive technologies	Nonexistent	Low	High, with many nonbank participants
Advertising/marketing	Moderate	Low	Very high

Source: "What Does the Future Hold For Retail Branch Banking?" First Manhattan Consulting Group presentation to the New York Bank and Financial Analyst Association (March 23, 1993).

As a first step in implementing a strategic plan for channel development, management needs to establish clear performance goals in terms of segment penetration, share-of-wallet, and cost-to-serve. Management information systems (MIS) that support and measure performance against these goals need to be designed and built. Key milestones that drive the reengineering and restructuring process should be established and managers held accountable for their achievement. At the same time, as the internal resources of the bank are being mobilized, management also must build regulatory support for any transition that affects protected groups. Obviously, as in other projects involving large-scale change, visible leadership on the part of top management will be essential in developing strategic vision, maintaining pressure for swift implementation, and overcoming organizational obstacles to success.

Managing the Transition

A key challenge for management is the pace of change. Moving too quickly could result in costly and embarrassing marketing debacles. Moving too slowly risks the erosion of the bank's customer franchise. Ultimately, factors such as changes in consumer preferences, acceptance and use of new channels, and financial constraints and requirements will determine the appropriate rate of change.

A Systematically Schizophrenic Approach is Required

Perhaps one of the most difficult aspects of managing a retail banking franchise in the 1990s is management's need to implement sometimes diametrically opposed approaches to channel management simultaneously. This schizophrenic approach is necessary because the value of the existing branch-driven delivery system must be defended tenaciously while, at the same time new delivery systems designed to replace branches are being developed. Thus, branches are both a key competitive strength and a network of albatrosses to be replaced as soon as possible.

The need for a deliberately schizophrenic approach to retail banking extends past the branch. Management must also balance short- and long-term requirements for profit and revenue as well as current profitability and the future value of the franchise. Should the value of the current franchise be harvested in the form of current earnings or reinvested in new or reconfigured distribution? Finally, management must emphasize the critical need to meet consumer demands at the same time it is seeking to change consumer behavior and preferences through incentives and managed behavior. If the mark of a creative personality is the ability to address two opposing ideas simultaneously, then retail bankers of the 1990s will be forced by their environment to become creative geniuses.

Perhaps one of the most difficult aspects of managing a retail banking franchise in the 1990s is management's need to implement sometimes diametrically opposed approaches to channel management simultaneously.

The Leadership Requirement

Technological expertise and marketing creativity will be necessary, but will not be the only qualities required for success in banking in the future. These qualities, while critical, will lead only to ineffective, ad hoc experimentation unless backed up by strong managerial leadership at both the strategic and operational levels. Only forceful leaders can marshal the necessary resources to make a strategic impact and overcome the organizational barriers to success. In setting its agenda, senior management needs to identify certain key areas where it must focus its attention.

Senior management must proactively lead the development of the new business paradigm and set strategic priorities. Because resource requirements to implement new distribution approaches will be significant over time, any doubts among the management group regarding the strategic role of retail banking within the bank's business portfolio must be resolved. Real and perceived risks must be identified and proactively managed. Hot issues, such as priorities for technological investments and cannibalization of existing businesses, must be explicitly addressed. If such key strategic issues are not resolved early on, they will inevitably emerge later to hinder effective implementation.

Once strategic issues are resolved and priorities set, management must aggressively address internal organizational barriers to swift implementation. Elimination of organizational silos and barriers to cross-functional cooperation is critical, and can best be addressed by special project teams and coordinating groups. In other cases, success may require the introduction of a completely new organizational paradigm. In all cases, development of appropriate MIS is essential; failure to address the MIS needs of channel managers may doom the evolutionary process.

At the end of the day, the constancy of CEO sponsorship is imperative if these initiatives are to succeed. Developing and implementing a new business paradigm, with its accompanying delivery channels, MIS, organization, and management processes, is a task requiring years rather than months. Any slackening in CEO attention will soon be perceived by line managers as lack of commitment. Thus, CEOs need to view the transformation process as a major accomplishment to be completed over their tenure, rather than as part of a budget process.

Owing to the complexities involved, resources required, and risks existant, most banks have chosen to postpone addressing delivery system issues until the consolidation process that is occurring throughout the industry is completed. But delay risks the loss of banking's traditional customer franchise to aggressive nonbank competitors. If banks do not move more aggressively, they may become irrelevant anachronisms in the emerging financial order.

In the industry's recent history, retail delivery issues were viewed principally as cost issues. Today, once again, they are being reframed as market share issues. Against this backdrop, getting maximum revenue from the bank's market share becomes the next challenge. In Chapter 9, we examine the industry's approach to the revenue growth challenge—relationship management.

9

The New Search for Growth: Relationship Banking

Consumer banking is different from many other consumer-oriented businesses because a large proportion of customers prefer to make their buying decisions based on personal relationships. While this is beginning to change with the advent of national brands (e.g., BANC ONE, NationsBank, and American Express), in many market segments it remains a dominant influence. A related issue for many banks is what effect will the proliferation of non-branch distribution have on their customer relationships. Will customer relationships wither as customers become less dependent on in-person branch service? Appropriately understanding consumer buying behavior is critical to the design of bank marketing and distribution strategies, organizational design, and even the basic profit model.

In corporate and commercial banking markets, a similar situation exists. For decades, personal relationships drove the corporate treasurer's selection of a banker. Today, like the consumer market, long-term personal relationships are being challenged by competitive pricing and expertise in the commercial customer's bank selection process.

What does the future hold for the traditional relationship approach that cemented together bank and customer? We argue that relationships need not necessarily be lost, but that banks must make greater efforts to understand the customer and to incorporate relationship-building elements into their new marketing, sales, and service approaches. Eventually, the now inconsistent approaches of relationship and product-management will be synthesized into an approach that emphasizes managing customer relationship profitability, regardless of the buying preferences of the specific market segment or customer.

What Is Relationship Banking?

A banking relationship is a mutually acknowledged, conscious commitment by both the customer and the bank to do business with each other over a sustained period of time. Banking relationships must be consciously acknowledged, especially on the part of the customer, if they are truly to exist and have operational implications. Many banks make the error of assuming that every customer who purchases a product from them constitutes a relationship. Internal measurement systems often reinforce this misperception. If these supposed relationships are surveyed, however, it is soon found that a large number of customers do not recall, at least on an unprompted basis, having purchased any product from the bank. Others remember having made past purchases, but consider them incidental and the bank as a secondary provider. Usually only a small proportion of customers actively identify their bank as being their primary financial services provider. It is only this small proportion of customers willing to acknowledge the bank as being their primary product provider that constitutes true relationships.

While some banks define their relationship customers by the number or type of products purchased from the bank—checking account holders or customers purchasing two or more products, for instance—these product-driven definitions are only approximations for what, in its most basic sense, is a conscious psychological commitment. To be a relationship, the revenues derived from the customer must be material and sustained. Often, product cross-selling ratios do not incorporate materiality of the revenues captured. Moreover, many institutions have misdefined their cross-sale ratio to almost delegitimize its use for strategic performance measurement purposes. For example, if a consumer's checking account counts for one product, should the inclusion of an ATM card count as two? Given the peculiarities of measuring true cross-sales, we argue later in this chapter for the adoption of a revenue-based measure, share-of-wallet, as the most appropriate measure of the depth of a customer relationship.

In a true banking relationship, current buying decisions are influenced by past occurrences. The time horizon of relationship customers transcends the current transaction and includes both historical transactions and expectations of future ones. Not all consumers wish to buy on a relationship basis, preferring instead a transaction basis in which each buying decision is made independently and is not affected by past purchases.

Not only do relationship and transaction customers have different time horizons, they also differ in their perception of value. Transaction customers focus more on tangible product features, price, and other explicitly measured sources of value-added service. In contrast, relationship customers are driven by intangi-

Banking relationships must be consciously acknowledged, especially on the part of the customer, if they are truly to exist and have operational implications.

Often, product cross-selling ratios do not incorporate materiality of the revenues captured. Moreover, many institutions have misdefined their cross-sale ratio to almost delegitimize its use . . .

bles usually associated with the way the product is sold and delivered. In many cases, the relationship customers' banking business is heavily directed by who does the selling and servicing—the long-term branch manager that has developed into a personal friend or the newly minted MBA business lender. In either case, relationship or product, success can be measured by increased revenues and resulting share-of-wallet gains. The marketing challenge is to match the appropriate approach with the needs and buying behavior of a specific customer or market segment.

Advantages to the Bank

Banks derive several important advantages from attracting relationship-oriented customers. The psychological commitment on the part of the customer to do business with the bank manifests itself in the customer essentially giving the bank the right of first refusal when purchasing new products to meet evolving financial service needs. That is, relationship customers prefer to bundle, or consolidate, their product purchases at their relationship bank; the right of first refusal gives the bank important competitive and economic advantages. For the bank, it is easier and cheaper to sell additional products to relationship customers than to attract new customers. The ability of banks to cross-sell products to relationship-oriented customers has long been a key determinant of franchise value in banking.

While the ability to cross-sell is an important benefit to the bank, relationships offer other competitive advantages. Because relationship customers value delivery-related intangibles, more than product features and price, they are usually less price sensitive than transaction-oriented customers. Also, relationships tend to be self-reinforcing in the sense that each successive transaction renews the customer's psychological commitment to the relationship and increases the likelihood of future transactions.

Finally, customers are often loath to change banks because of perceived high switching costs. These costs increase with the number of products involved, and so relationship customers are less likely to leave the bank than are transaction-oriented customers. Thus, forming and maintaining relationships is an important way to manage customer retention. Norwest, for example, believes that if it can establish a customer relationship that includes three or four different products, then it has effectively safeguarded that customer from competitive threats. Relationships are seen as a way to slam the back door, as well as sell new business.

Norwest, for example, believes that if it can establish a customer relationship that includes three or four different products, then it has effectively safeguarded that customer from competitive threats. Relationships are seen as a way to slam the back door as well as sell new business.

Advantages to the Customer

Many bank managers recognize the benefits that accrue to the bank from relationship banking, but do not fully understand the customer's benefits. What is clear is that customers are heterogeneous. As a result, the benefits—and the importance of those benefits—that they perceive from a banking relationship, both relatively and over time, will differ from customer to customer. For example, 40 years ago, when consumer lending was only quasi-respectable and credit was periodically rationed, many consumers believed that establishment of a banking relationship would give them preferred access to credit. By consolidating their deposit business at a particular bank, they believed they could increase the chances that the bank would extend them credit when they needed it.

Over time, the quid pro quo basis for banking relationships has eroded as consumer credit has become a commodity easily and widely available. The important exceptions to this trend are in private banking and small business. In the former, the willingness and ability to extend credit based on unique and hard-to-value collateral (e.g., race horses, art, collectibles) are often an important attraction to the customer. In the latter, although only about one-third of small businesses actually borrow, the perceived potential availability of credit repeatedly appears as a key concern of these customers.

Strategic Value of Adopting a Relationship Approach

If the quid pro quo basis for banking relationships has deteriorated because of competitive developments, then what has replaced it?

If the quid pro quo basis for banking relationships has deteriorated because of competitive developments, then what has replaced it? Common wisdom among many managers is that locational convenience, defined as physical proximity to the nearest branch, is an important factor. For those customers who use the branch for check cashing and other transactions, the frequent nature of such patronage creates a psychological awareness of the bank, and tends to build personal relationships with branch staff and present opportunities for selling additional products.

These considerations have led many banks to focus on attracting more checking accounts in order to establish more customer relationships. Marketing studies have shown that customers who purchase a checking account as their first product—in comparison to some other product such as a home mortgage—are much more likely to purchase a second product from the same bank within a one-year period.

Although physical proximity and locational convenience may be important in initially establishing a banking relationship, other factors may be more important in extending that relationship past the purchase of simple, commodity-like products. Relationships often play key roles in the purchase of complex, high value-added products. When purchasing such products, the customer often must depend on the sales representative for advice about an appropriate course of action. In such a situation, perceived integrity, expertise, and commitment to the long-term welfare of the customer are of paramount importance. Customers rightly perceive that they are more likely to find these qualities in a relationship environment than in a transaction-driven one.

The successful entry of banks into complex investment product areas such as mutual funds and annuities is an example of the importance of a trust-based relationship. Indeed, for the many customers who perceive banks as having a higher level of integrity than brokers, this perception is a deciding factor in their purchase of the product from a bank rather than from a nonbank. Professionals such as physicians, attorneys, investment bankers, and consultants, have long recognized the importance of being perceived as trusted advisers. As banks begin to seek an increasing share of their revenue from nontraditional, complex, high-margin products, they must add trusted adviser to their current role as a convenient, reliable provider of commodity products. The challenge is to lever banks' traditional relationship positioning into the role of trusted adviser. What may on the surface appear to be only a difference in semantics, however, will probably come to be understood as a major marketing challenge.

As banks begin to seek an increasing share of their revenue from nontraditional, complex, high-margin products, they must add trusted adviser to their current role . . .

Although empirical data are lacking, the relative importance of convenience, personal relationships, and trust/expertise in the establishment and maintenance of the banking relationship probably differs from customer to customer. For example, locational convenience and personal relationships may be more important in rural markets than urban ones. In parallel fashion, trust/expertise may be more important to less sophisticated customers. Banks striving to build relationships should determine not only who is relationship-driven, but also the exact nature of the benefits those customers seek from the banking relationship.

Relationship management is an integral part of the marketing strategy of the supercommunity bank. Anat Bird, a consultant with considerable experience in supercommunity banking strategies, emphasizes that banks are not size bound. That is, this approach to banking can be applicable to various size regional banks such as BANC ONE or Old Kent, as well as relatively small community banks (see Anat Bird sidebar, *Supercommunity Banking*, page 252).

Managing Share-of-Wallet

Ultimately, any customer strategy should be seeking to capture the maximum amount of profitable business from the customers served. Increasingly, this approach is referred to as managing "share-of-wallet." The term conjures up visual images of banks competing for maximum share of each individual customer's, either retail or commercial, financial services business.

Supercommunity Banking

Anat Bird
National Director, Financial Institutions
Consulting Group, BDO Seidman

Supercommunity banking is a strategic position which is designed to allow medium-sized banks to outlocal the nationals and outnational the locals. However, the strategy is not size bound, and the venerable BANC ONE is one prime example of a large, successful supercommunity bank. The supercommunity banking strategy is three-pronged: strong community orientation, customer-transparent cost savings, and a broad product line. This strategy is unique in that it provides defenses against large and small banks, builds value in the franchise, and generates strong earnings.

Supercommunity banks take the best of both the small bank and the megabank worlds to combine into a winning strategy. They are committed to a community orientation to serve their customers. Local decision-making authority and strong ties to the community are critical to success; hence, the presence of a local president and the support of a board comprised of local community leaders are very important components of the supercommunity banks. Although they represent a layer of overhead that could otherwise be eliminated, they also represent the bank's commitment to the service implications of community banking. Reduced customer turnover, improved cross-selling, and greater pricing flexibility represent the return on that investment. Local presence also facilitates growth of local market share through the use of the president's and the board's local contacts.

Another major competitive advantage of community banks is the accessibility of senior management and other decision-makers to customers. Small or large customers alike can speak with the department head and the president to gain access to the decision making and transaction flexibility resident only at the senior management level. The supercommunity bank ensures that those characteristics do not get lost in the process of creating a larger holding company. Much like the small community bank, the supercommunity banking organization strives to retain employees at the local level and maintain continuity of customer contact. The supercommunity bank is committed to keeping service continuity at each bank's level; therefore, mergers into a supercommunity bank are less painful to the small bank management since most personnel are retained.

The supercommunity bank remains close to the customer and maintains authority and control over the pricing decision with each bank. Although coordination across banks is important, and sometimes essential, especially in the case of overlapping markets, the guiding philosophy is to leave the flexibility of the pricing structure, both deposits and loans, at the local level. This approach takes full advantage of the community banking element of the supercommunity bank since it allows each bank's president and executive team to customize their pricing and transactions to individual customers and their market conditions. That is not to say that guidelines from the holding company are absent. They are often imposed, particularly regarding liquidity levels, credit quality, asset quality, and fees.

The supercommunity bank is geared toward building a relationship versus a transaction orientation. It is interested in attracting and then retaining the customer. Strong customer retention is followed by increasing cross-selling activities and declining acquisition costs. The bank is not interested in maximizing the fees of one transaction; rather, the strategy is an approach to maximizing long-term profits.

As mentioned earlier, the concept of the supercommunity bank is based on a three-pronged strategy. A broad product line is one cornerstone of the strategy. It is important to offer a wide array of products and services that will meet the customer's needs so that customers will not outgrow the bank and customer retention will be achieved. Retention is one way to maximize franchise value.

The supercommunity bank does not leverage the franchise at the expense of customer service levels; rather, it strives to maximize revenues through the franchise by combining effective relationship building with a broad, sophisticated product line. This combination provides the winning formula for defending the supercommunity bank against the small bank's service, since smaller banks cannot offer the product breadth and sophistication that can only be supported by a larger asset base. By the same token, that combination defends against the larger bank which can offer the product sophistication but loses the personal service and relationship management aspect. The effectiveness of this element of the strategy hinges on the bank's ability to offer training so that the staff is both knowledgeable and sales-oriented. The quality and salesmanship of the staff are essential to improve the leverage of existing resources, including distribution channels and customer bases.

The supercommunity bank does not aim to maximize the cost-effectiveness of its large asset base. In other words, it does not attempt to minimize human resource costs and centralize all operations and decision-making activities to maximize savings. Instead, it strives to reach a balance between cost efficiencies and relationship management. This tradeoff is typically achieved by centralizing functions that are transparent to the customer, ranging from accounting and investments to loan operations and data processing, which offer significant scale savings while being transparent to the customer. The consolidation of backoffice functions provides an effective tool to the supercommunity bank to capitalize on its size without sacrificing the community banking orientation. Technological investment is another scale-sensitive element to the strategy. Technological innovations represent high fixed cost. The greater the volume of assets over which the cost is spread, the greater the efficiency. In addition, technology can be used to improve customer service and sales effectiveness. Platform systems and imaging are two prime examples of such applications.

The supercommunity bank takes the community banking approach to the customer from the small bank and combines it with some measure of cost efficiencies, which are created by economics of scale and the breadth of product offering, from the large banks. That combination is a winning strategy for banks into the next century.

Essential to adopting a "share-of-wallet" approach is that share-of-wallet is tracked as part of customer profitability measurement system. Not only should share-of-wallet be tracked over time, market research should be employed to measure a bank's share-of-wallet compared to its competitors, both bank and nonbank. In the spirit of the "inspect what you expect" approach to MIS, share-of-wallet measurement gets a bank's relationship managers to focus on what truly matters—profitably expanding their relationships.

Of course, it should be noted that, from a measurement perspective, significant cross-functional coordination is required to develop meaningful share-of-wallet measurements. Marketing research, finance, product management, and business unit management must all collaborate to integrate product and financial systems with external research data. While a very reasonable task, it can represent a major challenge for institutions not skilled in cross-functional coordination. Perhaps, however, share-of-wallet measurement is the right vehicle to be used to rally the organization across traditional boundaries to deliver meaningful customer profitability.

Importantly, share-of-wallet is a strategy neutral measure. Regardless of one's approach to the marketplace, increasing share-of-wallet is an appropriate goal. Similarly, establishing a share-of-wallet measurement process commits one to neither a relationship nor a product approach to the marketplace. With either approach, share-of-wallet is the most focused measure of strategic progress. Importantly, the long-term profitability of a customer relationship will almost always move in parallel with share-of-wallet moves.

Relationship versus Product Approaches

The alternative to a relationship-driven strategy can be most simply defined as a product-driven one. These two approaches are perhaps best contrasted in terms of both their different marketing approach and underlying profit models. In a relationship-driven bank, growth is achieved through aggressive consolidation of customers' product usage. Consolidation is encouraged through incentives such as tiered or bundled pricing. Because of their dense distribution networks and high service levels, relationship-focused banks have relatively high cost structures. In successful relationship-focused banks, this cost is offset by higher revenues associated with premium pricing and greater customer penetration.

In product-driven banks, volumes are driven by attracting transaction-oriented customers and using aggressive product promotions. Individual products are often deeply discounted, and little use is made of cross-product incentives. Product-focused banks tend to have less dense distribution systems, lower levels of customer service, and, therefore, lower cost structures than their relationship-focused competitors. However, greater sales program structure and sales management is usually in place. In contrast to the high-cost, high-revenue approach of relationship-focused institutions, banks with product strategies follow a low-cost, low-revenue approach. Ultimately, the customers' wallet is fixed in size or available revenue potential. Each approach takes a distinct tact in attempting to capture a profitable share of the available revenue.

In addition to their differing marketing strategies and profit models, relationship- and product-oriented banks differ along a number of other dimensions. Ralph C. Kimball has worked and written extensively on the strategic implications of these two approaches.[1] For example, Kimball shows differences exist in products, distribution systems, internal organizational structure, and in the systems used to measure managerial performance. Relationship-focused banks' key players are the sales force and their managers, who operate out of the branches; the head of the branch is likely to have profit and loss responsibility. In contrast, in product-focused banks, the product managers are the key players with profit and loss responsibility for each product.[2]

The important point here is that relationship and product approaches are more than just superficially different. The different approaches each have strong implications for the whole way a

In successful relationship-focused banks, this cost is offset by higher revenues associated with premium pricing and greater customer penetration.

consumer or commercial business is managed. Indeed, the effectiveness of a bank's efforts will depend on the extent to which it recognizes such differences and moves aggressively to build an organization consistent with its basic marketing approach. If the bank mixes elements from one strategy with another, it causes confusion and creates a fuzzy image in the minds of both its employees and consumers.

The contrasts between relationship- and product-focused approaches are so extensive and so dramatic that the two are difficult to pursue simultaneously. Instead, many well managed banks have chosen one particular focus and then moved to design the organization and supporting systems to be consistent with its basic marketing strategy. Such a single-minded approach centers the entire bank around the needs of the customer and eventually builds a supporting culture.[3]

While one cannot readily implement both relationship- and product-focused strategies simultaneously, it is very important to note that there are gains to be had by cycling between them sequentially. That is, a bank may focus for some period of time on building relationships and then switch to a more product-driven approach. Several years of a product-oriented approach for the purposes of acquiring customers and gaining share can be followed by a more relationship-oriented approach to increase cross-selling and consolidate share gains. Similarly, when cross-selling stalls, a more aggressive product approach should be pursued to acquire new customers.

The logic of cycling can be very compelling. A product approach, emphasizing specific product benefits, and perhaps even attractive pricing, is used to acquire new customers. Having made the available gains in market penetration, a relationship approach is then pursued to deepen the customer relationship and increase share-of-wallet. There is neither a proper starting point nor endpoint. Banks must recognize, however, that they should evolve their positioning to pursue the largest incremental revenue opportunities.

A bank might sequentially cycle between a product- and relationship-focused approach as it iterates between the strategic priorities of seeking market share gains and increased profitability. Both Bankers Trust and Citibank have had success with this approach.

The reality is that most institutions must address this challenge. Few, however, actively manage the tradeoffs and explicitly sequence their strategies, which would require one know which strategy to emphasize at any point in time.

While this product versus relationship cycling risks confusion among both staff and customers, it tends to build a broader base of skills within the bank. The changing marketing strategy requires supporting organizational changes leading to a great deal of organizational flexibility. This is essential to maximize the value of the franchise. As a result, cycling between product and relationship approaches is less a strategic issue demanding resolution than it is an execution challenge requiring management attention.

The Consumer Market Challenge: Relationships in a Non-branch Environment

As discussed at length in the previous chapter on distribution, over time the branch system will become less important as more retail customers prefer to deal with alternative delivery channels. Will the adoption of non-branch distribution on a large scale mean the death of relationship banking, or will it simply transform the basis of the relationship? One could argue that as physical proximity to the branch becomes less important and face-to-face interactions less frequent, banking relationships will wither. Conversely, banks can still establish and maintain customer relationships if they are able to redefine the relationship to meet customer needs. We believe the latter is possible but that it represents a fundamental challenge for all banks. There are two key elements involved in successfully managing this transition in the definition of what consumers consider to be a valuable relationship. The first is consistent, quality service; the second is effective marketing and branding.

The experience of successful nonbank competitors demonstrates that it is possible to develop strong customer relationships without significant personal contact. Fidelity Investments, for example, was the first investment company to rely on direct response marketing rather than a commissioned sales force. But what has distinguished Fidelity from its competitors has not been just aggressive use of direct response, but its subsequent moves to add relationship-building elements. These include a broad product line and high levels of customer service using relationship-oriented features such as integrated account statements. Equally important, print and television advertising has made Fidelity a household brand name. By promoting the successes of Fidelity portfolio managers, such as the legendary Peter Lynch and his successors at the Magellan Fund, Fidelity's mass marketing and advertising have built brand image in the minds of consumers. As a result of their service and marketing efforts, Fidelity has built a large base of loyal customers who give it the right of first refusal when purchasing additional investment products.

The lessons to be gained from Fidelity, and other successful nonbanks such as American Express, is that customer relationships can be built using any delivery channel if the overall marketing and service approach addresses the relationship needs of the customer. Fidelity and American Express recognize that high levels of user-friendly customer service are essential to long-term

The experience of successful nonbank competitors demonstrates that it is possible to develop strong customer relationships without significant personal contact.

relationships. Both have also been successful in defining the concept of accessibility as one that emphasizes convenience of time (24 hours a day) and place (anywhere there is a phone). Indeed, as survivor banks develop alternative delivery channels, they must simultaneously incorporate and redefine traditional relationship concepts.

The Commercial Market Challenge: Simply Making Money

In no market is the need for both increased profitability and new marketing approaches greater than in commercial banking. Competition has significantly driven down margins over the past two decades. The resulting ability to shop price has eroded the traditional relationship loyalty that had long been a hallmark of this market.

Commercial and corporate customers have become increasingly sophisticated in recent years, especially those in larger firms. Capital-raising clients are more aware of the alternatives open to them, institutional investors have become more aggressive, and today's corporate treasurer tends to be better informed and more demanding than his predecessors. An excellent example of changing client expectations was manifest in the changing competitive environment for corporate securities underwriting following the establishment of 415 shelf registration. As a result of regulatory changes, major corporations have been able to "self-service" their securities underwriting needs. Thus, the major underwriters have experienced significant declines in their underwriting commissions.

Technology has also had a remarkable impact on the ways in which financial service firms do business. During the 1970s, it led to the creation of new products, such as electronic cash management and treasury management systems. At the same time, it began to open up new channels for the distribution of corporate financial services. Since the arrival of commercial satellite communications, financial and informational data can be transmitted around the globe within seconds.

Innovative commercial banks have recognized the value to customers of providing real-time access to both financial information and their major transaction accounts. Today, a significant proportion of corporate banking activities is conducted from computer terminals in the offices of corporate treasurers. Even the small business owner is realizing significant advantages from this technological revolution in the market for corporate financial services. All the while technology has been increasing the value provided to the customer, it has been reducing the role of personal contact in delivering banking services, and thereby undermining the basis for the traditional banking relationship.

The development of new technology-oriented products and distribution systems has also created an important opportunity for banks to develop the fee-based income necessary to replace declining net interest income. Investments in computer technology were initially based on the need for rapid data processing, improved documentation, and quality control. Many institutions are now attempting to pursue the opportunities for competitive advantage available through the application of computer technology. The development of new products, the creation of research data bases used to identify opportunities for cross-selling additional services to existing clients, and the automation of backoffice operations to reduce operating costs are all examples of how financial services firms are seeking to better lever technology for relationship purposes.

As a result of competitor and technological innovation, spreads in commercial loan markets are narrowing as even relatively small middle-market corporations can borrow large amounts from banks at thin spreads priced off the London Interbank Offer Rate (LIBOR). As a result, many companies that once had a borrowing relationship that involved rates above prime and compensating balances are now enjoying borrowing costs less than prime.

Most large companies now bypass banks and borrow directly from the capital market. In some cases they have better credit ratings than their commercial banks. In addition, many middle-market companies can issue short-term commercial paper into the capital markets and substitute for traditional bank borrowing. And the resurgence at the junk bond market has replaced many of the medium-term lending opportunities for banks. The shrinking opportunities to make loans have caused banks to compete even more aggressively for scarce earning assets, compensating balances, and fee income to augment the inadequate spreads from wholesale lending.

Historically, in the face of thin lending spreads, banks were able to increase profits by requiring companies to maintain large compensating balances on deposit. With improved cash management techniques, this area of traditional profitability has eroded. While banks are still able to require some middle-market and smaller companies to maintain balances, the deposit levels have lessened considerably. The historical reliance on compensating balances has complicated today's relationship profitability efforts. In the past, banks did not have consistent pricing programs for their loans or services, and bankers did not consider fees to be significant sources of income. The unrecognized dependence on compensating balances concealed the true costs and returns of lending. Given today's environment and profitability pressures, the historical reliance on compensating balances now looms as a major transitional issue for banks' commercial business lines. Exhibit 9.1

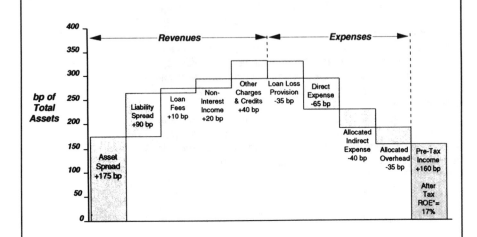

Exhibit 9.1

SOURCES OF EARNINGS OF TYPICAL MIDDLE MARKET BANKING CUSTOMER

Note: * This analysis assumed 6% equity to nominal assets and a 37.7% marginal tax rate.
Source: First Manhattan Consulting Group.

presents a breakdown of the typical sources of earnings for a middle-market banking customer.

The demise of traditional credit conventions centered on compensating balances has led to an explicit focus on customer relationship profitability. Uncertainty about whether compensating balances would continue to be available to take care of contingencies has forced banks to develop new, more aggressive customer profitability approaches.

The Next Frontier:
From Middle Market to Small Business

With large corporate lending eroding as investment banks lead major firms into the capital markets, many banks have chosen to focus in recent years on building relationships with middle-sized companies—companies with $50 million to $250 million in revenues. However, middle-market companies, following the lead of large corporations, are now also accessing the capital markets. As a result, the once attractive middle-market corporate lending segment is declining in profitability potential in much the same way the large corporate sector has over the past years.

The small business market (defined many different ways, but for our purposes those companies below $15 million in revenues) still provides potentially acceptable spreads. While the spreads may be wide, the average loan volumes may not be large enough, even at wide spreads, to generate sufficient net interest income to cover operating costs. Often, in an effort to make the small business model profitable, banks must also obtain the business owners' personal accounts and sell them other retail banking products. This relationship can become quite confusing to manage profitably because an individual's business and personal finances are highly interrelated. Essentially, to succeed in the small business market, a bank must not only capture a high share-of-wallet, but define the denomination of share-of-wallet to include both personal and business finances.

Essentially, to succeed in the small business market, a bank must not only capture a high share-of-wallet, but define the denomination of share-of-wallet to include both personal and business finances.

Small Business Lending Gains
Emphasis at Superregionals

As discussed in Chapter 5, Norwest and BANC ONE are two of the preeminent players and ultimate survivors in the consolidation game. BANC ONE is a premier lender at the small business level. Its focus and effectiveness with this market account for a significant part of its success story. Both Norwest and BANC ONE operated in this market long before it was fashionable and consequently know how to manage it well. It is interesting to note that when BANC ONE bought the failed MCorp in Texas, a significant middle-market lender, it immediately took steps to reshape MCorp in its own image of retail banking and small business lending. Norwest has a similar commitment to the small business markets; its strategic analysis appears to have determined that while middle-market loans were able to fuel profitability during the past decade, it may be unwise to rely on this segment in the future. Norwest and BANC ONE's small business focus and relationship banking approach helps explain why both banks are listed among the banks with the highest net interest margin (Exhibit 9.2).

The Final Frontier:
Managing for Relationship Profitability

Traditionally, commercial bankers have paid more attention to asset growth and prospecting for new customers than they have

	Exhibit 9.2	
	TOP NET INTEREST MARGINS	
	Bank	**Net Interest Margin**
1.	MBNA Corp., DE	7.23%
2.	BANC ONE, OH	6.22
3.	Wells Fargo, CA	5.70
4.	CoreStates, PA	5.61
5.	Norwest Corp., MN	5.58
6.	First Virginia	5.46
7.	Society Corp., OH	5.33
8.	KeyCorp., NY	5.30
9.	Huntington Bancshares, OH	5.27
9.	Firstar, WI	5.27
11.	First Security, UT	5.19
12.	National Community, NJ	5.16
13.	SunTrust, GA	5.11
13.	Barnett Banks, FL	5.11
15.	Banponce Corp., PR	5.01
15.	Union Bank, CA	5.01
17.	BayBanks, MA	4.99
17.	Southern National, NC	4.99
19.	First Alabama	4.98
19.	First of America, MI	4.98
19.	First Union, NC	4.98

Source: "Banking Makes Comeback," *Bank Management*, May 1993.

to managing the profitability of existing customers. An implicit tradeoff was being made in favor of market penetration over share-of-wallet and relationship profitability. In more recent years, however, the effective management of customer relationship profitability has become more and more critical to successful bank performance. As a result, management has begun to realize the importance of relationship management, and managing for maximum share-of-wallet, as a means of improving overall corporate profitability.

Bankers are necessarily taking a strict bottomline orientation toward handling their customer relationships. A variety of different analytical frameworks have been developed to help relationship managers identify opportunities to improve profitability and to guide them in developing customer relationship plans. By building and analyzing their portfolio of customer relationships, a relationship manager can develop more effective marketing plans, relationship management strategies, and profit planning.

Essentially, analysis of relationship profitability allows account officers to establish the profitability of individual customer relationships and to identify how each relationship contributes to overall business unit profitability. By understanding and managing each relationship in terms of its role in the portfolio, bankers can work to improve the financial performance of their total portfolio.

The two major dimensions along which customer relationship strategies must be designed are profitability and the size of underlying asset and deposit commitments. Successfully managing relationships requires linking the profitability and size of relationships in a strategic framework that allows managers to focus on performance.

Outside of the banking industry, multiproduct, multimarket companies developed customer and market profitability analysis to reduce the complexity of planning and resource allocation. Large diversified companies had hundreds of products serving different markets with widely varying profit potential. Some of these products were in a strong position relative to competitors; others were in weaker positions. The challenge was to deploy limited financial and management resources among these products to achieve the best performance possible. Dividing aggregate performance into manageable pieces led to a coordinated and integrated approach to the entire portfolio of products. With a typical portfolio, customer profitability prospects will be highly skewed. Exhibit 9.3 presents the typical distribution of profitability for the middle market.

Commercial banking's business unit managers who face a dilemma similar to that of managers of diversified companies can use the same profitability management concepts to analyze bank business units' customer relationships. Applying profitability analysis to commercial banking relationships provides the opportunity to quantify the importance of individual relationship strategies for customers and prospects. The allocation of the bank's limited financial and management resources becomes an explicit process.

Measuring Relationship Profitability

The basic framework for measuring relationship profitability is detailed in Exhibit 9.4. All of a loan customer's contributions or revenues must be compared with all the expenses involved in generating those revenues. Equity should be allocated to each relationship, and the resulting rate of return on equity can be computed. At first blush, this approach seems obvious and basic. However, the effective implementation of a relationship profitability model is complex and involves a number of financial systems, accounting, and training challenges. This accounts for the fact

However, the effective implementation of a relationship profitability model is complex and involves a number of financial systems, accounting, and training challenges.

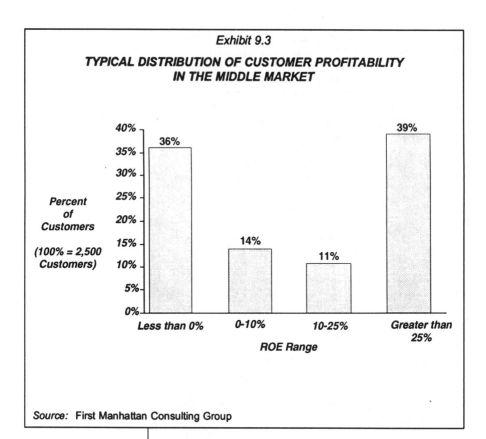

Exhibit 9.3

**TYPICAL DISTRIBUTION OF CUSTOMER PROFITABILITY
IN THE MIDDLE MARKET**

Percent
of
Customers

(100% = 2,500
Customers)

ROE Range

Source: First Manhattan Consulting Group

that banks experience varying success in developing and implementing relationship profitability management.

In Exhibit 9.4, the component parts of relationship profitability are indicated. Note first, the credit-interest contribution of a loan shown. Second, consider the operating service fees, which may include such fee generators as cash management, trust services, trading services, and data processing. Third, note the computed value of relationship balances. Collected balances generate investment earnings for a bank; however, these balances must be adjusted appropriately downward for required reserves. Finally, observe how revenue contributions earned from all other bank units are measured. These could include such items as corporate finance agent fees, advisory fees, offshore fees, and risk management revenues.

The largest expense involved in the lending business is the funding cost. While banks approach the measurement of funding cost in a variety of ways, most of the time they should support a loan with sources of similar or matching maturity. This serves to

Exhibit 9.4

CUSTOMER PROFITABILITY MODEL

REVENUE RESOURCES

- Credit Interest Income

- Operating Services Fees
  (e.g., cash management, trust, and wires)

- Value of Relationship Balances
  (adjusted for float and reserve requirements)

- Corporate Finance Fees
  (agent, adviser, offshore)

- Risk Management Services

- Other Sources of Revenue

LESS EXPENSES

- Funding Costs
  (match tenor; use of equity funds)

- Credit Risk Charges
  (by loan risk rating)

- Corporate Overhead Allocation

- Legal Expenses

- Marketing Expenses

PRE-TAX INCOME

EQUITY ASSIGNMENT

- Capital assigned must cover their
  loss variability (unexpected losses)

ROE (NET INCOME ÷ EQUITY)

isolate funding gaps from the pricing-profit equation. Banks that use pooled funds concepts for pricing sometimes neglect this point. The pooled funds approach also erroneously assumes loans—both individually and collectively—can be 100 percent debt funded. Accordingly, for the purposes of evaluating relationship profitability, a valid funding formula must be used to determine an appropriate leverage (debt-equity mixture) level for finding the true average funding costs.

Another important expense category is credit risk cost. Most banks only crudely estimate the true riskiness of a loan. Anticipated risk is usually derived from average net charge-offs over a historical period. Since most banks traditionally have risk-rated loans by loan types and industry categories, it is difficult for them to develop relevant risk charges. This has resulted in some fairly arbitrary risk-cost allocations. To get a handle on this variable, it is necessary to analyze each credit with respect to estimated future losses (defaults less recoveries), carrying cost estimates for periods of nonperformance, and workout costs pertinent to this type of credit. An effective credit risk management process, as outlined in Chapter 10, will establish probable loan loss costs to be used in the relationship profitability exercise.

Having factored in funding and credit costs, noninterest expenses must be explicitly considered in the profit equations as well. Relationship manager and marketing expense can represent significant costs. Product processing, and operating and systems costs must be assigned based on appropriate allocation methodologies. The total cost of selling and servicing the customer relationship must be established.

Finally, the loan unit must also absorb an appropriate portion of the general corporate overhead. For example, marketing and legal expenses should also be assigned. The objective is to establish a fully allocated customer relationship profitability measure.

Taken together, one can derive and project a customer relationship pre-tax income. To test it against standard ROE analysis, one must determine a loan capitalization level that is based on all unexpected loss variability. That is, conventionally risk charges are developed from expected, historical average (or mean) charge-offs, which do not reflect the fact that actual loss experience could vary greatly. The challenge is: how does one measure the unexpected loss? Perhaps loss volatility could be proxied by the number of standard deviations around the historical loss mean. In any case, all would agree that the use of one common equity rate for all loans would not be appropriate.

If a customer relationship profitability model is implemented with credible inputs, a bank can move rapidly toward discerning the more profitable customers from those who need to be improved through cross-selling or repricing, or exiting.

If a customer relationship profitability model is implemented with credible inputs, a bank can move rapidly toward discerning the more profitable customers from those who need to be improved through cross-selling or repricing, or exited.

The Discipline of Relationship Profitability

Once relationship officers understand what characterizes profitable and attractive relationships, how then is he or she able to identify additional opportunities in the marketplace? Using market information sources, account officers can screen the marketplace to identify the most attractive opportunities among their prospects and their existing, but less developed, customer relationships. Officers should then target the needs of this group of prospects on which business development efforts are to be concentrated.

As difficult as it may be, prospecting against nontargeted companies should be discouraged or—depending on resource availability—even prohibited. Formally establishing the calling capacity available to pursue new business, and then allocating it to specific prospects, is an effective check on unmanaged prospecting. All available business development efforts can then be concentrated on the most attractive opportunities.

Bank business unit managers may find it difficult to de-market low-priority/low-profitability customers. As every account officer or relationship manager knows, developing a customer relationship takes time and is highly personalized. Often, the decision to cut back efforts against a relationship is postponed several times. But, while letting go of customers who fail to meet established business development and profitability criteria is hard, it is a necessary step. It eliminates from a bank's portfolio customers who cannot generate attractive financial returns. It frees resources that can then be used to build more rewarding relationships. Repricing specific products and services often represent the most appropriate relationship management response to inadequately profitable relationships. Either profitability improves, or the size of the relationship is reduced.

Developing Relationship Strategies for a Portfolio of Customers

Customer profitability analysis not only drives the development of individual relationship management strategies but it also is the basis for evaluating the health of the customer portfolio. Evaluating the portfolio composition enables the relationship officer to manage the bank's marketing effort and resources. Bank account officers can identify both problems and opportunities in their customer portfolio and thus plan relationship management strategies accordingly.

The health of a bank's customer portfolio is indicated by the number of customers in different states of the relationship life-cycle, as well as by individual customer size and profitability. Comparing customer portfolios among account officers reveals opportunities to reallocate resources and to improve business unit

Often, the decision to cut back efforts against a relationship is postponed several times. But, while letting go of customers who fail to meet established business development and profitability criteria is hard, it is a necessary step. It eliminates from a bank's portfolio customers who cannot generate attractive financial returns.

performance. Bank officers should pay particular attention to mature relationships that consume too much time and effort.

Implications of Implementing a Disciplined Relationship Profitability Approach

Many commercial banks fail to match their customer relationship management approaches with customers' potential profitability. Bank officers overcommit resources to mature, but less profitable, relationships. They do not mount initiatives to find or develop new prospects. Ultimately, their traditionally large and profitable relationships peak in profitability. Bank resources and account officer efforts are spread too thinly across prospects and new clients. Also, if officers fail to perceive how important an individual customer relationship is to the full relationship portfolio, a bank may never fully realize the benefits of a relationship management approach to the business. In fact, for some institutions relationship planning risks becoming the ultimate "business as usual" exercise.

In the future, to be successful, account officers must focus on the profitability dynamics of their customer relationships. Their primary objective must be to identify opportunities for improving relationship profitability. When account officers become practiced in managing the profitability of their customers, they can readily identify—and capitalize on—opportunities for performance improvement.

Conventional relationship management often fails to affect the bottom line because account officers do not think strategically about their customer relationships and how they differ in size and importance to the bank, in profitability, and in responsiveness to marketing efforts. How often, for example, do limited bank resources (e.g., banker's acceptance, country risk, or tax-free availability), unique opportunities (e.g., new product introductions, attendance at special seminars), or even special favors (e.g., World Series tickets) get allocated to the same long-standing lead relationships without regard to chances of improving either tier position or the profitability of the bank's relationship?

To be effective, relationship management must be more analytical, more disciplined, and more profitability driven. Unless managers introduce formal profitability discipline into relationship management, the practices of the past will be perpetuated. As it is today, an account officer's approach to relationship management, begun at the same time the relationship is initiated, tends to remain constant through all stages of the relationship. For example, it would be extremely risky and, therefore, typically not considered in the account officer's interest, to direct resources away from long-standing and mature relationships to new future prospects.

Bank relationship management strategies are generally not designed with an eye on directing bank resources and an effort toward achieving maximum return. Only the exceptional account officer manages to allocate bank resources to less well-developed customer relationships. As a result, new relationships are pursued somewhat haphazardly. Without disciplined resource allocation, the account officer focuses on minimizing the risk that any customer relationship will be downgraded during his or her tenure, rather than marshaling the resources and taking the risks necessary to grow new relationships. Frequently, account officers continue to meet the credit requests of large, low-yielding customers without consideration of the impact of increased outstandings on business unit profitability.

Customer profitability analysis should be a regular part of any commercial bank business unit's relationship management efforts. It is a vital link between planning and marketplace execution.

Relationship management is more timely than ever today. Under increasing pressure to perform and, in many cases, facing declining profitability, commercial banks must make difficult resource allocation and management decisions. Customer profitability analysis can help instill greater discipline and a strategic perspective into day-to-day banking relationship management activities. Relationship management efforts should be designed such that profitability is no longer top management's charge alone.

Relationship Banking and Franchise Value

Analysts, and most shareholders, evaluate management in terms of its ability to generate shareholder value. What explains the ability of bank managements to manage their institutions to create shareholder value or the willingness of so many acquirers to pay a healthy premium over a target's book value? The answer lies in the concept of customer franchise, or an aggregate of individual bank customer relationships. To a great extent, shareholder value in banking is a direct reflection of the number and extent of the bank's customer relationships and the effectiveness with which these relationships are managed. In the end, to create shareholder value, bankers have two basic activities to perform: (1) establish and retain customer relationships and (2) manage those relationships effectively so they are economically viable. When a bank is acquired, the acquirer is not so much buying the bank's buildings, products, and systems as it is buying its customer relationships.

Not all banks, however, espouse a relationship-oriented strategy. How do these product-focused banks generate shareholder value if they lack long-term customer relationships? As discussed earlier in this chapter, product-focused banks follow a distinctly different profit model than do relationship-oriented ones. Ultimately, product-focused banks depend on their marketing and product management skills to generate a continuing stream of transaction-oriented customers. In contrast, relationship-oriented banks, reflecting the substantial period of time needed to establish customer relationships and their long-term nature once they are established, tend to experience fewer fluctuations in volumes.

Over the next decade, as shifts occur in customer preferences and the number of delivery options proliferates, management will be challenged to find new ways to create shareholder value. As discussed in Chapter 8, expertise in delivery channel management will become a key success factor for banks, both as a source of growth and as a way to defend their existing customer franchise. Relationship management skills will be required to transform the transactions stream in the new channels into customer relationships and then to leverage the new relationships into incremental product volumes. Product management skills will be needed to design product and channel features and to create effective promotional campaigns. Franchise management will require a synthesis of product, delivery channel, and relationship management skills.

In the end, the current, widespread distinction in banking between product-driven and relationship-driven banks will no longer be relevant.

In the end, the current, widespread distinction in banking between product-driven and relationship-driven banks will no longer be relevant. Instead, the primary difference will be between those banks that are able to synthesize both product and relationship management successfully into franchise management and those, whatever their orientation, who are not.

It should not be surprising that as the economics of the banking business evolve, the approach to handling the customer necessarily must also be reengineered. Cost-cutting has been the quick-fix response to industry margin and credit loss pressures. Now, a basic rethinking of a bank's relationship management processes will be necessary to ensure the industry's more customer-oriented businesses continue to create value for shareholders, and fit into the new paradigm.

10

Banker's Casino: Credit Risk Management

The commercial lending business has changed dramatically over the past 10 years, and it appears that even more changes lie ahead. The bottomline result of all of these changes is that a new system of credit intermediation is emerging, one that more efficiently links borrowers and suppliers of funds. While banks have lost traditional loan assets, new credit risk management approaches have evolved to produce more efficient methods of evaluating and mitigating credit risk. Adopting these more efficient approaches to credit risk management is critical to banks' efforts to succeed in the less regulated, more competitive marketplace. Successful banks, if they are to survive and thrive, must understand risk analysis and implement appropriate risk management techniques for all credit-related activities.

A Tough Credit Environment

The recent economic environment has been difficult for the banking industry, which has suffered through and endured several rolling recessions, as well as intense global competition and restructuring. Some banks have been clearly exemplary in their credit management and overall performance during this period of great challenge. Others lacking the essential management processes, credit analytical skills, and overarching credit culture have been vulnerable. No other major bank has been more successful managing its risk-adjusted returns than Wachovia. For this reason, we invited John Medlin, its CEO, to discuss credit management in a sidebar with a goal of learning some lessons from the Wachovia credit process (see John Medlin's sidebar, *Wachovia's Credit Mangaement Approach*, page 294).

The 1991–1992 recessionary period brought with it outsized credit costs attributable to problems in the industrial sector. Industrial portfolio losses came on the heels of heavy loan loss provisions for loans to less developed countries (LDCs) in 1987 and 1988. Other asset classes, such as commercial real estate and highly leveraged transactions (HLTs), also deteriorated in value and required substantial increases in reserves and write-offs.

Credit costs encompass loan loss provisions and explicit write-down costs. Write-downs reflect declines in the value of foreclosed property, including in-substance foreclosures. While recent regulatory guidelines state that foreclosures need not be reported unless possession has taken place, accounting practices have increasingly treated distressed property as foreclosed. Keefe, Bruyette & Woods recently compiled the credit/cost ratios of the largest 50 banks. They defined banks' credit cost ratio as the percentage of loan loss provision and write downs to risky assets. Risky assets were defined as loans plus other real estate owned (OREO). Exhibit 10.1 shows credit cost ratios of individual banks during the period from 1986 through the first quarter of 1993. These data exclude LDC provisions. Using the median numbers for 1986–1989 as a standard of comparison, Keefe concludes that the banking industry would ordinarily show a credit cost ratio range of 0.70 to 0.90 percent. The industry's .90 percent median credit cost ratio for the first quarter of 1993 indicates that the industry overall is normalizing.

Nearly all banks have gone through the cycle of first increases and then decreases in credit cost ratios during the past six years. From 1989 to 1991 credit costs, fueled by losses and write-offs, showed dramatic increases. Although most banks recently have experienced significant declines, certain ones still have room to lower credit cost ratios. With stricter underwriting standards and large loan loss reserves established, credit cost ratios continue to stabilize or decline. Strong mean reserves-to-loans and reserves-to-nonperforming loans (NPL) ratios suggest that there is potential for reductions in banks' loan loss reserves to be taken to earnings (Exhibits 10.2 and 10.3).

While industry profitability is currently at high levels, over time the variance in the profit performance of banks will widen. As a result, the difference in performance between weak and strong banks will become more apparent. While ROEs and ROAs are getting higher for many well-managed banks like Wachovia and Fifth Third, the aggregate numbers actually mask several banks that are substandard performers. Credit risk management is a critical operating lever against which to perform. All banks must ready their credit management processes for future economic swings.

Exhibit 10.1

CREDIT COST RATIOS FOR THE TOP 50 BANKS

SIZE RANK	BANKING COMPANY	1986	1987	1988	1989	1990	1991	1992	93-1
50	AMSOUTH BANCORPORATION	0.55%	0.48%	0.36%	0.79%	0.65%	1.37%	1.02%	0.45%
9	BANC ONE CORP	1.12%	0.83%	1.11%	1.11%	1.56%	1.81%	1.55%	1.06%
46	BANCORP HAWAII INC	1.26%	0.57%	0.85%	0.48%	0.52%	0.46%	0.76%	0.54%
20	BANK OF BOSTON	0.99%	0.61%	0.69%	2.76%	3.01%	2.06%	0.97%	0.46%
15	BANK OF NEW YORK CO INC	1.18%	1.28%	0.96%	1.10%	1.35%	2.71%	1.76%	1.34%
2	BANKAMERICA	2.56%	1.39%	0.80%	0.66%	0.81%	0.97%	0.92%	0.89%
7	BANKERS TRUST NEW YORK	1.19%	0.62%	0.10%	0.98%	0.91%	1.23%	1.31%	0.73%
21	BARNETT BANKS	0.72%	0.66%	0.64%	0.86%	1.83%	2.08%	1.55%	1.15%
33	BOATMEN'S BANCSHARES INC	0.95%	0.78%	1.02%	0.78%	0.76%	1.06%	1.28%	0.54%
6	CHASE MANHATTAN	0.96%	0.82%	0.61%	0.76%	1.72%	1.66%	2.04%	8.28%
3	CHEMICAL BANKING	1.37%	0.91%	0.88%	1.00%	1.43%	1.74%	1.97%	1.88%
1	CITICORP (INCL SEC'D CARDS)	1.50%	1.07%	0.93%	1.12%	1.94%	3.07%	3.37%	2.77%
26	COMERICA INC	1.13%	0.40%	0.57%	1.02%	0.65%	0.63%	0.70%	0.52%
30	CONTINENTAL BANK CORP	0.54%	0.13%	0.09%	0.27%	0.77%	2.32%	0.93%	1.80%
31	CORESTATES FINANCIAL CORP	0.75%	0.71%	0.83%	1.88%	1.87%	1.32%	0.86%	0.73%
45	CRESTAR FINANCIAL	0.56%	0.68%	0.70%	0.58%	1.68%	3.01%	2.34%	1.66%
35	FIRST BANK SYSTEM INC	3.45%	0.73%	0.54%	1.55%	0.92%	1.19%	1.29%	0.95%
11	FIRST CHICAGO CORP	1.84%	0.86%	0.57%	1.06%	1.65%	1.96%	4.51%	1.17%
24	FIRST FIDELITY BANCORP	0.66%	0.68%	1.54%	1.05%	2.59%	1.79%	1.46%	1.19%
10	FIRST INTERSTATE	1.52%	2.06%	1.97%	3.68%	1.99%	3.60%	1.83%	0.95%
34	FIRST OF AMERICA BANK CORP	0.59%	0.38%	0.39%	0.38%	0.34%	0.64%	0.60%	0.74%
12	FIRST UNION	0.78%	0.45%	0.42%	0.47%	0.77%	1.92%	1.42%	0.69%
43	FIRSTAR CORPORATION	0.76%	0.77%	0.80%	0.79%	0.70%	0.83%	0.64%	0.34%
14	FLEET FINANCIAL	0.69%	0.58%	0.57%	0.80%	3.81%	2.50%	2.38%	1.61%
41	HUNTINGTON BANCSHARES INC	0.51%	0.50%	0.46%	0.59%	0.95%	1.02%	1.69%	1.24%
49	INTEGRA FINANCIAL CORP	0.65%	0.49%	0.65%	1.52%	1.85%	0.91%	0.98%	0.83%
5	J P MORGAN & CO INC	0.75%	0.24%	0.64%	0.15%	0.16%	0.14%	0.19%	0.00%
27	KEYCORP	0.87%	1.11%	0.57%	0.74%	0.73%	1.21%	1.19%	0.79%
37	M N C FINANCIAL	1.24%	0.98%	1.24%	0.89%	6.05%	4.50%	2.86%	1.84%
23	MELLON BANK CORP	1.38%	2.68%	1.65%	1.64%	1.65%	1.52%	1.51%	1.21%
44	MERIDIAN BANCORP	0.40%	0.42%	0.57%	0.39%	1.61%	1.36%	1.12%	0.85%
39	MIDLANTIC CORP	0.74%	0.51%	0.71%	1.17%	4.13%	4.73%	2.07%	3.42%
17	N B D BANCORP INC	0.56%	0.48%	0.34%	0.37%	0.43%	0.74%	0.97%	0.76%
25	NATIONAL CITY CORP	0.78%	1.13%	1.07%	0.85%	1.05%	1.41%	0.94%	0.75%
4	NATIONSBANK	0.75%	0.66%	0.68%	0.68%	1.58%	2.42%	1.31%	0.79%
40	NORTHERN TRUST CORP	1.59%	0.70%	0.47%	0.32%	0.24%	0.54%	0.72%	0.37%
16	NORWEST CORP	1.81%	1.29%	1.01%	1.23%	2.33%	1.74%	0.89%	0.52%
13	P N C BANK CORP	0.92%	0.63%	0.70%	1.27%	2.87%	1.71%	1.51%	0.98%
19	REPUBLIC NEW YORK CORP	0.89%	0.48%	0.58%	2.50%	0.38%	0.72%	1.45%	1.23%
29	SHAWMUT NATIONAL CORP	0.47%	0.44%	0.38%	3.46%	2.70%	3.96%	2.56%	1.78%
48	SIGNET BANKING CORP	1.11%	1.11%	0.83%	0.88%	2.54%	5.90%	1.66%	1.17%
28	SOCIETY CORP	0.56%	0.47%	0.86%	1.17%	2.28%	1.59%	0.93%	0.56%
47	SOUTHTRUST CORP	0.82%	0.62%	0.57%	0.59%	0.99%	0.75%	0.78%	0.65%
38	STATE STREET BOSTON CORP	0.92%	1.09%	0.72%	0.79%	1.73%	2.83%	0.67%	0.49%
18	SUNTRUST BANKS	1.00%	0.81%	0.99%	0.89%	1.05%	1.05%	1.16%	0.94%
42	U J B FINANCIAL	0.73%	0.55%	0.58%	0.67%	2.99%	2.10%	1.98%	1.83%
32	U S BANCORP	1.36%	0.82%	0.80%	0.82%	0.83%	1.02%	1.13%	0.70%
36	UNION BANK	1.32%	1.60%	1.60%	1.20%	0.91%	1.51%	1.46%	1.49%
22	WACHOVIA CORP	0.89%	0.67%	0.48%	0.46%	0.73%	1.49%	0.64%	0.52%
8	WELLS FARGO & CO	1.29%	0.94%	0.86%	0.94%	0.79%	3.05%	3.19%	2.66%
	TOP 50 MEDIAN	0.90%	0.69%	0.69%	0.86%	1.33%	1.58%	1.30%	0.90%

Source: **Keefe, Bruyette & Woods, Inc.**

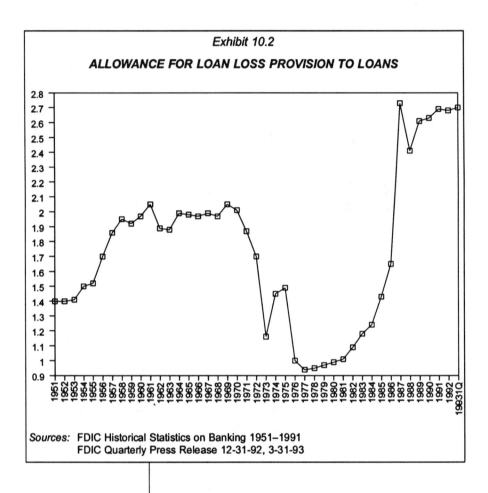

Exhibit 10.2

ALLOWANCE FOR LOAN LOSS PROVISION TO LOANS

Sources: FDIC Historical Statistics on Banking 1951–1991
FDIC Quarterly Press Release 12-31-92, 3-31-93

Fundamental Shift in Sources of Credit Supply

Demand for commercial and industrial (C&I) loans has declined
(Exhibit 10.4), and the impact of commercial paper and other
capital market substitutes for bank debt has been dramatic. Most
large and some middle-market companies have gained direct access to the capital markets. Additionally, nonbanks, particularly
insurance companies, are aggressively doing both term and spread
lending. This fundamental shift in the source of commercial credit
has dramatically changed the nature of banks' credit role and the
need to strengthen credit risk management. As banks have strug-
gled to maintain credit volumes in the face of their changing role,
over the past several decades, net charge-offs as a percentage of
total loans have continued to increase (Exhibit 10.5).

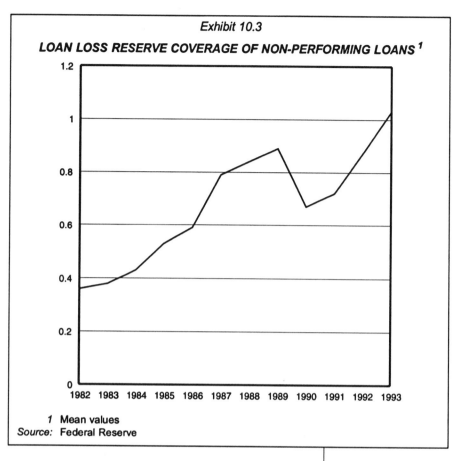

Exhibit 10.3

LOAN LOSS RESERVE COVERAGE OF NON-PERFORMING LOANS [1]

1 Mean values
Source: Federal Reserve

At the same time, three major challenges during the past 15 years have had a great influence on the current banking environment: globalization of individual country economies, major industrial restructuring, and new competitors to the traditional banking business. Globalization and industry restructuring trends have increased the complexity of analyzing risk. Additionally, heightened competition for traditional lending has come from nonbanks. In the past, inventory financing provided a solid source of loans. Now, more effective business practices, including just-in-time inventory management, have fundamentally reduced the overall corporate demand for credit. Companies are doing a better job of managing and raising cash throughout their operating environments. The initial public offering (IPO) market has been very strong as well. Many small and mid-sized companies are building solid equity bases, which further reduces the need for funding from commercial banks.

Credit Risk Management **275**

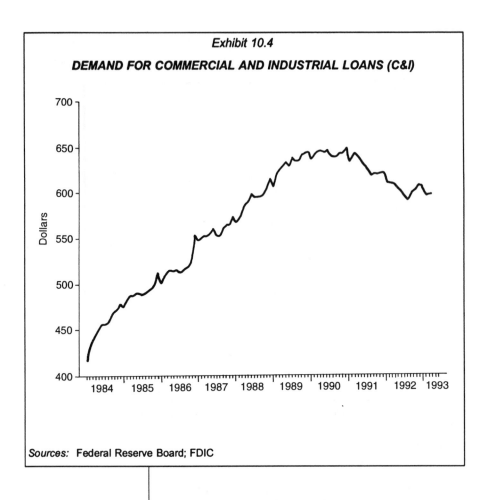

Exhibit 10.4

DEMAND FOR COMMERCIAL AND INDUSTRIAL LOANS (C&I)

Sources: Federal Reserve Board; FDIC

Building a Successful Credit Management Process

Banks, by their nature and design, exist to analyze and price risk within rapidly changing environments. They recognize the risks inherent in seeking credit business, beginning with the examination of individual loans. And they understand how important it is to generate, underwrite, and monitor individual loans within a solid credit risk management system. Originating and tracking the quality of each individual loan is an essential starting point for any institution. Successful banks are built upon effective credit risk management. Credit risk management must address two dimensions—evaluating the individual loan and building a prudent portfolio.

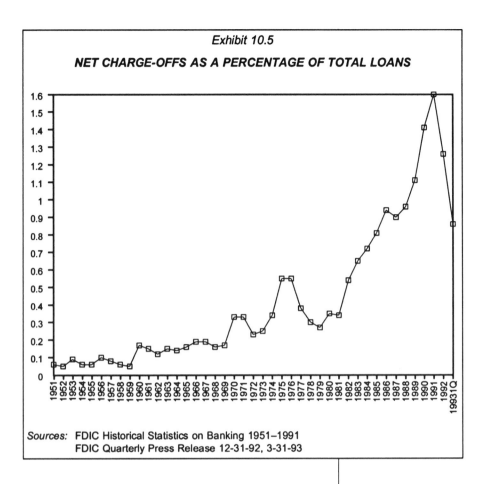

Exhibit 10.5

NET CHARGE-OFFS AS A PERCENTAGE OF TOTAL LOANS

Sources: FDIC Historical Statistics on Banking 1951–1991
FDIC Quarterly Press Release 12-31-92, 3-31-93

Evaluating the Individual Loan

Strong credit systems start with a process that assesses borrower strength at the outset of the loan. Credit-risk analyses are generally based on financial characteristics models. Balance sheet strength, cash-flow generating capabilities, and future business prospects are all evaluated with an eye toward the sources of loan repayment.

In addition to conventional financial analysis, individual credits require qualitative analysis of risk that requires the consideration of a borrower's competitive position, strength of management, product innovation, and customer perception. Generally speaking, a company with high market share and strong management represents low business risk to a commercial bank lender.

A bank will have a large number of credits within any given industrial sector that can provide evaluative criteria for de-

Credit Risk Management **277**

veloping industry-weighted risk categories. This can facilitate the origination of new loans to borrowers who have been risk-rated within their respective industries.

Zeta Analysis

In recent years, banks have sought out additional quantitative tools to assist in monitoring specific credits. One frequently used tool for ongoing credit analysis is Zeta analysis. Developed by Altman, Haldeman, and Narayanan in 1977, the Zeta model attempts to identify the bankruptcy risk of corporations by using multiple discriminant analysis (MDA) to differentiate between failed and nonfailed corporations.

The Zeta analysis approach examines seven variables: recent levels of profitability, long-term profitability, interest coverage, rate of return, liquidity, leverage, and size. Although these variables are comprehensive, even Altman cautions against relying on Zeta as a sole credit scoring device. Nevertheless, it can be a supplemental tool for the loan officer to use when reexamining total borrower creditworthiness.

Building a Prudent Portfolio

In a commercial loan portfolio, several individual credit exposures often share characteristics that can result in concurrent losses. Excessive concentrations in certain geographical areas, industrial sectors, and loan types present risks that banks should consider in planning their loan portfolio. By diversifying risks according to characteristics of individual industry performance, a more balanced portfolio that is insulated from economic hardships occurring in an industrial or geographic area can be constructed.

In addition, an effective credit management system constantly evaluates relevant portfolio characteristics. Early detection of weakening credits through efficient tracking allows for both prompt intervention in problem loans and limitation of new loans in affected industrial or geographic sectors.

Applying Portfolio Theory to Commercial Loan Portfolios

Similar to the portfolio theory practiced by equity portfolio managers, the concept of diversification and covariance management is applicable to loan portfolios and loan pricing. Industry and geographic concentration analysis is becoming an increasingly important part of estimating the economic value of a bank's loan portfolio. Both investors and regulators are wary of credits that are too concentrated and that share similar cash flow traits that could expose banks to common adverse economic conditions.

In the past, many banking problems were associated with high dependency on one industry. If that industry collapsed, the bank became very troubled or failed. While it makes little sense to lend a large percentage of available funds to a single industry, such as chemicals, agriculture, oil, automotive, furniture, or real estate, it does makes sense to have a diversified portfolio of loans from each of these sectors. The risk within each individual industry is mitigated because they are not highly positively correlated. Similarly, geographic diversification throughout the country can help reduce the inherent risk of concentrating within specific industries and serve as a buffer to regional economic cycles.

Unfortunately, because most U.S. industries are tied to the same macro fiscal and monetary policies, there are few negatively correlated companies (see Paul Ross' sidebar, *Enhancing Loan Portfolio Performance Using Covariance Analysis*, page 280). Just like stock market portfolio managers, credit portfolio managers must settle for those assets (loans) that have low positive correlation. The lower the positive correlation (or covariance), the greater the risk reduction from diversification.

Exhibit 10.6 displays simple historical correlations between a group of industries. As expected only a few negatively correlated cases appear—between nonferrous metals and lumber or textiles, for example. However, the several cases of low positive correlation suggest that diversification opportunities do exist. While application of portfolio theory does not fully address diversification challenges, it does provide a step forward in managing large commercial loan portfolios.

Managing Portfolio Concentration

Although banks generally appreciate the importance of the covariance characteristics of loans, current practice emphasizes underwriting and monitoring processes of individual credits to achieve soundness. Frequently only after these basic processes are functioning have banks examined concentrations of risk. In many cases banks have only reactively adjusted their exposures to an industry after they experienced widespread defaults as a result of concentrations. The real estate credit collapse demonstrated how quickly an institution can find itself in crisis management mode. It also demonstrated the limitations of "after the fact" portfolio management.

Some institutions have begun to focus on credit risk exposure as a percentage of capital. An industry concentration ratio is examined for the worst-case scenario—a maximum percentage of estimated loss—and credit limits are set to define each concentration's aggregate loss potential to a designated percentage of capital. Concentrations with lower expected loss rates receive greater percentages of capital investment.

Enhancing Loan Portfolio Performance Using Covariance Analysis

Paul Ross
Principal
DRI/McGraw-Hill

One of the key lessons learned by lenders during the 1980s is that active and careful portfolio management is critical to an effective credit policy. With the future course of economic events always uncertain, loan portfolio diversification is necessary to safeguard lending performance. Yet accurately assessing the diversification of a loan portfolio presents difficulties.

A key difficulty involves risk covariance—the tendency of different segments of a loan portfolio to behave similarly in response to economic events. These shared behaviors can cause a seemingly well-diversified portfolio to be highly vulnerable to a particular event, rendering it poorly diversified in reality. There are several approaches that lenders can use to measure industry covariance so that they can improve the risk management of their loan portfolios.

Risk covariance can come from several sources. The most obvious relates to regional economic interdependencies. The power of regional covariance was dramatically illustrated in the Texas debacle of the mid-1980s, when the collapsing energy sector triggered widespread difficulties in other segments of the local economy. In general, all industries with principally local markets were adversely affected, including retail, services, and real estate. As a consequence, even banks with modest direct exposure to the energy sector were vulnerable to the oil price shock.

Banks with national lending scope can also fall victim to shared risks if their loan portfolios contain concentrations in industries that are vulnerable to the same economic shocks. For example, a major West Coast bank's difficulties during the early- to mid-1980s were largely a consequence of industry positions—in real estate, agriculture, energy and shipping—that were all vulnerable to disinflation. Although the portfolio was geographically diversified and contained no single overwhelming industry concentration, the bank was devastated by its shared risk to disinflation.

With these and other examples serving as grim reminders of the power of covariant risks, and in response to regulatory pressure, banks are now seeking ways to identify and manage risk covariance. The benefits that lenders stand to gain include enhanced risk management, more stable earnings, and ultimately a higher stock valuation.

In general, an effective approach to analyze covariant risks should be reliable, predictive, actionable, and practical to implement. Because covariant risks are often hidden from casual scrutiny, the approach must be powerful enough to identify all significant sources of risk. Historical economic inter-relationships will not necessarily hold in the future, therefore an effective approach must be predictive in nature. The framework needs to produce information that motivates tactical and strategic actions, integrating the individual transaction decision-making process with the broader goals of the portfolio management precess. Finally, the approach needs to be workable and practical to implement.

The major methods employed to date to assess the covariant risks embedded in a loan portfolio fall into three classes: (1) historical correlations, (2) economic structure analysis, and (3) simulation-based approaches. Each possesses virtues as well as drawbacks and can provide valuable insights, although historical correlations and structure analysis are more limited and must be used with special care.

Historical Correlations

The historical tendency of different lending sectors to behave similarly can be measured with correlation analysis. In this method, correlation coefficients must be calculated for some historically available proxy for the credit risk of each segment to be analyzed. Possible risk proxies include variables such as sales or cash flow, charge-off rates, or market-based measures such as equity prices or bond risk premiums.

This approach is fairly straightforward and scores high on ease-of-implementation. The chief drawbacks include limited reliability and predictive power. Reliability suffers due to spurious correlations, that is, the possibility that sectors may have behaved similarly during the historical period used for analysis due to chance or other nonrecurring factors. Also, because the economic structure is constantly changing, industries that will be closely tied in the future may not have been in the past. As a consequence, the predictive power of an historical correlation is often low.

Structure Analysis

Better estimates of economic interrelationships can be derived from analysis of economic structure. An industry's performance is strongly influenced by the health of its principal customers, and, to a lesser extent, that of its suppliers. Analysis of patterns in customer-supplier relationships can identify sectors that are likely to be interlinked in the future.

Although this method is more forward-looking and less susceptible to spurious relationships than historical correlations, careful interpretation is still required. This is because commonality of customers does not guarantee similar performance. For example, two sectors with virtually identical customer profiles are oil refining and equipment leasing. Both sell in similar proportions to a range of industries including airlines and construction. Yet their fortunes are not equally impacted by the health of their customers—an ailing airline might defer leasing additional planes, but is less likely to forgo fuel purchases.

Simulation-Based Approach

This method examines industry and regional performance under a range of potential economic events, such as a significant shift in exchange rates, a Japanese financial collapse, a recession, or a pronounced regional downturn. The performance of the individual segments is then correlated across the range of scenarios developed by the set of potential events. In this manner, segments that are likely to suffer in the same economic environment can be identified.

This approach is by far the most reliable in our view. The resulting relationships are forward looking because they embody the full range of potential economic developments and are not limited to events in recent history. Moreover, spurious relationships do not pollute the analysis.

The chief drawback is the intensity of the analysis that is needed. This method requires an integrated, consistent economic modeling framework capable of translating economic events into industry and regional financial performance and credit risk. Few banks possess the analytical resources to undertake this effort without outside assistance.

Each of these methods can serve to enhance the assessment and management of the credit risk of a loan portfolio. The limitations of historical correlations and structure analysis seriously undermine the validity of these approaches, however. In order to gain a comprehensive understanding of the covariance risk lurking in its loan portfolio, banks should undertake an analysis of potential economic events and the impact on each key lending segment. The findings will form a key component to an effective risk management strategy by supporting decisions on credit approval, loan syndication, and portfolio restructuring.

Exhibit 10.6

HISTORICAL CORRELATIONS: IDENTIFYING COVARIANCES AMONG INDUSTRIES*

	1	2	3	4	5	6	7	8	9	10	11	12	13	14	15	16	17	18
Tobacco (1)	—	.23	.33	.40	.05	.00	-.06	.07	-.04	.25	-.04	-.03	-.10	-.02	.12	.03	.11	.08
Textiles (2)	.23	—	.33	.36	.09	.12	.04	.21	-.03	.06	-.04	.05	.07	.08	.15	.17	.17	.07
Lumber (3)	.33	.33	—	.33	.12	.06	.01	.06	-.04	.13	.02	.01	.05	.13	.18	.11	.22	.14
Paper Products (4)	.40	.36	.33	—	-.04	.35	.09	.15	.08	.19	-.04	.01	-.17	.00	.11	.10	.08	.02
Printing/Publ. (5)	.05	.09	.12	-.04	—	.17	.03	.17	.05	.04	-.02	-.03	.10	.05	.07	-.02	-.02	-.07
Chemicals (6)	.00	.12	.06	.35	.17	—	.23	.18	.11	.12	-.01	.24	-.04	.20	.22	.08	.08	-.02
Pet. Products (7)	-.08	.04	.01	.09	.03	.23	—	.04	.06	-.02	-.07	.10	-.03	.11	.16	.02	.18	.09
Rubber/Plastics (8)	.07	.21	.06	.15	.17	.18	.04	—	-.04	.04	-.04	.10	-.12	-.02	.12	.27	-.09	-.11
Primary Non-Ferr. Metals (9)	.04	-.03	-.04	.08	.05	.11	-.06	-.04	—	.07	-.05	.10	-.06	.05	.04	.00	-.02	-.11
Basic Steel Prod. (10)	.25	.06	.13	.19	.04	.12	-.02	.04	.07	—	-.04	.03	-.03	-.03	.03	-.04	-.02	-.05
Misc. Gen. Merchandise (11)	-.04	.04	.02	-.04	-.02	-.01	-.07	-.05	-.04	-.02	—	.08	.03	.03	-.03	-.06	-.07	-.15
Dept. Stores (12)	-.03	.05	.01	.01	-.03	.24	.10	.16	.03	.04	.08	—	.17	.56	.17	.20	.07	.16
Grocery Stores (13)	-.10	.07	.05	-.17	.10	-.04	-.03	-.12	.06	-.03	.05	.17	—	.29	.00	.02	.16	.22
Apparel/Accessory (14)	-.02	.08	.13	.00	.05	.20	.11	-.02	.05	-.03	.03	.56	.29	—	.18	.13	.28	.06
Furniture (15)	.12	.15	.18	.11	.07	.22	.16	.12	.04	.03	-.03	.17	.00	.18	—	.16	.15	.07
HH Appliance/Electronics (16)	.03	.17	.11	.10	-.02	.06	.02	.27	.00	-.04	-.06	.20	.02	.13	.16	—	.07	.08
Eating/Drinking (17)	.11	.17	.22	.08	-.02	.08	.18	-.09	.02	-.02	-.07	.07	.16	.28	.15	.07	—	.22
Drug Stores (18)	.08	.07	.14	.02	-.07	-.02	.09	-.11	-.02	-.05	.15	.16	.22	.06	.07	.08	.22	—

* Historical correlations based on 1992 industry cash flows.

Source: DRI/McGraw Hill Division of McGraw Hill; Lexington, MA.

Applying Portfolio Theory to Loan Pricing Practices

Perhaps more so than in underwriting and portfolio management practices, banks have been remiss in explicitly factoring risk into loan pricing. Loans are a fundamental source of income, and because there is currently overcapacity, banks are faced with either accepting the market price or not booking additional assets. In light of this overcapacity and the concurrent lack of sufficient alternative income sources, banks have tended to underprice risky credits and overprice good credits. Underpricing risky customers is ultimately likely to be unprofitable. Overpricing of strong quality credits tends to create incentive for these customers to use the capital markets. Loan Pricing Corporation (LPC) has done considerable work to dimension bank risk pricing. Exhibit 10.7 illustrates the comparison of bond risk pricing in the capital markets to similar risk-rated loans made by commercial banks. LPC's analysis and regular reporting of risk/pricing relationships has significantly raised the industry's consciousness in this area.

The most ambitious system of evaluating and managing risk concentrations to date is based on risk-adjusted return on capital (RAROC). Bankers Trust has been a leader in applying RAROC. This system has the advantage of integrating risk and return for across-the-board decision making. It assigns risk ratings and incorporates a loss probability distribution that assesses expected default experience and loss variability projections, including worst-case scenarios. Equity is then allocated to cover probable loan losses across a range of scenarios. Pricing on any specific loan is based upon minimum rates of return on equity allocated to each risk. Concentration caps, or boundaries, and loan pricing can be determined from the analysis of credit ratings. In addition, all credits in a particular industrial sector can be combined to determine whether pricing is sufficient to justify the capital allocated to the industry.

The banking industry's analysis of credit risk concentration is still in its infancy. The inherent problem in creating a reliable covariant loan loss model arises from the lack of historical default information. Only publicly traded debt can produce such information. However, the past problems of losses associated with concentrations make imperative continuing progress in the development of relevant information and refinement of risk management analytics.

Another key issue related to loan pricing involves distinguishing asset (or loan) specific borrowing cost from overall financing cost. Many loans are priced marginally over bank funding cost. The natural tendency for bankers is to fund loans through wholesale money markets, often at the London Interbank Offer Rate (LIBOR). A problem arises if the loan rate only reflects LIBOR and ignores any equity requirements. A bank has an equity cost

Exhibit 10.7

LOAN PRICING DATA SHOWS BANKS DO NOT GET PAID FOR RISK

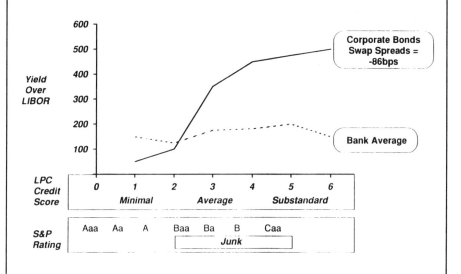

The corporate loan portfolios of banks show less than a 120 bps differential between loans with a credit score of 2 and 5. The bond market demands a spread differential of over 400 bps. The average bank overcharges its best customers and undercharges its worst customers, relative to the more efficient corporate bond market.

Sources: Loan Pricing Corporation, *Loan Pricing* Report, April 1988; Council on Financial Competition.

that is far greater than the short-term borrowing rate that it must not forget. Each loan must be evaluated according to its apparent incremental profit margin, including an appropriate equity allocation.

In many cases, credit pricing is related to the overall relationship between the bank and the customer. If a bank in an ongoing relationship can cross-sell various noncredit products to a customer at competitive rates, it can generate profits from the combination of loan interest spread and fees for other services provided. A problem arises when a bank that is tending to its relationships faces marketplace competitors prepared to price credit below what is required to meet risk-adjusted hurdle rates.

While there is no analytically derived proper pricing strategy, history suggests that one should always price to cover probable expected credit losses.

After the Deluge: The Potential for Credit Cost Reduction

Today, individual banks are in various stages of their recovery. Strong reserves for losses promise earnings increases for those banks that are just beginning to see declining losses on their loan portfolio. Many large banks, including Chemical Bank and Citicorp, have added billions to their loan loss reserves to absorb potential losses and may be close to turning the corner. Citicorp's action on LDC provisioning in 1987 had important implications for the industry's strategic and financial health. However, after Citicorp increased LDC reserves, it then experienced consumer, HLT, and commercial real estate difficulties. Provisioning for these loans has kept Citicorp's credit costs well above average (Exhibit 10.1). With the necessity to build reserves dwindling, Citicorp could lower credit costs and enhance earnings. This potential has not been lost in the stock market, where Citicorp has recently enjoyed a tripling of its stock price.

Using a Chainsaw: The Role of Bulk Loan Sales

It is expensive for banks to carry nonperforming assets. Essentially, there are two approaches that banks can follow to address this problem. One, used by Chemical Bank and Citicorp, among others, is to aggressively manage and sell off troubled loans in small or individual lots without deep discounting. Another approach involves bulk sales of weak and nonperforming assets to improve credit positions and get rid of the myriad costs related to problem loans.

Bulk sales imply heavy discounts. Loan values can be discounted as much as 40 to 50 percent. While some banks have consummated bulk sales at a 50 percent recovery rate, many sales contain significant portions of current loans as well as those that are underperforming. NationsBank, BankAmerica, First Chicago, and Shawmut are among the banks that have sold significant amounts of problem loans. This has enabled them to not only refocus on asset generation, but also downsize and reduce the costs associated with workout, such as legal, administrative, and real estate appraisal and management expenses. While real estate investors demand deep discounts, the costs of selling outweigh the substantial time and expense required to manage and sell troubled loans piecemeal. Additionally, removal of troubled assets reduces the amount of time management must spend with regulators and investors, who focus on asset problems.

For those banks that prefer to manage their way out of problem assets, selling individual pieces results in a much larger recovery of original loan balances. For instance, Citicorp recently sold a large troubled loan at more than $.70 on the dollar. This price greatly exceeds the typical 45 to 55 percent recovery rates from bulk sales.

Each bank must carefully assess the value of bulk sales in addressing problem loans. Quick reduction of problem loans lowers credit costs and can enhance investor confidence. However, some banks are better positioned to manage problem assets and may view the bulk sales market as too heavily discounted.

Recessionary conditions in the California economy have caused banks there to lag behind the nation in correcting credit cost problems. Wells Fargo, for example, with an above-average credit cost ratio, shows substantial underlying earnings potential. The California commercial real estate market may have bottomed out, and so the necessity for heavy reserving may cease, resulting in a boost to earnings. Over time, one should anticipate a rebounding of California's bank stocks in general.

Several banks in the Northeast also are in various stages of recovery, and their need for loan loss provisioning may soon decline. Midlantic Bank's ratio, because of serious credit setbacks, was among the highest in the country (Exhibit 10.1). As a result of the improving economy in the Northeast, there is hope for improvement. Reflecting the type of progress being made by the industry, Robert Albertson and Sally Davis Pope, bank stock analysts at Goldman Sachs, recently wrote of Shawmut, one of the New England institutions most troubled by credit problems, that, "credit quality (is) a non-issue . . . Declining credit costs will still have ample, positive influence on upcoming quantity results."

Fleet Financial is an example of a large bank still experiencing some credit cost problems from New England's economic and commercial real estate downswing. Eventually, Fleet's credit costs will return to normal levels and bring improved earnings. In the meantime, however, Fleet has been subject to potential merger rumors with NationsBank, reflecting both the potential severity of the bank's credit problems, as well as the strategic vulnerability that extended credit problems can impose.

Banks in the Southeast, as a whole, show little potential for further credit cost reduction. Similarly, the Midwest has led the nation in credit quality during the past six years, which leaves it little room for further improvement. In sum, by late 1993, the banking industry will have reaped most of the benefits of credit cost reduction. Although there are individual banks that still have room for improvement, the overall industry should be viewed as having recovered. What remains to be seen is whether the credit risk lessons of the 1980s have a permanent effect on banks' attempts to achieve proper risk-adjusted returns in the future.

Over-Reserving

Many banks have fought for a long time to bring their nonperforming loans down and their loan loss reserve provisions up. In many cases the ratio of loan loss reserves to nonperforming assets coverage has gone too high. Deposit Guaranty, a Jackson, Mississippi, bank holding company, recently found itself in this situation. It announced that it would reduce its allowance for loan losses in the second quarter of 1993 to produce a resulting sizable positive nonrecurring benefit to earnings. Both regulators and accountants had reportedly told the company that its allowance was excessive—based on June 1, 1993, circumstances—at over 407 percent of nonperforming loans and 136 percent of nonperforming assets.

Although often discussed, this is the first example in recent years of a major bank actually adjusting its reserve for loan losses to recapture a current estimated excess reserve back through the earnings statement. This initiative is probably precedent-setting for the rest of the industry. If so, we would expect similar announcements from other banks over the next several quarters as they address their generally over-reserved status.

The action taken by Deposit Guaranty may have informational content in itself. When a bank moves to build its book value by taking nonrecurring gains, it does so knowing that the market will not apply much of a multiple to such noncore earnings.

The action taken by Deposit Guaranty may have informational content in itself. When a bank moves to build its book value by taking nonrecurring gains, it does so knowing that the market will not apply much of a multiple to such non-core earnings. A very logical motivating factor may be a desire to boost book value with a view of selling the bank at a future date. Book value, right or wrong, remains an aspect of price in merger negotiations. The question remains as to where reserving levels will finally settle. Most believe that reserve coverage of less than one would be adequate.

The Emergence of a Secondary Market for Commercial Loans

In the midst of the credit problems of the late 1980s, a secondary market for commercial loans has arisen as an innovative response to financial pressures and regulatory forces. The loan sales market allows banks to benefit from the fees of a large underwriting, yet avoid portfolio concentration risks that result from holding large loans. However, the loan sales market is developing relatively slowly.

While some standard credit evaluation tools are available, few analytical methods are homogeneous across individual banks. The complex character and nonhomogeneity of corporate loan instruments mean they have to be structured uniquely for each borrower. As such, commercial loans are difficult to package, securitize, or trade. This challenge must be addressed for a loan asset market to proliferate. If banks are unable to form more homogeneous market standards, become more efficient, and work out inherent obstacles, nonbanks, such as security firms, could take over those parts of the commercial loan market.

As Chris Snyder of Loan Pricing Corporation has pointed out, investment banking firms—on a limited basis relative to the potential size of the loan asset market—have already actively entered this market. Merrill Lynch and Bear Stearns have recently been lead banks on syndicated loan transactions that are the first efforts by securities firms to package and sell portfolios of commercial loans.

Snyder sees two possible scenarios evolving. In one, several large money-center banks would arrange loan sales and sell off prearranged parts of loans to regional banks. By retaining fees on the overall deal, they could create greater effective yields on the loan portion held. In the other scenario, a marketplace where money centers play a key role is envisioned, but there would also be a relatively large number of regional banks with asset sales operations. A broader, more diverse loan sales market would evolve under this second scenario.

Market pressures, coupled with banks' increasing comfort with portfolio theory approaches, will eventually lead to a significant secondary market for commercial loans. The 1990s will see this market grow and mature as part of the broader paradigm shift the industry is undergoing.

Market Sources of Surge Capacity

Another interesting aspect of the evolving loan sales market emanates from the tremendous size amassed by several money-center and megaregional banks. Chemical Bank and BankAmerica, for example, have traditionally possessed large corporate lending skills. These skills can now be coupled with their huge size to create surge capacity. That is, when large deals appear (LBOs or corporate reorganizations, for instance), they are among only a few banks that can commit vast sums of money relatively quickly to win deals. As a consequence, they can earn large agent fees prior to subsequently syndicating out much of the credit risk. While this allows other banks, called "stuffees", to earn spreads on small parts of the loan, the "stuffer" banks capture all the management and related agent fees.

Regional banks have had difficulty profiting from the purchase of large corporate loans because the pricing on them is intense. Consequently, some have positioned themselves as restuffers, buying pieces of loans from banks like Chemical and BankAmerica and reselling smaller pieces to smaller banks.

As regional banks participate in the stuffing process they acquire expertise in engineering larger loan sales. A superregional bank that learns the game and gains enough size can approach corporations directly and do independent financing transactions. Thus, some large superregional banks, such as NationsBank, have graduated from being stuffees and restuffers to become stuffers themselves.

Regulatory capital constraints related to highly leveraged transactions (HLTs) also point to the need to access the liquidity that loan asset sales provide. Problems with real estate and less developed country loans further aggravate regulatory concerns about credit risk problems. The need for banks to develop structures that allow for the purchase and sale of large or risky loans is highlighted.

A willingness to overcome traditional barriers to sharing credit information and technical expertise is a key ingredient to developing a more fluid loan marketplace. Banks must close the gap in the evaluation of credit information if a trading market is to develop. A more rigorously applied national credit rating system would help this process. Existing credit rating agencies could play a key role in the process. Those banks that learn to deal with the complexities of this market will naturally dominate it as it develops. Should the economy expand in a manner that provides greater lending opportunities, those with the skills to do loan asset sales may be at an advantage.

Capital Market Evaluation of Bank Credit Risk

Among bankers, the nature and limits of market discipline are increasingly subjects of discussion. Expanded use of market discipline, for example, may restrain financial institution risk-taking and lower potential losses to the FDIC. Opponents of market discipline favor traditional regulatory supervision. They doubt the ability of investors to judge the credit risk in commercial bank portfolios.

Does the market notice problems in a bank's loan portfolio before regulators do? The academic literature suggests that monitoring stock market returns of publicly traded bank holding companies may be a method of identifying problem banks early. Some studies have found evidence suggesting that unexpectedly low stock market returns may precede a bank's inclusion on the problem bank list and, thus, could be used as early warning signals. If so, then vigilant shareholders could help identify problem banks earlier and assist in scheduling examinations to where they are needed most.

Traditionally, bank supervisors have relied heavily on site examinations to identify problems and ensure compliance. Federal examiners assess five key aspects of a bank's operations—capital, assets, management, earnings, and liquidity—rating them on a scale of one to five, with one being highest. A composite rating of these five aspects, known as CAMEL, an acronym derived from

> *As regional banks participate in the stuffing process they acquire expertise in engineering larger loan sales. . . . Thus, some large superregional banks such as NationsBank have graduated from being stuffees and restuffers to become stuffers themselves.*

the first letter of these five key elements of bank performance, is then assigned. A rating of four or five indicates a problem bank.

In recent years, the deteriorating credit quality of bank loans in many regions of the country has placed an increasing burden on limited regulatory resources. Given those limitations, if it were possible to identify deteriorating banks prior to scheduled examinations, examiners could concentrate their efforts more efficiently on those banks most in need.

Toward that goal, two economists of the Federal Reserve Bank of Boston, Katerina Simons and Stephen Cross, examined stock returns for a sample of 22 problem banks for the time period before their downgrade.[1] Their findings, however, indicated that, in the aggregate, investor returns failed to anticipate bank downgrades by examiners. In addition, examination of individual problem banks failed to reveal convincing examples of specific information known to investors before the downgrade.

The study analyzed publicly traded bank holding companies in which the lead bank was a national bank that had its composite CAMEL rating downgraded to either four or five between 1981 and 1987. Weekly market returns were studied for two years, and cumulative residuals were found to be consistently negative in only 12 cases. They were generally positive in the other 10 cases studied, suggesting no systematic directional capability of detecting problem banks prior to an examination by looking only at security returns.

Managers and directors themselves were found to show no pattern of trading that indicated they were aware of the deterioration in their bank's condition before examination. Of the 12 banks with negative stock return residuals, only three showed clear selling patterns. Of the other nine, six showed clear patterns of stock purchases, and the other three had mixed patterns.

One must conclude that there is no reason to believe that the prices of bank stocks can be analyzed to improve supervision of commercial banks. Moreover, neither the market nor the management of these banks seemed to be aware of impending problems before examinations took place. This research casts doubt on the strength of market discipline by investors over bank regulators in monitoring bank risk. It also further underscores that most banks must strive to upgrade their own credit risk management and monitoring systems.

Is There a Credit Crunch?

The concept of "credit crunch" has been popularized by the business media. Richard F. Syron, President of the Federal Reserve Bank of Boston, for one, has written and testified extensively on the credit crunch. He accurately notes that even during periods of rapid credit expansion, some credit requests are denied. So anecdotal evidence of credit denials is not, per se, evidence of a credit crunch.

To be fair, the determination of a credit crunch can really only be made by comparing current lending patterns to those of previous similar recessions. Because credit extension naturally varies over the course of a business cycle, restrictive credit conditions in a recession do not necessarily imply a credit crunch. If credit extension under restrictive conditions was compared to that of expansionary periods, all recessions would qualify as credit crunches.

Unlike previous cases of credit supply problems that were associated with disintermediation and loss of bank deposits, however, the recent tight credit period is connected more with bank capital losses and deficiencies. Capital adequacy concerns have probably limited credit availability.

A 1992 study by Herb L. Baer and John N. McElravey of the Federal Reserve Bank of Chicago supports this capital crunch thesis.[2] Taking into account higher capital requirements, capital deficiencies, losses, and asset recycling, these authors estimate the depository system needed an additional $65 billion in equity to have remained in equilibrium from June 1989 through June 1991. Lacking this capital, the industry evolved more conservative lending practices to avoid exacerbating the already overextended situation.

The steep yield curve of 1991–1993 is also mentioned as a contributor to the credit availability problem. Banks have enjoyed the large spreads between short-term costs of funds and yields on longer-term government and agency securities. While current investing activity is profitable, a flattening of the yield curve will eliminate these profits. One should remember that this type of investment behavior by banks has been seen, to a lesser extent, in similar stages of past business cycles. Fortunately, many economists are now predicting that the yield curve will flatten. The combination of a flatter yield curve, a stronger economy, and higher bank capital levels should result in banks seeking and achieving more loan growth.

One should remember that this type of investment behavior by banks has been seen, to a lesser extent, in similar stages of past business cycles. Fortunately, many economists are now predicting that the yield curve will flatten.

The Credit Process as a Management Challenge

In any bank there must be a firm understanding of risk and return. Performance in handling risk/return tradeoffs relates directly to its capacity to evaluate and manage risk. These skills are the foundation of future success in commercial lending.

There is no one credit process that anyone can prescribe as the single best model, but one thing is clear: those banks that have an effective credit management process will be among the most successful players in the industry. John Medlin's sidebar, *Wachovia's Credit Management Approach*, page 294, presents a perspective on the very successful Wachovia credit model. Here we present a comprehensive model that addresses the key aspects of credit management and provides useful insights into managing the credit process.

The overall approach to engineering an effective and efficient credit risk management process must start with a well-defined and communicated philosophy. Top management should not only understand, but also define and articulate the process it designs. The roles of key credit personnel, technology, policies, and procedures must be understood by both line and credit management if successful implementation is to occur.

Moreover, a bank's business strategy and credit administration must be linked so that collaboration provides a consistent ongoing credit risk evaluation. Effective communication ensures that line lenders and credit risk managers follow the same discipline. The supporting management infrastructure must provide timely and accurate information for monitoring performance and allow for checks and balances between the sales (lending) and underwriting functions. Senior bank managers must be able to identify problems early.

Structuring Loan Portfolios

Bank portfolios should be constructed around the salient dimensions of both industry and geographic exposure. Management needs to place limits on total exposure and outstandings, with sublimits for existing and new credits. Industries need to be weighted according to average risk ratings. Regional economic differences and considerations should be considered. And detailed analysis should be conducted on how new credits and current industry performance affect these risk ratings.

A bank should assess an industry's credit characteristics by examining its history, present status, and future projections (12 to 36 months). Regression analysis is an excellent tool for examining an industry from a historical perspective and developing a macroeconomic model that predicts change. Such a model can assess both the input/output and credit quality of the industry over time. Consideration of key macroeconomic variables—GNP growth, interest rates, and the trade-weighted value of the dollar—and their behavior is essential. From this model, one can extrapolate a view of the future of the industry during periods of recession and growth.

Each industry sector to which the bank has, or is considering, exposure should be categorized in terms of future economic conditions on a probability continuum from most to least likely. On this basis a bank can determine and weight scores on how a targeted industry credit will perform in the anticipated economic future. The bank can then use these distinctions to determine risk

Wachovia's Credit Management Approach

John G. Medlin, Jr.
Chairman and Chief Executive Officer
Wachovia Corporation

Although as bankers we are basically buyers and sellers of funds, to describe us simply as traders would be an understatement. A charter to provide banking services is a special privilege and carries with it near-sacred responsibilities. Our friends and neighbors have granted us this franchise with the expectation we will safeguard their deposits and lend them money for worthwhile purposes. Our stewardship of depositors' and stockholders' money places both limits and demands on the types of risks that should be assumed with the resources entrusted to us.

Our duty is to balance the interests of our stockholders, customers, employees, and communities. At times, the interests of these diverse constituencies can seem contradictory. However, common threads are their desire first for a steady, dependable source of financial services and, second, for rewards that are relatively stable despite the inevitable swings in the economy.

Our approach to ensuring such reliability is to pursue progressive business strategies within a framework of sound banking principles. Our emphasis is on soundness, profitability, and growth, in that order of priority. We strive to be equally good at risk management, cost control, and business development and to maintain an appropriate balance that prevents our preoccupation with quality from inhibiting growth and our overobsession with growth from hurting quality.

A business culture designed with these underlying disciplines can meet the long-term responsibilities and goals of banking. We are not saying our approach is the only structure that bank's should consider; we are saying it has worked well for us.

The issue of proper credit quality will always be central to achieving excellent performance in banking. A sound loan portfolio produces a steady, annuity-like stream of quality and dependable profits. A portfolio burdened by significant levels of problem assets and credit losses can devastate earnings and capital.

A bank is basically a blind pool of credit risk that varies depending on external conditions and internal practices. While it is important to understand the nature and magnitude of bank credit exposures, it is more important to understand the philosophies, processes, and people involved in managing the credit risk of a financial institution.

In our organization, the first line of offense and defense is the account officer, who is held personally responsible for developing and maintaining all customer relationships. The account officer is also responsible for properly analyzing all facets of credit proposal—industry, management, financial, and economic—and for recommending a proper structure of repayment terms, documentation, collateral, and pricing.

Throughout this process information is shared with loan administration, the credit review side of our bank. This information flow is supplemented by direct discussion between the account officer and loan administration, which acts as a second line of defense and conducts it own simultaneous review of the data generated by an account officer.

Upon completion of the credit analysis, the account officer makes a recommendation regarding the proposed credit. Loan administration may either concur with the recommendation and offer suggestions for enhancement to the proposal or indicate disagreement with the loan. Disagreements generally are resolved at this point, and a loan proposal satisfactory to the sales and credit functions is agreed upon and communicated to the customer.

Analysts and regulators place great emphasis on the level of nonperforming assets as an indication of the health and weakness of a bank's credit exposures. However, it is important to remember that a loan has reached a mature state of deterioration by the time it is classified as nonperforming.

Wachovia's system of review is comprehensive and diverse, with emphasis on early detection of a deteriorating credit and prompt action to strengthen such loans before they reach a stage of severe deterioration or loss. It involves a series of actions by numerous individuals and functions within the company, beginning with the account officer. This broad and deep surveillance process gives us balance and protection from the possibility that one individual may be lax or misguided in his or her duties. Attention to detail and vigilance by lending and loan administration officers are the key ingredients in the maintenance of sound income-producing loans.

While the primary purpose of the review process is to detect any elements of credit deterioration, it also raises and broadens the level of knowledge about our customers and prospects within our organization. In addition to permitting us to spot a problem credit in the early stages of deterioration, this knowledge is a very powerful offensive weapon for selling multiple bank services and allows us to enhance customer service by shortening our response time to customer requests.

Wachovia does not have a workout group for problem loans. Whenever possible, such loans are handled by the account officer who originally made the loan. Problem loans do receive a higher degree of attention and handling by loan administration than do satisfactory loans. However, account officers remain actively involved because of their intimate knowledge of the relationship and because it is considered an excellent learning and character-building experience.

Our top priority emphasis on soundness has caused some to characterize us as conservative. In reality, we are creative but disciplined and informed risk takers who have both good loan growth and good credit quality. We can sell more aggressively and lend more safely because our bankers are well trained and highly skilled in evaluating and managing risks.

We aspire to provide superior service, to know our customers well, to build broad and enduring relationships, to have above average loan growth, and to maintain below average operating costs and credit losses. Along with capable people, these are key ingredients for excellence in banking over time.

ratings and approval guidelines for new or continued exposure. The idea is to use data to create statistical scoring models that allow credit policy committees to set exposure and outstanding limits for each industry. The credit officers and policy committee can then review the limits and targets on a regular quarterly basis.

The Loan Underwriting Process

Industry ratings are based on credit quality sensitivity in various economic climates. Individual companies are rated on a scale based upon the bank's risk rating standards. These two guidelines are used to establish client categories. Some may receive normal approval while others may fall into classes that require further examination. For instance, if both the industry and company ratings are at the top of the scale, approval should be streamlined. If the company falls somewhere in the middle of the rating range, an additional evaluation tool such as a Zeta score may be required to evaluate the credit. Ratings below certain levels or a new credit relationship—either new to the bank or a new type of exposure—require a much higher level of scrutiny. These circumstances require approval from a senior credit officer.

To analyze significant individual loan requests, a bank needs to assign a team composed of a senior line officer, economic analyst, and portfolio manager to prepare a joint credit policy document that sets exposure limits for each industry. Additionally, appropriate debt service parameters must be developed to be part of required underwriting standards. In order to determine specific underwriting standards, the instrument must assess both industry and company credit characteristics. Analysis of both the economic structure of the industry and operating life cycle of the company is important.

Underwriting policy documents can serve only as a guideline, not hard and fast rules. Credit officers have to use judgment. It is in the exercising of judgment that the process often breaks down. In many instances, people feel exposed to criticism if they do not follow the credit policy document religiously. Officers should remain focused on the risk factor involved and design a plan to mitigate it.

Zeta scores or other quantitative techniques are sometimes useful for testing credit judgments and flagging potential errors. New credits and certain categories of risk renewals also may require Zeta calculations. Zeta scores, for example, could be compared to loan risk grades, and officers should have to explain their rationale for assigning risk grades that are inconsistent with Zeta or other quantitative scores.

Establishing Formal Signing Authorities

Commercial banks use different types of credit granting authorities. Whether a bank relies on individuals or committees can produce vastly different results. Regardless of the approach, a signature system ensures responsiveness and accountability.

The level of authority required from the line signatories is usually designed around several factors: (1) the size of the exposure; (2) whether the relationship is new or existing; (3) industry risk characteristics; and (4) credit condition of the company relative to the industry.

Senior credit management will initially assign credit approval authorities. Additional authority will be assigned overtime based on each officer's performance, line management recommendations, and senior credit officer confirmation.

Maintaining Loan Portfolio Quality

The foundation for maintaining a quality portfolio is early identification of potential problems. To achieve this objective, teamwork among line officers and credit specialists is essential. Early diagnosis and evaluation of problems is critical. Both lenders and credit officers must stay on top of each and every credit and anticipate what lies ahead. Management processes should be designed to ensure this happens.

One way to accomplish this is by segmenting each industry into thirds according to creditworthiness. In the top-third are the premier industry members; these firms should be cross-sold and built into more profitable relationships. The middle-third include noninvestment-grade companies, local entities, and current or former HLTs. Middle-third clients should be managed toward the top of the category and cross-sold as well. The lower-third are

The foundation for maintaining a quality portfolio is early identification of potential problems.

weaker credits where new exposure should be avoided. If a lower-third company cannot be migrated up, it should be moved out of the bank's portfolio. The bank should make every attempt to help the customer restore its financial health, while maintaining the ultimate objective of restructuring the bank's exposure. Uncooperative borrowers should be allowed to be stolen by the competition, or terminated whenever possible.

Credit quality can range from investment grade, to attention zone, to watch list, to problem loan. Attention zone credits require assessment by both the relationship manager and a credit officer to determine whether they should be watch-listed. The goal of the watch-list process is to provide early identification and elimination of potential credit problems by planning and teamwork-building among the line, credit, workout, and legal staffs.

The credit monitoring process should contain incentives urging line officers to take early and aggressive action to avoid weakening credits having to be watch-listed. A change in the status of the credit quality rating of a borrower can be recommended either by a line officer or mandated by a credit officer based on early warning devices that set priority processes. For example, companies that are late with financial statements or whose Zeta score update shows a lower grade than assigned could be flagged for attention and reviewed as soon as possible. This process requires discipline to make certain that annual reviews are done on time. Acceptable but weak credits should be reviewed first. The key is to accelerate the process so that potential problems can be flagged and monitored early. In that way, the bank can take appropriate action before it is too late.

Involving the Credit Policy Officer

When the credit policy officers understand a deal from its inception, it is likely they will maintain an effective liason with relationship managers. Relationship managers and credit officers shall work closely with each other to move credit problems along. Wachovia's effective process emphasizes this approach. However, no matter how smooth the process, disputes occur that need resolution. The chief credit officer and respective commercial group head must cooperatively mediate appeals.

An organizational system of checks and balances must be developed to ensure the integrity and effectiveness of the line vis-a-vis credit administration people. Credit and line people should evaluate each other and cooperate in the constant monitoring and improvement of credit quality and inform the credit officer of weaknesses in any lending units so that corrective action (coaching and training) can occur. This organizational framework ensures that the credit officer becomes personally involved in first-time and ongoing credit decisions, thereby improving decision quality. Identification and remediation of problem credits requires early application of expertise. Again, the emphasis should be on improving response time at every juncture of the credit process.

Organizational Approaches to Building a Credit Culture

Creating a premier credit organization requires functional discipline. The organization should impose the discipline to implement and monitor systems its framework provides. Wachovia excels at organizational discipline in monitoring and spotting problems early. The best decision makers need to be positioned and supported with both technical expertise and a system of checks and balances. Banks must create a culture that encompasses an ability for individuals to understand their common and individual roles.

Credit and line people have many similar objectives. They need to work together in the creation of a quality portfolio. This means they are meeting customers and not just pushing paper. In a good credit model, deputy credit officers align with line officers and report to both credit administration and the line in being responsible for: (1) monitoring and improving credit quality; (2) coaching line personnel on effective credit risk management; (3) assisting line people in meeting revenue targets; and (4) achieving nonrevenue goals.

Required Infrastructure and Information Systems

An effective organization requires efficient and evolving information systems ready to assess and manage risk. Technology needs to be fused into the credit process along with judgment and common sense. Risk analysis for evaluating and managing borrowers requires an information base that includes: (1) exposure, creditworthiness, and company trends; (2) performance and compliance (early flags for problems); (3) industry trends; and (4) competitive information. A data base needs to track and follow industry trends, exposure limits, and sublimits. Additionally, terms, covenants, collateral, and, if applicable, remedial plans for each exposure should be machine automated.

Bankers understand the importance of gathering and using information, but they often fail to reorganize information that could help create more efficient and productive systems. Banks must continually develop better ways to manage constantly growing quantities of information. Documentation, where possible, needs to be standardized to facilitate transactions and reduce inaccuracies and costs. And as is well known, unfortunately, the generation of large amounts of data is ineffective without analytical and timely methods of evaluation.

Centralized support functions need to check documentation and resolve exceptions. Finally, ongoing credit training is necessary. Inexperienced new hires and experienced transfers require the basic foundation of credit training. In the future, banks who can integrate new technological information systems with well-trained people should have an important competitive advantage.

Credit Risk Management from the Shareholder's Perspective

Investors know, generally, that some banks control risk well, and others do not. The determination an investor must make is how to distinguish between the risk management practices of individual banks. For investors, this is a difficult, but necessary, exercise. Investors often see loans as nothing more than a blind pool. Knowing loan profit margins are thin, they quickly lose confidence when they read a scare headline about an industry or a weak regional economy.

In banking, this blind pool characteristic circumscribes credit risk and often causes overdiscounting and lower stock valuations. Since investors do not know how much principal will be lost or recovered, they will discount suspect bank loan portfolios heavily. An investor wants to be constantly assured of a growing and stable cash flow from a bank's loan portfolio.

To address this problem, banks need to continue improving the visibility of their balance sheets through greater disclosure. To an increasing extent, some banks are showing their loan concentrations in finer segments and greater detail. For instance, some holdings are classified by industry proportions, while others are classified by geography or bank product type.

Asset quality position is expressed by ratios of allowance for loan loss reserves to nonperforming assets or nonperforming loans. Information related to specific categories of nonperforming loans and their specific allowances is often given. Usually banks have a designated amount of reserving that is unallocated to suggest further comfort. The goal is to make the blind pool risk more visible. Demonstration that a bank is well reserved produces a more comfortable investor.

Another notion of better expressing value involves market value accounting (MVA). Just as securities firms mark assets and liabilities to market at the end of each day, banks should do likewise, contend MVA proponents. There is a problem with this idea, however, because it is not feasible for loans; there is no tradable market that generates daily loan prices. The inherent complexity and nonhomogeneity of loans inhibits the quick development of such a market. Nevertheless, several forces in the industry are pushing in this direction. Earlier, Loan Pricing Corporation's attempt to price loan risk was noted. Citicorp has

Investors know, generally, that some banks control risk well, and others do not. . . . Investors often see loans as nothing more than a blind pool. . . . In banking, this blind pool characteristic circumscribes credit risk and often causes overdiscounting and lower stock valuations.

established a U.S. corporate loan market index that uses prices derived from public debt markets. Also, Bankers Trust, Continental Bank, and others have attempted to price, trade, and distribute various specific credits—HLTs, for example—for other banks. We expect, over time, that risk pricing sophistication will sufficiently grow to allow the development of a broad and deep secondary market. Such a development would certainly be in the interests of customers and shareholders.

Summing Up

The discipline of credit management represents yet another area in which the performance of banks varies widely. A review of the status of bank credit quality and related credit costs suggests that the majority of banks have weathered the 1990–1992 national recession, as well as various regional downturns. Indeed, one could expect to see several reversals of the over-reserved positions of individual banks.

Despite strong current credit positions, the banking industry faces numerous challenges in this core banking function. Aggregate loan demand may not be sufficient to support the lending capacity of the industry. Large and middle-market loan spreads are increasingly narrowing. Profit pressures historically stress credit conservatism. Instead, it should generate an increase in risk/pricing sophistication.

Our review of the credit management arena highlighted several challenges related to the profitability of the loan function that must be addressed. Loan pricing, in particular, deserves much attention. In many cases, rates that are charged do not result in profitable business. The pricing of risk is a key aspect of this problem. Increasingly, banks will have to better measure the default potential of individual loans and do more work to rid themselves of unexpected loan loss volatility by better developing portfolio strategies.

Although many banks have elaborate credit management systems, bottomline effectiveness will require greater discipline in execution. A review of John Medlin's essay on credit management clearly indicates that careful management of the credit process results in a variety of offensive as well as defensive opportunities.

There is heightened awareness of the blind pool nature of bank loan accounts by bank stockholders. Despite increasing analysis, disclosure, and even market making, the inherent limitations on establishing loan values probably prevent a complete substitution of market discipline for bank examination. Nevertheless, the relentless pressure of investors, along with the substantial progress in the reporting of loan values and quality, promises to foster even more efficiency in this important area.

The pricing of risk is a key aspect of this problem. Increasingly, banks will have to better measure the default potential of individual loans and do more work to rid themselves of unexpected loan loss volatility by developing better portfolio strategies.

This completes our discussion of the key internal levers that bank management can pull to achieve operating success. Thoughtful, innovative, and disciplined practices applied to the areas of cost, distribution, relationship, and credit management will greatly improve an organization's prospects, and ultimately determine where a bank fits into the consolidation landscape.

11

Managing
Wall Street

Only in recent years have bank stocks taken their rightful place alongside corporate stocks in terms of portfolio importance. As competition for capital and corporate performance has grown more intense, bankers have concentrated on increasing the effectiveness of their dialogue with analysts, institutional investors, and retail investors.

Today, bankers are still learning how to attract new equity by courting the investment community. Likewise, analysts, and institutional investors are still developing sophisticated measures to incorporate into their evaluations of banks.

As the financial community concentrates on bank profitability over asset growth and stresses management strength, asset quality, and overall safety, banks themselves are growing more sophisticated in managing the Wall Street analyst and institutional investor communities. The investor is expecting much more than just asset quality and capital adequacy. As deregulation and increased competition has eroded the traditional industry profit model, both Wall Street and banks themselves have worked to upgrade their coverage of the strategic, business economics, marketing, and operating aspects of a bank's story for investors.

The Evolution of the Bank Equities Market

The capital structure of banks is unique in American business. Until the early 1960s, bank stock ownership was decentralized and fragmented. Community banks were essentially owned by a handful of local business leaders. Not so long ago, presidents of those small institutions made markets in their stock out of their top desk drawers by matching sellers with buyers and influencing control over who owned the stock, which was usually priced at a 10 to 15 percent premium-to-book value. It was deemed an honor to hold a sizable stock position in the local bank. Large ownership usually equated to a board membership or status as a large borrower and/or community leader. Since ownership conferred status and influence in the community, there was a waiting list of buyers for local bank stock.

As a result of the ravages of the Great Depression, privately owned banks essentially became an extinct breed. The surviving 14,000 banking concerns each had a small and highly select shareholder base, assets in the $100 million to $150 million range, and about 300 shareholders. Yet, few grew large enough to attract stock analysts' attention, let alone have established markets trade in their stock. In fact, the only major difference between banks and other local businesses in America's small towns was that the bank had to be incorporated in order to limit its own liability and the personal liability of its owners to depositors.

Reflective of this small town approach to raising equity capital, as recently as 1970, only 13 banks were listed on the New York Stock Exchange (NYSE). Today, 40 of the top 50 banking organizations are listed on the NYSE. Many more institutions are listed on the American and NASDAQ stock exchanges.

Evaluation of Bank Stocks: A Brief History

Until recently, few people realized that bank stocks had the potential to attract a broader range of investors. The first analyst to focus in depth on the banking business was Morris Shapiro. He was the evangelist of the fledgling bank equity market and championed the inherent investment value of community bank stocks. His disciple, Harry Keefe, established Keefe, Bruyette & Woods (KBW) in 1962. The firm grew to be one of the nation's most respected brokerage firms specializing in bank stocks. Today, KBW is one of the leading investment banking firms covering the banking industry.

Keefe showed his own commitment by investing all the firm's pension money in bank stocks. "In 20 years," he said, "1961 was the only down year, and in 17 of those 20 years the pension fund outperformed Standard and Poor's 500 stock index." Over time similar comments led others to realize that the business franchises represented by bank stocks could attract a far more widespread group of investors than the relative few who lived within a short distance of the community bank's home office. While banking was fragmented by state regulations and the crazy-quilt jurisdiction of different federal agencies, an embryonic national market for bank stocks was beginning to emerge. A small dedicated analyst community was also forming.

In addition to a growing and increasingly sophisticated analyst following, the advent of the NASDAQ system in 1971 quickly modernized the over-the-counter market and provided its hundreds of bank stocks with better liquidity and more credible pricing. The screen-based NASDAQ system attracted the largest securities firms in the world to the over-the-counter market, bringing quality market making as well as better sponsorship to bank stocks. The introduction of last-sale pricing and a full regulatory transaction audit trail to NASDAQ in the early 1980s meant that bank stocks, one of the largest components of that market, could be traded in a pricing and regulatory environment basically comparable to that of the New York Stock Exchange. The ability to efficiently make markets in small bank stocks created significant trading opportunity as well as greater investor interest.

In 1970 national rating agencies—Standard & Poor's, Duff & Phelps, Moody's—joined the new banking environment, providing an independent means of valuation and an additional force for broader bank ownership. Until that time, rating agencies had been concerned that a low rating or downgrade could cause consumers to lose confidence in an institution and possibly even cause a run on a bank.

Even in the early 1970s, all indications suggested that ratings were based solely on size. Large money-center banks were rated AAA, medium-size banks were rated AA, and small banks merited only an A. The ratings had little to do with profitability, just size.

Deregulation, of course, has notably changed the pattern of bank ratings. Moreover, now bank ratings are pivotal to a bank's access and cost of funds. This was dramatically in evidence during the October 1990 bear bank capital market. Many large regional and money-center banks slipped below the lowest A rating, with some prominent banks rated below investment grade, or junk. To the extent that a bank relies on external funds as opposed to retail sources, capital market disciplines are binding. Between the growth of the industry and the emergence of stronger capital market forces, over the course of two decades the banking industry went from being totally insulated from Wall Street to being both fully exposed and rather dependent on capital market scrutiny.

The Sell-Side Bank Analyst Comes of Age

Traditionally banks had been viewed as homogeneous, making it easy to compare one to another. Not only was the playing field limited and structured by regulation, but banks were also required to report financial results in essentially the same manner. The contrast with the rest of corporate America was obvious: if you compare two tire companies like Goodyear and Firestone, you might well find that one derives more of its income from chemicals than the other. But a bank was a bank, wherever you looked.

The great similarity actually made it both easy and difficult for the growing number of bank analysts—easy because analysts could develop massive, performance-driven data bases for measur-

. . . over the course of two decades the banking industry went from being totally insulated from Wall Street to being both fully exposed and rather dependent on capital market scrutiny.

ing individual bank performance against the norm; but difficult because they found it virtually impossible to determine the quality of the asset base, which was primarily loan receivables. While the depth of one's analytical efforts might be limited, there was a broad recognition of the need to conduct more in-depth analysis to support banks' increasing need for capital to support growth and acquisitions.

Because of the apparent lack of differentiation among banks, the difficulty of asset quality analysis, and the central role of government regulations and Federal Reserve policy in determining profitability, the growing number of securities analysts following banking turned to other measures in their selection process. During the 1970s, many stock analysts recommended banks on the rather soft basis of geographic location. Until the real estate investment trust (REIT) problems surfaced, the higher-growth Southeastern banks commanded the highest multiples. Later, California banks became the investments of choice until the technology sector concentrated in Silicon Valley began to cool. Then there was a time when Texas with its oil strength made Texas bank stocks a popular investment.

In reality, growth area geography may be a reverse indicator. The fact is that banks in the high-growth areas, such as Arizona, Florida, and Texas, have not fared as well as banks in areas of moderate growth. Naive indicators of market strength and growth potential can actually be more misleading than helpful. The key is differences in management matter significantly. It is more difficult to manage for profits in a slow growth area. Fast-growing markets can temporarily mask management problems. When growth slows, however, weak management teams are exposed and certain to find trouble. Building a strong management team is critical to achieving enduring success. Demonstrating to Wall Street that you have the management depth necessary to meet the rigors of the market is also important.

Fast-growing markets can temporarily mask management problems. When growth slows, however, weak management teams are exposed and certain to find trouble.

To gain the respect and investment attention of analysts and investors, bank CEOs face the challenge of divesting low-margin and unprofitable operations, concentrating on return on assets rather than size, emphasizing credit quality, and pursuing sound and distinctive business strategies. And it is just as important to effectively communicate the strides made in those areas to the investment community. Communicating strategic and operating progress requires providing more specific measures of progress and milestones, as well as having the right long-term story to tell the Street.

In the 1990s, analysts evaluating banks will increasingly apply measures used in other industries. Business line profitability, a variety of corporate productivity and efficiency measures, service quality and customer satisfaction, and market segment share-of-wallet will all be tracked and evaluated. Today, there is significant pressure on banks to disclose more performance and profitability information.

At the same time, beyond quantifiable measures, analysts are seeking to gain more insights into banks' long-term stories. Quality and measurement depth will take on greater importance. Banks with specialty areas that give them competitive advantages in certain markets will draw the attention of investment professionals, as will banks with proprietary technology and/or ventures or agreements that provide access to technology.

Notable Analysts' Work

The analyst community is small and relatively tightly knit. In this community, a handful of analysts stand out for their notable work.

Montgomery Securities, under the leadership of J. Richard Fredericks, has done much to strengthen the conceptual framework for bank stock analysis. In particular, his survival-of-the-fittest "Darwinian Banking" thesis appears to be on point. More recently, he and others have stressed the importance and value of a "fortress balance sheet" and a small-loan orientation, or granularity, in the loan portfolio to achieve diversification. The stock market has validated these themes. If a measure of the impact of an analyst is the number of new concepts and jargon that they introduce to an industry, Fredericks has certainly had impact (see J. Richard Frederick's sidebar, *Where We Are and Where We Are Going in the Banking Industry*, page 308).

There have been several other notable analytical breakthroughs that have enhanced bank equity analytics. George Salem of Prudential Securities has contributed valuable weighted scoring models to assist in the assessment of the various segments of credit risk. Tom Brown and Frank DeSantis have produced models that appear to be superior in the detection of bank turnaround situations. Morgan Stanley, through its analysts, Art Soter and Dennis Shea, did much to separate revenue functions of financial institutions into those that derive from net interest margin products and those that are fee or processing related. Bill Weiant, formerly of First Boston and now with Dillon Read, developed several useful tools for a better understanding of bank credit exposure and funding implications. Led by Judah Kraushaar, Merrill Lynch's team, including Sandra Flannigan and Livia Asher, has demonstrated remarkable understanding of the role of bank strategy in producing high sustainable required returns.

The top analysts are issue-driven. They focus their work on critical P&L issues. Banks that are properly prepared to address the analysts' earnings concerns are rewarded. If, however, the analyst is working an issue for which a bank has not yet developed an appropriate strategy or response, management should expect to be criticized.

Where We Are and Where We Are Going in the Banking Industry

J. Richard Fredericks
Senior Managing Director
Montgomery Securities

Could it get much better? Profits and profitability in the banking system have never been better. Once rates started to decline, the profitability of our nation's 11,000 banks surged. A widening of margins and reduction in problem assets and net charge-offs have greatly contributed to record profits. Fueled by a historically wide yield curve, the banking industry has posted the highest returns since the FDIC started keeping data nearly 60 years ago. The full year 1992 return on assets was 0.96 percent, a record, but one which will easily be eclipsed by the results of 1993. The median return on assets at the top 50 banking companies was 1.24 percent, and 1.18 percent in the first and second quarters of 1993, respectively. Third quarter ROA exceeded both earlier periods, coming in at 1.26 percent.

With profits soaring, balance sheet strength has improved as capital ratios are higher than they have been for 30 years. Additionally, reserves have never been higher relative to problem assets (relative to loans, too). The reserve levels are so lofty that bankers have the option of matching or underproviding for charge-offs, possibly for years to come. If that were not enough, other reserve types—tax reserves, legal reserves, OREO reserves, accounting reserves (stepped up write-offs of deposit intangibles, purchase mortgage servicing rights, more conservative treatment of discount rates for pension plan assumptions, etc.)—have been bolstered, while even foundation grants have been stepped up.

Managements, reflecting the good news, have responded as well. Dividends are expanding at a rapid clip, dividend reinvestment programs are being canceled, preferreds are being called, and capital rich concerns are even repurchasing common stock.

Reflecting all of the above, bank stocks have responded. From their lows in October of 1990, the median stock market performance for the top 50 banks has been nearly a 200 percent gain. Only three banks in this group have not enjoyed a rise of at least 100 percent.

The Near to Intermediate Term: More of the Same

Thankfully, nothing on the immediate horizon seems likely to derail the record profits/profitability being generated by the industry. Few, if any banks, are reaching for profits as the earnings reports appear conservatively stated. Margins continue at historically high levels and earnings allow banks the flexibility to "bridge" income forward despite the absence of loan demand. Having strengthened their balance sheet, the high income flow is even allowing for the financing of some R&D projects to develop new income sources as well as give banks the time to rationalize their expense base. Importantly, as noted above, banks have been able to share their good fortune with their owners in the form of increased dividends (in some cases, substantially so).

Looking Forward: Some Predictions

Any view into the crystal ball, by definition, is clouded. The issues we see playing a role going forward are manyfold:

Prediction 1

The pace of net interest income generation will remain modest. In the decade of the 1980s, the growth of debt rose well above trendline. Traditionally, the long-term ratio of debt creation relative to our country's gross national product has been approximately 1:1 to one. The rapid rate of growth of borrowing in the decade of the 1980s pushed that relationship to nearly 1:4 to one. The culprit: real estate. Banks aggressively pushed for growth and notably lifted real estate loan exposure within the loan totals. To achieve that end, real estate growth at all banks was large enough to represent a lion's share of all the growth recorded in the industry. The hangover from that lending binge will definitely have a tempering influence on loan growth for some time to come. Having said that, we *do* anticipate loan demand to resume, but the growth will come from small business categories, consumer borrowing, and single-family lending. Other reasons that loan demand remains soft and could remain so are: banks continue to purposefully unwind large commercial real estate and commercial loans and replace them with smaller consumer credits and single-family real estate loans; incursions into the traditional banking domain by nonbank competitors; the resurgence of the junk bond market; low inflation; and better corporate inventory controls.

Without doubt, margins should add little impetus to the net interest income equation. Some skeptics go so far as to say that margins will narrow sharply. On that score we disagree! Margins will indeed recede some from the high current levels, but the contraction should be tempered by (1) the large buildup of core deposits, which, unlike past cycles, are now priced in an oligopolistic manner; (2) a higher level of loans in the asset mix financed out of balance sheet liquidity; and (3) a better mix of loans favoring higher-yielding instruments such as consumer loans and small business credits. Those factors will be further supplemented by more common equity support and less of a drag from problem assets. An interesting issue for banks relative to the future direction of margins is how sensitized core depositors have become to rate movements and whether they will defect in a rising rate environment to seek higher returns. Banks cannot count on the same core depositor loyalty in a rising rate period.

Prediction 2

Revenue growth from other products, services, and revenue sources may not be enough to shore up for slow net interest income growth. Currently the top 50 banks generate noninterest income that comprises 33 percent of total revenues. Similarly, the figures for all 11,000 FDIC-insured are 34 percent. Some of the industry's proposed answers to the profitability challenge are to recapture revenues lost from population shifts. Due to an aging baby boomer population, borrowers have become savers, but the preferred savings vehicle has become mutual funds. While banks are scrambling to introduce investment products, do they have the systems in place to properly promote those products without overselling? Will the customers balk at dealing with banks without the insurance coverage of the FDIC? Won't some customers believe the investment products have government insurance?

Prediction 3

While one can question the near-to intermediate-term growth prospects of loans, and therefore revenues, the larger question is whether the banks are not outflanked altogether by more agile nonbanking competition. Banks run the risk of becoming the "brand" names of the financial industry while other non-bank purveyors ("discounters") offering low pricing continue to steal share. Nonbank competition is formidable and arguably can compete effectively against banks in virtually any financial product area with better results. Why? Because banks are burdened by high deposit insurance costs, high costs of regulatory filings, and government CRA costs. We do not see a near-term solution to that unfair advantage.

Prediction 4

Consolidation will continue! Simply stated, our country is overbanked. The United States has 35 banking companies per million people, while other industrial countries generally have less than one per million people. In an era where revenues will be harder to come by, managements will turn toward consolidation in an attempt to engineer profits. Furthermore, many managements are becoming more comfortable in extracting costs from combinations. Some acquisitions, however, may cause indigestion to those who are not diligent in the integration process.

Prediction 5

The economic cycle has not been repealed, so the seeds of future loan losses will again be sown as banks push for volume. In the interim, however, losses may come in below historical norms for several years before an increase resurfaces.

Prediction 6

Scale and scope will increasingly become critical to success in banking. As an example, we envision a shakeout in mortgage banking after the current round of refinancing runs its course. The day is coming when a mortgage loan goes from the broker packaged/securitized directly to Fannie Mae or Freddie Mac, electronically. Thus, future players in the mortgage area will have to possess advanced, cost-effective software to process customers and be able to disperse funds quickly to compete at all against scale players. That format is the same in credit card, student loans, and even large corporate loan customers. Fewer players, with scale, will dominate the business.

Prediction 7

All of the discussion above indicates a sales/marketing culture is vitally important for future success, but it must be accompanied by a cost-effective delivery structure backed by a line of business approach. Many merger combinations in the late 1980s were made possible by management error that manifested itself in loan quality problems. In the future, the difference between above-average returns and mediocre returns will be in the cost area. Those banks that have bloated cost structures will become the merger targets for the better run, sales oriented, efficient organization.

In a world where revenues are hard to come by, where sales culture needs desperately to be imposed on sleepy organizations, and merger acumen in both pricing and integration is a prerequisite . . . MANAGEMENT MATTERS!

Reflections on "Darwinian Banking"

Ten years ago, I coauthored a treatise entitled "Darwinian Banking." Over the course of a decade, much has changed, but much remains the same. We espoused in that piece that banks that would thrive and survive would first be backstopped by a "fortress balance sheet" and exercise discipline in the areas of costs, credit losses, and the acquisition process. Additionally, expertise would be required in some non-inflationary product type.

Interestingly, while the darlings of Wall Street are the cyclical, recovery names and the industry now approaches fortress balance sheet strength, those who were leaders when we penned our original piece, remain so today. For the greater part, they managed through the turbulent 1980s without problems in the credit arena, without disruption from ill-conceived mergers, and their high profit product strength has enabled many to achieve ever higher profits. Indeed, many are among the first to buy back some of their stock and have continued to steadily, if not rapidly, increase dividends. Those same names have provided some of the best total returns that can be found over the 10-year measurement period. Is Darwinian Banking out of vogue? We think not!

Houses that are superb in providing broad, regular, and timely coverage of the banking universe are Salomon Brothers, Keefe, Bruyette & Woods, Montgomery Securities, and Goldman Sachs. Salomon's work, initially developed by Tom Hanley who is now with First Boston, in the area of detailing performance reviews as well as in-depth segment studies, such as their landmark research piece, *Technology in Banking*, is noteworthy. John Leonard and Diane Glossman have done a superb job maintaining Salomon's excellent reputation in bank research since Hanley's departure. Goldman Sachs's effort, under the leadership of Robert Albertson, in unbundling the value components of banking companies has the potential of better identifying sources of shareholder value.

These analysts and investment banks do not constitute an exhaustive list. There are several other strong analysts and brokerage houses doing very good work (for example, Smith Barney, Lehman Brothers, Fox-Pitt Kelton, and Bear Stearns). In particular, regional investment bank analysts at Robinson Humphrey, J.C. Bradford, Stifel Nicolaus, Alex Brown, McDonald & Company, A.G. Edwards, Advest, Chicago Corporation, and many others warrant more attention and discussion than can be provided here.

The New Role of Capital

Fortunately for some banks—and unfortunately for others—the trend among bank analysts to delve deeper into individual institutions coincides with banks' increasing dependence on capital raised through the stock market. As regulators asked banks to meet higher minimum capital standards, equity capital grew in importance. As equity capital grew in importance, so did the role of Wall Street in determining a bank's future.

Equity capital has become a prime determinant of growth, even survival, in the new banking environment. The need to live up to tougher capital standards will limit the field of competition and provide a new basis for assessment of comparative financial strength. Banking organizations with the strongest capital positions have the most options as the industry continues to consolidate. Indeed, they will be the survivors.

The central importance of equity capital to the future success of a bank's strategy, and the increasing sophistication of sell-side bank analysts, account for the fact that superregional bank executives often turn to those analysts for strategic as well as financial advice. The most successful sell-side analysts often also find themselves playing a strategic advisory role with the superregional banks.

On the other hand, money-center institutions still rely more on the corporate finance side of investment banks for advice. It has been interesting to observe the strategies of money-center banks as they maneuvered to meet new capital requirements. Before the Basle agreement, some money-center banks believed capital adequacy was an issue of limited importance. The money-center banks' managements believed in market share and control of business in their respective markets, sometimes at the expense of profits, and played the leverage game aggressively. Even if this belief was valid on an intellectual level, the investment community and the regulators had a more cautious view. Money-center banks were required to hold, at least, minimum levels of capital. Many of those banks have had to scramble to find enough capital to meet the new minimums. Competition for capital will become even more intense in the future.

The new capital rules also changed basic banking business strategy. Banks now have to make sure that each new piece of business is profitable. Poorly capitalized banks will have trouble raising money in the capital markets and will not have the option of pursuing market share at the expense of profit. This will also be true for banks competing all over the world. As a result, loan and deposit pricing will probably become more rational and uniform. Uniformity in pricing is a major concern. It potentially leads to commoditization, a dangerous trend.

. . . the increasing sophistication of sell-side bank analysts, account for the fact that superregional bank executives often turn to those analysts for strategic as well as financial advice. The most successful sell-side analysts often also find themselves playing a strategic advisory role with the superregional banks.

Ownership Issues and the Evolving Role
of the Institutional Investor

For well-run banks, the current investment environment is nearly ideal. Institutions are more interested than ever in buying equity in banks of different sizes, because returns have been attractive and predictable. Deregulation has created an industry structure that allows the top banks to differentiate and outperform their competitors. Value-creating growth, funded by external capital, is possible.

Today, institutional investors own 35 to 50 percent of most of the superregional banking organizations and one-half to three-quarters of many money-center banks (Exhibit 11.1). Until the late 1970s, only money-center banks had large enough market capitalizations to attract institutional investors.

Superregional banks are now actively traded and have enough outstanding shares to attract a broad set of institutional investors. The critical mass for significant institutional participation appears to be about 10 million shares outstanding and a market capitalization of about $500 million. Continued consolidation of banks will further enlarge institutional ownership.

As a result, buy-side analysts today have great influence in the banking industry. Their portfolio recommendations are a major determinant of the relative values of bank stocks and increasingly represent a running evaluation of management. More recently, the traditionally passive role of institutions as stockholders has changed to a point where many institutional shareholders now take an active role in issues of corporate governance; voting rights; change-of-control provisions; and, increasingly, management performance and compensation. Similar to the cases of GM and Sears, bank directors and management will face increasing performance pressures. To bankers, the emergence of institutions as the dominant shareholder voice has been swift and dramatic because of the relatively short period of accumulation of bank stock by institutions.

The trend toward institutional ownership poses a challenge for bank managers: they must communicate effectively with both the sell-side analysts who influence growing groups of institutional owners and the buy-side analysts who work directly for big investors. Exhibit 11.2 displays a cross-section of institutions that are today's major bank stock investors.

Communicating with Wall Street

In the late 1980s, credit quality and capital strength were every analyst's most important evaluation criteria. It is now common conventional wisdom that in the future analysts will become even more short-term oriented, looking for performance quarter-to-

Exhibit 11.1

INSTITUTIONAL INVESTMENT IN BANKS
Top Bank Institutional Investors

Ranked By Market Value of Bank Holdings as of December 31, 1992

Rank	Investor	December 31 Shares Owned	% Chng Shares Owned[1]	December 31 Mkt. Value ($M)	% Chng Market Value[1]
1	Wells Fargo Inst Tr NA	116,260,100	4.89	4,078.22	18.32
2	Fidelity Mgmt & Res Corp	125,946,133	-2.89	4,047.43	19.78
3	Bankers Trust N Y Corp	92,184,350	4.23	3,524.89	18.85
4	Capital Research & Mgmt	71,668,000	2.11	3,462.27	12.42
5	Wellington Management	72,884,000	5.09	2,807.81	18.36
6	Mellon Bank Corporation	60,887,500	1.62	2,314.13	14.20
7	College Retire Equities	53,544,000	7.32	2,122.55	23.56
8	Bernstein Sanford C & Co	59,959,750	-6.80	1,997.09	9.42
9	Janus Capital Corp.	43,788,000	14.19	1,982.33	32.20
10	Alliance Capital Mgmt.	44,590,750	2.01	1,762.56	12.22
11	Delaware Management Co	41,020,000	-8.38	1,741.69	1.48
12	Barrow Hanley Mewhinney	37,158,000	0.71	1,542.83	17.33
13	Morgan J P & Co Inc	39,214,150	0.77	1,379.06	17.72
14	New York St Common Ret.	33,281,000	4.32	1,367.74	16.36
15	Nationsbank Corporation	29,355,200	-0.51	1,309.57	13.81
16	Calif Public Emp. Ret.	34,095,000	9.41	1,302.28	26.55
17	State Farm Mut Auto Ins	30,080,000	-0.67	1,292.50	11.86
18	Boston Company Inc	31,190,000	3.58	1,290.70	20.76
19	State Street Boston Corp	32,223,150	-2.42	1,273.90	15.23
20	Calif State Teachers Ret	30,360,500	1.10	1,134.32	15.40
21	Michigan State Treasurer	29,562,000	-1.11	1,030.64	17.56
22	New York St Teachers Ret	24,125,500	5.64	1,000.02	22.89
23	Capital Guardian Trust	22,465,000	6.62	990.23	13.97
24	Shearson Lehman Hutton	23,935,750	20.31	979.38	31.61
25	Prudential Ins Co/Amer	25,868,600	4.89	978.64	17.01
26	Banc One Corporation	18,891,900	-15.59	930.06	-2.32
27	Miller Anderson&Sherrerd	22,062,500	7.67	912.98	21.07
28	Capital Growth Mgmt	22,256,000	-21.05	894.18	4.62
29	Northern Trust Corp	21,207,650	1.54	884.39	12.70
30	Lazard Freres & Co	22,699,500	-7.77	884.03	11.68
	Total For All Publicly Traded Banks:	**3,490,877,680**	**4.97**	**133,690**	**19.16**

[1]Percent change from September 30.

Source: CDA Investment Technologies, Rockville, MD, and SNL Securities

---

quarter rather than simply year-to-year. In part, this increasing short-term orientation reflects the growing percentage of bank shares controlled by institutional investors. Some might argue that a short-term performance orientation might lead bank managements to become even more short-term oriented than they are today. We question whether such an adverse course will unfold.

More generally, analysts will increasingly focus on quality of bank management and its ability to formulate and articulate strategic plans and future direction. Analysts want to know what management believes is important and how management plans to

Exhibit 11.2

TOP BANK INSTITUTIONAL INVESTORS

Institutional Investment in Banks

Ranked By Percentage Owned as of December 31, 1992

Rank	Ticker	Bank	ST	Percent Owned	Shares Out	Owned by Inst. Invstrs	Chng from Sept 30
1	UBNK	Union Bank	CA	79.85	32,429,000	25,893,000	278,000
2	BK	Bank of New York Company	NY	79.54	80,355,985	63,915,000	3,155,000
3	I	First Interstate Bancorp	CA	76.53	75,181,138	57,533,000	3,197,000
4	KRB	MBNA Corporation	DE	73.21	99,000,000	72,474,000	1,542,000
5	BT	Bankers Trust New York Corp.	NY	71.29	82,873,988	59,080,000	550,000
6	NOB	Norwest Corporation	MN	70.79	140,116,125	99,193,000	291,000
7	NCC	National City Corporation	OH	70.59	79,083,590	55,822,000	1,016,000
8	CHL	Chemical Banking Corp.	NY	67.86	246,800,000	167,481,000	4,447,000
9	STBK	State Street Boston Corp.	MA	67.60	75,061,000	50,741,000	995,000
10	NTRS	Northern Trust Corporation	IL	66.29	52,832,000	35,024,000	720,500
11	JPM	J.P. Morgan & Co. Incorporated	NY	65.06	191,610,298	124,660,000	-1,329,000
12	USTC	U.S. Trust Corporation	NY	63.87	9,272,322	5,922,000	497,000
13	FNB	First Chicago Corporation	IL	63.45	82,331,001	52,237,000	985,000
14	WFC	Wells Fargo & Company	CA	63.27	55,191,173	34,918,000	-592,000
15	SRCE	1st Source Corporation	IN	62.68	7,200,800	4,513,500	-28,500
16	BOH	Bancorp Hawaii, Inc.	HI	59.30	28,056,190	16,638,000	-241,000
17	SNC	Shawmut National Corporation	MA	58.94	92,528,000	54,533,000	4,472,000
18	KEY	KeyCorp	NY	58.41	72,460,000	42,327,000	1,355,000
19	FTU	First Union Corporation	NC	57.95	136,051,813	78,838,000	5,527,000
20	CSFN	CoreStates Financial Corp	PA	57.72	58,415,000	33,716,000	2,732,000
21	MEL	Mellon Bank Corporation	PA	57.55	54,962,761	31,631,000	1,041,000
22	BKB	Bank of Boston Corporation	MA	56.68	84,732,000	48,027,000	1,648,000
23	PNC	PNC Bank Corp.	PA	55.95	232,573,253	130,128,000	2,351,136
24	BAC	BankAmerica Corporation	CA	55.89	348,603,000	194,828,000	889,000
25	NB	NationsBank Corporation	NC	55.83	252,990,000	141,235,000	4,526,000
26	FBS	First Bank System, Inc.	MN	55.62	93,982,486	52,277,000	7,774,000
27	FSCO	First Security Corporation	UT	55.56	38,296,000	21,277,000	1,694,000
28	MNCO	Michigan National Corporation	MI	55.23	14,908,000	8,233,000	323,000
29	LBNA	Liberty Bancorp	OK	55.09	8,815,399	4,856,000	590,000
30	BBNK	BayBanks, Inc.	MA	55.00	18,507,002	10,179,000	1,562,000

1 Percent change from September 30

Source: CDA Investment Technologies, Rockville, MD, and SNL Securities

differentiate their bank from its competition. They are looking for signs that a bank will be able to generate better-than-average returns on a sustained basis. If they think a bank has the ability to capitalize on a unique strength, its stock will sell at a higher multiple. And those banks with the highest multiple will have many more strategic options than other banks.

One of the major problems faced by superregional banks has been convincing analysts that their existing business lines will continue to produce the earnings that they have in the past.

Analysts will focus more and more on individual banks' areas of expertise. They realize that financial performance will depend more on the success of a particular bank's business lines than on the general health of the industry.

Deregulation has broken old geographic barriers and created a new species of bank in the superregional. It has pushed banks to specialize and capitalize on the specific activities they do best. Individual banks are now specializing in mortgage banking, student loan processing, credit cards, cash management, and trust processing, among other lines of business. Moreover, several of the leading high-growth superregionals, notably BANC ONE and Norwest, also describe their acquisition activities as a "line of business."

Wall Street hates surprises. An analyst or portfolio manager who is surprised more than occasionally will be encouraged to find another line of work. The career-threatening aspect of surprise has caused the investment community to put great emphasis on the credibility of the management with whom they deal. Once lost, credibility from the investment community is seldom, if ever, regained by the same management—a reality that has career-threatening aspects of its own for bank senior management.

It is important to present a well-articulated strategic plan to analysts. If investors have a clear understanding of where management is headed, a negative quarter is more easily digested—up to a point. A continuing refrain of "We are sure that it will turn around next quarter," erodes credibility as quarters become years and gaps between promise and performance are established. The lesson is: keep communication lines open, and set accurate expectations that you intend to meet.

The CEO and Investor Relations

A CEO should play the primary communications role with the investment community. He or she is expected to have a firm grasp of financial performance (the more detailed, the more impressive) and be able to articulate the future direction of the company. It is his or her performance and message that establishes the credibility of the organization. Because investor interaction involves much more than review of recent financial results, the CEO normally has a wide range of opportunities to be personally involved. Many bank investor programs now include more one-on-one meetings with key investors. Consequently, a proactive investor relations program can easily consume 10 to 15 percent of a CEO's time.

When analyst presentations are given, a bank needs to provide two things: complete financials and a clear, strategic direction for the company. Analysts complain that many banking companies provide the financials without a strategic framework, leaving doubts as to the existence of a bank strategy. Given the

Wall Street hates surprises. An analyst or portfolio manager who is surprised more than occasionally will be encouraged to find another line of work. The career-threatening aspect of surprise has caused the investment community to put great emphasis on the credibility of the management . . .

complexity of today's banking environment, to overlook the strategic dimension would be a major oversight.

The investor road show team generally includes the CEO, the chief financial officer, and an investor relations officer. Some banks may vary the mix to include executives who can address specific concerns of investors. If a particular loan category—commercial real estate or highly leveraged transactions (HLTs), for example—is of keen interest, a senior lender should participate. Similarly, if a significant merger is to be addressed, the executive who is coordinating it should be available.

Because of the relatively large increase in superregional bank stock float and corporate financing needs, many banks have begun to market themselves periodically in Europe and Asia. To the extent that bank equities become increasingly integral to global investment programs, this trend will most likely continue.

Other Investors, Individuals, and Employees

It is probably a mistake for a bank to limit all of its investor relations resources to analysts and institutional investors. Individual investors are also important. Institutional investors often follow trends, running toward and away from various types of stocks as a group. By contrast, individual investors are much more stable. They want to invest in a company for the long run, and can provide an anchor in good times and bad. One of the major reasons for a small bank to affiliate with larger regional banks is that by joining others it can offer individual shareholders immediate liquidity. This is important, especially to shareholders who have significant positions in the acquired bank. These acquisitions constantly add to the number of individuals who hold the stock of the acquirers.

Hosting regional shareholders' meetings where small investors get a chance to ask senior managers about their companies provides an opportunity for actively courting the retail investment community. It is important for management to make certain that these investors receive as much pertinent information about their banks as possible. This type of effort has proven effective in attracting new retail shareholders and is an excellent opportunity for maintaining relationships with people who receive stock through an acquisition.

While solid recommendations from analysts are flattering and healthy, the mark of a truly strong bank is substantial employee and management ownership. It signals loyalty and faith in the business strategy.

The bank analyst community tends not to focus on ownership of bank stock by management and employees. Occasionally, an individual shareholder at an annual meeting, usually hoping to make an issue, will zero in on management and employee ownership. In contrast, very few analysts even ask the question.

Working with Wall Street

Wall Street is not going to determine the future of the banking industry; individual banks will. At the same time, however, banks' ability to communicate with Wall Street may prove decisive. While Wall Street's role is relatively new to the banking industry, it should be expected to continue to increase as consolidation unfolds.

Living by your stock price is a double-edged sword. Performance improvement translates into share price gains to support acquisitions and growth. Performance declines, however, can undermine a bank's market capitalization throttling growth plans downward. Given this reality, Wall Street must be managed. It is a key dimension against which high performance must be delivered. It is another important element of the new industry paradigm.

12

CEO Leadership Matters

Given the banking industry's historically regulation-dominated management culture, it is helpful to look outside the industry for examples of competitively driven, market-focused management approaches. With so many significant changes occurring in banking today, the ability to adapt and evolve is of paramount importance. When the challenge is managing change, the focus is on the CEO. In periods of change, CEO leadership matters.

Business observers and management experts have frequently cited the Disney organization as a corporate role model. Through the years Disney has maintained a culture that places customers first. By placing customers first, it facilitates the company evolving in response to new market needs. It is no wonder then that the company has a long history of producing superb financial results. Consumers equate Disney with value and are willing to pay premium prices to enjoy the experience the company provides.

Perhaps banking is not as much fun as the Disney experience, but many of the company's management principles apply to any business. Moreover, the problems that Disney addresses every day are the same problems that bank CEOs will grapple with during the next decade. Clearly, the best forward-looking role models for those who run banks are not necessarily to be found in the banking industry. Fierce competition for the core business of most banks will continue to demand a higher level of innovation, market responsiveness, and management discipline than the industry has traditionally required.

In the 1990s, CEOs and senior managers will also have to cope with cultural and morale issues that result from an unprecedented wave of banking mergers. The industry would do well to strive for the kind of well-defined and integrated corporate culture that the Disneys of the world have built. As the consolidation process continues, one should expect increasing emphasis to be placed on building strong, even domineering, bank corporate cultures and management organizations. The responsibility for building the banking organization of the 1990s rests squarely with the CEO.

As a strategic decision maker in a deregulated environment, today's chief executive officer has to define for his or her managers the bank's strategy, goals, and sources of competitive advantage. Beyond strategic issues, however, the CEO plays an extremely critical organizational leadership role. For an industry in transition, the CEO's organizational role could well be more important than the strategic role.

Popular management literature provides an extensive set of frameworks with which to evaluate and characterize organizations. In looking at the requirements for building and managing successful banking organizations—and while keeping in mind the hostile competitive environment of the 1990s—four areas warrant special attention: market responsiveness, innovation, performance measurement, and people. Careful attention to these four critical organizational variables can help top management achieve great competitive advantage and marketplace success. Ultimately, the challenge is to weave these features into a compelling corporate culture. This is where CEO leadership matters the most.

Market Responsiveness:
A Real Opportunity for Differentiation

Commoditization is the road to nowhere. Investing in branding and differentiation is banks' only defense against competitive oblivion. Marketing success should be measured in market share gains. Traditionally, fragmented markets and regulatory constraints made the achievement of annual share gains exceeding one percent unusual. Today, as a more oligopolistic market structure emerges, annual share gains in the one to two percent range should be targeted by the ambitious banking organization. To compete effectively in this crowded environment, a bank chairman must chart a focused, distinctive, and well-researched course and stick to it with conviction. The truly successful superregional banks provide evidence of this requirement for success, BankAmerica, BANC ONE, Wachovia, Norwest, and Wells Fargo are each excellent examples of the power of this long-run market perspective. In each case, the CEO has played an important role in establishing this market perspective.

The importance of market responsiveness can be best demonstrated in the consumer marketplace. Retail banking is more dynamic and complex than the trust or commercial lending businesses, which change slowly and usually only in response to new regulations or laws. Most commercial-oriented banks, that are used to dealing with fewer customers and products, simply have not been very successful in the retail marketplace. In the 1980s, the industry made a tremendous investment in the development of sophisticated data processing and distribution systems needed for competing in the retail marketplace. In the 1990s, executive leadership is essential for managing and capitalizing on this infrastructure.

If a financial institution is to stand out and remain successful in an increasingly crowded financial services industry, it must be dedicated in its focus on the market. Superior knowledge of customer needs and competitive offerings is almost certainly the best opportunity for gaining real, sustainable competitive advantage. That knowledge includes understanding both what customers want and the ways in which they perceive the service that they receive. The ability to deliver and maintain a perception of value is crucial to financial success in a deregulated environment and defines the major way in which bankers differ from one another. Since concentration on quality is still rare in the industry, it becomes a useful tool to use in determining how customers differ in their willingness to pay for superior service.

The successful bank studies the financial services offered by its competitors very closely. After all, the real competition for its more profitable lines of business comes from the automobile, communications, securities, and insurance companies that have the latitude to compete across the financial services landscape. The bank measures the success of its efforts to build a differentiated market franchise by tracking their own customer retention, depth of relationships, and levels of customer satisfaction. These three measures are the bases for judging the effect of the quality effort throughout the organization. Results should affect the salaries of top management, which, in turn, ensures attention throughout the organization. The CEO must drive the linkage of marketplace performance and executive compensation.

When it comes to achieving marketplace success, CEOs can provide leadership by paying attention to every point of customer contact. For example, they should let it be known that quality of service is really their main priority, not simply an abstract concept. Since CEOs cannot decree quality, they must demonstrate their commitment by example. At BANC ONE, the CEO visits companies known for offering outstanding service and selects some of their best procedures or concepts for consideration and implementation by the bank. He personally reviews customer statements to gauge the message they convey or do not convey; answers every letter received, whether it is a compliment or a complaint; and returns every phone call to a customer within 24 hours.

BANC ONE solicits feedback from more than 200,000 customers each year, urging them to comment on what they like and do not like about the bank's service. Some are unpaid volunteers, and others are part of paid focus groups. Based on those interviews, the bank adjusts its procedures and priorities. Such research enables BANC ONE to stay focused on the market and the priority needs of consumers.

The banking industry is only just beginning to understand the linkages between branding, pricing, and profitability. Consumer marketing companies such as Pepsi, McDonald's, Proctor & Gamble, and Nike have long understood the linkages; American Express, far ahead of other financial services competition, also understands. Banks, as the industry consolidates, must begin to manage these critical linkages as well. It is the responsibility of the CEO to ensure the required linkages occur.

The banking industry is only just beginning to understand the linkages between branding, pricing, and profitability. Consumer marketing companies such as Pepsi, McDonald's, Proctor & Gamble, and Nike have long understood the linkages . . .

Making an Imperative of Innovation

We are living in a quality and services revolution. Nearly every recent business publication includes an article on quality, service, or both. Most indicate that businesses must better focus on their customers if they are to succeed in the 1990s. Banking is no exception.

One of the most critical contributors to marketplace success is having the systems and technology in place that will enable the company to capitalize on opportunities as they arise. Taking a long-term view of new product development is a significant challenge to an industry long comfortable with a regulatory-mandated product set. A long-term view is necessary if the company is to place appropriate emphasis on innovation and automation. In 1970, for example, BANC ONE was one of the first banks to install cash dispensing machines and for the past several years has been working with Electronic Data Systems (EDS) to create software that it hopes will set a new standard in retail banking. The system envisioned will provide a level of integrated customer, product, and credit information that simply does not yet exist.

Although advanced technology often is available, the market sometimes is not ready for it. For instance, home banking has been pursued and then dropped several times over the past two decades. Recently, however, banks have reentered the field in a small way by becoming part of a third-party service called Prodigy, a joint venture of Sears Roebuck and IBM. Prodigy computerizes a wide array of services from home information and shopping to banking. It is also testing a range of access devices, such as personal computers and advanced phones with computer capabilities, for use in home banking and shopping services. CEO leadership is necessary to allow a thin-margin provider to experiment with exploratory ventures like advanced data processing systems, futuristic branches, and home banking.

Pricing of bank products and services will increasingly border on commoditization as competition for the financial services dollar intensifies. In the final analysis, effective strategic marketing and brand management are the sources of successful differentiation in the consumer products arena. Banks can best differentiate by bundling attractive combinations of convenient services in an array of segment-priced products. Tailored, packaged accounts aimed at seniors or young households are examples of opportunities for differentiation.

It used to be that banks developed products and services for very broad, poorly defined markets. Commodity systems approaches begat commodity products. Now the systems exist to build products for very well-defined market segments and to microidentify those customers who are most likely to be interested in particular products. This permits systems-based differentiation, a critical issue for bank CEOs to focus on during the coming years.

Performance Measurement: The Critical Management Tool

An effective management information system (MIS) both measures and motivates. MIS tracks all balance sheet and income statement data as well as high-impact productivity and loan quality ratios. This moving picture of financial performance forces constant comparisons of results with budgets and forecasts. At PNC, for example, management demonstrates its near passion for management information systems with the saying, "If you can't measure it, you can't manage it."

Multibank holding companies are particularly advantaged in applying MIS toward improved operating performance. Texas Commerce and First of America each represented strong commitments to the use of MIS for managing multibank holding companies. From a line-of-business perspective, notable MIS have been developed at CoreStates, First Chicago, Chemical, and Shawmut. Developing strong MIS is the hallmark of a management committed to achieving high performance.

But developing MIS is one thing; actively using MIS to gain the insights necessary to strengthen operating performance is another. BANC ONE'S MIS, called Management Information Control System (MICS), is one of the banking industry's best examples of an actively used MIS.

BANC ONE's MICS

BANC ONE's MICS data are assembled for each affiliate bank and made available on computer screen to every other member of the system. At BANC ONE it is common knowledge which bank is

But developing MIS is one thing; actively using MIS to gain the insights necessary to strengthen operating performance is another. BANC ONE'S MIS, called Management Information Control System (MICS), is one of the banking industry's best examples of an actively used MIS.

best and worst in each performance category. Instead of measuring itself against other local competitor banks, a new affiliate bank measures itself against the best performing affiliate banks in the country, all of them in the same business, selling the same products. Whatever intracompany peer pressure may be engendered by MICS is viewed by management as positive. It drives the process of self-analysis and integration to begin directly after acquisition.

While BANC ONE's MICS highlights problems, it also offers opportunities for solutions. A bank affiliate experiencing operating problems can learn from the best bank in the system. A newly acquired bank ranking high in delinquent loans might complain, "You don't understand my local market; we're having a regional recession here." Across a far-flung franchise, there are always executives who have experienced or are experiencing similar situations.

Management information gives the officers of each affiliate more than just a computer system that churns out financial data; it also provides the stimulus for proactive thinking about how the bank makes money.

Management information gives the officers of each affiliate more than just a computer system that churns out financial data; it also provides the stimulus for proactive thinking about how the bank makes money. Effective MIS becomes an important piece of the corporate financial structure and culture that allows feedback and input from across the organization. In short, it is a tool—albeit not the final decision maker—that allows management to run the institution in the most profitable way possible.

BANC ONE applies its MICS in precisely this way. Using MICS, each affiliate reports its actual data for the just completed month and then forecasts what it believes monthly earnings will be for the remainder of the year. A monthly reforecast of the remaining months of the year is unique discipline. Moreover, banks forecast the drivers of financial performance rather than just financial performance itself. Drivers help identify the root causes of successes and problems for each business product unit. This enables the bank to identify the key aspects of that business or product and focus its efforts on improving them.

This key performance measure (KPM) approach to managing the business has been popularized by academics such as Bob Keplar of Harvard Business School and John Rockhart of MIT's Sloan School of Management. Among consulting firms, First Manhattan Consulting Group has been most notable in its promotion of the use of KPMs.

In order to arrive at an assessment of corporate performance, each affiliate's individual performance is consolidated into its respective state holding company; the consolidation of those holding companies then represents the corporation's total performance. All levels of management have the opportunity to review each bank's results on a comparative basis. This bottom-up approach to financial reporting allows senior management of both the individual bank and the corporation to review the results of that particular affiliate.

At BANC ONE, MICS provides the common formats and account mapping that make comparisons across banks possible. Whereas it has been customary across bank holding companies not to reveal individual bank financial results, just the opposite is true at BANC ONE. There, banks are encouraged to share information and expertise with others within the system who request it. State and corporate management can review results and analyze those banks found to be strong performers. They can then meet with other banks to review the strengths they may have in particular areas that enhance performance. Peer bank pressure definitely creates a desire to avoid being at or near the bottom of key performance measures. This peer group structure helps the poorer performing banks become more adept at improving earnings.

A focus on credit quality

Credit quality, not surprisingly, is a critical focus of most banks' management information systems. Key reports for credit quality comparative purposes include nonperforming loans, problem loans, and delinquent loan analyses; year-to-date (YTD), full-year forward (FYF) forecast, and annualized net charge-offs.

The credit quality, delinquent loan, and lease analyses allow each affiliate to compare its percentage of delinquent loans by product. Also, breaking out the percentages delinquent by categories (30–59 days, 60–89 days, 90–119 days, 120+ days, and cumulative >90 days) enables the bank to evaluate trends and probable future credit quality conditions.

The nonperforming loan analysis ranks individual banks according to nonperforming assets (NPA) as a percentage of the bank's total assets. Included in the NPAs are nonaccrual loans, renegotiated loans, and other real estate owned (OREO).

Problem-loans-by-affiliate is another tool that is useful when evaluating the total problem loan portfolio and its relationship to capital. These rankings enable the bank to compare its loan portfolio in relation to other banks in each state holding company.

The corporation also ranks the affiliates by total percentages of delinquencies. This allows management of the affiliate to get a better understanding of the ways in which their collection operations are performing in comparison to other banks and to see if any unusual credit problems may have developed in a product category.

Banks use YTD and FYF net charge-off percentages to evaluate their ranking by loan products measured against net charge-offs. When compared to reports from other affiliates, this valuable summary allows individual banks to see whether any product in their portfolio is creating excess losses.

MIS key to managing profitability

Beyond credit quality, the BANC ONE Corporation peer group comparison report (see Exhibit 12.1) provides a comparative financial breakdown of affiliates by size and lists their results by current quarter and full year using key financial measures that include equity/assets, net income, ROA, ROE, NIM, and NIE/Revenue. Banks are very conscious of the performance they attain in each category.

Again, peer pressure is managed as a very positive aspect of being a bank affiliate of the BANC ONE Corporation. There is no hiding below-average performance from fellow banks. Yet there is a very strong commitment among those banks that are performing well to make themselves available to help their peers. The camaraderie among BANC ONE CEOs and CFOs is very strong. Without that sense of trust, BANC ONE affiliates would not be as successful as they are today.

To be successful nowadays, a bank must be a performance-driven organization. Measuring results is a critical factor in achieving financial success. To be truly effective, every CEO and CFO should be cognizant of his or her bank's performance, not only on a monthly basis, but daily as well. It is this sense of knowing precisely where the bank's earnings for the month stand that separates average performers from top performers.

Measuring these results is a key driver in this process. Each bank has a target for most key performance measures that requires it to stretch. These targets, at times, seem unattainable to some affiliates. However, without them it is doubtful the bank would ever attain its maximum potential earnings power. Experience has shown a bank can do surprisingly well when its focus is centered on improving key performance ratios.

On the 20th, 25th, and last business day of each month, the CFO is responsible for updating the corporation on its earnings projection for the month. Any variance from the MICS-forecasted, pre-tax earnings target requires an explanation. Having this process in place allows the affiliate time during the latter part of the month to try to address the variance. This financial responsibility drives the management team at the individual banks to seek to achieve the earnings projected in the forecast. Without this discipline, many more variances would likely occur as earnings totals were rolled up to the corporation, thereby creating investor and analyst concern. MICS is a critical tool in the attempt to manage both earnings and Wall Street's expectations.

When new affiliates are brought into the BANC ONE fold, most experience a much higher level of financial reporting than they were used to providing. MICS is the first financial tool they

Peer pressure is managed as a very positive aspect of being a bank affiliate of the BANC ONE Corporation. There is no hiding below-average performance from fellow banks. Yet there is a very strong commitment among those banks that are performing well to make themselves available to help their peers.

Exhibit 12.1

BANC ONE CORPORATION
PEER COMPARISON
December 1992
($ Thousands)

	Current Quarter							Full Year						
Affiliates*	EOQ Assets	Equity/Assets	Net Inc	ROA	ROE	NIM	NIE/Revenue	EOY Assets	Equity/Assets	Net Inc	ROA	ROE	NIM	NIE/Revenue
1	$2,374,206	7.91	$12,482	2.12	26.66	6.65	44.94	$2,374,206	7.91	$38,956	1.67	21.78	6.74	51.56
2	$915,658	9.34	$2,148	0.98	11.53	6.86	63.63	$915,658	9.34	$9,103	1.03	13.17	6.57	63.22
3	$2,294,988	6.89	$10,586	1.89	26.46	6.82	51.16	$2,294,988	6.89	$34,782	1.59	23.30	6.84	54.47
4	$5,875,651	8.31	$26,266	1.89	21.62	7.26	52.90	$5,875,651	8.31	$118,513	2.12	26.00	8.34	48.32
5	$6,905,424	6.47	$30,440	2.01	30.19	5.21	41.36	$6,905,424	6.47	$97,859	1.94	30.09	5.37	46.61
6	$2,885,217	7.94	$15,936	2.28	27.63	9.49	46.01	$2,885,217	7.94	$51,506	1.86	23.34	9.18	46.49
7	$1,173,720	7.45	$2,575	0.92	11.82	6.36	75.64	$1,173,720	7.45	$10,217	0.91	12.05	6.00	76.20
8	$2,064,338	6.28	$287	0.07	1.27	4.57	93.01	$2,064,338	6.28	$6,544	0.63	11.67	4.62	73.28
9	$4,687,831	7.36	$12,376	1.14	16.87	5.21	54.42	$4,687,831	7.36	$41,360	1.06	16.48	5.44	57.78
10	$4,597,023	9.55	$16,117	1.46	14.69	6.27	62.37	$4,597,023	9.55	$75,496	1.79	18.08	6.49	53.24
11	$1,674,534	8.67	$2,513	0.59	7.00	5.31	69.25	$1,674,534	8.67	$7,936	0.45	5.51	4.96	76.42
12	$3,266,548	8.38	$13,083	1.66	19.32	6.51	49.68	$3,266,548	8.38	$46,625	1.56	18.33	6.51	51.15
13	$1,193,005	8.96	$5,428	1.85	20.13	6.75	52.88	$1,193,005	8.96	$15,184	1.31	14.11	6.52	60.41
Total Large Banks	$39,908,142	7.82	$150,236	1.61	20.20	6.35	54.04	$39,908,142	7.82	$554,080	1.58	20.41	6.61	53.32
% of Total Banks	66.21%		67.81%					66.21%		65.57%				
1														
2	$452,300	8.03	$1,122	1.06	12.32	5.54	61.75	$452,300	8.03	$6,030	1.46	17.12	5.78	54.85
3	$247,110	6.96	$1,026	1.62	23.25	6.60	54.34	$247,110	6.96	$3,790	1.47	22.00	6.49	51.47
4	$1,109,584	5.83	$3,808	1.58	28.14	5.22	58.20	$1,109,584	5.83	$13,528	1.70	33.21	5.47	57.11
5	$474,031	10.08	$1,772	1.45	14.41	6.32	54.74	$474,031	10.08	$6,297	1.67	16.44	6.64	51.25
6	$604,788	7.06	$2,452	1.74	23.39	5.88	61.10	$604,788	7.06	$9,459	1.75	22.99	5.93	61.87
7	$299,796	10.30	$1,254	1.69	16.21	5.70	50.59	$299,796	10.30	$5,616	1.85	18.34	5.42	50.73
8	$517,397	7.45	$2,281	1.79	24.34	5.58	61.94	$517,397	7.45	$8,401	1.74	24.57	5.40	63.00
9	$287,854	9.56	$1,477	2.00	21.55	7.09	48.13	$287,854	9.56	$5,897	2.02	22.19	7.18	46.79

Continued

Exhibit 12.1 Continued

| | Current Quarter | | | | | | | Full Year | | | | | | |
Affiliates*	EOQ Assets	Equity/ Assets	Net Inc	ROA	ROE	NIM	NIE/ Revenue	EOY Assets	Equity/ Assets	Net Inc	ROA	ROE	NIM	NIE/ Revenue
10	$617,118	9.60	$1,525	0.99	10.33	5.85	61.85	$617,118	9.60	$12,860	1.98	23.53	5.30	48.05
11	$479,454	8.19	$1,334	1.14	13.54	5.31	56.77	$479,454	8.19	$6,359	1.39	16.63	5.43	54.23
12	$674,832	9.32	$2,555	1.52	15.39	7.65	51.85	$674,832	9.32	$13,026	1.99	21.96	8.70	48.76
13	$613,288	6.68	$1,867	1.24	18.45	5.62	54.45	$613,288	6.68	$6,705	1.20	17.87	5.28	55.96
14	$912,006	6.93	$2,331	1.02	15.61	6.01	59.54	$912,006	6.93	$10,485	1.71	20.66	6.76	55.44
15	$309,041	8.32	$1,107	1.45	17.34	5.70	60.70	$309,041	8.32	$4,596	1.55	18.63	5.83	57.78
16	$433,523	8.46	$1,824	1.62	19.73	6.86	48.35	$433,523	8.46	$7,656	1.76	20.81	6.65	50.10
17	$624,025	9.12	$2,694	1.89	18.76	6.32	52.02	$624,025	9.12	$7,907	1.45	14.05	6.61	56.57
18	$770,336	5.93	$2,184	1.21	21.76	5.18	65.86	$770,336	5.93	$10,048	1.55	29.26	5.70	59.63
19	$280,561	6.89	$596	0.89	12.31	4.90	68.86	$280,561	6.89	$2,112	.80	11.18	4.70	74.73
20	$246,292	9.20	$1,144	1.85	19.63	8.17	46.85	$246,292	9.20	$4,655	1.87	20.13	7.80	48.32
21	$357,613	8.64	$1,347	1.49	17.50	5.57	60.89	$357,613	8.64	$5,426	1.55	18.17	5.57	56.72
22	$289,744	8.72	$280	0.38	4.29	6.55	75.69	$289,744	8.72	$3,070	1.07	12.03	6.71	65.98
23	$573,317	6.75	$2,734	1.86	27.06	7.05	57.20	$573,317	6.75	$10,365	1.75	27.49	7.25	56.09
24	$312,501	5.43	$1,882	2.32	30.06	5.89	47.38	$312,501	5.43	$7,955	2.37	31.90	6.45	45.89
25	$724,979	9.39	$3,607	2.00	21.10	6.19	59.76	$724,979	9.39	$15,441	2.21	23.41	5.83	58.91
26	$250,806	9.45	$995	1.54	16.83	7.31	54.64	$250,806	9.45	$4,109	1.63	17.52	7.08	54.51
27	$418,746	5.69	$1,553	1.63	22.98	4.99	49.29	$418,746	5.69	$5,945	1.89	23.94	6.06	47.57
28	$357,140	8.61	$1,664	1.90	22.01	5.71	47.97	$357,140	8.61	$6,193	1.75	22.19	5.27	45.95
Total Mid-Size Banks	$13,238,185	7.83	$48,415	1.50	18.72	6.04	57.03	$13,238,185	7.83	$203,932	1.70	21.27	6.19	54.76
% of Total Banks	21.96%		21.85%					21.96%		24.13%				
All Small Banks	$7,130,781							$7,130,781						
% of Total Banks	11.83%							11.83%						

* Data (percentages) for affiliate banks only.

Source: BANC ONE Corporation

encounter. While some of these new affiliates may have thought they were inundating their management with financial information before the acquisition, the volume and degree of complexity they experience following the acquisition is sometimes a shock, not only to senior management but throughout the financial management function.

It is the financial area that will usually see an increase in head count after acquisition by BANC ONE. The CFO and his or her staff are responsible for supplying the required information to the corporation within the time frames set by policy. Lateness in reporting holds up the entire consolidation. The staff must quickly become accustomed to time pressures of the financial reporting process.

In this regard, MICS is a major performance tool used in developing the BANC ONE culture within the affiliate. Finance people visit the new affiliate and begin integration of the process by meeting with the CFO and other senior management. Once the acquisition is completed, the CEO, CFO, and other key members of management receive monthly visits from a holding company finance representative who reviews the monthly earnings, forecast, and any risks or opportunities. The representative also receives an update on any issues that may arise in the near future either from the standpoint of the affiliate or the corporation. These meetings stress the importance of accurately forecasting earnings to the affiliate's management. Cooperation among all divisions in the affiliate is crucial if the affiliate CFO is to provide BANC ONE a reliable forecast of earnings.

Too often we measure everything and understand nothing. A key phrase that is used in the financial culture is "no surprises." The CFO can use MIS as a key tool to analyze risks and opportunities, be it pricing, volume, or fees. However, the CFO must also have a strong enough relationship with the division heads that those people will notify him or her of any potential earnings impact during the month or full year. Therefore, developing a P&L culture throughout the bank is a major challenge. Once this is accomplished, the bank has a much better chance of enhanced performance. Effective MIS is a major tool in this process. The ultimate implementation responsibility, however, is the CEO's.

Management Talent:
The Real Performance Constraint

Market responsiveness, innovation, and measurement are critical elements of a competitive banking organization. People, however, are what make the organization move forward. One of the ultimate responsibilities of the CEO is to make certain the organization is filled with the best management talent available. While

Too often we measure everything and understand nothing. A key phrase that is used in the financial culture is "no surprises." The CFO can use MIS as a key tool to analyze risks and opportunities, be it pricing, volume, or fees.

that may sound like an obvious statement, knowing who are the best people is not always immediately apparent. In the midst of an industry paradigm shift, traditional thinking about people issues may no longer be relevant. There is often the need to look beyond the industry, not just within it.

Human resource-related matters can occupy a considerable portion of the CEO's time. The objective is always to match the right people to the right jobs. Given the competition for management talent today, people decisions will undoubtedly occupy an ever increasing amount of the CEO's time.

Today's work environment is a difficult one in which to find top talent. Not only has the population decline caused a shortage of young workers, but the ones who are available are often not well trained for the increasingly service-oriented banking business. Contact people need to be more sophisticated now because of the broader range of services they must sell and the complexity of problems they encounter in serving customers.

By the end of the decade, almost all bank customer-contact people will be college graduates who will be required to have significant general training as well as sales training. Pay-for-performance plans in banking may expand until they parallel those of insurance and brokerage firms.

The ultimate challenge a chief executive faces is hiring the best top managers, who, in turn, can build winning management teams. While it is best to try to develop excellence from within, with the challenges facing the banking business, management often must recruit talent from outside the organization or, increasingly, outside the banking industry. They come from manufacturing, insurance, brokerage, retailing, and consulting and usually add a new perspective to the business. A CEO's natural inclination is to take his or her best bankers and train them in new fields that the bank is entering. The tougher—but more productive— option may be to keep the best bankers as managers of traditional banking businesses and hire new talent to face the new challenges.

In banking today, the selection and management of the senior management team is undergoing more frequent and critical review. Since the senior team must orchestrate and execute the CEO's agenda for performance, it is imperative that this team be able to implement the bank's plan. A recent (October 19, 1993) bold shakeup of the top management of Bank of Boston demonstrates how crucial this point is. In requesting the resignation of an entire layer of his senior managers, its CEO, Ira Stepanian, demonstrated that conservatism can no longer be the industry standard. Significant change may require more than incremental action. In seeking radical change, Stepanian argued that "you really have to start at the top."

A CEO's natural inclination is to take his or her best bankers and train them in new fields that the bank is entering. The tougher—but more productive—option may be to keep the best bankers as managers of traditional banking businesses and hire new talent to face the new challenges.

In the search for management talent, CEOs should also view directors as key advisers and resources. There was a time when boards of directors of most banks were made up of close business and professional associates of the chief executive. Often there were more inside officers than outsiders serving on boards. Frequently, from the CEO's viewpoint, the critical selection attribute for directors was simply that they could be trusted.

What is needed now are smart and insightful individuals who have proven track records in their chosen professions. To run a superb banking business, it is essential that directors have a thorough understanding of all the businesses the bank serves. For example, when the bank loans money to a specific business, it must have a deep knowledge of its market and its future. The best way to obtain this expertise is to place competent people from that industry on the board. Not only does having such people on the board provide the bank with an ad hoc internal advisory resource, but their presence instills investor confidence in the bank.

Even the chairman's office is not immune to the need for a broader perspective. Thirty years ago, bank chairmen were corporate bankers because bank customers were primarily businesses. Twenty years ago, the average CEO had corporate lending and experience and was adept at working with regulators. Now, with mergers in the banking industry leaving a stronger set of players competing in a more complex environment, the best CEOs are those who know how to manage opportunity and provide products of outstanding quality and perceived value. Marketing and organizational skills are increasingly more valued than more traditional sales and credit experience. Again, even at the CEO level, key people will likely come from outside banking.

The trend in external recruitment has already begun. For instance, in 1989 National Westminster Bank, the United Kingdom's second largest clearing bank appointed Lord Alexander of Weedan, a barrister with no formal banking background, as its chairman. Other notable banking senior executives recruited from outside traditional industry circles include Richard Braddock, formerly of Citicorp, Richard Kovacevich of Norwest, Leo Mullin of First Chicago, Eileen Friars of NationsBank, and Paul Kerins of Barnett. In the early 1990s, beyond the most senior executive ranks, there has been a major influx of nontraditional industry talent. Reflecting the need to pursue a rapid paradigm change, a faster and, in many instances, necessary way to pursue needed structural and cultural changes is the hiring of new talent.

The bank CEO should consider himself or herself as much the chief strategic personnel officer as anything else. Given the fierce competition for the limited pool of talent, the next-generation CEO must increasingly think this way.

Ultimate CEO Responsibility:
Building a Competitive Corporate Culture

Getting the best people on board is one thing; empowering them to do their best for the bank is another. To make it all work, employees must be given the autonomy and authority to make their ideas flow and work. For the successful institution, this empowerment is usually achieved through a strong guiding culture. Troubled institutions often have cultures that could be characterized as both dysfunctional and as a debilitating obstacle to change. As a result, for the CEO, managing the corporate culture is perhaps the most important responsibility.

But before taking on a lot of responsibility, employees need to really know their company, its strategy, and goals. General Electric and Xerox are two industrial firms renowned for putting their new employees through rigorous orientation and training. Employees at Disney often train three weeks before coming in contact with their first customers. These companies consider training an investment in customer service and retention, not an expense.

Training and management development programs can be used to bring together a select cadre of senior managers each year. An environment designed to generate networking and trust among participants will ultimately prove valuable to the bank. When all participants are encouraged to share ideas, organizations can abound.

To be successful in a rapidly changing environment, banks must vest a tremendous amount of autonomy and accountability with people in line positions. For such empowerment to succeed, a much greater investment in training and management development will be required.

In contrast, unfortunately, most new employees of banks go through a concentrated orientation process designed to get them on the floor, or platform, or behind a teller window as soon as possible. Not only is their actual training usually done on the job, but they are not properly indoctrinated into their bank's corporate culture and guiding beliefs.

Senior bank executives should look hard at the programs of leading service companies in the nonfinancial sector because the management style of the next generation of bankers needs to resemble that of today's leading service corporations more closely. To be successful in a rapidly changing environment, banks must vest a tremendous amount of autonomy and accountability with people in line positions. For such empowerment to succeed, a much greater investment in training and management development will be required.

Once employees are part of the corporation, it is very important that they feel they have a stake in it. Stock ownership is the most powerful way to impart that feeling. Incentives would spur managers into action. If incentive plans are well designed, management actions will translate into shareholder value. Research suggests, however, that most banks' compensation plans reward the achievement of goals not necessarily tied to shareholder value. Moreover, the incentive compensation arena has been dominated by industry benchmarking techniques and other forms of ultimately inward-looking analyses. Benchmarking, for example, almost inevitably leads to the incremental redesign of one's compensation system to make it similar to competitors'. Not much of an opportunity for breakthrough can be found with this approach.

Even in the most decentralized banks, problems drift to the top. An important element of CEO leadership is the ability to exercise authority. Frequently a judgment call may be required. The successful CEO relies on consistency of intent as well as a supportive culture to provide needed guidance.

Organizational politics exists everywhere. Consistent leadership, however, can probably limit its dysfunctional impact. Turf battles and parochial interests can be squelched by clear, strong corporate direction.

At the end of the day, an element of excellent leadership is visibility. Visibility is necessary to understand firsthand the requirements of line managers. Management by walking around provides the opportunity to learn directly what is going on in the bank as well as to project desired CEO visibility into the organization.

In the country's most successful corporations, a high percentage of equity ownership rests with the officers and employees. For example, well over 95 percent of BANC ONE's officers are shareholders, and more than 70 percent of all employees own stock. Similarly high stock ownership percentages can be found in other leading banks.

The Ultimate CEO Test:
Merging Banks and Corporate Cultures

In Chapter 6, we discussed the 1990 study by First Manhattan Consulting Group for the Bank Administration Institute of the largest bank mergers between 1982 and 1988. The study contained bad news for would-be acquirers: the average stock price of acquirers fell 8 to 15 percent in the first year following acquisition. As a matter of fact, by 1988 the average price of an acquirer's stock was at a 38 percent discount when compared to that of its peers. Moreover, 12 of the 26 banks that made big acquisitions in 1982 were themselves later acquired. Another nine of the 26 experienced slower than average asset growth through the remainder of the decade. From a financial perspective, making acquisitions work is a major challenge.

Greater than the financial test is the organizational test. Consider the 1990 merger of Citizens & Southern with Sovran Financial Corporation, a classic example of a merger gone wrong. The troubled C&S/Sovran was acquired by NationsBank in 1991.

Beyond credit problems and unnecessary layers of management, however, the two companies never succeeded at merging and defining common goals . . . The corporate culture was put in play, disempowering management from taking the decisive action that would have been necessary to address serious performance problems . . .

After the fact, analysts are now saying that the C&S/Sovran merger points out that problems can occur when banks of nearly equal size, but from completely different markets, merge—Citizens & Southern was from Georgia and Sovran was from Virginia. From a credit perspective, C&S had no idea how troubled Sovran's Washington, D.C., area real estate loan portfolio was. Also, a form of golfcourse etiquette prevented the prompt elimination of unnecessary and expensive top management. After all, one of the goals of a big merger is to create operating and personnel efficiencies, and that is impossible to accomplish with an overabundance of poorly functioning, highly paid managers.

Beyond credit problems and unnecessary layers of management, however, the two companies never succeeded at merging and defining common goals, strategies, and cultural mores. The corporate culture was put in play, disempowering management from taking the decisive action that would have been necessary to address serious performance problems effectively. As management consensus languished, so did the chance for a successful turnaround.

Many lessons can be drawn from the wreckage of failed bank mergers and acquisitions of the late 1980s and early 1990s. In addition to C&S/Sovran, Connecticut Bank & Trust-Bank of New England, and Midland-Crocker, are testimony to the operating, financial, credit, and organizational risks that carry the potential to derail and destroy significant opportunities to create shareholder value through merger and acquisition efforts.

Several institutions have exemplary track records on the acquisition front. BANC ONE, Norwest, First Bank System, First Fidelity, and BankAmerica have all demonstrated a proven ability to successfully acquire, integrate, and create value for their shareholders. We can cite BANC ONE's acquisition strategy as a useful case example of success. Its track record is good: overall improvement in return on assets for acquired banks from the year prior to purchase through June 1993 approximates 50 to 60 percent.

From an organizational perspective, an explicit and paramount goal of BANC ONE is to ensure that not only its culture survives, but it strongly takes root in acquired banks. A targeted institution must operate in a familiar, attractive market and have a strong, committed management and good asset quality. The BANC ONE philosophy states that it will not acquire any bank that is larger than one third of the resulting combined asset size.

The most important acquisition variable is quality of management—not surprising, given the premium that should be placed on attracting and retaining top talent. Buying a bank is really just buying people. Failure to motivate and control acquired management is the chief pitfall in most unsuccessful acquisitions. Mergers and acquisitions succeed or fail on the basis of people.

The failed mergers of the past strongly prove this point. BANC ONE's acquisition history of both potential and actual deals well demonstrates these key principles. The history of the MCorp, Bank of New England, and Valley National transactions each provides useful insights.

When the idea of a BANC ONE-MCorp deal was first broached in 1989, BANC ONE's CEO opposed the idea because it did not fit neatly into its standard acquisition profile—it was outside BANC ONE's familiar midwest operating territory and it was a failed institution. Naturally, there were concerns raised about the quality of MCorp's management. Adding to the concern was the fact that Texas, traditionally the seat of big-ticket energy and real estate lending, was not generally viewed as a retail banking market.

Management by dissent—not consent—is an important part of the BANC ONE culture. Could MCorp's management succeed in the BANC ONE environment? A team of analysts and executives studied the MCorp operations, interviewing top people at every MCorp bank and sometimes probing deeply into the ranks of the bigger banks in the holding company. The study team found that the best people had remained and retained their motivation, primarily because there really were no other good career options in banking to be found in Texas at the time. Once convinced of the quality and compatibility of the MCorp people, BANC ONE made the purchase.

On the other hand, when BANC ONE took a hard look at the failed Bank of New England in 1991, it was not interested in that opportunity for two reasons. First, it was not possible to predict the end of the recession in New England—it appeared that it could be years before the economy would turn around. Second, BANC ONE did not have a high level of confidence in the management team running the bank—many had been on board for just a short time, and most had not moved permanently to the area. These two factors indicated a lack of personal commitment to the job at hand, namely, turning the bank around. The other potential suitors already operating in this market, Fleet and Bank of Boston, understandably rated the management factor of lesser importance and anticipated very large in-market cost savings.

The exact opposite of the Bank of New England case was true at Valley National Corporation in Arizona. A new management team had been put in place by Valley National's board. They had fundamentally restructured the company along the lines of a typical BANC ONE affiliate before merger discussions began. In addition, the Arizona economy had started to improve, and future prospects for the region were excellent. Valley National met all the affiliation benchmarks, including being less than one third BANC ONE's asset size at the time of the affiliation.

Managing a Multibank Holding Company

The whole issue of corporate culture, quality employees, and autonomy has taken on new importance in this age of bank mergers and acquisitions. As the pace of consolidation in the industry quickens, it has become increasingly clear that the track record to date for mergers and acquisitions is mediocre at best.

BANC ONE's treatment of acquired banks and affiliates is a good example of effective, decentralized management style. After more than 100 acquisitions, it has been exposed to a range of management structures, from full centralization to total decentralization. Centralization always looks better on paper for cost reasons. However, decentralization is more advantageous because it generates motivation and a sense of ownership of the process. BANC ONE has evolved a style it calls "uncommon partnership," under which it tries to operate in as decentralized a way as possible. A common culture, corporate goals, and management information system bind the corporation together.

The large, multimarket, multibank holding company is much more willing to test new and innovative products and services because it can try them in a single market with local banks, thereby avoiding bet-the-bank tryouts of unproven ideas. And the great freedom it allows its top managers when making lending, pricing, and personnel decisions provides the best training for high-level managers of the future. Ironically, failure to develop adequate management depth for succession purposes represents one of the greatest risks faced by a large bank. As distressing as it may be to some central corporate staff, the benefits gained from affiliate executives operating as independent business persons outweigh what may be lost in organization time and consistency at headquarters.

Ironically, failure to develop adequate management depth for succession purposes represents one of the greatest risks faced by the large bank. As distressing as it may be to some central services people, the benefits gained from affiliate executives operating as independent business persons outweigh what may be lost in organization time at headquarters.

Managing External Constituencies

In the 1990s, CEOs will have to be more aware than ever of politics at the national and local levels because the industry will continue to experience wrenching reforms throughout the decade. Historically, banks have been content to use trade associations and lobbyists to carry a simple set of shared messages to Washington. With bank failures, mergers, issues of capital, and interstate banking, a common industry perspective shared by all bank executives continues to be illusive. Banking industry trade associations are experiencing a decline in their influence that can be expected to continue. Equally important, trade associations have splintered across the wide variety of different perspectives.

In October 1991, for example, President Bush asked 12 bank chief executive officers to visit with him at the White House to help determine what should then be done about the so-called credit crunch. Banks of all sizes were represented at the meeting, and their chief executives were very impressed with his working knowledge and understanding of the critical issues that face the banking industry. It was an ideal opportunity—away from the need to influence layers of staff support—for an honest discussion about today's opportunities in banking. President Clinton has continued the tradition of meeting and listening to all types of business leaders, including bankers. Several excellent and new ideas have come from those meetings. Time will tell if they will be implemented and produce a positive impact on the economy.

Beyond the White House, a vast array of regulatory agencies—the Fed, the OCC, HUD, and the Department of Justice, not to mention state or local authorities—are all playing increasingly active roles in this supposedly deregulated environment. Banking leaders need to be aggressive in pursuing direct access with the top policymakers and regulators. The CEO must play a critical role in developing perspectives and delivering them to the key external constituencies.

Evolving Role of the CEO

Banking, just like other businesses, is going through an evolution in the kind of CEOs required to run a competitively successful company. In the early days of automobiles, engineers ran the business. At the inception of air travel, pilots ran the airlines. Future banking CEOs will need to be highly astute managers capable of running any kind of major company. They will come from a broad cross-section of the banking industry or, just as likely as not, from outside the industry.

Gone are the days of the CEO whose most important talent was attracting borrowers and knowing a good credit risk. Bank chiefs now have to be marketers and innovators, human resource and organization experts, and politicians—and all the while maintain a shareholder's perspective. Not surprisingly, a key responsibility of bank CEOs is the management of the investment community. Perhaps most important, they must be effective leaders and delegators.

Neither the management style embodied by the hands-on chief executive nor that of the executive who works by consensus is up to the challenges of deregulation and intensified competition in financial services. A mixed, variable approach is going to be necesary. To be successful, today's CEO must invest time studying and understanding their markets in search of differentiation opportunities and time focusing on recruitment and development of senior managers. They must rely on delegation and empowerment, and place more emphasis on accountability through financial systems that measure competitive performance.

Gone are the days of the CEO whose most important talent was attracting borrowers and knowing a good credit risk. Bank chiefs now have to be marketers and innovators, human resource and organization experts, and politicians—and all the while maintain a shareholder's perspective.

In today's environment, timidity may cause mistakes. A CEO is the leader and orchestrator of change. It may be an error for a CEO to want to be liked and thought of as reasonable. Seeking to have too many constituencies on board is an unnecessary constraint on the pace of change. Less focus should be placed on consensus and more effort made toward empowerment. The challenge of the 1990s is to engage the effort of every manager and employee.

Change has no natural constituency. Most people, even if they recognize the need for change, prefer the status quo, if only because it is familiar. Moreover, significant change cannot be successfully pursued on an incremental basis. If the change is not great enough, inertia and preexisting bureaucracy will win out. The role of the CEO as manager will be crucial throughout the paradigm shift already underway in banking. In separating the winners from the losers in consolidation, CEO leadership will make the critical difference.

13

Paradigm Regained

Despite the plethora of statistics and proliferation of industry pundits, no one can forecast with certainty the endpoint of the industry's evolution. While the 1980s deregulation has sparked increased competition and dramatic industry change, market forces once unleashed cannot really be managed. In this context, financial services consumers are king as they make explicit their needs and demands, and regulators referee. Competitors are left to seek solutions to the resulting product and capital market challenges.

Bank management faces enormous challenge. Throughout this process of industry change, shareholders must be satisfied. For many management teams, this high-stakes competitive game is a new one. Because an old paradigm must be replaced, the game promises to be rich and intense. As has already been pointed out, there will be winners and losers.

Although there may not yet be a defined endpoint, one can begin to observe the emergence of a new industry paradigm. Equally profound as the new paradigm, new rules of thumb are gaining acceptance as part of the new conventional wisdom that is evolving to guide industry competition in the 1990s. Usually conventional wisdom is not to be trusted, reflecting that it is too often out-of-date when changes in thought or conduct are required. However, the new guidelines are fresh and have only recently developed as a response to the competitive marketplace. As a result, they constitute the leading edge of the emerging new paradigm.

No new solutions manual is going to be issued. Across the industry, there will be those competitors who press on boldly into the future, and those that remain shackled by the practices and policies of the past. A keen sensitivity to the evolving environment, and the challenges and opportunities it presents, will be critical. When travelling at exceptionally high speeds, one must keep their eyes on the road out ahead.

In reflecting on both the corporate and business line challenges of today, we see 10 new guiding rules that should receive great focus. These 10 themes are receiving increasing attention throughout the industry. They constitute the outline of the paradigm regained:

1. **In an industry that is undergoing massive consolidation and restructuring, the critical limiting resource is management talent.**

In the late 1980s, the industry's need for increased capital drew great attention. The Basle Accord took the regulatory step of mandating higher bank capital standards. Through equity offerings, restructuring, divestitures, dividend cuts, and increased profitability, most institutions spent the past five years building and strengthening their capital position. Reflecting implementation success, by 1993 many analysts were writing about the industry's excess capital problem. With record earnings, achieved through the decline in interest rates and a steep yield curve, as well as strong loan reserves, one can expect most banks' capital positions to continue to strengthen through the mid-1990s. Obviously, capital is no longer the critical constraining resource.

In contrast, the changing economics of banking has continued to ratchet up the need for flexibility and creativity from management. The pace of the paradigm shift that the industry is undergoing requires much more aggressive and proactive management than the industry has traditionally had available. Increasingly, decisions must be made with a view of what the future environment is going to be like, rather than what worked in the past. Moreover, at the same time, most banks' compensation and reward systems are designed for a different era. As a result, even when the management horsepower has been available, too often it has been trained, developed, and acculturated in a manner that leaves management ill-equipped for today's challenges. Now that the capital problem has been resolved, attracting and developing management talent presents itself as a potentially more intractable problem.

Importing talent from outside the industry has been a necessary step for many institutions. And while a CEO must be careful to avoid the radical upset of an organization's prevailing culture, at the same time, he or she should recognize that the chief executive's ultimate responsibility is the proactive management, not passive stewardship, of that culture. If culture is the performance constraint, then an effective culture must be developed.

In addressing cultural issues, the recruiting of external talent can play a critical role. Notably, management talent has been

. . . while a CEO must be careful to avoid the radical upset of an organization's prevailing culture . . . he or she should recognize that the chief executive's ultimate responsibility is the proactive management, not passive stewardship, of that culture. If culture is the performance constraint, then an effective culture must be developed.

recruited into banking from the packaged goods, computer and technology, investment banking, and management consulting industries. In addition, within banking it has become increasingly acceptable to recruit talent from one institution to another. In this case, what was once taboo is now commonplace.

The recruiting of external talent has been critical to managing a successful turnaround. Some of industry's dramatic strategic turnaround stories tell of the importation of external management talent—Mellon, First Fidelity, First Bank System, Barnett, and Shawmut are notable examples. In each case, while there was probably resistance to bringing in outsiders, the moves were critical to gaining both new perspective as well as much needed expertise and energy for the institution.

Both our analytical discussions and review of the empirical evidence related to performance throughout earlier chapters strongly suggest that management can make the difference in an institution's ability to achieve superior results. If the management talent necessary to achieve high performance levels is not in place, it must be acquired. There is really no acceptable alternative.

2. The stock market is the key performance barometer and ultimate arbiter of success.

A new breed of top management is emerging within the banking industry. These leaders understand the intricate economics of managing risk and creating value for shareholders. Management's focus is on the bank's stock price, and it embraces the stock market as both the vehicle and ultimate arbiter of success.

In the current consolidation environment, every bank faces a challenge to be among the survivors. Meeting this challenge requires achieving a high stock valuation. Resources must be allocated appropriately or restructured to achieve that objective. At the same time, perspective must be maintained on both the short run and the long run to ensure that one does not become a constraint on the other.

As part of the process of building shareholder value, most large banks need to evaluate their business portfolio mix very critically. Too often breakup-value analysis reveals there are business lines destroying value, while high-value lines are not receiving enough investment. In these cases, focused restructuring can add significant market value within a relatively short time period. A careful blending of high-value-creating business units was found to be at the heart of the success of Chapter 4's four case study banks—Fifth Third, Wells Fargo, Banker's Trust, and State Street. Undoubtedly, careful analysis of most bank's business portfolios would reveal parallel sources of values, as well as opportunities for restructuring.

From the perspective of the new breed of bank executive, the Wall Street analyst community is viewed not so much as an adversary, but an ally. Effective communication with the analyst community is critical to achieving success. Management must strive to address investors' and analysts' questions about how value will be created. Tangible examples of both strategic and tactical initiatives to achieve higher values must be evident.

From Wall Street's perspective, to be successful, a bank must be clearly pursuing a value-creating corporate strategy. There is also great value in building a reputation as a strategically managed company. Most importantly, in working to gain and maintain Wall Street's confidence, a bank must deliver on the promise of earnings. For the successful institution, a positive reinforcing cycle of delivering on earnings commitments must be established. Steps to achieve an even higher level of performance must also be prepared and publicly presented. The old adage—live by the sword, die by the sword—seems apropos. Except substitute stock price for sword. In today's shareholder-oriented world, you must deliver consistently.

The old adage—live by the sword, die by the sword—seems apropos. Except substitute stock price for sword. In today's shareholder-oriented world, you must deliver consistently.

3. Acquisitions, given profitability pressures and low growth prospects, should be an important source of earnings growth.

The 1970s and 1980s were both marked by waves of growth driven by the oil, defense, and real estate sectors, as well as demographics-driven growth provided by baby boomers. Each surge in demand provided an impetus for balance sheet and earnings growth. Management that grew up during the past two decades has really not experienced either deregulated or low-growth environments until now.

The 1990s most likely will not feature sector-specific or broad-based sources of growth that have characterized the past. Indeed, it may well prove to be a decade principally marked by restructuring and retrenchment. In this environment, the usual sources of growth will probably not prove adequate to support shareholder value goals. While internal restructuring and cost cutting may prove to be effective in the short run to boost earnings, they are not long-run strategies. In this context, an important source of earnings growth will depend upon acquisitions.

Successful acquisitions, however, are not a given. Targeting, pricing, transaction structuring, and integration are all critical steps to ensuring that acquisitions create value. Today BANC ONE, Norwest, Wells Fargo, and NationsBank are among a small set of major regionals that have demonstrated the ability to grow their earnings consistently through acquisitions. The focus and discipline that these institutions have brought to the acquisition process are now emulated by many. Both the strategic importance and the need for a disciplined methodology are well recognized by leading acquirers. Without any doubt, to be a survivor in the low-growth 1990s requires a value-creating acquisition program.

4. Attention to the financial mechanics of mergers is required to ensure that transactions create value.

Strong, negative stock market reaction to the earnings dilution that characterized many deals in the early consolidation waves of the 1980s appears to have brought substantial discipline to the bank acquisition pricing process. In general, most deals in recent years have involved little dilution, and, to the extent that it does surface, acquirers are taking aggressive cost-saving actions to eliminate any permanent dilutive effects. The industry apparently internalized the message sent by Wall Street's reaction to those early deals.

Nevertheless, pressures are building for several second- and third-tier superregional banks to expand their franchises and size in order to remain independent or safe from takeover. Given that the alternatives are to sell out or merge as an equal, which can be tantamount to selling out for no premium, an increased number of "stretch" transactions should again be anticipated. In these cases, dilution effects and cost-saving estimates are pushed to extreme limits. Similar to the acquirers of the 1980s who overpaid to win deals, some of these firms, too, will find that winning deals is not by itself enough to create shareholder value. When strategic transacations require stretch pricing, integration and cost-cutting skills are put to the test.

As the bank merger landscape enters its mature phase, banks increasingly must face the end game head-on. Because very few sizable targets remain, more regional and even superregional banks will themselves become targets. In a game of chicken, the competitor that blinks first loses. In the bank consolidation game, you cannot blink, but neither can you pursue a course that fails to reward your shareholders. Like the high-wire acrobat, one must balance and trade-off growth, acquisition pricing, capacity to absorb dilution, and the demonstrated ability to successfully integrate acquired banks to create shareholder value. The calculus of success will undoubtedly be complex.

Our work illustrated that, assuming reliable input data, a mixture of dilution, acquiree enhancement, and discounted cash

Given that the alternatives are to sell out or merge as an equal, which can be tantamount to selling out for no premium, an increased number of "stretch" transactions should again be anticipated. In these cases, dilution effects and cost-saving estimates are pushed to extreme limits.

flow analyses can frame most merger propositions appropriately. However, because of inherent investment banker transaction biases, the existence of multiple stakeholders, and limitations of the data used for financial analyses, the board of directors is inevitably left with a difficult decision. What is often left to carry the day is the strategic vision that management has developed to provide context to what otherwise might just be viewed as merely a financial transaction. While strategic vision may not be formally in the algebra of a valuation model, it must be at the heart of any deal.

5. Successful cost management requires both budget discipline and potentially radical resource allocation. It is also imperative.

Given the existence of multiple approaches for either incremental or radical cost management, a lack of action can only be explained by indifference. The late 1980s were marked by industry attempts at downsizing in the face of credit losses and limited growth prospects. Countless *American Banker* headlines were written about different institutions' cost cutting and layoffs. In some cases, the cost reduction impacts were effective and permanent. More often than not, however, the P&L results were both temporary and less than anticipated.

To be effective, cost management cannot be a one-time or five-year-cycle event. Effective cost management requires both near-term incremental discipline and a longer-term perspective, necessarily a radical one that allows the questioning, examination, and reengineering of some of the basic ways business is conducted. It is in the careful blending of this call for discipline and radicalism that management faces as its challenge.

At the same time, however, budget discipline cannot be allowed to imply resource rigidity, or else the achievement of more aggressive long-term goals may be put at risk. Ultimately, effective cost management must encourage sufficient radical thinking to eliminate all potential sources of resource rigidity.

Discipline in budgeting is necessary not only to ensure hitting targeted performance levels, but also to instill the accountability required to manage against the budget. At the same time, however, budget discipline cannot be allowed to imply resource rigidity, or else the achievement of more aggressive long-term goals may be put at risk. Ultimately, effective cost management must encourage sufficient radical thinking to eliminate all potential sources of resource rigidity. Process reengineering is the most commonly employed technique for pursuing radical cost restructuring. But whether pursuing short-term incremental gains or longer-term restructuring, management commitment is always the differentiating factor across institutions.

In Chapter 7, our examination of bank efficiency ratios revealed that over time banks find it difficult to maintain consistent low-cost positions. Several banks that had either high- or low-cost positions in 1988 found their performance substantially different (either better or worse) five years later. Only about 20 percent of the top 50 banks were able to sustain both superior and improving efficiency ratios. Banks have been criticized for behaving like lemmings. In statistics parlance, the observed "reversion to the mean" phenomenon provides evidence of such behavior. Superior performance can be achieved and sustained, but only through a superior commitment.

To achieve the dual objectives of discipline and flexibility, new management processes and analytical tools must be adopted and embraced by the industry. External benchmarking and process reengineering can be two helpful tools. In an industry undergoing significant economic change—indeed, where the underlying business paradigm is being redefined—the ability to restructure and reallocate resources in line with the new business economics is critical.

Viewed from senior management's perspective, cost management must be part of a broad strategic framework that includes a search for expenditure opportunities and profitable revenue streams. More importantly, cost management and the pursuit of increased efficiency cannot be allowed to be merely a tactic to be employed. Rather, for the successful bank, it must be bred into the institution's culture. A high sense of urgency must be created. Tolerance cannot be shown for sacred cows or tradition-protected practices that no longer have any economic logic.

Effective budgeting and resource allocation become the key management processes for managing change. The approach to cost management certainly has explicit impact on a bank's P&L, but perhaps an even more profound influence on the corporate culture. No operating activity deserves greater top management attention.

6. A clear understanding of customer behavior and market potential, as well as the real cost of doing business, may be the greatest source of competitive advantage.

Long driven and, as a result, protected by regulation, critical resource allocation and pricing skills were never essential to bank management. Moreover, the strategic market orientation required for survival in other competitive industries has developed late in banking. It is the exceptional institution that really understands how much a customer relationship is worth, or how much it costs to provide products or relationship services. But in the land of the blind, the one-eyed man is king. Superior knowledge of costs and profitability by product or customer, with its obvious

But in the land of the blind, the one-eyed man is king. Superior knowledge of costs and profitability by product or customer, with its obvious strategic implications for pricing and resource allocation, can become an important source of competitive advantage.

strategic implications for pricing and resource allocation, can become an important source of competitive advantage.

The CEO who emphasizes the use of effective pricing and resource allocation as operating levers for achieving superior performance has identified the two with the highest impact. Unfortunately, traditional industry MIS and analysis are weak on these important dimensions. Consequently, if the recommended financial analysis is developed and implemented, an opportunity to outperform competitors should result. Building superior MIS and profitability models may appear to be an intangible investment. However, because institutions seeking to survive the 1990s cannot afford the risk of being outdated, it may be a wise investment with rapid payback.

Consider, for example, how retail banking represents an area in great need of critical reevaluation from a management information perspective. The MIS and related profitability models advocated earlier have great application to this line of business. The forces of deregulation, changing technology, and shifting consumer behavior have served to change the profit model of consumer banking dramatically. Management must develop systematic approaches for addressing these environmental and behavior changes. As discussed in Chapter 8, the task required can be characterized as a schizophrenic exercise. Traditional delivery networks must be simultaneously viewed as a competitive weapon and a costly albatross. Management must extract profits from the present franchise in the short-run while transforming the traditional distribution paradigm into one that has long-run or future value. Reporting and tracking progress on such an undertaking is essential to ensuring success. Because a new world is unfolding, past intuition is limited in value. Real-time MIS needs are critical.

Strong MIS that addresses the customer behavior, product profitability, and P&L implications of the way a bank does business, is the appropriate response to the challenge of unwinding seemingly intractable problems. Cost allocation schemes must be upgraded. Systems investments must be made to capture and report the data needed to run the business, not just satisfy regulators and shareholders. MIS must be repositioned, front and center, as a defining element of the new paradigm.

7. Marketplace forces provide the opportunity both to differentiate with superior products and delivery and to improve the alignment of revenues and costs.

Deregulation unleashed marketplace forces that were too long ignored or incorrectly assessed as irrelevant. The forces of change, once set in motion, require the industry to be flexible in its reallocation of resources toward the greatest opportunities for revenues and profits. At the same time, a lowering of industry growth prospects has translated into greater resource allocation scrutiny, head count reductions, and general downsizing. It would be a mistake, however, to assume that the forces of the market are not also creating opportunity.

In the drama of industry change, several important market-driven growth opportunities merit special attention:

- investment products to meet the saving and retirement needs of the baby boom generation of Americans;

- increased self-service convenience in providing bank service to younger consumers;

- home equity-based credit products that allow home-owners to access the major investments they have made in their homes;

- the banking needs of small business that have long been required to be satisfied with either the large size of retail banking products or miniaturized versions of corporate banking products, neither of which works appropriately.

The list of opportunities goes on. The point, however, is that market change also provides opportunities for growth.

Pursuing these opportunities requires effective target marketing and high standards of analytical rigor in allocating resources and making P&L decisions. The upgrading of the banking industry's marketing talent that started in the 1980s will continue. As the basis of competition becomes increasingly brand- and image-related, the importance of strategic marketing and positioning decisions will increase. Coca-Cola CEO Roberto C. Goizueta wrote the book *The Cola Wars* to characterize competition between major brands in the beverage industry in the 1980s. In parallel fashion, the late 1990s will be "The Bank Wars" as major brand names aggressively compete for consumers' share-of-wallet.

Relationship management, a traditional industry tactic to manage for share-of-wallet, will remain a critical lever. Higher-level franchise and brand management considerations, however, will take precedence over a one-customer-at-a-time approach. High-share positions, somewhat ironically, will lead to more visible and overt competition. This competition will put a premium on real differentiation and sustainable service quality. In this competitive marketplace, there will be no rest for the weary.

High-share positions, somewhat ironically, will lead to more visible and overt competition. This competition will put a premium on real differentiation and sustainable service quality.

But there will also be much opportunity. Stealing share, differentiated service levels, premium pricing, and segmented approaches to the marketplace will all be real opportunities, not always available in the past's more stable, structured, and regulated market environment. The bottomline benefit for well-managed banks in the 1990s can be a period of expansion and earnings growth, not just a continuation of 1980s' retrenchment.

8. Credit risk should be managed to maximize risk-adjusted returns. Better pricing of risk will continue to be a critical determinant of performance.

In perhaps no other area are the challenges of the 1990s greater than in the area of credit policy. Coming off the credit problems of the 1980s, and with a low loan growth environment anticipated, credit conservatism will inevitably be identified as one of the causes of limited growth. Not surprisingly, the whole arena of credit risk management is concurrently undergoing a revolution in both philosophy and analytical approach.

Like the investment management field before it, credit risk management is undergoing a change that is driven by the concepts of modern portfolio theory. The central principle being advanced is that in maximizing profits, banks should explicitly manage risk-adjusted lending spreads rather than simply work to minimize loan losses—a straightforward concept that is profound in its implications.

The redefined objective of maximizing risk-adjusted returns is increasingly accepted and embraced. Yet the banking industry needs much improvement in several key areas if it is to successfully achieve this necessary objective. First, the industry has been found by the Loan Pricing Corporation and others to fail consistently in pricing risk correctly. Second, owing to its historic fragmentation and focus on individual loan risk, the industry has been slow to adopt the pricing and diversification lessons of modern portfolio theory. For example, application of covariance management principles promises to improve the profitability of loan portfolios. Third, there must be a much higher adherence to rigorous credit management processes. Teamwork, discipline, and communication in this regard are crucial.

It is important to note, however, that the changes in credit risk management are market driven. The growth of the commercial paper market that increased private companies' access to public capital markets, and the accelerating development of a secondary market for commercial loans, both contribute to the need for increased market responsiveness and discipline in managing credit risk. The changes occurring in the credit risk management area

Yet the banking industry needs much improvement in several key areas if it is to successfully achieve this necessary objective. First, the industry has been found by the Loan Pricing Corporation and others to fail consistently in pricing risk correctly. Second, . . . the industry has been slow to adopt the pricing and diversification lessons of modern portfolio theory.

are not about newfangled finance concepts but, rather, about the industry's efforts to stay competitive and profitable in the face of an increasing array of market sources of credit. The revolution occurring in credit risk management should not be characterized as "the revenge of the nerds," but rather, "market forces again prevail."

While changes in the credit risk management area may be initially slow to come, they will eventually occur, and they will be profound. In commercial lending activities, banks face fierce competitive conditions. Failure to adapt and evolve will produce an unwanted Darwinian outcome.

9. More powerful than the corporate strategy is the underlying corporate culture; changing the traditional culture of banks is key to performing in the 1990s.

Much has been written about the need to develop a value-creating corporate strategy. In *Bottomline Banking* we have put forth analytical tools as well as conceptual models and discussed at length the need for their disciplined application. The discussion, however, risks incorrectly discounting the human element from the management equation. More specifically, it is organizations that implement value-creating strategies, not academics, consultants, or even bold CEOs. To be successful, the entire organization must be engaged in implementing a chosen strategy. The real challenge immediately becomes one of managing the evolution of the corporate culture.

In the management literature, there has been a great debate about whether a corporate culture should, or even can, be managed. In examining this discussion, there is only one useful conclusion for the banking industry—a bank's corporate culture *must* be managed. Given the dramatic economic paradigm shifts under way in banking, failure to manage change within the corporate culture is like trying to compete in the 1990s with an organization designed decades earlier for an environment that was much different and more forgiving. Failure will most likely follow.

Public declaration of a decision to change corporate culture is not going to be popular. Ideally, a transforming bank would have in place the measurement and compensation systems necessary to support an evolutionary approach to maintaining a competitive organization. Having available a turnkey cultural solution is not the real world. If change is required, strong CEO leadership is necessary. Resistance should be expected and managed.

Books have been written on the subject of managing change and successfully transforming organizations. There are im-

Public declaration of a decision to change corporate culture is not going to be popular. . . . Having available a turn-key cultural solution is not the real world. If change is required, strong CEO leadership is necessary.

portant lessons to be learned and taken to heart. For example, even when radical change is necessary, respect for historical strengths is important. And change can be best managed when the CEO has a true game plan, even if a private one.

Managing change is the ultimate challenge and may be a CEO's most critical test. Some management tasks such as the building of MIS systems can be purchased and critical strategic analysis can be contracted out to consultants and experts. However, only a CEO can provide leadership.

10. Management must embrace change; proactively define new, more appropriate business paradigms; and lead the difficult transition of the organization.

While it still may be too early to declare a paradigm regained, an outline for the future is emerging. It is a paradigm that is simple in its focus on and responsiveness to market and competitive forces. The magnitude of change required to succeed with it, however, will be extreme for many, perhaps even beyond the grasp of some.

In an industry undergoing change, one in which leadership is critically important and the stakes high, how one thinks about organizational change is the inevitable litmus test of management's prospects for survival. Sometimes events seem beyond our control. Change, however, does not simply happen; successful change is always managed. The bottom line in *Bottomline Banking* is that, to be successful, management must embrace and lead change. Paradigms do not shift in response to gravitational forces or laws of chemistry. Paradigms shift when leaders lead.

To respond to deregulation and market forces, banking needs to search for new paradigms, and banks need their managers to lead the discovery process. There is not much certainty in being a bank executive in the 1990s, other than knowing that if you are not prepared to make the necessary tough decisions and learn to compete in today's hostile environment, another management group that is will be knocking at the door.

At the end of this decade, when the pundits review the industry leadership of the 1990s, two attributes will be viewed most favorably as factors contributing to an institution's success— strategic vision and ability to manage change. The industry's future can be seen today, but not all are prepared to wrestle with it. Given all that is known about the industry's prospects, today's fitness test is boldness in embracing the future.

While it still may be too early to declare a paradigm regained, an outline for the future is emerging. It is a paradigm that is simple in its focus on and responsiveness to market and competitive forces. The magnitude of change required to succeed with it, however, will be extreme for many, perhaps even beyond the grasp of some.

Eventually, change provides opportunity. In our industry, our economy, and indeed, our whole way of life, change is to be championed for the opportunities it provides. Change can intimidate, but it can also inspire. For the inspired, banking provides a period of unprecedented drama. The 1990s will see the culmination of forces kicked into motion decades earlier. The institutions and managements that will lead us into the next century will be those that have stepped up to the decade's challenges.

If the new paradigm is not yet fully clear today, it will be by the end of the decade. Of course, once the new paradigm becomes embedded in conventional wisdom, one risks inertia again setting in. If stability ever again arrives, therefore, we should expect to again see the market and competitive forces of change unleashed. The cycle is an inevitable one. An ever stronger industry will evolve out of it.

Endnotes

Chapter 1

1   Larry A. Frieder and Phillip Petty, "Determinants of Bank Acquisition Premiums: Issues and Evidence," *Contemporary Policy Perspectives* (April 1991).

Chapter 3

1   Kenneth A. Letzler and Michael B. Mierzewski, "Antitrust Policy Poses Greater Burdens for Bank Mergers and Acquisitions," *Banking Policy Report* Vol. II, No. 8 (April 20, 1992): 1, 14–18. Edited by Secura Group, Washington D.C.

Chapter 5

1   Larry A. Frieder, et al, *Interstate Bank Expansion: Market Forces and Competitive Realities,* The Report of the Interstate Banking Study Group, Florida A and M University (Tallahassee, FL, January 1984).

Chapter 6

1   David C. Cates, "Can Bank Mergers Build Shareholder Value," *Journal of Bank Accounting and Finance* Vol. 5, No. 2 (Winter 1991–1992): 3–11.

Chapter 7

1   Stephen A. Rhoades, "The Efficiency Effects of Bank Mergers: Rationale For a Case Study Approach," *Proceedings of Conference on Bank Structure and Competition* (1993), Federal Reserve Bank of Chicago (forthcoming).

Chapter 9

1   Ralph C. Kimball, "Relationship versus Product in Retail Banking," *Journal of Retail Banking* Vol. XII, No. 1 (Spring 1990): 13–25.

2   Eric Berggren and Robert Dewar, "Is Product Management Obsolete?," *Journal of Retail Banking,* Vol. XIII, No. 4 (Winter 1991–1992): 27–32.

3   Ralph C. Kimball and William T. Gregor, "Emerging Distri-
     bution Strategies in U.S. Retail Banking," *Journal of Retail
     Banking* Vol. XI, No. 4 (Winter 1989): 4–16.

Chapter 10

1   Katerina Simons and Stephen Cross, "Do Capital Markets
     Predict Problems in Large Commercial Banks?" *New Eng-
     land Economic Review* (May/June 1991): 51–56, Federal
     Reserve Bank of Boston.
2   Herbert L. Baer and John N. McElravey, "Capital Shocks and
     Bank Growth—1973 to 1991," *Economic Perspectives*
     (July/August 1993): 2–19, Federal Reserve Bank of Chicago.

Index

About the Authors

John B. McCoy, Chairman and Chief Executive Officer of BANC ONE CORPORATION, is one of banking's most visible and highly respected executives. He assumed the responsibilities of Chairman and CEO in January 1987. Previously he was President and CEO beginning in 1984.

Prior to joining BANC ONE CORPORATION he had been president of Bank One, Columbus, NA and Bank One Trust Company, NA. He is the third generation of McCoys to be associated with the BANC ONE organization. McCoy joined Bank One (then City National Bank) in September of 1970, and during the ensuing seven years had numerous responsibilities in the bank's many areas which later prepared his various presidential positions within Bank One.

McCoy has a B.A. in History from Williams College in Williamstown, Massachusetts. He later earned his M.B.A. in Finance from Stanford University, Graduate School of Business.

Larry A. Frieder is considered a pioneer and authority on interstate mergers, bank strategy and financial deregulation. He is Professor of Banking and Finance at Florida A and M University where he is currently Head of the Finance Program.

A study Dr. Frieder directed for the Florida legislature on Interstate banking has been used as a blueprint for numerous states and regions. He has given testimony before the U.S. Congress as well as several state legislatures.

Dr. Frieder consults widely and is a frequent speaker before bank associations and senior management retreats. He has co-authored major books on banking. His articles appear in several financial publications, including *Journal of Corporation Law, Economic Review, Journal of Financial Research.*

Frieder received B.B.A. and M.B.A. degrees from the University of Michigan and his Ph.D. from Arizona State.

Robert B. Hedges, Jr. is a leading analyst and innovator in consumer financial services. After more than 10 years in management consulting to banks, brokerage firms and insurance companies, he joined Shawmut National Corporation as Executive Vice President, Consumer Banking Group, in 1993.

Prior to joining Shawmut he was a vice president with First Manhattan Consulting Group, the renowned New York firm responsible for many of banking's most insightful studies and new directives. Prior to joining First Manhattan, he spent nine years with The MAC Group as vice president and banking practice leader.

Hedges completed his undergraduate degree in Economics at Dartmouth College and received his MBA from the Sloan School of Management at MIT.